Outdoor and Nature Play in Early Childhood Education

BEVERLIE DIETZE

Okanagan College

DIANE KASHIN

Ryerson University

May you days with children be filled with outdoor + nature play! Be an advocate!

Diane Kash

 Pearson

VICE PRESIDENT, EDITORIAL: Anne Williams
PORTFOLIO MANAGER: Keriann McGoogan
MARKETING MANAGER: Euan White
CONTENT MANAGER: Madhu Ranadive
PROJECT MANAGER: Ainsley Somerville
CONTENT DEVELOPER: Christine Langone
PRODUCTION SERVICES: Cenveo® Publisher Services

PERMISSIONS PROJECT MANAGER: Integra Publishing Services, Inc.
PHOTO PERMISSIONS RESEARCH: Integra Publishing Services, Inc.
TEXT PERMISSIONS RESEARCH: Integra Publishing Services, Inc.
INTERIOR DESIGNER: Anthony Leung
COVER DESIGNER: Anthony Leung
COVER IMAGE: Karen Eilersen

Pearson Canada Inc., 26 Prince Andrew Place, North York, Ontario M3C 2H4.

978-0-13-474208-3

1   18

Library and Archives Canada Cataloguing in Publication

Dietze, Beverlie, 1957-, author
    Outdoor and nature play in early childhood education / Beverlie Dietze,
Okanagan College, Diane Kashin, Ryerson University.

Includes bibliographical references and index.
ISBN 978-0-13-474208-3 (softcover)

    1. Outdoor education—Textbooks. 2. Nature study—Textbooks. 3. Play—Textbooks.
4. Early childhood education—Textbooks. 5. Textbooks. I. Kashin, Diane, author II. Title.

LB1139.35.P55D527 2017   372.21   C2017-907508-X

Dedication

The authors dedicate this textbook to all the early learning students and teachers that we have had the honour to know and who have joined the movement to help children reconnect to nature and to experience the joys of outdoor play. We also dedicate this textbook to the children who over the years have touched our lives and helped us see outdoor play from their perspective. We look forward to seeing a new generation of children growing up and connected to nature especially Griffen Lucas Kashin, Maya Andruchow, and Justin Andruchow.

Finally, we dedicate this textbook to our families, especially our husbands Lorne and Peter, who have provided us with the encouragement, time, and support to follow our desire to write about early childhood education topics that support children's optimal experiences in early learning environments.

Brief Contents

Detailed Contents

Preface

As an early learning teacher, do you remember playing outdoors by the ocean, climbing trees, or splashing in large puddles? Do you remember experiencing feelings of empowerment, freedom, and joyfulness, as you felt the coolness of the ocean, the feeling of accomplishment when you climbed high up the tree, or the sense of delight when splashing and puddle jumping? As children, you may have moved from one backyard to another to play with or without adult supervision. Now move the clock forward to this generation of children and consider their experiences outdoors today. They spend less time outdoors than ever before. Outdoor playtime has been reduced and replaced with indoor play experiences or group activities that have either a cognitive or team sport orientation. Children have lost the freedom to explore their outdoor environments, connect with nature, and engage in many necessary play experiences that adults have now classified as "risky". There is great debate among professionals, researchers, and families about outdoor play. Where should children play? Will outdoor play provide children with the foundational skills needed for later academic performance? Do children become ill from being outdoors? Isn't it a time for children to "run off steam"? These are all important questions that require discussion so that, collectively, families and early learning teachers have a clear understanding of the importance of outdoor play to children's overall learning and development.

Outdoor and Nature Play in Early Childhood Education is timely because it is backed by new research, both Canadian and international, that reinforces the importance of outdoor play in the lives of children. Outdoor play has been shown to be vital for children's health, wellness, development, and connectedness to their childhood space and place. Indeed, outdoor play is so important to children's daily living that we have written this book to present the core concepts that will support educators in post-secondary institutions, student teachers, and teachers in collectively examining outdoor play within their environments and beyond.

In addition to outdoor environments connected to early learning programs, there are many places and spaces that can offer children the wonders and joys of nature. Not all programs have access to forests or beaches; however, early learning teachers may be able to consider even a small enclave of trees, a brookside, or ravine as a space to cultivate a pedagogy of place and nature. Children who have teachers that love and respect nature will grow to be adults who love and care for the planet.

The text is rooted in the work of well-known theorists who have made invaluable contributions to the study of early childhood education and have advocated for children to have opportunities for playing and learning outdoors. We situate the discussion about the benefits of outdoor play and the breadth and depth of learning it provides in a Canadian and local context. As well, we introduce readers to many Canadian and international researchers from various disciplines who are engaged in influencing the current theoretical concepts and perspectives on outdoor play.

As we began writing this book, we wanted to provide emerging early learning teachers with a combination of theory, practice, and reflection. We believe that in order to position outdoor play as a vital part of programming and for children to have the opportunities for outdoor play, early learning teachers must have theory, practice, and passion from which to draw upon. We view outdoor play and the diverse environments in which it can occur as both a right and a need of all children. Therefore, this textbook emphasizes that wherever children play, they have opportunities to explore, discover, wonder, imagine, and create in their outdoor places and spaces. We hope this book provides early learning teachers with insight into how theory informs the application of outdoor play curriculum and what experiences support children in their play, their quest for curiosity, and their learning and desire to care for our environment. In addition, this text is intended to support early learning teachers in expanding their philosophical perspectives and approaches to working and learning with children in the great outdoors.

We have been inspired by the knowledge and skills that we have gained from working with early learning students, graduates, early learning teachers, colleagues, and children who share our passion and desire for outdoor environments that are rich in opportunity and experiences. This book represents many of the theories and applications of theory into practice we have grappled with during our journey to promote outdoor play.

Finally, we hope that this text will inspire further discussion, debate, and research, as you determine what aspects of the material presented you will embrace and transfer to your work with the children, families, colleagues, and environments that are part of your context.

OUR VISION FOR THIS BOOK

As we began research for this book and sketched out the potential content and areas of concentration, we felt it was essential to examine outdoor play from a Canadian perspective, and to acknowledge the diversity among the children, families, and communities who access early learning programs. We knew that the theory and practices presented had to be transferrable to many of our communities—urban, rural, and remote, as well as to our provinces with warmer climates and provinces and territories with the beauty of long, cold winters. We also wanted to draw upon key elements of Indigenous ways of knowing and learning and how such principles may be related to early learning programs. We are confident that this book will continue to be a resource for students when they begin their practice, as it will:

- Support early learning students in exploring the various components that contribute to an outdoor play pedagogy;
- Create opportunities for readers to question, imagine, reflect, and explore further research that would support them in gaining insight into the depth and breadth of outdoor play;
- Combine the historical roots of outdoor play with contemporary research in order to facilitate discussions on outdoor pedagogy and nature, approaches to outdoor play programming, and how the outdoors positions children for later academic learning;
- Present discourse and perspectives that would stimulate discussions among early learning students and teachers on the why, how, when, and where of outdoor play;
- Emphasize how the attitudes and values that early learning teachers and students place on outdoor play influence the extent to which children embrace this phase of their programming;
- Share photos of children engaged in a variety of outdoor play experiences, as many of the photos can trigger opportunities to emulate similar options for children through materials, questioning, and role modelling; and

- Assist students in early childhood education in developing a new lens for outdoor play and acquiring a passion for and commitment to ensuring children have quality outdoor play experiences on a daily basis, in all kinds of weather.

APPROACH TO THE TEXT

The underlying theoretical foundation of *Outdoor and Nature Play in Early Childhood Education* is constructivism. Our approach to the text is to create learning that can be constructed through reflection and co-constructed through dialogue. We acknowledge the ever presence of new technologies and have included opportunities to continue thinking and conducting research with search engines and online resources. We created a text that is comprehensive, visual, and interactive to entice readers to enhance children's experiences in nature. Combining theory with practice and in outlining suggestions for outdoor play and nature pedagogy that are featured in each chapter will support early learning students in their practicum experiences and spark new thoughts, perspectives and approaches to outdoor play by those readers already working with children.

CONTENT AND FEATURES

There are 12 chapters in the textbook:

One	Introduction to Outdoor and Play and Nature
Two	Historical and Philosophical Foundation for Outdoor and Nature Play
Three	Canadian and International Research on Outdoor Play
Four	Loose Parts—Using Natural and Found Materials in Outdoor and Nature Play
Five	The Relationship of Outdoor and Nature Play to Development, Health, Learning, and Thinking
Six	Outdoor Play That Involves Challenge, Adventure, and Risk
Seven	Nature-Based Early Learning Places and Spaces
Eight	Sustainability and First Nations—Teachings
Nine	Programming from a Four-Season Perspective
Ten	Supporting Families and Others in Connecting Children's Play to Their Development
Eleven	Documentation and Assessment of Children's Outdoor Play Environments
Twelve	Outdoor and Nature Play—Looking to Research and Practice to Inform the Future

Each chapter begins with a childhood memory that is intended to be evocative for the reader, followed by our vision for outdoor play today and information related to positioning outdoor play in the lives of children. To introduce theory to early learning students, we feature a different influential theorist in each chapter. In terms of practical applications, each chapter of the textbook features standards and principles of practice. Place-based learning is a thread throughout the textbook: in different chapters we present various places where children make a connection—emotionally, physically, and spiritually—such as the garden, the neighbourhood, the park, and the forest.

To support the rights of all children to have outdoor play and nature in their lives, the chapters include information related to accessibility and design, as well as suggestions to support families in encouraging more outdoor play in nature. We want our text to be simultaneously theoretical and practical and therefore include tips and tools for early learning teachers and specific programming suggestions. Every day early learning teachers take children outside to experience the joys and wonders of nature. In each chapter, we include a narrative that highlights the statement "Why I love Outdoor Play" for students to understand that outdoor play programming is possible.

Each chapter contains the following features:

Epigraph	A quote from a key historical figure in early childhood education to support the antecedents of the concept of outdoor play
Learning Outcomes	Six to eight learning outcomes for the reader that are intended to outline the core concepts of the chapter and guide their learning. To outline the core content that supports to be learned in the chapter.
Childhood Memories	A childhood memory to evoke reflection on the benefits and importance of outdoor play learning in and with nature.
Chapter Preview	A chapter preview to provide the reader with an overview of what to expect in the pages ahead.
Setting the Stage for Outdoor Play	Examples of how outdoor play experiences, environments, and people in the environments contribute to children's experiences and learning opportunities.
Our Vision for Outdoor Play	The authors' vision as it pertains to the focus of the chapter for early learning programming outdoors.
Positioning Outdoor Play in the Lives of Children	An introduction to the importance of children being engaged in an array of outdoor experiences that support their overall health and development.
Theoretical Foundation	A section that provides background to the content of each chapter and a historical perspective detailing the influence of theorists who have contributed to the current movement for active outdoor play.
Practical Applications	Descriptors of how theory informs practice and how early learning teachers draw upon theory to inform their outdoor play planning and practice.
Principles of Practice	Different sets of principles of action or conduct for those working with children outdoors to support children's active play and learning.
Learning in Place	Possible places where children can develop an emotional, physical, and spiritual connection.
Programming	Various programming experiences described and illustrated, using a framework focused on planning, engagement, exploration, and reflection.
Family Support and Engagement	Suggestions for students to engage and enlist families to fully support children's learning, growth, and development.
Accessibility and Design	Answers to questions about accessibility and design in the provision of outdoor play for children with exceptionalities.
Tools and Tips for Outdoor Play	Suggestions for using technology and tools to enhance outdoor programming and professional learning around outdoor play.
On the Ground— Professional Reflections: "Why I Love Outdoor Play"	Real stories from practising early learning professionals who think deeply and intentionally about the ideas and concepts presented.
Case Studies	Case studies that invite the reader to reflect on related questions as they situate outdoor play in various contexts.
Take It Outside!	Suggestions for adult-centred outdoor experiences to help increase the comfort level early learning students have with nature.
Key Terms	Key terms that reflect the chapter's contents.
Summary	A bulleted summary of the points discussed in the chapter.
Quiet Reflection	Questions on which the reader can personally reflect that foster an outdoor learning mindset, while recognizing that self-reflection is an important feature of professional learning.

Community Dialogue	A focus on the perspectives of others to provide a broader, more complex understanding of the chapter's contents, including suggestions that support the development of a community of learners.
For Further Thought and Action	Links that may lead to further thought, as well as suggestions for action. Changing societal norms as they relate to active outdoor play requires advocacy and action.
Resources	Descriptions and links to additional resources that can add to the discussion of the importance of outdoor play to children's development.

Also scattered throughout the chapters are textboxes to assist the reader in further reflections on outdoor play such as "Think About It! Write About It! Read About It!;" "Curious?;" and "Shedding Light on Outdoor Play—Points of Reflection."

SUPPLEMENTS

- An Instructor's Manual is available to support the delivery of the content in an experiential way that supports outdoor learning.

ACKNOWLEDGMENTS

The authors wish to acknowledge Pearson Canada for the opportunity to support a growing and important movement to reconnect children to outdoor play and nature. Our work would not be possible without the support of our families and all the early learning students, teachers, and children that get outside every day to play. We thank the reviewers whose feedback helped us shape the content and the layout of the text: Tricia Dumais, Conestoga College; Alison Gaston, Sheridan College; Mary Lou Lummiss, Fleming College; and Kathryn Markham-Petro, St. Clair College.

CHAPTER 1
Introduction to Outdoor Play and Nature

There should be a garden attached where they may feast their eyes on trees, flowers, and plants . . . Where they always hope to hear and see something new.

(Comenius, The Great Didactic, 1632)

LEARNING OUTCOMES

After exploring this chapter, you will be able to:

- Discuss key reasons why outdoor play and nature is important in the lives of young children.
- Explain what is meant by "a child's right to experience the outdoors" and how this influences the role of early learning teachers.
- Describe Banning and Sullivan's (2011) standards for outdoor play and how they are visible in early learning programs.
- Outline what is meant by rights-based principles of practice.
- Discuss ways in which early learning teachers may program for outdoor play that considers the children, families, and program pedagogy.
- Explain how and why accessibility and design are integral to children's right to play and the United Nations *Convention on the Rights of the Child*.

CHILDHOOD MEMORIES

I live in a big neighbourhood with lots of houses. I have two younger brothers, and we love to play street hockey outside. I am in Grade 4 now. The school that I go to is only five minutes from my house. I like going to school so that I can see my friends, but I wish we could play outside more. In the summer when I was five I went to a camp, and we spent every day outside in a forest. It was only one week, but I remember it so well! I loved exploring outdoors. We found so many interesting bugs, and once a chickadee landed on my hand! One day we arrived in the morning and it had rained the night before. Everything was so muddy! I thought we were going to have to stay inside all day but we didn't. We played in the mud! Now when I go to school sometimes we don't even get to go outside for recess. The teacher says that we have to study more especially when we don't do well on our spelling tests. I miss playing outside.

CHAPTER PREVIEW

Imagine a day of not being outdoors—perhaps missing the opportunities to hear the sound of the snow crunching under our feet or to feel the raindrops softly falling on our heads? Or seeing a fabulous puddle and deciding, should I or should I not make a big splash? Imagine not getting to observe the beauty of the birds that come to the feeders? What are you missing in your life without such experiences? Now think about the lives of children in Canada. How accessible is the outdoors and what opportunities are available to children? What types of outdoor play experiences are children exposed to? What level of freedom do children have to explore their environments—to look at, observe, experiment, discover, and wonder why, what, when, and how about all the things in their environment? Examine the three photos of children playing in puddles. Think about what children learn from these sensory experiences and how such experiences in the early years influence their later learning.

Dana Barratt

Photo 1.1 Splashing in a puddle.

Gill Robertson

Photo 1.2 Playing in a puddle.

Gill Robertson

Photo 1.3 More puddle play.

Now think about the learning possibilities that evolve when children are given the freedom to splash in the puddle. Reflect on your ideas and think about the questions posed in Figure 1.1. Can children experience these same types of learning indoors? Why or why not? If so, how? If not, why not? What can children learn from a puddle?

Even though a puddle might seem to you as commonplace and mundane, it is a reflection of the world of possibilities for children. Vecchi (2010) described puddles as "an upside fragment of the world" (p. 121). Vecchi challenges adults to think what children can observe when they move closer to the puddle and the image appears to become larger. Children can reflect upon why, when they move away from the puddle, that the order is reversed. Children can also observe the changes in the puddle and their reflections as the weather changes. This supports their development of scientific knowledge. By becoming connected to a puddle, children can experience environmental stewardship as they care for the puddle similar to how they would care for other parts of the environment. In this chapter, we will introduce you to the wondrous world of outdoor play and nature pedagogy. You will be introduced to the benefits and importance of these types of experiences for children. You will begin to see how outdoor play in and with nature leads to learning. You will consider the role of the early learning teacher in making outdoor play accessible to all children as is their right!

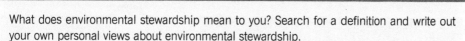

Are there scientific principles that children are learning? If so, what are they?

Are there opportunities for children to learn about environmental stewardship? If so, what are they?

Are there aspects of splashing in a puddle that can be used in other play? If so, what might they be?

Figure 1.1 What children learn from a puddle.

THINK ABOUT IT! READ ABOUT IT! WRITE ABOUT IT!

What does environmental stewardship mean to you? Search for a definition and write out your own personal views about environmental stewardship.

CURIOUS?

What do you think is the connection of outdoor play to later academic performance? How is children's outdoor play related to the future of the planet? Satisfy your curiosity by searching the Internet for answers.

SETTING THE STAGE FOR OUTDOOR PLAY

Children's social, emotional, cognitive and physical development is influenced by their connections to nature. Children are hardwired to need nature and to be part of natural environments (Smirnova & Riabkova, 2016). In nature, children can build significant relationships with each other, their animal friends and with the adults who care enough to make sure that they spend time outside. Imagine this: a group of children are playing outdoors in a large meadow, surrounded by trees. Look at Photo 1.4. What do you see? How might the actions of the child in the photo influence other children? Now read more to see what happened.

Tessa carried sticks that she had collected to the opening where the other children were sketching their surroundings. As she arrives with the sticks, they look up and Mario asks, "Where did you find those sticks?" Tessa points to the woods and all the children jump up and run to find more sticks. All of the sudden, the children decide to create a fort. They discuss their plans with their early learning teacher and together consider

Photo 1.4 Outdoor playing with branches.

Photo 1.5 Building a fort.

THINK ABOUT IT! READ ABOUT IT! WRITE ABOUT IT!

What learning do you envision happened from this experience with the sticks? Read this article to think deeply about sticks: https://www.psychologytoday.com/blog/friendship-20/201405/why-sticks-are-good-kids

Write out a creative follow-up experience that you could provide these children if you were their teacher.

which branches would be best for the fort. After discussing their plans, the children determined that the best branches to use would be those as long as their bodies. Children took turns measuring the branches by having each child lie down beside one. Then, they determined whether the branch would be used or discarded. Think about this experience. How did it support children's learning?

In this example, children are building relationships with each other and with their early learning teacher. As well, they are making connections to nature. They are practising math skills and engineering processes. They are connecting words with math principles such as length, width, thick, and thin. Their early learning teacher takes photos while some of the children retrieve their sketchbooks to draw their creation. This experience is captured in the images and documented by the teacher. More significantly, children will have those memories for life. Can you remember an experience from your childhood that lives on in your memory? As a point of reflection (see Box 1.1), think back to that time.

In each chapter, we will include vision statements for outdoor play. Vision statements are related to utopian thinking in early learning (Dietze & Kashin, 2016). When we put forth these statements, it is to articulate what we imagine outdoor play and early learning would be like in a perfect world. As outlined in Photo 1.6 our utopia is as follows:

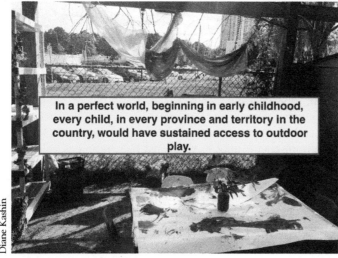

In a perfect world, beginning in early childhood, every child, in every province and territory in the country, would have sustained access to outdoor play.

Diane Kashin

Photo 1.6 In a perfect world.

THINK ABOUT IT! READ ABOUT IT! WRITE ABOUT IT!

Do a search online by putting the words *utopian thinking* in early childhood education. Read the results. Now think about it. What does utopian thinking mean to you? Write a paragraph about your utopian vision for children.

When ideals are envisioned, efforts can be made to work towards their realization. Since outdoor play is not part of every child or adult life, in order to bring outdoor play back into the lives of children, we need to:

■ Change adult and children's attitudes about outdoor play;

■ View all outdoor play spaces and places as possibilities for play; and

■ Offer children access to outdoor spaces and places that will support their sense of curiosity and related experiences outside.

As we work towards this vision, early learning teachers and student teachers can make a difference by embracing the outdoors on a daily basis as the preferred place for play and learning to occur.

OUR VISION FOR OUTDOOR PLAY

Play is in peril, especially outdoor play. Children's indoor environments offer much entertainment coming through electronic devices. In contrast, the outdoor environment offers children real-life experiences that include different sounds, smells, ideas, thoughts and ways of knowing that cannot be replicated indoors and especially not through their screen experiences. Larimore & Sobel (2016) suggest that play is being shunted aside in early learning programs in many parts of North America in favour of more teacher-directed instruction in order for children to meet standards. Do they know their colours? Can they count to 10? Can they spell their name? Meeting academic standards according to Larimore & Sobel (2016) is becoming the focus of many teachers, which leads them to regard play, especially outdoor play, as less important than academic work. At home and at school, children spend more time indoors than outdoors (Gundersen, Skår, O'Brien, Wold, & Follo, 2016). At home and at school children are staying indoors for too long.

Across Canada, early learning program policies are under the direction of provincial and territorial governments. If there are outdoor play standards that identify the amount of time children are required to be outdoors, they may or may not be adhered to due to such things as interpretation of what the standard means. In school, children might, in many circumstances, spend much of their time indoors being instructed. Some children are even missing out on recess. This is occurring in spite of children's right to play outdoors. At this pivotal time in history, governments across Canada, and society at large, can either remain silent on outdoor play or chart a new direction. Charting a new direction may require

Canada to examine how other nations of the world have put policies and practices in place to protect children's rights to play and, more specifically, to play outdoors.

All children have a right to outdoor play. They have a right to the benefits and the joy that playing outside brings. Learning how other countries view outdoor play is fundamental to our ability to advocate for the return of outdoor play to the lives of children in Canada. Broadening our perspectives on outdoor play by examining how it is embedded in other cultures provides early learning teachers and students with ways in which they can make a difference to the children in this country (Chawla, Keena, Pevec, & Stanley, 2014; Gundersen et al., 2016). For example, in some countries, such as those in Scandinavia, playing outdoors is an important part of childhood. As mentioned earlier, in some areas of North America outdoor play is valued less than time devoted to academic learning (Larimore & Sobel, 2016). Such trends add to the significant erosion (Prince, Allin, Sandseter, & Ärkemalm-Hagsér, 2013) to the amount of time devoted to outdoor play.

You can play a role in shaping the course of history in your own community. Yes, you can contribute to saving outdoor play from extinction. No matter how much the indoor learning environment is set up with open-ended and naturalistic materials in aesthetically pleasing ways, it is not a substitute for playing, discovering, and wondering outdoors. Throughout this textbook, you will be introduced to the history, theories, and research connected to outdoor play. You will also be presented with practical suggestions to help you program for outdoor play. Early learning teachers and students who examine outdoor play in and with nature are able to develop knowledge and a positive viewpoint that will influence their ways of supporting children and families in outdoor play. Families of course want what is best for their children (Ontario Ministry of Education, 2014). When families understand the importance of outdoor play to children's development and feel supported and engaged in their children's learning, they too will honour the rights of children to be outdoors.

POSITIONING OUTDOOR PLAY IN THE LIVES OF CHILDREN

Children's play experience in outdoor environments is becoming increasingly recognized as the foundation for their healthy development (Brussoni, Olsen, Pike, & Sleet, 2012; Dietze & Kashin, 2017). Over the past decade, there have been a number of research studies connecting the benefits of outdoor play to children's social, emotional, physical, spiritual, and cognitive development (Brussoni et al., 2012; Li, Hestenes, & Wang, 2016). Research is now connecting the relationship of children's outdoor play experiences during their early years to later academic performance (Pacini-Ketchabaw & Nxumalo, 2015; Shanker, 2016) and even to the future of our planet.

If we agree that children's play experiences with and in nature are so important, then why are more and more children having less and less contact with the natural world (Louv, 2005)? Compared to the 1970s, children are spending 50% less time engaged in unstructured activities outdoors (Chiao, Li, Seligman, & Turner, 2016). In some jurisdictions in Canada outdoor play is not required in early learning programs, and as children enter grade school, with the decline in the amount of time allotted to recess, there is even less unstructured outdoor play opportunities. Many school settings are choosing to offer children structured outdoor experiences such as sports activities in place of unstructured play, but this is not the same as play. "Children age 10–16 years now spend, on average, only 12.6 minutes per day" playing outside (Chiao et al., 2016, p. 62). Do you think children should be outside more? Do you think children want to play more outside? What do you think would be the positive and negative implications for children if they were to have greater access to outdoor play? Children's disconnect with nature has serious implications for their health, wellness, and development and will be explored in future chapters. In this chapter, we ask you to consider outdoor and nature play from a *rights perspective*.

THINK ABOUT IT! READ ABOUT IT! WRITE ABOUT IT!

What does a rights perspective mean to you? When you search this on the Internet, what occurs to you? Write out a rights statement about children and outdoor play. Start your statement with these words: Children have a right to …

Time and space to play outdoors is now being recognized both as a need and a right of children and one that is central to their well-being and development. Across the globe, children's need to play is recognized as a basic childhood right (Brussoni, Olsen, Pike, & Sleet 2012; Krechevsky, Mardell, Filippini, & Tedeschi, 2016; Ontario Ministry of Education, 2016). Focusing this introductory chapter on the rights of children to spend time in nature is deliberate. Every child has the right to experience the joys and wonders of the outdoors. Such experiences have incredible benefits to children (Smirnova & Riabkova, 2016).

Those who are studying early childhood education and those who are working as early learning teachers are in a unique position to support children's right to outdoor play. Think about children in early years programs who would rather be outdoors than indoors. Then think about what happens to them when their outdoor play time is cancelled. What happens to children's sense of spirit and curiosity?

THINK ABOUT IT! READ ABOUT IT! WRITE ABOUT IT!

What are some of the challenges that children have when they are required to stay indoors for a day, two days, or several days? Ask this question in a search engine: What are the negative effects of children spending too much time indoors? Why might a teacher feel that being outside is not as important as being indoors? Write down your ideas.

There is so much learning to be gained from outdoor play experiences in nature. Think about what would happen if the teacher described in the childhood memory opening this chapter combined learning to spell with outdoor experiences? Perhaps the children could do a scavenger hunt to find discoveries in nature? Look at Photo 1.7. These children have just found a cicada. Would learning to spell something that is tangible to the children be more meaningful to them than being exposed to words they may not have connections with for the sake of language and literacy goals?

Children have a right to experience the joys and wonders that outdoor play can bring. There is a whole exciting world to discover, and we owe it to children to share it with

Photo 1.8 Enjoying outdoor play.

Photo 1.7 Children discover cicadas during their outdoor explorations.

them. We also owe it to the environment. Children who grow up engaged in nature and having an affinity for it will become stewards of the environment. They will learn to care for the environment, rather than destroy it. Children can make an emotional connection to a place within nature. This supports them in developing an **ecological identity**. Early learning teachers support children in developing ecological identities by providing them with a place to observe and opportunities to experience the gifts of nature. This place can be in their outdoor play spaces in their early years programs; it can occur on walks in their neighbourhoods or in a forest, a meadow, a hillside, a ravine, or a creek; even just by a small enclave of trees. Children require the time and opportunity outdoors, as well as adults who support their explorations and inquiries so that they can develop their ecological identities.

> Ecological identity refers to the ecological self, which can be described as an individual's connection to and attitudes toward the natural environment (Wilson, 2012).

Many environmentalists today are concerned with the types of life experiences that children are exposed to, particularly when access to the outdoors is minimal. According to David Suzuki (2014) computers, video games, and increased access to the Internet offer entertainment in a virtual world without "all the joys that the real world has to offer" (p. 194). Suzuki suggested that, "unless we are willing to encourage our children to reconnect with and appreciate the nature world, we can't expect them to help protect and care for it" (p. 194). Larimore & Sobel (2016) argue that children require time to connect to nature so that they can learn to love the Earth before being asked to save the Earth. There is a movement to reconnect children to nature (Sobel, 2016). Early learning teachers are central to this movement—they provide children access to and opportunities to be outdoors, to play and to embrace their natural world.

THEORETICAL FOUNDATION

Researchers and theorists have long supported the importance of play and, specifically, children's outdoor play (Kemple, Oh, Kenny, & Smith-Bonahue, 2016; Whitebread, Basilio, Kuvalja, & Verma, 2012). Given the benefits of outdoor play, consider the consequences when children are denied it. When children play, they exercise their rights to play for play's sake—to play for the pleasure and joy of being able to play. Play is not mere indulgence; it is essential for children's health and well-being (Kellert, 2012; Lester & Russell, 2010; Palmer, 2015). With a growing body of literature outlining the emotional and physical health benefits for children and adults from real contact with nature, it is essential that children in the early years have connections to it (Dennis, Wells, & Bishop, 2014; Dowdell, Gray, & Malone, 2011; Gill, 2014; Kellert, 2012; Larimore & Sobel, 2016).

All children have a right to outdoor play. If you asked children about this right, what do you think their answer would be? Would they agree? When we take a **rights-integrative approach** to early learning (Di Santo & Keanelly, 2014), we stand up for every child, whatever gender, whatever background, whether rich or poor. Margaret McMillan (1919) (see Box 1.2) understood this concept and made it her life's work. Almost 100 years ago, she worked with her sister Rachel in promoting outdoor play because they believed that the health benefits should apply to all children.

Over the centuries, there have been many theorists who have written about the benefits of outdoor play for children. We begin by introducing you to the great Margaret McMillan. She is often quoted as saying that the best classroom and the richest cupboard are roofed only by the sky (McMillan, as cited in Schweizer, 2009, p. 3). She declared "that the sky really is a canopy, that whispering trees are often a good substitute for walls" (McMillan, 1919, p. 325).

Rights-integrative approach refers to "a teaching and learning practice that acknowledges the CRC [*Convention on the Rights of the Child*] explicitly and puts it into action, regardless of the philosophical framework that guides the program" (Di Santo and Kenneally, 2014, p. 396).

Diane Kashin

Photo 1.9 The sky as a canopy.

For McMillan (1919), the problem was that those who lived in crowded, improvised neighbourhoods were cut off from the "all that is most healing and uplifting in nature" (p. 325). Why would McMillan, who started one of the first open air nursery school programs in the world, proclaim the outdoors to be the ultimate classroom? Is it because relationships seem to be intensified outdoors and children feel stronger connections to the adults in their world when they experience outdoor learning together, as depicted in Photo 1.10? Is it because playing with the elements of nature is an exhilarating experience, as you can see in Photo 1.11, as Zoe feels the mud? Might it be the ultimate classroom because it provides children with the opportunity to interact with animals that they meet during the course of their day? How important is it for children to realize that they share this world with non-human species (Pacini-Ketchabaw, Taylor, & Blaise, 2016)? Look at Photo 1.12, as Alexis, after finding a frog and interacting gently with it, returns it to its home in the tree.

Re-examine the photos of the children in the chapter. Now think about the types of learning that children may have acquired from each experience. For example, when you look at Zoe, she may have experienced new sensory experiences, such as how mud feels when it is harder, gooey, drippy, or cold. She may have examined different consistencies in the mud, such as thick, dry, and runny. She may have discovered what happens to mud when water is added to it. And, she may have learned new language, such as gooey or slimy. When adults carefully examine how outdoor play experiences contribute to children's development, they gain a better appreciation of its importance and how it sets the foundation for lifelong learning.

For reasons that will be explored in the upcoming chapters, early learning teachers can contribute significantly to reversing the trend towards an indoor childhood to one that will be rich in outdoor play experiences and environments. Advocates for outdoor play are calling for a movement to reconnect children with nature (Louv, 2005; Frost, 2009, Sobel, 2016). More than 10 years ago, Richard Louv wrote *The Last Child in*

Diane Kashin

Photo 1.10 Relationships are intensified outdoors.

Tanya Murray

Photo 1.11 Zoe experiences mud.

Diane Kashin

Photo 1.12 The frog is released to go back home.

Nature deficit disorder refers to a term coined by Richard Louv (2008) that relates to the human costs of alienation from nature.

the Woods (Louv, 2005), where he made popular the term "**nature deficit disorder**". Children with a nature deficit disorder, as outlined in Figure 1.2, would experience an absence of core experiences and values necessary for lifelong learning. These types of experiences are not attainable indoors.

If adults do not develop a comparable understanding of the importance of outdoor play as did past generations, then as a society we are countering our genetic predisposition to be outdoor players and learners. Children come to this world with instincts to observe, explore, play, and converse with others.

These instincts were shaped by natural selection during the hundreds of thousands of years in which our ancestors survived as hunter-gatherers (Gray, 2008). Accordingly, it is not children's natural instinct to be indoors, engaged primarily in sedentary activities (Gray, 2008). When children's play takes place outdoors, it becomes the ultimate

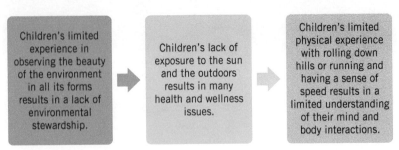

Figure 1.2 Children with nature deficit disorder.

Photo 1.13 Children observing with a magnifying glass.

environment for learning, play, building relationships, and contributing to health and wellness (Chawla, 2015).

Across Canada, governments at all levels, health care providers, and education and early childhood experts are expressing concerns about children's lack of outdoor play with the concomitant increase in childhood obesity and related diseases (Tremblay et al., 2015). Providing children with a healthy start during their early years is essential for the current and future social, environmental, and economic health of Canada. Early learning teachers play important roles in supporting children to establish healthy living practices during the early years. Health Canada describes 'healthy living' as making choices that enhance physical, mental, social, and spiritual health. There are many researchers (Burdette & Whitaker, 2005; Dietze & Kashin, 2016; Fjortoft, 2004) who have extolled the wide range of health benefits children gain from outdoor play (see Figure 1.3).

Numerous studies point to the growing trend towards the institutionalization of children's time and space, such that they do not have the opportunity to roam and play freely (Lester & Russell, 2010; Murray et al., 2013; ParticipACTION, 2015). This concern has led research groups in Canada to come together to develop a position statement on outdoor play, which will be reviewed in Chapter 3. The statement illustrates how researchers, medical experts and advocates are worried about the future of childhood (Gray et al., 2015). Although this textbook will focus on outdoor play from a Canadian context, we will also examine theorists, research, and perspectives from other nations in the world. By the end of the text, it is our intent that you will have a deeper knowledge and perspective on the importance of outdoor play, which will help to inform your practice.

Children are fitter and leaner.

 Children exhibit lower stress levels.

 Children have stronger immune systems, reducing the number of colds, flus, and related illnesses.

 Children create more intriguing play that is multi-faceted.

 Children express more active imaginations and communication skills.

 Children develop play partner relationships that include expressing respect and empathy for others.

 Children exhibit more freedom to explore.

 Children exhibit higher levels of curiosity and a sense of wonderment.

Figure 1.3 The benefits of outdoor play.

PRACTICAL APPLICATIONS

Play is the primary vehicle that children use to explore and make sense of the natural world. Margaret McMillan understood this at the turn of the 20th century (Schweizer, 2009). Now, in the 21st century, we are still learning about play and what it means. It takes a knowledgeable adult to be able to interpret the importance of play in the lives of children and all of its intricacies. Although it may appear simple, children's play is in fact complex and sophisticated (Holmes, Romeo, Ciraola, & Grushko, 2015).

Photo 1.14 Children test their ideas.

Table 1.1 Standards for outdoor play and learning.

1. Curiosity and Initiative Standard

2. Engagement and Persistence Standard

3. Imagination, Invention, and Creativity Standard

4. Reasoning and Problem-Solving Standard

5. Risk-Taking, Responsibility, and Confidence Standard

6. Reflection, Interpretation, and Application Standard

7. Flexibility and Resilience Standard

Source: Excerpt from *Lens on Outdoor Learning,* Banning & Sullivan, 2011.

When children play outside they test out ideas and theories, refine their understanding, and develop skills. "Nature provides ongoing teachable moments, endless opportunities to make discoveries and limitless reasons for critical thinking" (Banning & Sullivan, 2011, p. 9). As outlined in Table 1.1, Banning and Sullivan (2011) identified a series of standards for outdoor play. They designed them to help improve the quality of education for young children and to support the identification of benchmarks for children's growth and development. These learning standards are not meant to be static but dynamic "qualities, attitudes, and habits" that early learning teachers "can promote and extend in children by planning environments that purposefully focus on them" (Banning & Sullivan, 2011, p. 10). Each of these seven standards, listed in Table 1.1, will be featured in subsequent chapters.

As you think about each of these standards, ask yourself which are new to you? What do each of them mean to you? What core questions arise for you? Early learning teachers examine the standards to guide and inform their practice with children. For example, they think about why is it important for children to be curious and to take initiative. Why is it important for children to engage and persist? Think about what happens to children when they use their imagination, invent, and create. The outdoor play environment provides many opportunities for children to reason and problem solve. How are these standards related to and helpful for children's development? Examine the options in Table 1.2. What are your views of children? Column 1 and Column 2 feature two different views of children. We ask you to consider each column and decide what you wish children to experience and why. The final column is left empty for you to consider the reasons for your choice.

Table 1.2 Reflecting on different views.

Column 1 Do you want children to experience this?	OR	Column 2 Do you want children to experience this?	Column 3 Why?
Do you want children to be confident and active?		Do you want children to be passive, doubtful, insecure, and timid?	Why?
Do you want children to problem solve and take risks?		Do you want children to depend on adults to guide their decision-making?	Why?
Do you want children to participate in environmental sustainability practices?		Do you want children to take the environment for granted?	Why?

When children take risks and responsibility for their own actions, their problem-solving skills and confidence increase. In your studies, you are asked to reflect, interpret, and apply theory to practice. Why are actions, problem solving, and confidence important to your learning and development? Now, consider how they would be important to children too. Think about children who are inflexible and lack **resiliency**. What behaviours do they exhibit? Reflect upon what it means to be resilient. Why is this important for all children to achieve? When children have exposure to rich outdoor play environments, they can meet these standards. This potential reinforces the argument that all children living in Canada deserve the right and access to play in nature.

Resiliency means that children are quick to recover from difficulties and exhibit strength and toughness.

PRINCIPLES OF PRACTICE: RIGHTS-BASED PRACTICE

The United Nations *Convention on the Rights of the Child* was officially approved by the United Nations in 1989. In 1991, Canada ratified it (United Nations Treaty Collection, 2014). The ratification signified a commitment by the Government of Canada and subsequently by the Canadian provinces and territories to agree to bring laws, policies, and practices in line with the standards of the *Convention* (Di Santo & Kenneally, 2014). By ratifying the *Convention*, Canada made a commitment to protect and enhance the rights of children. Although all articles of the *Convention* are important, we list Articles 3, 12, 19, 23, 30, and 31 below in Table 1.3, as they are particularly relevant to outdoor play and learning.

Viewing children as rights-holders is a move towards a rights-integrative approach to early learning. This requires a shift in thinking from a focus on children's needs and academic outcomes to a conceptualization of the child as having rights. From this perspective, there will be consideration of the child's rights in the program. Early learning teachers will actively listen to children and ask questions that deepen their knowledge. This approach will influence how adults think about organizing the learning environment indoors and outdoors for children's active engagement and ownership (Di Santo & Kenneally, 2014). Children not only need outdoor play to reconnect with nature and all the benefits it has to offer, they also have a right to learning outside! We begin this textbook with a rights perspective as a principle of practice, and in each subsequent chapter we will expand on a multiple perspective framework for outdoor play and learning.

Table 1.3 United Nations Articles.

Article 3	States that in all actions concerning children, the best interests of the child shall be a primary consideration.
Article 12	States that the child has the right to express his/her views freely and have them considered.
Article 19	States that adults have the responsibility to ensure that children have safe environments for their play episodes.
Article 23	States that children with disabilities have the right to recreation and the fullest possible social integration and individual development.
Article 30	States that children of ethnocultural minorities, or of indigenous origin, have the right to their own culture. This includes their forms of play/recreation.
Article 31	States that every child has the right to rest and leisure, to engage in play and recreational activities appropriate to the age of the child, and to participate freely in cultural life and the arts. That member governments shall respect and promote the right of the child to participate fully in cultural and artistic life and shall encourage the provision of appropriate and equal opportunities for cultural, artistic, recreational, and leisure activity.

CURIOUS?

Learn more about the United Nations' convention on children's rights. The link that follows will take you to a PDF of the UN *Convention on the Rights of the Child* in child-friendly language: https://www.unicef.org/rightsite/files/uncrcchilldfriendlylanguage.pdf

LEARNING IN PLACE: THE NEIGHBOURHOOD AS PLACE

Tim Gill is considered one of the United Kingdom's leading thinkers on childhood. He advocates for positive change in children's everyday lives. In his book, *No Fear: Growing Up in a Risk Averse Society* (2007), Gill recommended that children be given more opportunities to engage in outdoor play. Gill discussed how children's spaces for outdoor play in their neighbourhoods are disappearing. Since the days of their grandparent's generation, children's access to neighbourhood spaces has shrunk dramatically. To counter this societal trend, early years teachers can support families and children with place-based education.

CURIOUS?

Do you want to read this book *No Fear: Growing Up in a Risk Averse Society*? Do a search to find a free downloadable copy. Click on this link for a free downloadable copy: https://timrgill.files.wordpress.com/2010/10/no-fear-19-12-07.pdf

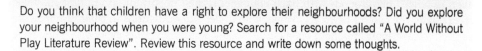

THINK ABOUT IT! READ ABOUT IT! WRITE ABOUT IT!

Do you think that children have a right to explore their neighbourhoods? Did you explore your neighbourhood when you were young? Search for a resource called "A World Without Play Literature Review". Review this resource and write down some thoughts.

Place-based education is the process of using the local community and environment as a starting point for learning in all areas of the curriculum. Emphasizing hands-on, real-world learning experiences, this pedagogical approach supports children in making a stronger connection to the natural world in a way that will increase environmental stewardship. Learning in place takes advantage of the natural space that children have access to during their outdoor play experiences. When given choices about outdoor space, children form connections with the positive features of the space (Pelo, 2013). When children make these connections, it increases their motivation to explore, while giving them purpose in their learning (Ontario Ministry of Education, 2014).

CURIOUS?

Search images on the Internet using these key words "children draw pictures of their neighbourhoods" and see what you find! What do these drawings tell you about children's perspectives of their neighbourhood?

THINK ABOUT IT! READ ABOUT IT! WRITE ABOUT IT!

Think about the importance of place. Do you want to read more about place-based education. Look for a resource online called Place-based learning: Learning Kids Can Put Their Hands On.

Write about a place in your neighbourhood that could be a source for learning.

Changing urban environments prevent many children from engaging freely in their neighbourhoods (Sandseter, Ärlemalm-Hagsér, Allin, & Prince, 2012). When these changes restrict children to 'islands' such as homes, early learning centres, and schools, their access to outdoor play decreases (Larimore & Sobel, 2016). Children benefit from having opportunities for outdoor play in their neighbourhoods. How can early learning teachers support children's opportunities to play outdoors and learn about their own neighbourhoods?

PROGRAMMING

If all early learning teachers considered children's play from a rights perspective how would it change the way early learning teachers plan for time spent outdoors? Early learning teachers plan a program of experiences throughout the day that support children's engagement, expression, well-being, and sense of belonging (Ontario Ministry of Education, 2014). However, these experiences often take place indoors. Outdoors, when children are taken to fenced playgrounds with fixed equipment, their opportunities are limited. Take, for example, the case of Myra and Paige, who under the regulations in their province are required to take their preschool-aged children outside for two hours every day. They have scheduled one hour in the morning and one hour in the afternoon. On the planning form all that is written is "outdoor play". The rest of the form is filled in with detailed descriptions of planned indoor activities. When Myra and Paige go outside, they stand together and watch the children climb on the climber and play in the sandbox. The children are often bored when they are outside. Aside from the climber, slide, and the sandbox, there isn't anything for the children to do. In the winter months, the sand gets frozen and there are even less play possibilities. The children complain about being cold so the decision is made to shorten the time outdoors. With a little thought, creativity, and relatively little cost, materials could be added to the outdoor environment that would engage the children, keep them moving, trigger their curiosity, and maintain their right to play outside.

The early learning teachers could have programmed for the conditions outdoors. They could have ensured that the children spent enough time outdoors to reap the

Photo 1.15 Children playing outside.

benefits it contributes to their development. In each chapter of this textbook, we will explore how early learning teachers can program for outdoor play using what we term the "PEER Principle" illustrated in Figure 1.4.

Taking into consideration time, space, and materials, an initial plan is put into place for children's outdoor play experiences. Thinking back to the scenario of the children complaining that they were cold and having their outdoor play time cut short, what could the teachers have planned, not only to engage the children for the full hour in the morning and the afternoon, but also to increase the time spent outdoors? Myra and Paige decided to take an outdoor online training program and came to understand that there are many things for the children to do outside. They started to appreciate that they

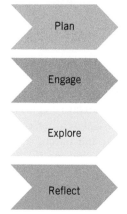

Plan

Engage

Explore

Reflect

Figure 1.4 The PEER principle.

Table 1.4 PEER—snow and ice sculptures.

PLAN	Compose a plan to invite children to create snow and ice sculptures.
ENGAGE	Invite children to chop at the ice or snow to create chunks that can be used in their creations. Once the buckets are filled, engage the children in a dialogue of what they can make. Record their ideas and give them an opportunity to either vote on what they want to do or reach consensus. Explain to the children what the differences are between majority rules and consensus. Another day, give children the freedom to decide spontaneously about their creation.
EXPLORE	The children explore with ice and snow when filling the buckets. Explore how the children worked collaboratively or independently to create their sculptures.
REFLECT	Consider the decisions the children made, the process involved, and whether there was a difference in the experiences.

had a role to play outdoors, aside from supervision, and that they could take children beyond the playground to explore. Consider what might have occurred if there had been a written plan that involved placing buckets and shovels in the outdoor environment for children to collect snow and ice? Once the snow and ice had been collected, children might naturally want to construct a sculpture or create a design, especially after Myra and Paige enthusiastically invite them to chop, chisel, and collect. Review Table 1.4 to think further about the possibilities of the snow and ice sculpture plan.

As noted earlier, Myra and Paige shortened the time outdoors because the children were complaining about being cold. They were at a point that they too did not want to go outside. It just didn't seem worth the effort. However, they found that when they were able to engage the children in active play, the complaints stopped. What might be another reason why early learning teachers were reluctant to go outdoors? There are many reasons that they might verbalize. They may suggest that the children do not all have the proper clothing for the weather or that families do not want the children outdoors. These are valid perspectives, but not acceptable given the cost of keeping children indoors. The authors of this textbook suggest that barring severe and dangerous weather conditions, such as hail and lightening, children go outside. When children are dressed properly, they can enjoy the benefits of outdoor play. Families benefit from having encouragement or support in understanding the importance of outdoor play. This helps families to understand why the correct clothing is necessary. We need to believe that all families want what is best for their children. Early learning students and teachers support families through the change of attitudes and practices towards outdoor play (Gundersen, Skar, O'Brien, Wold, & Follo, 2016).

FAMILY SUPPORT AND ENGAGEMENT

There is a popular saying in the outdoor play and nature world that *there is no bad weather, only bad clothing.* Healy (2016) suggested this proverb originates from Norway, "Det finnes ikke dårlig vær, bare dårlig klær!" which translates to "There is no bad weather, only bad clothes"! There is a similar saying from Sweden: "Det finns inget dåligt väder, bara dåliga kläder"—"there is no bad weather, there are only bad clothes". Norway and Sweden are home to many forest and nature schools, where children's programming occurs outdoors, all day, every day (Knight, 2013). With these types of programs now growing in Canada, early learning teachers provide detailed lists of appropriate clothing for the various weather conditions. Some programs fundraise to keep a class set of clothing such as raincoats and rubber boots on site for families who might need that type of support.

CURIOUS?

What type of clothing is recommended in programs that spend the majority of their time outdoors? Follow this link to find out: http://www.tirnanogforestschool.ca/clothing-at-forest-school

We encourage all early learning teachers to advocate for and support increased outdoor active play and to help families be more active. If we take the position that all children have the right to outdoor play, then it stands to reason that we should provide families with access to the information that will support them in understanding why daily outdoor play is necessary for their children. It is important for early teachers to model why outdoor play is vital and to embrace practices that make outdoor play accessible to children and their families.

ACCESSIBILITY AND DESIGN

The outdoor play environment is one of the most important spaces and places for children to learn; to connect with people and with nature; and to develop socially, emotionally, cognitively, physically, and spiritually (Ergler, Kearns, Witten, & Porter, 2016). Cooper Marcus (Acar, 2013) observed that children are deeply affected by their environment. For example, children who have many play experiences outdoors learn where different animals live in the forest and why some trees have leaves that change colours and why others are evergreen. Children's behaviour and the way they connect to people in their community and use their space are influenced by their physical surroundings. The design, **accessibility**, usability, and materials within the outdoor space influence how children connect with peers, cultivate relationships, and embrace diversity in play ideas. The depth and breadth of the interactions the children have with others and with their outdoor environment are affected by their surroundings.

Today, early learning teachers consider the outdoor space not only from the perspective of the physical experience that children may have with nature, but also from a practice perspective of **inclusion**. This means that the outdoor space is designed to support all children having access to the space and play experiences equally. The space design accommodates children and families who have a variety of disabilities, such as visual impairments, physical challenges requiring the use of mobility devices, speech and hearing impairments, or autism.

As outlined in Figure 1.5, Woolley (2013) suggested that early learning teachers apply three criteria to their design thinking and practice. When the outdoor space presents barriers to children, it reduces their opportunities to engage in the social aspects of play, to actually play, and to gain a sense of the overall connectedness to outdoor play

Accessibility refers to one's ability to approach, enter, and exit the outdoor play space in a functional manner (Prellwitz & Skar, 2007). The Canadian Standards Association (2007) describes an accessible route as "a continuous unobstructed pathway from the perimeter of the use zone to the equipment" (p. 3).

Inclusion is "the philosophy that all people have the right to be included with their peers in age-appropriate activities throughout life" (Miller & Schleien, 2006). Outdoor play spaces that are designed to encourage all children to have the opportunity to play together, rather than being segregated by ability, age, or interests contribute to an inclusive practice.

All children are able to access and play in the outdoor space.	All children are able to access the space and take part in the experience.	All children are able to choose from a range of options within the space.

Figure 1.5 Requirements for design practice.

environments, peers and community. These attributes are strongly tied to the development of sustainable and inclusive practices of play and the feelings associated with belonging (Dietze, 2013; Woolley, 2013).

Throughout this text we will demonstrate how design principles influence aspects of children's play, such as their desire to act upon their curiosity, explore, problem solve, and embrace risk-taking. Early learning teachers benefit from becoming familiar with the principles of **universal design** and how those principles can be incorporated into outdoor space that is designed and presented to children. The intent of universal design is to simplify life for everyone by making products and creating environments that are usable by as many people as possible at little or no extra cost. Universal design benefits people of all ages and abilities (Bringolf, 2008). As outlined in Table 1.5, Dietze & Kashin (2016) examined the seven principles of universal design and determined how they may influence outdoor play space design.

Early learning teachers who embrace universal design principles examine each component of the outdoor space to ensure that all children have equitable access to the play

Universal design is a framework of principles professionals use to design program space, including outdoor play space, to ensure that the space includes all children and families.

Table 1.5 Universal design principles in outdoor play environments.

Universal Design Principles	Outdoor Play Application
Equitable use The space provides all children with identical or equivalent use whenever possible.	The accessibility of the outdoor play space allows all children to make use of it. Children are not segregated because of the materials, equipment, or placement of the items in the outdoor play space. The environment has interesting features that are appealing to the varying interests of the children. The space is designed to engage all children.
Flexibility in use The space is designed to accommodate a wide range of individual preferences, interests, and abilities.	The outdoor play space is designed to allow for change in its usage, depending on children's interests and types of play episodes. The space is also designed to accommodate the differing energy levels, sensory-motor, and related abilities that will allow for children to exercise outdoor play at their pace without interfering with other children's play.
Simple and intuitive space The design and flow of space is easy to understand.	The outdoor play space has a flow to it that is simple and understandable to children through visual, auditory, or sensory observations and experiences. As changes occur to the outdoor space, children and adults engage in communication about the changes and how the changes inform their play.
Perceptible information The design communicates necessary information to the user through different modes such as pictorial, verbal, and tactile, regardless of sensory abilities.	The outdoor play design clearly communicates the different elements of the space. The space can be altered to meet the needs and interests of children and their play.
Tolerance of error The design minimizes hazards and the adverse consequences of accidental or unintended actions.	The outdoor play spaces are accessible to all and are arranged in ways that encourage children to engage with their peers. No child feels isolated because of physical barriers. Observation of the space is continuous to eliminate hazards and potential unsafe conditions.
Low physical effort The design can be used efficiently and comfortably and with a minimum of fatigue.	The outdoor play environment provides children and adults with ease in accessing resources and space. The aesthetics of the space provide comfort to the users. Access to and manoeuvering through the space occurs with a minimum of effort.
Appropriate size and shape for approach and use Appropriate size and space is provided for approach, reach, manipulation, and use, regardless of user's body size, posture, or mobility.	The outdoor play space and organization of the materials, equipment, and resources support all children having access to what they require to support their play. The space is organized to provide a clear line of sight of children in their play, no matter what the children's body position is. The space pathways and equipment accommodate children and adults that use assistive devices or have personal assistance.

Table 1.6 Essential qualities of universal design and implications for outdoor play spaces in early learning environments.

Essential Quality	Implications for Outdoor Play Spaces
Visibility Outdoor play curriculum is visible and presented in multiple means of representation to support all children's abilities and interests.	The outdoor experiences of children are displayed in a variety of ways, such as through pedagogical documentation. Displays are placed at outdoor entry and exit points and throughout the outdoor play space.
Expression Outdoor play curriculum provides children with multiple means of expression.	The environment, materials, and people within the outdoor environment engage in outdoor play experiences that lead to exploration and discovery in diverse ways. A variety of potential experiences to engage with are present daily that offer challenges and encourage children to experience ideas that require them to move from a simple to a more complex approach. This contributes to the achievement of new knowledge and skills.
Engagement Outdoor play curriculum provides multiple means of engagement.	The outdoor play space is designed to support all children in being comfortable in the space, having options for connecting with others, and having access to time, resources, peers, and adults. There are many opportunities for children's curiosity to be aroused and options for play and learning.

areas. This may result in some adjustments to the spaces, which, in essence, offer rich play opportunities that may not have been previously considered. For example, there may be ramps placed in strategic areas of the outdoor play spaces to accommodate individuals with a mobility apparatus. They become places for children to learn about many scientific principles such as speed, angles, or velocity. Using the core principles of universal design, in Table 1.6 Dietze & Kashin (2016) further identified three essential qualities of universal design for outdoor play environments.

Early learning teachers take part in many decisions with children and colleagues that contribute to ensuring that the outdoor play space and place benefit all children. These include the following:

- The outdoor physical space ensures that all children have access and equitable opportunities to engage in a variety of outdoor play experiences offered within the space and place. The materials, resources, structures, and permanent and non-permanent equipment are available to children without requiring adult intervention.

- The outdoor space promotes safety and opportunities for healthy risk-taking by ensuring that all children may use the space with minimal hazards to them. The outdoor space accommodates all children's desire to play outdoors regardless of health or disability.

- The outdoor play space is a place that supports children's development of socio-emotional skills by offering children equitable access to the space, experiences, and peers.

- The outdoor play space encourages exploration, discovery, and learning by enabling all children to have equitable access to the environment and opportunities for play within the environment. There are multiple ways in which children may express their ideas and engage in outdoor play.

Early learning teachers may find it beneficial to think about and reflect upon questions such as those below as a way to ensure that due consideration is made when planning accessible and usable space for all children:

- What types of considerations need to be made to ensure that the space is designed and equipment placed to accommodate all children?

- What types of motor and learning abilities need to be considered to ensure inclusive practice is evident?
- What types of designs for physical space should be evident so that all children may manoeuver the space safely?
- How are all children supported and engaged in making the outdoor play space inclusive?

Creating opportunities for all children to have access and a variety of experiences in their outdoor play environments is a complex process. As part of early learning practice, teachers and student teachers ensure all children have access to nature and to play.

TIPS AND TOOLS FOR OUTDOOR PLAY

Technology refers to the invention of things to solve problems. Technology is understood as that which is not created by nature.

We view digital devices and software applications as tools to support early learning teachers in their planning and documentation of outdoor experiences. When considering technology integration in early learning programs, it is important to understand that the broad definition of **technology** is that which is not created by nature. Technology is all around us, from the chairs that we sit in to the pencils that we use to write. Technology is not just computer and digital screens. It is true that digital technologies (which include computer and digital screens) are contributing to keeping children inside (Palmer, 2015). However, these devices can be seen as tools to support outdoor play by offering children ways to include their affinity for technology outdoors. For example, having a smartphone camera ready to take close-up photos of nature's beauty can spark the imagination of children and encourage them to wonder about the mystery and beauty of nature.

ON THE GROUND—PROFESSIONAL REFLECTIONS: "WHY I LOVE OUTDOOR PLAY"

We asked early learning teachers from across the country and beyond what they love about outdoor play. In each chapter, we feature a short narrative from these teachers who are passionate about children's outdoor play experiences. Barbara Routliffe eloquently shares her story in Box 1.3.

>> **BOX 1.3**   **Why I Love Outdoor Play**

It's simple. The natural landscape provides wonderful opportunities for learning. It provides its own rich curriculum. Where else can you find such an array of colour and texture as you would outside? The feel of bark, as you caress a tree, the sight of dew drops on a tiny leaf, or the humming of a grasshopper in the lazy, summer afternoon. Nothing in the classroom can even come close. And children know how to look for the beauty in nature. To stand in wonder and amazement at the landscape and yearn to know more, without the need to be coerced or forced. If self-directed learning is at the heart of knowledge, then the outside world is a wonderful place to begin. Nature is brimming with math, literacy, art, gross motor, social, emotional, and spiritual experiences. It begs to be discovered, and one has to simply observe children as they play and delight in nature to know deep down that children intrinsically desire to discover it.

Barbara Routliffe
Early Childhood Educator
Used with permission from Barbara Routliffe

CASE STUDIES

Read Case Study 1.1 below and consider the questions that follow.

>> CASE STUDY 1.1 | Nature Hikes

Georgina feels it is important for the children in her family home child care program to spend time outdoors, especially because she has a nice fenced yard with a sandbox and lots of loose parts. The children spend hours outside. The two babies that she cares for even nap outdoors. Beyond the fence, Georgina's house backs onto a conservation area with a trail system. At least once a week, in all seasons, she takes the children on a nature hike. They take pails and baskets for collecting. They don't go too far into the woods. They stop at an enclave of trees and almost every tree has a cavity or hollow that reminds Georgina of a place where elves can make cookies! Every time she takes the children on the hike, this is where they stop and turn around. Georgina worries that the children will get too tired if they go any further. As soon as they reach the hollow tree enclave, she says it is time to go back. When they return home, they put all their collections in a pile so that the children can use them for loose parts or nature art.

1. Is there something missing in the experience of the nature hike that Georgina could be sharing with the children?
2. What do you recommend she consider doing differently that would help the children develop a sense of place and their ecological identities?
3. If the children did not immediately turn around when they got to the enclave of trees what could they do there?

>> BOX 1.4 | Take It Outside!

Take a walk to a field, forest, lake, or nature reserve. Slow your pace down and notice the sights and smells. Take the time to touch the trees and to feel the drops of water on the grass. Listen for the sounds of nature: the tweeting of the birds, the croaking of the frogs, and the chirping of the crickets. Sit for a few minutes in silence on your own. This is your "sit spot". Hopefully, you can make an emotional connection to that spot. This experience that you have in nature is beneficial to children. Share it with children so that you can help them develop an ecological self or identity.

KEY TERMS

Ecological identity
Rights-integrative approach
Nature deficit disorder
Resiliency
Accessibility
Inclusion
Universal design
Technology

Diane Kashin

Photo 1.16 Key terms.

Summary

- Children have a right to receive the developmental benefits of outdoor play.
- Outdoor play supports learning.
- Margaret McMillan (1919) believed that the greatest classroom for children was the outdoors.
- When children lack experience outdoors, they can develop nature deficit disorder (Louv, 2005).
- Banning & Sullivan have identified seven standards for children's outdoor play and learning.
- Children learn from place. A child's neighbourhood offers multiple experiences for learning.
- Early learning students and teachers can plan experiences for children outdoors that engage children and offer opportunities for exploration and reflection.
- Families that receive support from early learning students and teachers will understand the importance of outdoor play for their children.
- Outdoor play environments that are inclusive pay heed to universal design principles and accessibility.

QUIET REFLECTION

Find a quiet spot in nature and sit comfortably with your eyes closed. Breathe deeply to spend a few moments decompressing. Open your eyes and look around while contemplating this reflective question: What would life be like for children who are disconnected from nature?

COMMUNITY DIALOGUE

With others, enter into a dialogue about children's lack of connection to nature. When children are spending more time indoors, what does their world look like? From the perspective of the child, describe this world with each member of your dialogue community, adding detail to the description. Create a picture of the indoor world of the child. Create a list of what you can do to reverse the trend of childhood becoming an indoor culture.

FOR FURTHER THOUGHT AND ACTION

You can become an advocate for outdoor play. Changing the culture of childhood from one that is predominately indoors to one that takes place outdoors can begin with you. This may seem like a daunting task for one person to take on, but if all early learning students and teachers were able to articulate and stand up for children's rights, change would follow. Become part of this movement that is seeking to reconnect children to nature and to enhance children's outdoor play possibilities. Think about how it would feel to be an agent of change that will improve not only the future health of the children but also the health of the planet! You can act now by increasing your knowledge base about outdoor play. In each chapter we will include resources for you to continue your journey as an advocate.

RESOURCES

The Canadian Child Care Federation offers outdoor play training modules written by the same authors of this textbook. Having access to these modules will support you in your studies and your practice. To find out more: contact the Canadian Child Care Federation at http://www.cccf-fcsge.ca

CHAPTER 2

Historical and Philosophical Foundation for Outdoor and Nature Play

Lead your child out into nature, teach him on the hilltops and in the valleys. There he will listen better, and the sense of freedom will give him more strength to overcome difficulties. But in these hours of freedom let him be taught by nature rather than by you. Let him fully realize that she is the real teacher and that you, with your art, do nothing more than walk quietly at her side.

(Johann Henrick Pestalozzi, 1746–1827)

LEARNING OUTCOMES

After exploring this chapter, you will be able to:

- Discuss how outdoor play has evolved over the course of history.

- Describe how children's play experiences, types of play, and learning are connected to outdoor play.

- Explain how your current philosophy of outdoor play reflects a living document.

- Explain how theorists and theories have influenced outdoor play today.

- Outline the benefits of gardening with children and the concept of the garden as place.

- Describe how children's interests can emerge from experiences outdoors.

CHILDHOOD MEMORIES

When I think back to my childhood I remember that one of my favourite pastimes was to lie under the big tree in our backyard and watch the clouds. I would watch them move and play around with the sun, sometimes covering it, sometimes letting the rays shine through. When I was older, my parents took me outside one night when it was dark and the moon shone brightly and the stars twinkled above. I realized then that I was part of something big—that the universe was magical and I was connected to it. Now whenever I get a chance, I watch the sky. It is like having a live theatre performance in my backyard that changes all the time. It never ceases to amaze me.

CHAPTER PREVIEW

Children belong in nature; it is in their nature (Louv, 2005). Being able to play freely in and with nature is vital to children's healthy development while supporting their learning in wondrous ways (Gray, 2013). As Pestalozzi suggested in the early 1800s, nature is a teacher (Elkind, 2015). Pestalozzi was an educational reformer whose influence on early childhood education continues today. Nature embeds teaching within it, so that when children are engaged in outdoor play in and with nature, the opportunities for learning are bountiful. Children have been learning from nature and playing outdoors since the dawn of time (Cohen & Solnit, 1993). For example, archaeological evidence reveals that children in the time of ancient Greece and Rome played with objects. More than likely, some of the objects (similar to those featured in Photos 2.1 and 2.2) would have come from nature. Children in Greece played outdoors with balls made from pigs' bladders, while children in Rome played with toy soldiers. Children 2500 years ago participated in running and jumping games and piggyback fights (Cohen & Solnit, 1993).

Diane Kashin

Photo 2.1 Rocks are historical objects for play.

Diane Kashin

Photo 2.2 Sticks have historical roots in children's play.

THINK ABOUT IT! READ ABOUT IT! WRITE ABOUT IT!

You can find Rousseau's book by searching online. Skim the contents to get a sense of what Rousseau thought about play and nature.

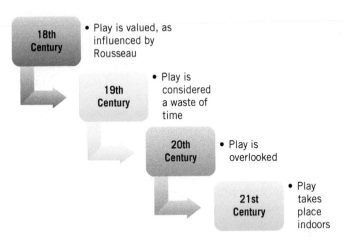

Figure 2.1 Societal attitudes towards play in Europe and North America.

Early learning teachers benefit from viewing the historical evolution of play as it influences our understanding of play today. A historical perspective reinforces why early learning teachers today advocate for children to have opportunities to participate in outdoor play. As outlined in Figure 2.1, there have been a number of shifts in how play has been regarded in society through the centuries. As you review the historical perspectives presented, think about how the changes cited relate to play and to outdoor play today.

In this chapter, we explore how historical perspectives have influenced the past and present and will contribute to the future of outdoor play in the lives of children. Learning from history is important, as it gives us a context for how outdoor play has evolved and will continue to evolve. Understanding the past gives us a fuller perspective upon which to ground our philosophy and build our practice as early learning teachers (Lascarides & Hinitz, 2013).

SETTING THE STAGE FOR OUTDOOR PLAY

Historians provide information on how historical perspectives influence outdoor play today. An examination of the historical literature shows a notable absence of comment on play. When historians examined medieval art from the thirteenth century, children were seen at play, but only on the periphery of the art pieces. By the sixteenth century, artists were painting children playing games, suggesting that children during that time period may have had more opportunity to play. However, in the seventeenth century, diarists recorded that children were to have their minds raised above the sillier diversions of play. This counsel suggests that during this time, play was considered a diversion rather than a vehicle for learning (Cohen, 1993). Jean-Jacques Rousseau's book, *Emile* (1762) depicts a world in which the children should roam freely, explore the woods and fields, and learn to read through play. Rousseau, an enormously influential figure at the time, believed that play was a child's right. He wrote that Emile should be taken outdoors every day, "far out into the fields" instead of suffocating in the "exhausted air indoors" (Rousseau, 1762/1889, p. 41). The ideal world for children was to play outside. He suggested to

...let him run about, play, fall down a hundred times a day; oftener the better, as he will sooner learn to get up again by himself. The boon of freedom is worth many scars. My pupil will have many bruises, but to make amends for that, he will always be light-hearted. Though your pupils are less often hurt, they are continually thwarted. Fettered; they are always unhappy.

(Rousseau, 1762/1889, p. 41)

While Rousseau's work (1889) was influential, in the following century, there was a shift in thinking about play and its importance to children. Play was now considered frivolous. As outlined in Figure 2.1, societal attitudes towards play have evolved since the eighteenth century when Rousseau was influential. At each phase, change in societal attitudes influenced children's access to and type of outdoor play.

For the Victorians, in the nineteenth century, play and leisure were rare, as they were regarded as a waste of time. For working class families, survival was at the forefront. Children often worked in mines and factories. For the children of middle-class and rich families, leisure time for children was used for self-improvement. If there was play, it was to be purposeful (Cohen & Solnit, 1993). At the turn of the twentieth century, and with the advent of the industrial revolution, schools were designed to introduce children to the new industrial order. There was a great migration from farms and rural communities to the cities, and immigrants from European nations came to North America to take positions in factories. With the increase in land usage devoted to factories and housing, there was a lack of play spaces in cities for children. In an effort to provide city children with safe places to play and keep them away from dangerous city elements, concerned citizens started what was known as the child-saving movement (Frost, 2010). Throughout history there have been many **social movements** (Opp, 2009). In Box 2.1, as a point of reflection, think about whether we are on the cusp of another movement connected to children.

Social movements are characterized by a group of people who get together to advance their shared ideas intended to bring about change.

>> **BOX 2.1** **Shedding Light on Outdoor Play—Points of Reflection**

Are we in the midst of another movement? Do we need a return-to-nature movement or a twenty-first century version of the child-saving movement? Do children need to be saved from a childhood that is increasingly becoming characterized by indoor experiences?

In the twentieth century, advocates for children worked hard to change the culture of childhood, where children's access to play environments had become replaced by work in the factories or unsafe city surroundings. When playgrounds were not available, children played in the streets, the fields, and in the neighbourhood slums, if they were not working as child labourers. In the early decades of the twentieth century, the numbers of child labourers peaked; these numbers gradually declined with the advent of the child labour reform movement, as social reformers sought to ban the employment of children in the workforce (Frost, 2009).

From a Canadian perspective, social reform had a positive influence on reducing child labour. For example, at the start of the twentieth century most provinces had enacted labour laws to restrict the employment of children. Legislation restricting child employment in mines was enacted in Nova Scotia in 1873, followed by British Columbia in 1877. By 1929, children under 14 years of age were legally excluded from working in factories and mines in most provinces. From the early 1870s to the mid-1920s, all provinces enacted legislation requiring school attendance (Barman, 2011).

THINK ABOUT IT! READ ABOUT IT! WRITE ABOUT IT!

What does it mean to be overscheduled? Have you ever felt that you had too much going on in your life? Do a search on the Internet using these words "overscheduling children" and read a few articles on the topic. Now write a letter to families informing them of the issue. Write the letter as if you were an early learning teacher.

The United Nations *Convention on the Rights of the* Child (UN General Assembly, 1989) as featured in Chapter 1, indicates that the right to play is necessary for a child's development. As we examine childhood in the present, we can see many differences that have developed over the centuries. However, two key questions remain regarding the status of play today: 1) Are the children playing? 2) If so, where are the children playing? In 2009, Miller and Almon wrote "The Crisis in Kindergarten". In that article, they claimed that play needed to be restored. They indicated that in kindergarten, play has been replaced with a focus on teaching literacy and academic skills. In fact, the authors suggested that the trend away from play was happening with children at an even younger age. In 2017, Gronlund and Rendon wrote *Saving Play* as a way to address the decline of play, both indoor and outdoor, in children's lives. Today, the notion of play appears to be in jeopardy.

In the twenty-first century, children's outdoor play has been drastically reduced and replaced with indoor activities or organized sports. Research is clearly identifying that children require much more time playing and learning outdoors (Brussoni et al., 2015; Nedovic & Morrissey, 2013). There is recognition amongst many that childhood today is in crisis due in part to the lack of outdoor play (Frost, 2009; Gundersen, Skar, O'Brien, Wold, & Follo, 2016). With children experiencing "an unprecedented decline in opportunities for play—outdoor free play in particular," there is mounting concern amongst child development experts and play advocates and a conviction that change is needed (Belknap & Hazler, 2014, p. 218). This new generation of children is more scheduled, stressed, and involved in adult-directed activities than ever before. They are now being referred to as the "play deprivation" generation (Belknap & Hazler, 2014, p. 218). Just as the child-saving movement evolved at the turn of the twentieth century to help children who were left alone in the streets while their parents worked in factories (Carr & Luken, 2014), we are in the midst of a new movement for the twenty-first century to preserve children's right to play. This movement seeks to get children outdoors more often in order to reverse current trends (Frost, 2009; Sobel, 2016). Will you become a part of this movement? Will you help change history?

CURIOUS?

What does virtual nature look and feel like? Find out by using the words "virtual nature" in a search engine. Watch a video. Is this a good substitute for real nature?

Today, children can access nature via the Internet and experience it virtually (Pearson & Craig, 2014). As new technologies advance, are the virtual reality versions of babbling brooks and the pitter-patter of rain a substitute for the real experience? Eliminating technology from children's lives is effectively impossible (Houghton et al., 2015). When children actually sit by a babbling brook and hear the sounds in real time, will they be thinking about computer simulations? When children stand in the rain and feel the raindrops on their tongue, will they feel bored and wish that they could experience rain virtually? It is our vision that given the opportunity to experience and play in the outdoors children will realize how much more fun it really is!

OUR VISION FOR OUTDOOR PLAY

It is our vision that outdoor play in and with nature becomes the dominant way children play today and into the future. Children require environments where they feel a sense of belonging and have positive and empowering relationships with others. These environments are essential to support children in optimal exploration and engagement for outdoor learning experiences. We view outdoor play in nature as a time when possibilities are open for both children and adults to examine their worlds and to investigate areas of interest that intrigue them. It is our vision that early learning teachers will embrace the outdoors and support children in having intriguing experiences there that captivate them. Early learning teachers will balance between child-led and adult-facilitated outdoor experiences. They will understand that their role is instrumental in facilitating access to and opportunities for children to play and learn in the great outdoors. Early learning students and teachers will see their role as co-constructors of play and learning in nature.

Philosophically, we approach this textbook from a social constructivist worldview. We suggest that learning in a social context has numerous benefits to children including developing competencies and risk-taking and self-regulation skills (Dietze & Kashin, 2016). From a constructivist approach, early learning teachers serve as provocateurs and facilitators to support children in identifying interests and in experiencing rich and intriguing explorations and discoveries. Constructivism refers to knowledge that is acquired through active involvement with content and experimentation (Kashin, 2009). Social-constructivism, based on Vygotsky's (1978) perspective suggests that early learning professionals and children "co-learn, co-research and co-construct knowledge" (Stuhmcke, 2012, p. 7). This means that the social context and environmental factors are highly influential in children's level of engagement with their environment (Stuhmcke, 2012).

Photo 2.3 Playing together in the forest.

Diane Kashin

Social constructivist learning occurs through intense participation with people and the environment. It is recognized as a powerful form of learning (Barkley, Cross, & Major, 2014). When children's strengths and talents are acknowledged, full engagement is more likely to occur, especially when their interests are supported and embraced within their family, culture, and society. The ways in which children express their ideas, interests, and sources for creating knowledge about their world will vary amongst children.

Creating environments where children feel a sense of belonging and have empowering relationships with others is essential for optimal exploration and engagement in outdoor play and learning.

Diane Kashin

Photo 2.4 Vision statement.

POSITIONING OUTDOOR PLAY IN THE LIVES OF CHILDREN

Play-based learning has been described as an approach to teaching that involves playful, child-directed elements along with some degree of adult guidance (Pyle & Danniels, 2016).

Play is recognized as a vehicle for learning (Dietze & Kashin, 2012; ACDE, 2013). Provincial curriculum frameworks demonstrate support for play-based learning (Dietze & Kashin, 2016). Play and learning are inextricably linked for children. Increasingly, early learning teachers understand their role is to support play-based learning. Now, it is beneficial for early learning teachers to recognize the importance of **play-based learning** occurring outdoors. There are multiple benefits of outdoor play as illustrated in this chapter, but if these benefits are not recognized or acted upon, children's experiences outdoors may be limited. For example, are children at home playing outdoors? Are children in early learning programs having outdoor play daily? When children are not attending early learning programs, they might be playing but are they playing outdoors? If early learning programs do not take the children outdoors daily, what are the children engaged in? What will be the long-term effects on children and childhood if we become an indoor culture? We are advocates of children being outdoors because research is clear about the developmental and health benefits of outdoor play that can't be achieved indoors (Palmer, 2015). Children miss out on numerous learning possibilities inherent in nature if they do not have ample time and experiences within it.

Compounding the issue of the lack of outdoor play is the impact that this indoor cultural shift will have on the planet. More than 20 years ago, David Sobel (1996), a leading environmental educator, expressed concern for the future if children do not learn at a young age to love and respect the natural world. Unfortunately, the connections to nature and children playing outdoors have further deteriorated since Sobel's expressed concern (Belknap & Hazler, 2014). If children are to grow up and have the responsibility to protect the environment, they benefit from developing dispositions that include a desire and an appreciation of outdoors. Will they take care of something they do not know and love? Although these seem to be questions that are being asked currently and in many disciplines, two decades ago, in his seminal work, Sobel reminded us that we need to "allow them to love the earth before we ask them to save it" (1996, p. 10). It is through having experiences and connections with nature and the environment that children learn to love it so that they can grow up and protect it. Think about the childhood memory that begins this chapter. Do you have a memory from your early years with a nature connection?

Since the time of the early philosophers, much has been written about play, and increasingly over time the links have been made between play, learning, and development (Eberle, 2014). Play that is mediated by early learning teachers can become a purposeful experience connected to emergent literacy, numeracy, and inquiry skills (Ontario Ministry of Education, 2014). However, for children, play is intended to be "an activity that is purposeless, voluntary, outside the ordinary, fun, and defined by rules" (Eberle, 2014, p. 229). Undiyaundeye (2013) identified that in order for an activity to be considered play, the experience needs to include a measure of inner control, an ability to bend or invent reality, and a strong internally based motivation for playing.

Play is spontaneously created by players in "direct response to the human need to have fun, simply for its own sake" (Nell, Drew, & Bush, 2013, p. 6). When you think back to your play experiences as a child, where did you have the most fun? Many of you will probably recall that you were outside. Where children play is also an important consideration (Brown & Kaye, 2017). Play is the way children learn. What children learn outside cannot be duplicated inside (Wilson, 2012). Reflect upon the childhood memory that opens this chapter. What was learned from the experience of watching the sky? Could this same learning be accomplished through an instructional lesson presented by a teacher? It would then no longer be play but work, and consequently much less pleasurable for children and less likely to transfer learning to knowledge creation.

Photo 2.5 Where are the children playing?

Photo 2.6 Watching the sky.

THINK ABOUT IT! READ ABOUT IT! WRITE ABOUT IT!

What do you think play from a cultural perspective means? Read this study from the Encyclopedia on Early Childhood Development (2013) http://www.child-encyclopedia.com/play/according-experts/play-and-cultural-context. Write a summary of the article.

Play has been a teaching method since the time of Plato, the ancient Greek philosopher, who believed that children learn best in playful activities (Hunnicutt, 1990). Now, centuries later, in many societies, including that of North America, Plato's message is being forgotten. Children today are spending less time playing and more time interacting with screens indoors (Brindova et al., 2014). When screens are being turned off, children are playing with "highly realistic replicas of what they have seen on screens – often with electronic push buttons, and bells and whistles" (Levin, 2015, p. 227). Gone are the days when children played freely in their neighbourhoods with their peers. Researchers and experts have expressed much concern over the effect of this decline (Belknap & Hazler, 2014).

What is the current and future societal impact of children having a lack of time to play outdoors? What experiences are children missing? Whitebread, Basilio, Kuvalia, & Verma (2012) examined play from a historical and cultural perspective and suggested that studies of play over time have revealed that wherever children play, they are all engaging in the same types of play! As illustrated in Figure 2.2, in different manifestations, the following types of play can be found in all cultures.

Photo 2.7 Playing together outside.

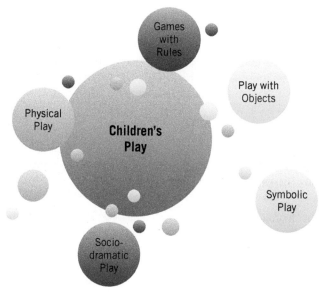

Figure 2.2 Children's play.

Looking at these types of play, do you think that they could occur more so outdoors than indoors? In fact, the outdoor environment supports these types of play in ways that are not possible indoors (Henderson, Grode, O'Connell, & Schwartz, 2015). In the outdoor environment, children have room to be physically active and to play with objects, large and small. Outside, children have access to environments that lead them to explore and discover in ways that will enhance their symbolic and socio-dramatic play (Moyles, 2014). The outdoors lends itself to games that have been played for centuries. As illustrated in Table 2.1, Dietze and Kashin (2017) adapted the work of Whitebread et al. (2012) to expand on the five types of play as they relate to outdoor play environments.

Table 2.1 Types of play.

Types of Play	Description of Play	Outdoor Possibilities
Physical Play	Includes active exercise play.	Jumping; climbing; dancing; skipping; bike riding and ball play; rough-and-tumble play and construction.
Games with Rules	Young children are strongly motivated to make sense of their world and, as such, they are very interested in rules. They enjoy games with rules and like to invent their own.	Playing Hide-and-seek, Catch, Hopscotch, London Bridge, Simon Says and Red Rover; playing games with rules that children make up.
Play with Objects	Involves children's developing explorations, as young scientists, of the physical world and the objects they find within it. When playing with objects, children set themselves goals and challenges, monitor their progress towards them, and develop an increasing repertoire of cognitive and physical skills and strategies.	Collecting pinecones; sorting sticks; balancing rocks.
Symbolic Play	The use of symbolic systems including language, reading, writing, number, visual media (painting, drawing, collage) and music are an important element of children's play.	Playing musical instruments outside; painting and drawing outside; counting sticks, rocks, and pinecones; reading and writing outside.
Socio-dramatic Play	This is the most prevalent type of play, emerging around one year of age and closely associated with cognitive, social, and academic abilities.	Building small worlds for fairies and other woodland creatures; pretending to be animals; pretending to fly; enacting stories.

Source: Adapted from Jones, M., & Shelton, M. (2011). *Developing your portfolio: Enhancing your learning and showing your stuff.* New York, NY: Routledge.

Critical reflection An extension of critical thinking. To question and challenge. To be descriptive and analytical.

Critical thinking To examine reality beyond the surface. Pondering questions of who, what, where, when, how, and most importantly, why.

Imagine a world where children do not engage in these types of play. Think about what children would be missing if they spent all their time indoors, "playing" with screens? Reflect on children's day-to-day experiences in early learning environments. Are they being given enough time and options to play outdoors? What are they doing when they are outdoors? Critically consider the early learning program featured in this case study scenario. Here is an opportunity for you to engage in **critical reflection**, which is an extension of **critical thinking**. The first scenario appears in Case Study 2.1

≫ CASE STUDY 2.1 Frustration During Outdoor Play: Scenario One

Fatima is an early learning teacher who works in an urban setting. With her partner, she has 16 preschoolers in her program. Most of the children arrive early in the morning, and they begin their day indoors. At 9 a.m., Fatima and her partner gather the children for morning circle and take attendance. Afterwards, they sing a good morning song and discuss the calendar and the weather. Every morning one child gets to put the appropriate number on the calendar and another child gets to look out the window to report on the weather. This usually takes about 20 minutes. Then, depending on the day of the week, they follow up with show and tell, French lessons, and the letter of the week

or sign language lessons. Then the children are told about which centres are open that morning and they play indoors for another half an hour. Then the children are told to line up and go to their cubbies to get dressed for outdoor play. Once everyone is dressed, they line up to go outside. They wait in line while Fatima or her partner do a safety check of the playground. When the children get outside they go directly to the fenced in playground that has a climber, sandbox, and three tricycles. The children are always fighting about who gets to use the bikes. Most days, the teachers get so frustrated that they tell the children to line up to go inside before the scheduled time for outdoor play is over.

When asked about how long the children spend outdoors, Fatima identified that it is less than an hour, since much of the time set aside for outdoor play is taken up with getting the children dressed and lined up. As well, sometimes the teachers take the children inside earlier than scheduled because their behaviour outside is not appropriate. Fatima explained that outdoor play is not really an important part of the children's day because, more importantly, it is indoors that they can be taught information that prepares them for kindergarten and meets family expectations. Outdoors, they just play—but indoors they REALLY learn.

Think about the case study.

1. Was outdoor play valued in this early learning program?

2. Did the early learning teachers believe that children could learn while playing outside?

3. Did they schedule enough time for outdoor play and keep to this schedule?

4. Did they program for outdoor play?

Keep thinking about the above scenario where there was a lack of outdoor play and compare it to Case Study 2.2, where children spend most of their day outside!

Diane Kashin

Photo 2.8 Learning from the pond.

Greg teaches kindergarten in a school situated in a small town. Adjacent to the yard is a large forested nature reserve. This is Greg's third year at this school. Each year he takes the children out for longer and longer periods of time during the day. Almost every day the children go outside for two hours in the morning and two hours in the afternoon. Last year, Greg was able to fundraise for a class set of waterproof coveralls that the children wear in all weather conditions. When the children move on to other grades, the coveralls stay with Greg for the next group of children to use. The children love to play outside. Probably their favourite thing to do is to run in the open field leading to the nature reserve. They know that when Greg howls like a wolf, that they are to stop and gather into a group. Often, they will go into the nature reserve to build dens or gather found materials. Sometimes they help carry the big loose parts that are stored in the shed near the yard to the open field where they build more shelters. Sometimes it's hard for Greg to get the children to go inside at the end of the day. He struggles with whether he should take the children back inside or let them continue to learn and explore outdoors. He knows that so much learning happens in a collaborative way outdoors.

Compare and contrast the two scenarios. They offer two different perspectives about the value of outdoor play.

1. If you were a child, which program would you like to attend?
2. How might a family's experiences and culture influence where the child would like to spend time?
3. What do you think the children were learning in Scenario One?
4. What do you think they were learning in Scenario Two?
5. What were the benefits for the children in both scenarios?

Thinking about both programs, is play a tenet of the philosophy of the program? Philosophy is defined by Jones and Shelton (2011) as educational beliefs and values that are clarified and articulated. Your philosophy defines you as a professional and is reflected in your practice. A philosophy underpins what happens in practice. For many early learning programs across Canada, having a philosophy statement is required as part of the provincial or territorial licensing requirement. These statements are intended to be reviewed regularly. Here is a list of questions adapted from Dietze and Kashin (2016) that help to examine and critically reflect upon philosophical perspectives. How would you answer each of the questions and why? Afterwards, record your answers. What do you value about children?

Photo 2.9 Playing outside in the forest.

Diane Kashin

- How do you believe children learn?
- What do you believe is the relationship between outdoor play and learning?
- In what ways do your values and beliefs reflect theoretical perspectives?

Later in the textbook, you will have the opportunity to revisit these guiding questions and to critically reflect up on your answers. You may decide to change or add to your **living document** that represents your developing philosophy of early learning and play.

Living document refers to a document that is continuously edited, added to, and updated.

THEORETICAL FOUNDATION

Up to the mid-nineteenth century, many programs had been based on philosophical, spiritual, and romantic ideals of the Froebelian kindergarten (Kernan, 2007), discussed later in the chapter. Margaret McMillan's original nursery garden school established in London, England was inspired by Froebel's work. McMillan believed that a nursery garden provided children with sensory stimulation and opportunities for physically active play and challenge (Kernan, 2006).

Between the 1930s and 1950s, psychoanalytic ideas, represented initially in the work of Sigmund Freud, that emphasized emotional needs and natural development were making an impact upon those who worked with children. Susan Isaacs, a psychoanalyst, believed that children's play was essential for their healthy emotional development (Kernan, 2006). Now, at the beginning of the twenty-first century, play remains a standard clinical practice in child psychotherapy. Play is used to help children who are dealing with complex psychological difficulties (Carr, 2015). Play continues to be considered a right for all children, with its benefits extending well beyond emotional development. As play theories continue to evolve, there is an increased understanding about the benefits of play and its importance to children's well-being (Smith, Cowie, & Blades, 2015).

Historical theorists have been influencing early learning program philosophies and continue to influence practice. Throughout history, great thinkers have influenced the way society has responded to children and outdoor play. Today, this tradition is continuing as researchers and advocates from all over the world support and advocate for a societal shift to the move towards children having more outdoor play (Rogers, Waite, & Evans, 2017) in their daily lives.

It is important to note the pioneers of early childhood education whose work continues to influence the present. These are the giants on whose shoulders we stand (Spodek & Sarracho, 2003). Listed below, we introduce you in chronological order to these great thinkers and educators.

Diane Kashin

Photo 2.10 Opportunities to play outside: Seneca College Newnham Lab School.

Theorists

John Comenius (1592–1670)

John Comenius was a Czech philosopher, pedagogue, and theologian who was the originator of the concept of natural education and believed that children could learn holistically through all their senses (Solly, 2015). There is no better way to learn through your senses than being outdoors.

Jean-Jacques Rousseau (1712–1778)

Jean-Jacques Rousseau was an eighteenth century Francophone philosopher, writer, and composer from Geneva, Switzerland, whose philosophy influenced the Enlightenment era across Europe and the development of modern political and educational thought. His ground-breaking book, *Emile*, contributed to the idea that children were capable of making informed decisions about choices in their play, particularly their natural play (Solly, 2015). Rousseau's philosophy stressed the importance of play as an instrument for the development of the senses, the exercise of judgment through sensory experience, and contact with things. He believed that children learn best in the natural world. Rousseau's work influenced Pestalozzi, Owen, and Froebel (see below).

Johann Pestalozzi (1746–1827)

Swiss pioneer Johann Pestalozzi believed that the aim of education was to develop thinking rather than just knowledge and skills. Pestalozzi suggested that education should be carried out according to nature and a child's development (Elkind, 2015). As a writer, philosopher, and defender of the poor, Pestalozzi valued play, indoors and outdoors, as central to human fulfillment and achievement at each stage of development.

Robert Owen (1771–1858)

Robert Owen was an English social reformer and radical thinker. In 1816, Owen established a workplace nursery school in Scotland. He was opposed to child labour and encouraged the children of his workers to spend hours playing outside, where there was an emphasis on physical activity (Solly, 2015).

Friedrich Froebel (1782–1852)

German educator Friedrich Froebel grew up with a strong interest in nature. He created the first kindergarten to reflect his philosophy about young children. He stressed that children should primarily be allowed to be children. He emphasized that curriculum be based on first-hand experience with nature, music, spirituality, the arts, and mathematics (Solly, 2015). Froebel believed play to be fundamental to all growth. He highlighted the necessity of interconnectedness and harmony between the inner and outer worlds of the child. The role of adults was to provide environments in which children could explore "in areas not yet known but vaguely surmised" (Liebschner, 1991, p. 15). The environment was crucial to the child's development and learning. "The educator only has to learn how to provide the widest opportunities and means, as well as the fullest freedom for such play" (Froebel cited in Lawrence 1952, p. 192). Outdoor learning environments offer children freedom to explore and discover, with wondrous opportunities for play and learning.

Rudolf Steiner (1861–1925)

Rudolf Steiner, an Austrian philosopher, has had a significant influence on early childhood education. He believed in an education that focused on real life experience. For Steiner, whose philosophy is evident in Waldorf schools today, play was valued and the imagination considered the cornerstone of child development. Steiner believed that learning should occur at a natural pace. He also advocated that the printed word not be introduced to children until age seven (Solly, 2015). Children in Waldorf schools spend time outside, learning naturally in nature.

John Dewey (1859–1952)

John Dewey, an influential educational theorist from the United States, is called the father of the progressive movement for his role in espousing a less traditional approach to school. His approach is aligned with the constructivist theory. According to Dewey, an ideal school would have a garden surrounded by fields. Dewey understood the value of the outdoors in children's education. He believed that schools were disconnected from the real world. The real world, outside the school building, was where children should learn and play (Rivkin, 1998).

Margaret McMillan (1860–1931)

In 1914, Margaret McMillan and her sister Rachel started the first open-air nursery in London, England. Influenced by both Froebel and Dewey, the sisters believed in the "importance of the garden, wholesome food, baths, fresh air, light and regular sleep/exercise periods to improve children's health and well-being" (Solly, 2015, p. 5). They created gardens with children to grow vegetables. They arranged space for children to play on climbing equipment, in sandpits and on the "heap", and where they could explore natural and manufactured objects (Solly, 2015).

Maria Montessori (1870–1952)

Maria Montessori, born in Italy, was a trained physical anthropologist and a doctor of medicine. Perhaps her greatest influence to early childhood education was to introduce a scientific approach that emphasized observation and experimentation. Her influence continues in the many Montessori programs around the world today. These programs incorporate a specific Montessori methodology of introducing children to particular materials known as apparatuses and how the apparatus is used. Often, the majority of Montessori programs take place in a controlled indoor environment (Elkind, 2015). For Montessori, her scientific approach called for children to experience a sense of wonder with nature, and it was her expectation that children had open access from indoors to outdoors, throughout the entire day (Tovey, 2014).

Susan Isaacs (1885–1948)

Susan Isaacs was a British psychologist and educator. In the 1920s, she was one of two founders of the Chelsea Open Air Nursery. As outlined earlier in the chapter, Isaacs believed that play was of crucial importance to children's emotional well-being. Of her many contributions to outdoor play, she was one of the first to provide a climbing apparatus for young children. She believed that schoolrooms should be open to the outdoors. In the open-air nursery, in addition to the climbing frame, there was a sandpit, seesaw, and plots for children to grow their own vegetables. Children were encouraged to use adult tools. Isaacs gave children ages 2 to 10 years of age an "unusual degree of freedom to explore outside and indoors too" (Solly, 2015, p. vii). Isaacs saw play as an outlet for strong impulses and emotions. It was a place to reduce anxieties. For Isaacs, the garden was a safe place to be curious as well as to express feelings of jealousy, hate, fear, or anger (Tovey, 2014). She viewed the outdoor environment as a place to support the healing of children's inner selves, and developed into what is known today as self-regulation skills.

Jean Piaget (1896–1980)

Jean Piaget, a Swiss psychologist, has had an enormous influence on many fields of study, including early childhood education. It is his theories related to constructivism that attest to children learning through play and discovery. It is not enough for a child to be taught about nature inside a classroom; the child must learn in the outdoor environment. Piaget was an environmentalist. He believed that the outdoors nourished, stimulated, and challenged children. Children build their own cognitive structures, and play is the vehicle in which they expand their mental abilities. Piaget's work put to test the basic question of epistemology, which is how we come to know the external world (Elkind, 2015). Piaget was clear that children learn from hands-on exploration of their environment, whether indoors or outdoors.

Lev Semenovich Vygotsky (1896–1934)

Russian psychologist Lev Vygotsky was a social constructivist who emphasized the influence of culture and society on human development. Although he did not live long enough to fully articulate his innovative theories or to support them with a substantial body of research, his influence is still felt today. His ideas have been influential to early childhood education (Elkind, 2015). Through the use of **scaffolding**, which is a tool adults use to help children cross their **zone of proximal development**, experiences outdoors can lead to children being able to take on greater challenges and engage in deeper thinking, exploration, and learning.

Scaffolding can be defined as a process whereby an adult or a more capable peer helps a child solve a problem, carry out a task, or achieve a goal that the child may have otherwise been unable to achieve (Bakker, Smit, & Wegerif, 2015).

Zone of proximal development refers to a concept developed by Lev Vygotsky where a more capable peer or teacher helps children learn to operate at a higher level than they could do on their own. This allows them to cross the zone and operate independently at this level (Wass & Golding, 2014).

Loris Malaguzzi (1920–1994)

Loris Malaguzzi is considered one of the most important educational influences of the twentieth century. He was devoted to early childhood education and to the pre-primary schools in Reggio Emilia, Italy, that have now become world renowned. Born at the end of World War I, Malaguzzi's formative years were spent under Mussolini's fascist World War II regime (Moss, 2016). The Reggio Emilia approach to early childhood education is based on children initiating ideas while their teachers facilitate and encourage their learning through play. According to Knight (2013), the approach is not centered on outdoor environments or natural materials only, but it has parallels to outdoor approaches advocated in various types of outdoor play programs, including forest and nature schools. For example, in forest schools and in Reggio Emilia schools, it is the children's ideas that drive the curriculum and learning experiences, rather than a teacher-led **prescribed curriculum** (Knight, 2013).

Prescribed curriculum A prescribed curriculum is given to the teachers for implementation with the children without input from the teachers and or the children.

Photo 2.11 Mixing potions at forest school: Ottawa Forest and Nature School.

Diane Kashin

The Reggio Emilia approach values and believes in the image of the child as competent and capable of complex thinking. Malaguzzi (1994) proposed that the image of the child is where teaching needs to begin. The approach utilizes **pedagogical documentation** as a means to make the image of the child, the learning and thinking visible. This approach and the underpinning theories have become influential in the twenty-first century.

Pedagogical documentation refers to a process whereby early learning teachers make children's learning visible in a way that impacts curriculum and pedagogy. The process involves observation, documentation, and interpretation.

Theories are bodies of ideas derived from studying facts or from speculating on thoughts or ideas about a particular topic.

Theories

In the nineteenth and twentieth centuries theorists were concerned with explaining the reason that play exists (Santer, Griffiths, & Goodall, 2007). **Theories** help early learning programs and early learning teachers analyze practices and develop programs that support philosophies of teaching and learning. Examining past and current theories affords opportunities to critically think and reflect upon practice while developing an ever-evolving personal philosophy of your own. Theories about play have been divided into three categories: classical (nineteenth and early twentieth century), featured in Table 2.2; modern (after 1920), featured in Table 2.3; and contemporary, representing more current thinking about play, shown in Table 2.4.

Theories and theorists form the basis of philosophical orientations to outdoor play and learning. The study of philosophy is complex and requires deep thinking about the nature of reality, the nature of knowledge, and the nature of values (Jones & Shelton, 2011). Two of the most common philosophies that you may see in practice in early learning

Diane Kashin

Photo 2.12 An outdoor play space for children.

Table 2.2 Classical theories of play.

Theory	Description
Surplus Energy	This theory proposes that children's need to play is because they have excess energy, and active play is needed to eliminate the surplus. This early theory of play proposed that, as our lives became easier, obtaining food and shelter did not require all of a person's energy. Play occurred to use the children's excess energy.
Recreation/Relaxation	This theory suggests that play is a mechanism to replenish energy after hard work. When children engage in activities that are more cognitively focused, they need time to play actively to replenish energy.
Practice	This theory proposes that play is a mechanism for children to practise adult roles. Children play the roles of significant people in their lives such as mothers, fathers, and teachers, based on observations.
Recapitulation	This theory suggests that children engage in play that has them revisit the developmental stages their ancestors passed through in ways that help them alleviate negative behaviours and develop correct processes that support society.

Table 2.3 Modern theories of play.

Theory	Description
Cognitive Development	This theory views play as a vehicle for children to use materials and interact with people as a way to build their knowledge about the world they live in.
Neurobiological	This theory based on new developments in neuroscience suggests that the environment that children are exposed to positively or negatively impacts brain development. Children who are engaged in quality play experiences are strengthening their neural network.
Psychoanalytic	This theory examines how play enhances emotional release and esteem building as children act out their feelings and work through areas of challenge by role switching and repetition.

Table 2.4 Contemporary theories of play.

Theory	Description
Critical Educational	This theory examines how play is influenced by gender, class, and racial inequalities within society. Children should have freedom and control of their learning while adults facilitate opportunities for children to examine inequalities.
Sociocultural	This theory suggests that children learn about the social and cultural contexts of their world through experiences in daily living. It is through play that children encounter problems and work through strategies that support them in their problem solving.

programs are constructivism (also known as progressivism) and behaviourism, which can be described as instructivism. Constructivism and instructivism are on the opposite sides of the philosophical continuum. These theoretical perspectives are illustrated in Figure 2.3, adapted from Dietze and Kashin (2016).

The instructivist theoretical perspectives are most often associated with behaviourism. Based on the work of Pavlov (1849–1936), Thorndike (1874–1949), Watson (1878–1958), and Skinner (1904–1990), behaviourism is a branch of psychology that has influenced early childhood education. "Behaviourists believe that all behaviour, no matter how complex, can be reduced to a simple '*stimulus-response' association*" (Gray & MacBlain, 2015, p. 4). In early childhood, you may see children being rewarded either by praise or something more tangible such as food, stickers, or gifts for what is deemed good behaviour. The emphasis is on meeting outcomes identified by the early learning teacher (Gray & MacBlain, 2015). In contrast, constructivism offers "a considerable departure from that of behaviourism" (Gray & MacBlain, 2015, p. 4). Constructivist early learning teachers view children as an active participant in their own learning. Our featured theorist in this chapter as depicted in Box 2.2 is Friedrich Froebel. Although he is not usually associated with the theories of constructivism, do you think he believed that children should be active players and learners?

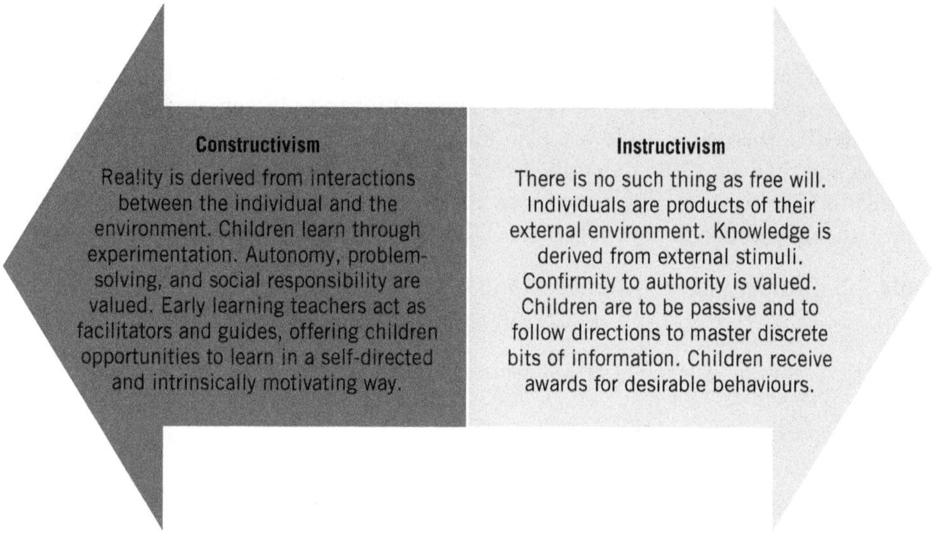

Constructivism

Reality is derived from interactions between the individual and the environment. Children learn through experimentation. Autonomy, problem-solving, and social responsibility are valued. Early learning teachers act as facilitators and guides, offering children opportunities to learn in a self-directed and intrinsically motivating way.

Instructivism

There is no such thing as free will. Individuals are products of their external environment. Knowledge is derived from external stimuli. Confirmity to authority is valued. Children are to be passive and to follow directions to master discrete bits of information. Children receive awards for desirable behaviours.

Figure 2.3 Constructivism and instructivism.

Source: Adapted from Dietze and Kashin (2016). Empowering Pedagogy for Early Childhood Education.

>> BOX 2.2   Featured Theorist: Friedrich Froebel (1782–1852)

Friedrich Froebel is known as the father of kindergarten. He first used the term and it has now become an accepted part of education. The word is derived from *kinder* (children) and garden. Froebel introduced the concept of gardens for children. He advocated for them to be incorporated into spaces that are used for play and learning. Froebel turned to nature because he had an unhappy and lonely childhood. In his solitude he found comfort from plants, flowers, and trees. For Froebel, the soul is freed from the oppression and contradictions of life when in nature. He saw the garden as the ideal learning environment for children. He saw the most viable method for children to learn in kindergarten was through play. When children are actively playing, they tend to freely express their ideas, creativity, and feelings (Omatseye & Momodu, 2014).

Photo 2.13 Gardening with children.

PRACTICAL APPLICATIONS

What does it mean to be curious and to take initiative? How will you see this in children during your observations? How can you encourage children to be curious and to take initiative? What experiences could you plan for children that would support this standard? Banning and Sullivan (2011) identified seven standards of practice for outdoor learning as listed in Chapter 1. In this chapter we feature the Curiosity and Initiative Standard of professional practice from that list (see Table 2.5). As you define your philosophy and

Table 2.5 Curiosity and initiative standard.

Curiosity and Initiative Standard

1. The child shows an eagerness to learn as demonstrated by questions, developing ideas, and exploring objects and materials.
2. The child expresses interest in others and initiates interactions.
3. The child wonders about the world and is open to new experiences.
4. The child uses multiple senses to explore and experience.
5. The child takes initiative to create and works on creations with growing independence.

Source: Banning & Sullivan, 2011, p. 201.

build your practice as an early learning teacher, we encourage you to revisit the standards as they relate to children's learning in and with nature. We recommend that early learning teachers maintain a professional portfolio.

Your **professional portfolio** can include each standard from Banning and Sullivan (2011). You can illustrate how you have worked towards these with photos and descriptions of experience. You can also work to create your philosophy statement about outdoor play and learning by reflecting on the principles of practice that are featured in each chapter. In this chapter, we introduce experiential learning as inspired by the work of John Dewey, who, as discussed in the Theorists section, was an early constructivist and progressive educator, and considered the father of the progressive movement in education.

Professional portfolio A professional portfolio documents your beliefs, professional learning, experience, involvement in the profession, and programming (Priest, 2010).

CURIOUS?

What is the progressive movement in education? To learn more about this interesting time in history follow this link: http://education.stateuniversity.com/pages/2336/Progressive-Education.html

PRINCIPLES OF PRACTICE: EXPERIENTIAL LEARNING

Theorists such as John Dewey wrote about experiential learning in relation to the importance of learning in place. Dewey (1916) identified that, "Education is not an affair of 'telling' and being told, but an active and constructive process" (p. 46). Children and educators can be co-constructors of pedagogy that emerges from nature and occurs in a specific place. Place-based educators often refer to Dewey as their ideological ancestor due in part because of his support for democracy, experience, and the learning environment connects to their theories (Jayanandhan, 2009). Place-based education is hands on and inquiry-based. It is closely connected to sustainability and nature (Smith & Sobel, 2014).

Dewey valued learning from outdoor experiences. He suggested that good schooling was dependent on the outdoor world because that is where life occurs (Rivkin, 1998). He wrote that:

> The life of the child would extend out of doors to the garden, surrounding fields and forests. He would have his excursions, his walks and talks, in which the larger world out of doors would be open to him.
>
> (Dewey, 1980, p. 35)

For Dewey, gardens, fields, and forests made up the ideal world for children to learn in. Today, these spaces still exist beyond the fenced-in playgrounds that are all too commonplace in early learning programs. He espoused the need for teachers to provide children with access to natural environments that "ought to be in a garden, and the children from the garden would be led on to surrounding fields, and then into the wider country, with all its facts and forces" (Dewey, 1980, p. 75). It is in these spaces that early learning teachers build on the experiential learning principle of practice. Through observations, discussions with children, and support and encouragement, children's experiences in and with nature flourish.

LEARNING IN PLACE: THE GARDEN AS PLACE

The garden has historically been considered a place for learning. Exposure to gardens in the early years helps us grow a green generation! There are so many benefits to children having experiences in place, in a garden. Nimmo and Hallet (2008) indicated that the garden is a place:

- For play and inquiry;
- To take safe risks;
- That lifts our expectations of children;
- To develop diverse relationships;
- To develop community;
- To invite and uncover diversity; and
- To widen social views.

There are different types of gardens for children to experience such as butterfly, vegetable, herb, and grass gardens (McClintic & Petty, 2015). Imagine the experiences that each could offer. Which garden would you like to play in? Just like Froebel advocated years before, all children benefit from having access to gardens. Gill (2014) conducted a systematic literature review on the benefits of children's engagement with nature. One of the findings supported in the literature is that children who take part in gardening projects have greater scientific learning skills than those who do not have gardening experiences. They also have healthier eating habits. The findings also indicated that when children have exposure to gardens their social, self-control, and awareness skills improve.

Diane Kashin

Photo 2.14 A children's garden.

PROGRAMMING

Early childhood teachers influence children's experiences and depth of play and exploration in early learning programs (McClintic & Petty, 2015). The attitudes towards play and exploration expressed by adults and the environmental conditions provided can either facilitate opportunities for children and their desires to be curious or create barriers that reduce their desire to act upon their sense of curiosity. When children's curiosity is sparked and heightened, more in-depth, long-term exploration occurs (Cremin, Glauert, Craft, Compton, & Stylianidou, 2015). Children have higher levels of exploration, discovery, and learning in environments with unique resources and experiences that trigger curiosity and in environments where curiosity is honoured (Alexander & Grossnickle, 2016).

Curiosity piques children's interests. It is incumbent upon the early learning teacher to discover and cultivate children's authentic interests that are worthy of attention. Children are, and can be, interested in many things. Building on interests that emerge outdoors supports children's learning and development. This is called **child-led learning**. In this approach, early learning teachers take a leading role but at the same time leave room for the children to voice and influence what happens next.

Using the PEER Principle that was introduced earlier in Chapter 1, how could an early learning teacher plan to support children's curiosity? How will the children engage in the experience? What materials can be explored? What will guide the reflections that the early learning teacher will make after the experience takes place? We offer the following experience (see Table 2.6) as an example of one that is planned to pique curiosity.

Even with carefully thought plans, children's interests and focuses can change, especially outdoors where nature has a tendency to be unpredictable. Early learning students and teachers take in consideration that curriculum is emergent and the importance of co-constructing experiences or opportunities with the children.

Photo 2.15 Looking closely in the forest.

Child-led learning also called child-initiated learning, in this approach children make choices about how to play and who to play with and what they are interested in learning about. Child-led or child-initiated does not mean that the adult does not have an important role to support and frame children's play.

Emergent Curriculum

Emergent curriculum is an approach to teaching and learning that emerges from the interests of the learner and is co-constructed with the teacher (Jones & Nimmo, 1994). By focusing on interests worthy of investigation, possibilities for play and learning can emerge (Wien, 2015). Together with children, early learning teachers create a program and experiences that are not prescribed, but unique to them. This approach provides an opportunity to give the ownership of play to children. Deciding on what is of interest to children is not a simple or rapid process. An emergent curriculum can be limiting if it is based only on things or topics in which children show an interest. For example, if the children have found a frog in the forest and show an interest, it does not mean that this should become

Emergent curriculum refers to a way of planning that builds on children's interests (Dietze & Kashin, 2016).

Table 2.6 Plan, engage, explore, reflect—in the forest.

PLAN	Prepare for an experience where you will invite the children to look closely in the forest.
ENGAGE	Share the book *Looking Closely Through the Forest* by Frank Serafini or one of the author's other books about the garden, shore, or pond depending on your context. Invite children to look closely using magnifying glasses.
EXPLORE	Encourage the children to look closely and notice detail. Ask the children what they see, what they think, and what they wonder about a variety of natural items. Record the children's response to what they see, think, and wonder. Use a camera to capture close-up photos of the natural items to create your own looking closely book. Encourage children to tell stories of what they see, to count, look for patterns, and to wonder.
REFLECT	By exercising their natural curiosity, triggered by looking closely at nature, children will have many inquiries stimulated that can lead to more experiences and long-term projects. Record their questions, wonders, and ideas, and reflect on the next possible round of plan, engage, explore, and reflect (Dietze & Kashin, 2016).

the focus of the curriculum moving forward. What are the children thinking about? What and why are they curious about the frog? Time needs to be taken to think deeply and to encourage the voice of others in the play community, including the children and their families before making the judgment call of what interests will lead the curriculum.

FAMILY SUPPORT AND ENGAGEMENT

Families are important to children, and therefore early learning teachers create places that families feel welcome in. A positive relationship with families contributes to their gaining a sense of belonging and connectedness to the early learning place. In order for families to feel that they are part of a community, they must feel engaged and supported. Engagement requires dialogue and communication. Engagement goes beyond "parent involvement" to a position where there is a reciprocal relationship of interconnectedness (Pushor, 2012). There are many ways to engage families in the support of children's outdoor play and learning. Inviting families to be part of children's outdoor experiences is a good first step. Adults, too, learn from experience. Perhaps they do not see the play and learning possibilities that exist in the great outdoors? Rather than teaching them by telling, adults and children learn from experience.

CURIOUS?

Early learning teachers need to be advocates for play. Learn more about the importance of play and how to support families by following this link: http://pediatrics.aappublications .org/content/119/1/182

As early learning teachers build their knowledge about the importance of outdoor play and learning, they are in a better position to support families in ensuring that outdoor play becomes a focus of children's experiences at home, too. There may be many reasons why children are not playing outdoors when they are at home. Imagine a childhood without play!

ACCESSIBILITY AND DESIGN

Over 150 years ago, Herbert Spencer espoused the surplus energy theory, which suggested that the main reason children need to play was to release energy (White, 2004). Even though this theory has been since rejected by most researchers and child development theorists, it has had a lasting influence on the design of children's outdoor play environments (Mulryan-Kyne, 2014). As a result of the lasting effect of Spencer's theory, playgrounds have been seen as areas for physical play, where children can burn off excess energy rather than to support the other domains of cognitive, language, social, and emotional development. When playgrounds have manufactured climbing equipment, they limit children's experiences. Often these playgrounds are designed with artificial ground cover and lack natural elements such as grass, plants and trees. They are not green but gray and more analogous to a parking lot than a playground (White, 2004).

These fixed equipment playgrounds are not only unattractive, they are also often inaccessible. Many municipalities across Canada have created neighbourhood playgrounds that are intended to offer children and families a place to play, meet other families, and participate in activities that support the establishment of a healthy lifestyle. Despite the purpose of neighbourhood playgrounds, the structural designs of many of these neighbourhood playgrounds restrict or eliminate their use by children or adults who have mobility restrictions. Structural barriers include the placements of the sidewalks, pathways, ground surfaces, and elevated frameworks around the playground equipment (Olsen, 2015; Dietze, 2013). Addressing these design issues is of utmost importance to communities across Canada. **Accessibility** in neighbourhood playgrounds supports early learning teachers in building capacity for all children to experience play beyond the playground as potential play spaces. This is essential for inclusive practice.

Accessibility The design of products, devices, services, and environments that are inclusive.

TIPS AND TOOLS FOR OUTDOOR PLAY

Technology is a tool that can support outdoor play and learning. Technology has been around since the very first humans made tools, and new technologies continue to be invented. We use technology to live. We use technology to learn and to play. Technology is used for communication and entertainment. How much technology is too much? Today, there is concern about technological integration into early learning environments. In the late 1960s and early 1970s, television was the newest technology, and educators and families worried about children's obsession with TV. Today, children are growing up in a digital age with a variety of new technologies. These are attracting children's attention away from outdoor play experiences.

Banning these new technologies from children would be difficult. Instead we recommend integrating technology to enhance experiences for children outdoors. Children are born into a world of new technologies. Children enjoy the functions and benefits of technology. Technology however, does not replace the teacher; rather, it is considered a tool that supports children and their learning options. Technology is also not a substitute for outdoor play and hands-on experiences (Goldstein, 2013). Rather, it can be used to enhance outdoor play learning. For example, if when the teacher is outside with children they notice a colourful bird, the teacher could then take the opportunity to use technology to assist children in identifying its name and characteristics. They can share their findings with families digitally. Authentic and meaningful learning begins with the experience, and technology is introduced as a tool to support children's interest in and exploration of a topic such as learning more about the birds. We consider technology as a tenet of play; it maintains the principles of constructivism, experiential learning theories, and the progressive education movement (Dietze & Kashin, 2013).

ON THE GROUND—PROFESSIONAL REFLECTIONS: "WHY I LOVE OUTDOOR PLAY"

Why do some early learning teachers love outdoors and others not? How do previous life experiences influence early learning teachers' outdoor play dispositions? Do children exhibit different types of behaviours outdoors from indoors? Read the professional reflection featured in Box 2.3 as an early learning teacher reflects on why outdoor play is important to her practice.

BOX 2.3   Why I Love Outdoor Play

As an early childhood educator, former kindergarten teacher, and current ECE faculty member, I have spent most of my life being with children, playing with children, and learning with children of all ages. With over 30 years of experience, I have learned that outdoor play completely transforms the learning experience. Once the formal classroom walls are removed and learning and play are taken outside, everything becomes alive. Outdoor play is never the same from

(Continued)

BOX 2.3   Why I Love Outdoor Play (*Continued*)

one day to the next. It is always changing, with a new story to tell about what can be seen, felt, and heard. This not only impacts the child's learning but the educator's learning as well. Our brains are engaged, alive, and alert. Suddenly, the senses are immersed in sight, sound, smell, touch, and temperature; even taste can be experienced if you dare to catch a falling snowflake on your tongue. I have experienced school-age children who struggle with concepts in the formal classroom setting come alive with understanding when given the opportunity to apply concepts in an outdoor setting through their own natural curiosity. I have seen a spark ignite in the ECE students I teach, when they are given the opportunity to play outside and reflect on how they will inspire environmental stewardship in children, as future Early Childhood Educators. Personally, as an adult, I can't imagine a world without outdoor play. For me, cross-country skiing through a wooded trail, biking down a hill with the wind through my hair, or kayaking at the break of dawn across a quiet lake is true nourishment for my soul.

Cheryl Herder
Fleming College Early Childhood Education Program
Used with the Permission of Cheryl Herder.

CASE STUDIES

Read Case Study 2.3 and consider the questions below to critically reflect on the possibilities for the early learning teacher and the children involved.

CASE STUDY 2.3   Tree Stumps

One day when Ravi, an early years teacher, was driving to work, he saw a bunch of tree stumps at the side of the road. The owner of the house must have taken down a tree. He slowed down and saw a man on the lawn. Immediately, he became curious about how the children would use these stumps. Ravi began thinking of possibilities such as if they put them in a circle, they could have their meetings outdoors! The children could also climb on them or use them as surfaces for loose parts. He stopped his car and spoke with the man about the work he did with children and asked whether he would donate the tree stumps for the children to use in their play. The man told him "of course" and that he would be so happy that children would be playing with his tree. He helped Ravi put the stumps in his car. There were so many pieces that Ravi had to return to pick up a second carload. He was excited to set these pieces up for the children in a round formation and then see what happened! Ravi planned to share with the children his story of how he acquired the tree stumps.

1. Would you have stopped and asked the owner of the house for these tree stumps? Why or why not?
2. Can you think of different possibilities for the use of the tree stumps other than what is listed?
3. How might the children be encouraged to thank the owner of the house for the tree stumps?

BOX 2.4   Take It Outside!

Don't be afraid of weather! Even if it is raining, go outside. If it is muddy, put your boots on and mess about. Splash in the puddles and feel the raindrops on your tongue. If is windy, fly a kite. Is there snow on the ground? Build a snow sculpture. If you become comfortable in the outdoor environment in all types of weather, you can be a role model for the children.

Social movements
Play-based learning
Critical reflection
Critical thinking
Living documents
Scaffolding
Zone of proximal development
Prescribed curriculum
Pedagogical documentation
Theories
Professional portfolio
Child-led learning
Emergent curriculum
Accessibility

Diane Kashin

Photo 2.16 Key terms.

Summary

- Over the course of history, societal attitudes towards play and outdoor play have fluctuated until the present time, when children are spending more time indoors.

- Play and learning are linked for children.

- Children belong in nature. They have been learning from nature and playing outdoors since the dawn of time.

- Examining the history of outdoor play provides valuable information about its importance to children's development, well-being, and learning.

- Children today, more than ever before, have less access and opportunity to be exposed to nature or engage in outdoor play. Research is identifying that there are long-term, negative effects on children, society, and our environments when children are deprived of these experiences.

- In early childhood education there are more than a dozen theorists dating back to the 1600s who continue to be influential today in the promotion of outdoor play and nature in the lives of children.

- Examining classical, modern, and contemporary theories of play provides context for understanding the complexity of play and why outdoor play is vital for children during their early years.

- Two of the most common philosophies that are used in early learning programs are constructivism and behaviourism, which is also described as instructivism. A constructivist approach supports children playing in nature and the outdoors through experimentation and problem solving.

- Friedrich Froebel is known as the father of kindergarten and first introduced the concepts of gardens for children.
- Understanding the importance of curiosity and initiative supports early learning teachers in planning and facilitating intriguing outdoor play experiences.
- The garden is a place for learning with numerous benefits to children, including as a place for play, the taking of risks, and the development of community.
- Emergent curriculum is an approach to teaching and learning that emanates from the interests of the learner and is co-constructed with the early learning teacher.
- All children require equal access to outdoor play equipment and spaces.

QUIET REFLECTION

Wherever you are, take a few moments to look out the window. What do you see? Is it a place where children might play? What would they do if they were playing in this space? What would they be learning? As an adult, how would you play in this place? If what you are looking at is not green but gray, like a parking lot, what would you do if you could transform it into a space for children to play?

COMMUNITY DIALOGUE

With others, enter into a dialogue about children's play, considering how to help families support children's opportunities to playfully learn in, and with, nature. As a group reflect upon these questions:

1. What do families need to know about the long tradition of children's outdoor play and the benefits of playing outside?
2. How can you communicate this information to families in a supportive, understanding, and non-judgmental way?
3. What does it mean to be non-judgmental?

FOR FURTHER THOUGHT AND ACTION

Are there organizations in your community that offer workshops on outdoor play? Have you ever considered taking a workshop on outdoor play? Before signing up, make sure that you will be learning, at least some of the time, outdoors. Why would it be difficult to learn about outdoor play indoors? Begin amassing names and links of organization across Canada that support outdoor play. Check the resources section for a few recommendations.

RESOURCES

Evergreen, an internationally known Canadian charity, has a mission to transform public landscapes into thriving community spaces with environmental, social, and economic benefits; in doing so, it supports children's outdoor play. https://www.evergreen.ca/about/

The Child and Nature Alliance of Canada is an organization that aspires to foster meaningful connections to the outdoors for children and youth. Learn more here: http://childnature.ca/

CHAPTER 3
Canadian and International Research on Outdoor Play

Enforced learning will not stay in the mind. So avoid compulsion and let your children's lessons take the form of play.

(Plato, 428–347 BCE)

LEARNING OUTCOMES

After exploring this chapter, you will be able to:

- Describe the influence of academic research on outdoor play.
- Discuss the types of research being conducted in Canada and internationally that are informing outdoor play practices.
- Describe what is meant by qualitative and quantitative research relative to outdoor play.
- Explain the connections between current practices in outdoor play and historical perspectives.
- Discuss the theory of biophilia and the influence of the featured theorist, Rachel Carson.
- Compare current theories that are informing practice regarding the importance of outdoor play in the lives of children.

CHILDHOOD MEMORIES

When I was a little girl, I would spend hours at the creek, watching the flow of the water, stepping across while balancing precariously on stones, looking closely for tadpoles and minnows. Time was suspended while I collected rocks, pebbles, and other treasures. I remember getting wet and dirty but not being concerned about what my mother would say. I knew that eventually I would have to make my way home, which was a few blocks away. I would go home when I got hungry. When I was by the creek it was like my sensory perception was amplified. I could hear the babbling of the brook and the sounds of the frogs and the buzz of the bees. I noticed the butterflies fleetingly flapping by and I vividly recall the brightness of the colours of their wings. This was a place that I loved to visit with my friends sometimes and also by myself. We moved away a few years later, and I missed that place. I will always remember the sights and sounds. Now when I think back to that time, the memories are nostalgic and soothing.

CHAPTER PREVIEW

Early learning theorists and researchers have long recognized the value of outdoor play (Ernst, 2014). In Chapter 2 we examined the many theorists who have been important advocates for outdoor play and nature pedagogy. Despite these historical roots and the continued interest shown among researchers, there has been a steady decline in children's access to and opportunities for outdoor play. Now, in the twenty-first century, we have alarming rates among children of Type 2 diabetes, depression, being overweight, obesity, hyperactivity, and academic challenges (Sahoo et al., 2015). These childhood conditions are leading policy-makers, educators, and health professionals to turn to research as a way to seek answers to questions such as how outdoor play influences children's health, wellness, and development (Chawla, 2015). Increasingly, research findings are suggesting that today more so than any other time in history, it is vitally important for children to get outdoors to play. This means, as early learning teachers, we have an obligation to halt the decline and actively promote outdoor play in nature (Lewis, 2017).

Research has an influence on practice. Examining current research on how children learn outdoors supports the position expressed by Whitebread and Coltman (2015) that suggest effective teaching is always based on an understanding of how children learn. Understanding the theory and application of the **pedagogy** of outdoor play and nature supports adults in their work with children (Moyles, 2014). Therefore, it is important to consider the type and scope of research that is being conducted on outdoor play. For example, how do children learn outside? What does the research say? Do children learn best if the play is unstructured or structured? Does time and place make a difference? How is pedagogy linked to programming? The literature on this topic is expansive. In this chapter we seek to help you navigate the research terrain.

The concept of research can be daunting for those new to the study of early childhood education. Yet, we encourage early learning students and teachers to engage in research as part of their daily practice. Research occurs when we look to answering a question or solving a problem by collecting information, analyzing it, and interpreting it to reach a conclusion and make recommendations for new ways of practising. This occurs throughout our lives (Mukherji & Albon, 2014); we just may not call it research. Assuming a view of ourselves as researchers when working in the early childhood education sector supports an elevated image and a thoughtful, analytical approach to practice (Edwards & Gandini, 2015).

There are distinctions between research conducted in practice and academic research. Both are valid forms of research and will be examined in this chapter. What is of significance is that never before has the research on the various facets of outdoor play been so relevant to the interdisciplinary groups, including early learning, health, education, and psychology professionals. Examining questions about outdoor play, analyzing results, and producing findings are necessary to advance knowledge, skills, and practices

Pedagogy is an early learning teacher's understanding of how learning takes place. It involves the philosophy and practice that supports one's understanding of how learning happens (Ontario Ministry of Education, 2014).

THINK ABOUT IT! READ ABOUT IT! WRITE ABOUT IT!

What does "teacher as researcher" mean to you? Search for an article called "Teacher research in Reggio Emilia, Italy: Essence of a dynamic, evolving role" and read it to understand the term.

The authors describe the image of the teacher as researcher as one that is dynamic and evolving. Write about what those words mean in relationship to your practice.

(Kellert, 2012) concerning the relationship of outdoor play to children's development and wellness (Park & Riley, 2015).

Taking the position of a researcher who collects, analyzes, and interprets information, imagine observing the children in Photo 3.1. What types of information can you collect to inform your practice? What questions would you ask in your analysis of the observation? How and why would you interpret your findings? Where might these interpretations lead you in your continued efforts to understand the children and plan for further outdoor play and learning experiences?

If early learning students and teachers adopt a lens that view outdoor play as a laboratory of potential research, the richness of possibilities for play can be revealed through their own research methods. When early learning students and teachers use the knowledge gained from outdoor play and academic research, they have a theoretical and philosophical foundation upon which they may carry out their experimental practices.

Photo 3.1 Playing with sand and water.

Diane Kashin

SETTING THE STAGE FOR OUTDOOR PLAY

Research is a concept that underpins most early learning program philosophies and methodologies. For example, research is central to the Reggio Emilia approach and to the role of the educator. In this perspective, research is "considered a way of thinking and approaching knowledge oriented to the future" (Edwards & Gandini, 2015, p. 92). Research is a way of understanding oneself in relationship to your context of practice. It offers multiple perspectives on research questions and problems (Edwards & Gandini, 2015).

CURIOUS?

Lilian Katz, who is considered a giant in early childhood education studies, wrote about attitudes and dispositions (1993). Her work emphasizes the importance of developing positive dispositions and offers "helpful definitions of both dispositions and attitudes that highlight the breadth and stability of dispositions and the directionality and specificity of attitudes" (Georgeson & Campbell-Barr, 2015, p. 321). Into a search engine, put the words "Lilian Katz and dispositions" to find out more.

Taking inspiration from the educators of Reggio Emilia, research can be seen as a part of everyday life. Rinaldi (2012) described it as an attitude or "way of thinking for ourselves and thinking jointly with others, a way of relating with other people, with the world around us, and with life" (p. 245). Rinaldi suggested that research is an attitude. What does that mean to you? Attitudes and dispositions as they relate to your beliefs about outdoor play will influence your practice. What is your attitude towards outdoor play? When was the last time you played outdoors, as an adult?

Ann MacDonald

Photo 3.2 Adults playing outside.

Diane Kashin

Photo 3.3 Outdoor play involves risk and challenge.

Georgeson and Campbell-Barr (2015) compare the definitions of attitudes and dispositions. A disposition refers to a broad, enduring tendency to behave in a particular way when responding in a variety of situations. For instance, if you believe that play is a waste of time, you will be reluctant to play as an adult outdoors or indoors. This influences how you support children's play indoors and outdoors. An attitude, according to Georgeson and Campbell-Barr, refers "to elements of a system of beliefs about ideas, things and people in the world that have different components (emotional, motivational, intellectual, and evaluative) and are differentially open to change" (p. 321). Figure 3.1 summarizes the concept of attitudes and dispositions.

You can develop a positive disposition to outdoor play and nature pedagogy. Early learning teachers who have a desire to change their attitude and embrace outdoor play develop a strategy to engage in adjusting their system of beliefs. This may take time. We encourage you to begin the journey of seeing yourself as a researcher in the pursuit of learning more about outdoor play. In the process, there will be disposition development and attitudinal change.

Introduction to Research Methods

Research is a complex process. Early learning students and teachers benefit from understanding types of research categories and principles associated with high quality research.

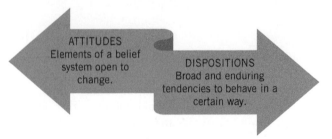

ATTITUDES
Elements of a belief system open to change.

DISPOSITIONS
Broad and enduring tendencies to behave in a certain way.

Figure 3.1 Attitudes and dispositions.

There are two basic categories that are associated with research: **quantitative research** and **qualitative research**. Quantitative research generally refers to data that are created based on descriptors or stories in response to specific questions asked (Hartas, 2015). Qualitative researchers are curious about seeking answers to *why* questions that may be triggered or evolve from their philosophy, vision, observations of children and environments, conversations with children and adults, or questions that evolve with colleagues, children, family, or community partners. The data collected are generally analyzed by making comparisons within the data and by examining the context of the emerging themes that surface. Qualitative research aligns well with many of the core questions associated with children's engagement in outdoor play, such as in their use of equipment, children's play choices, staff attitudes toward outdoor programming, play space designs, and programming strategies.

Quantitative research requires some form of measurement where the data are assigned a numerical value to the topic being researched. Researchers engaging in this form of research focus on seeking knowledge from complex and diverse data. Quantitative and qualitative research can work together when researchers use qualitative studies to help identify what needs to be measured (Maxwell, 2012). In outdoor play research, quantitative studies measure specific concepts, such as children's time in using playground equipment or the duration of engagement in a particular type of play experience.

> **Quantitative research** is used to quantify a problem by using numerical data that is measurable. Data collection is more structured than in qualitative research (Wyse, 2011).

> **Qualitative research** is exploratory research that is used to generate ideas or develop hypotheses. Data collection methods are often unstructured and sample sizes often small (Wyse, 2011).

›› BOX 3.1   Shedding Light on Outdoor Play—Points of Reflection

Why would measuring time spent outdoors be important? How do you think researchers gather this data? What percentage of a full day from 8 a.m. to 6 p.m. should children be engaged in outdoor play? In the research conducted by Tandon, Saelens, Zhou, Kerr, & Christakis (2013), 45 children (average age 4.5 years; 64% boys) from five early learning programs wore portable accelerometers with built-in light sensors and a separate GPS device around their waists. These devices accurately measured time spent outdoors versus indoor time. The rationale for the research was to understand the relationship between outdoor time and an improved measurement in health.

Accessing and reading research on outdoor play has the potential to advance your understanding of the theory and practice of outdoor play and nature pedagogy. Research is the systematic investigation of a topic that is intended to inform practice. Early learning teachers are encouraged to examine the research and to incorporate core findings from the research into their practice. Ultimately, this will result in children living in Canada having outdoor play experiences and resources that are meaningful, intriguing, and supportive of their levels of curiosity and interests (Dietze, 2013).

Until recently, much of the research on outdoor play occurred primarily in countries such as Norway, Scotland, England, and the United States. Since the beginning of the twenty-first century, there has been a significant increase in the number of researchers in Canadian college and university settings who are studying, advancing, and adding to outdoor play research. Outdoor play research crosses disciplines such as education; behavioral psychology; the political, environmental, and health sciences; and early childhood education. Figure 3.2 provides a sampling of the types of topics being researched related to outdoor play.

Do any of these topics pique your interest and curiosity? What are researchers finding in their studies of these various aspects of outdoor play? We hope that you will become familiar with the current research literature on outdoor play. Many aspects of it will inform your practice and enhance your vision of the possibilities for children when they play and learn outdoors.

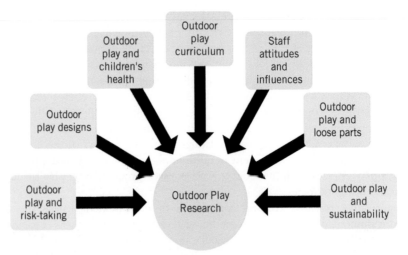

Figure 3.2 Types of outdoor play research.

THINK ABOUT IT! READ ABOUT IT! WRITE ABOUT IT!

What type of research would you be interested in conducting? Find out more about research methods in early learning by following this link: http://www.oecd.org/education/school/49322754.pdf

In one paragraph, write a description of the research that you would be interested in doing.

OUR VISION FOR OUTDOOR PLAY

It is our vision for outdoor play that early learning teachers and students create their own visions by examining beliefs and research and then aligning research with beliefs. This is done in recognition that decisions made in practice are driven by perceptions and beliefs. Your beliefs affect your planning, interactions, decisions, and practices. Beliefs about outdoor play, children's learning outdoors, and environmental connections influence child and adults actions and behaviours in the outdoor play environment. "Each person constructs their reality as a result of past experiences and how they interpret those experiences" (McClintic & Petty, 2015, p. 27). What you believe and learn from research can influence your outdoor play practice with children.

McClintic and Petty (2015) conducted a qualitative case study to explore how early learning teachers' beliefs and practice influence outdoor play. The researchers found early learning teachers' recollections of their own outdoor experiences indicated that they valued the freedom outdoor play provides. However, they saw their current role with children as supervisory. They believed that outdoor play was important but emphasized the reinforcement of rules during children's experiences. The findings indicated that the early learning teachers had minimal knowledge of the benefits and possibilities of outdoor play, creating this juxtaposition between beliefs and practice.

The findings in the McClintic and Petty (2015) study suggested that there was not belief alignment with practice. To bring practice, beliefs, and research together there needs to be passion for outdoor play. What impact would it make if a passion for outdoor play was in the hearts and minds of all early learning students and teachers? Would children get to play more outdoors? How would this benefit the children? It is our hope that early learning students and teachers will align their own childhood experiences about outdoor play with research and enhance their current practice by reflecting on the past and creating a vision for the future. Visions are dreams. Sometimes dreams transpire from negative experiences. For some, the most powerful and meaningful childhood memories took place outdoors. While for others, they may not have spent much time outdoors and are a product of the societal shift in the culture of childhood. When you turn dreams into visions you go beyond how things are, to how you want them to be. If you believe that children deserve outdoor play, creating a vision statement is an important step (Carter, Cividanes, Curtis, & Lebo, 2010).

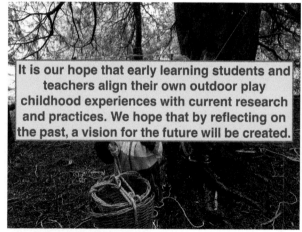

It is our hope that early learning students and teachers align their own outdoor play childhood experiences with current research and practices. We hope that by reflecting on the past, a vision for the future will be created.

Diane Kash.n

Photo 3.4 Vision for outdoor play.

THINK ABOUT IT! READ ABOUT IT! WRITE ABOUT IT!

What do you think should be in an early learning program's vision statement? It is not difficult to find sample visions statements online. Read five or six and then write your own.

POSITIONING OUTDOOR PLAY IN THE LIVES OF CHILDREN

Surveying the recent research literature on topics related to outdoor play can serve as a way to expand **professional vision**. According to Seidel & Stürmer (2014), professional vision is the use of knowledge to notice and interpret significant features of situations as they occur in the learning environment. The three aspects of a professional vision as identified by Seidel & Stürmer (2014) are outlined in in Figure 3.3.

Professional vision in teaching is the specialized knowledge that helps to make sense of day-to-day practice. This occurs through attention and knowledge-base reasoning. (Seidel & Stürmer, 2014).

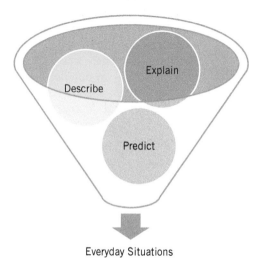

Everyday Situations

Figure 3.3 Three aspects of professional vision.

Literature Reviews

Research literature related to outdoor play serves as a means to a professional vision. Reading all the academic articles on multiple topics within the broader category of outdoor play may seem like a daunting task. Narrowing down the broad topic of outdoor play as illustrated in Figure 3.2 is a recommended first step. Next, you will need to do a **literature review**, or written overview of significant academic sources, for your topic. For example, take the category of loose parts for outdoor play and conduct or write a literature review. Either exercise will increase your professional knowledge and vision about loose parts and their importance to children's outdoor play.

There is a distinction between conducting a literature review and writing one. Conducting involves locating appropriate and relevant academic sources (research literature), reading them, and mentally analyzing them. Writing a literature review involves the same steps, in addition to the process of composition that includes: a) planning; b) organizing; c) drafting; d) editing; and e) redrafting (Galvan & Galvan, 2017). In many instances, you can find academic literature reviews that have already compiled a survey on the topic of your interest. For example, Houser, Roach, Stone, Turner, & Kirk (2016) have written a review on the implementation of loose parts to promote physical activity. Literature reviews help early learning students and teachers enhance their understanding of topical issues related to outdoor play and nature pedagogy.

Literature reviews are written overviews of specific topics that include a survey of academic sources.

CURIOUS?

Read a literature review on loose parts by searching using these words "literature review on loose parts". How has the process of reading a literature review helped you learn more about loose parts?

As a result of two systematic literature reviews, an important *Position Statement* has been published in Canada that supports outdoor play. A diverse, cross-sectorial group of partners, stakeholders, and researchers collaborated to develop an evidence-informed statement on active play for children aged 3–12 years. The *Position Statement* development process was informed by reviews; a critical appraisal of the current literature and existing position statements; engagement of research experts and cross-sectorial individuals/organizations; and an extensive stakeholder consultation process. There was overwhelming evidence and support for active play outdoors (Gray et al., 2015).

In April 2015, the *Position Statement* was published in the *International Journal of Environmental Research and Public Health,* which is available from: https://www.participaction.com/en-ca/thought-leadership/research/2015-position-statement-on-active-outdoor-play.

The *Position Statement* "was created in response to practitioner, academic, legal, insurance and public debate, dialogue and disagreement on the relative benefits and harms of active (including risky) outdoor play" (Tremblay et al., 2015, p. 1). Stakeholders from a variety of sectors including health, education, and physical activity were

Photo 3.5 Loose parts from nature.

>> BOX 3.2   Position Statement on Active Outdoor Play

POSITION STATEMENT ON ACTIVE OUTDOOR PLAY

Position

Access to active play in nature and outdoors—with its risks—is essential for healthy child development. We recommend increasing children's opportunities for self-directed play outdoors in all settings—at home, at school, in child care, the community and nature.

PREAMBLE

We conducted two systematic reviews to examine the best available scientific evidence on the net effect (i.e., balance of benefits vs. harms) of outdoor and risky active play. Other research and reviews were also consulted. The Position Statement applies to girls and boys (aged 3-12 years) regardless of ethnicity, race, or family socioeconomic status. Children who have a disability or a medical condition should also enjoy active outdoor play in compliance with guidance from a health professional.

CONTEXT

In an era of schoolyard ball bans and debates about safe tobogganing, have we as a society lost the appropriate balance between keeping children healthy and active and protecting them from serious harm? If we make too many rules about what they can and can't do, will we hinder their natural ability to develop and learn? If we make injury prevention the ultimate goal of outdoor play spaces, will they be any fun? Are children safer sitting on the couch instead of playing actively outside? **We need to recognize the difference between danger and risk. And we need to value long-term health and fun as much as we value safety.**

Risk is often seen as a bad word—by parents, neighbours, care providers, insurance providers, schools and municipalities. But in play, risk doesn't mean courting danger—like skating on a half-frozen lake or sending a preschooler to the park alone. It means the types of play children see as thrilling and exciting where the possibility of physical injury may exist, but they can recognize and evaluate challenges according to their own ability.¹⁴ It means giving children the freedom to decide how high to climb, to explore the woods, get dirty, play hide 'n seek, wander in their neighbourhoods, balance, tumble and rough-house, especially outdoors, so they can be active, build confidence, autonomy and resilience, develop skills, solve problems and learn their own limits. It's letting kids be kids—healthier, more active kids.

EVIDENCE

» When children are outside they move more, sit less and play longer⁵¹¹—behaviours associated with improved cholesterol levels, blood pressure, body composition, bone density, cardiorespiratory and musculoskeletal fitness and aspects of mental, social and environmental health.¹⁹ ⁴³

» Outdoor play is safer than you think!

o The odds of total stranger abduction are about 1 in 14 million based on RCMP reports.²³ Being with friends outdoors may further reduce this number.

o Broken bones and head injuries unfortunately do happen, but major trauma is uncommon. Most injuries associated with outdoor play are minor.²⁴⁻³¹

o Canadian children are eight times more likely to die as a passenger in a motor vehicle than from being hit by a vehicle when outside on foot or on a bike.³²⁻³⁴

» There are consequences to keeping kids indoors—is it really safer?

o When children spend more time in front of screens they are more likely to be exposed to cyber-predators and violence, and eat unhealthy snacks.³⁵⁻³⁹

Position Statement on Active Outdoor Play   1

Used with permission from Participaction and its Partners.

consulted in the development of the Position Statement (Gray et al., 2015). Box 3.2 provides a screenshot of the position statement. The final *Position Statement on Active Outdoor Play* states: "Access to active play in nature and outdoors—with its risks—is essential for healthy child development. We recommend increasing children's opportunities for self-directed play outdoors in all settings—at home, at school, in child care, the community and nature" (Gray et al., 2015, p. 1). The full statement provides context, evidence supporting the statement, and a series of recommendations intended to increase active outdoor play opportunities that promote healthy child development.

THEORETICAL FOUNDATION

Many researchers are now emphasizing that it is crucial that early learning teachers understand the differences between programming for indoor and outdoor environments. The types of play, motor function, learning, sense of curiosity, level of environmental consciousness, and exploration differ significantly if children are exposed to outdoor environments that support exploration and connectedness to the space and place (Derby, Piersol, & Blenkinsop, 2015). As well, the role of early learning teachers differs within the two environments. This chapter highlights some aspects of the research that supports

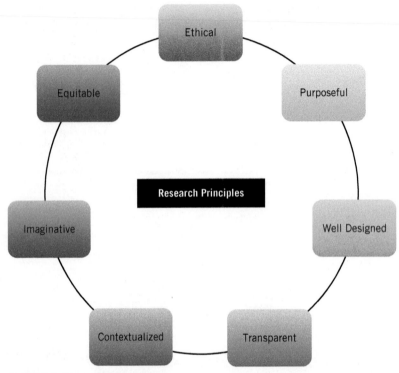

Figure 3.4 Research principles.

outdoor play as an essential component of early learning programs. Figure 3.4 illustrates these aspects of research as principles. Early learning teachers are encouraged to use **peer-reviewed articles** to inform their practice because the process of peer review ensures the research has been examined from a variety of perspectives. In this case, the topic is outdoor and nature play.

Peer-reviewed articles refer to those articles that have been evaluated by several academic researchers, prior to the article being published, to validate worthiness of publication.

Action Research

Action research will help you answer questions about your practice and children's play. When you engage in action research you are the research subject. According to Dietze et al. (2014) "action research begins with a sense of curiosity and wonderment," (p. 3) making it particularly aligned with children's approach to outdoor play. Dietze et al. (2014) suggested that action research is the study of one's own practice in relationship to children's learning. The goal of action research is to improve the practice of teaching and learning (Dietze et al., 2014).

Researchers are required to meet ethical guidelines to protect the research subjects. They obtain ethics approval from a university, college, or school board. Ethical principles are always required in all research. With action research being common educational practice involving the gathering of data and making pedagogical changes, it assumes that the process will be ethical. The action research should be conducted with protective concern for the children (Dietze et al., 2014). If the data obtained from action research results in publication, ethical approval would be required.

Action research can be both qualitative and quantitative (Stepaniak, 2015). It has a reflexive nature with an iterative cycle of plan; act and observe; reflect (Rose, Spinks, & Canhoto, 2015). As depicted in Figure 3.5, it is an ongoing process.

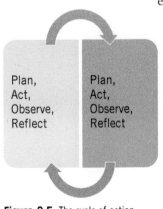

Figure 3.5 The cycle of action research.

The plans for action research begin with a question or problem that causes you to pause and to wonder (Rose, Spinks, & Canhoto, 2015). In thinking about outdoor play, an early learning teacher might wonder what would happen if the outdoor play time was increased. A plan would be created. Then, the plan would be put into action and would include observing children to determine if there is an impact. Observations would be recorded and then reviewed. At that point, written reflections derived from the observations lead to changes in practice.

National and international researchers have been instrumental in advocating that children's outdoor play experiences be examined and changed to offer more varied experiences, time, and opportunities within natural play settings (Waller, Sandseter, Wyver, Ärlemalm-Hagsér, & Maynard, 2010). In the following section, we will provide a selection of research that is contributing to the development of new knowledge about the relationship of outdoor play to children's development.

Photo 3.6 Children spending time outside playing.

For more information on Dr. Ellen Sandseter put her name into a search engine.

National and International Research Influencing Children's Outdoor Play

A qualitative study by Sandseter (2010) examined risky play amongst preschoolers in Norway. The findings of the study suggested that risky play primarily takes play outdoors, is thrilling and exciting, and may include a possibility of physical injury. However, the findings revealed that there is a difference between risk and hazard. Observations and interviews with preschool children and educators led to the identification of categories and subcategories of risky play. The categories are outlined in Table 3.1

For more information on David Sobel see: https://en.wikipedia.org/wiki/David_Sobel

Sobel (2008), an American author conducted research that revealed that children engage in more creative forms of play in green areas, as opposed to manufactured play areas. This finding led to the development of seven principles/themes that emerge when children experience free time in nature. These play motifs are featured in Figure 3.6 and explained below.

Table 3.1 Categories and sub-categories of risky play.

Categories	Risk	Sub-categories
Great heights	Falling	Climbing Jumping Balancing
High speed	Uncontrolled speed that could lead to a collision	Swinging Sliding Running
Dangerous tools	Injuries such as cuts and bruises	Cutting tools Hammers Ropes
Dangerous elements	Falling Exposure to water or fire	Cliffs, hills, ledges Deep water Fire pits
Rough-and-tumble play	Injury to others	Sticks Rough housing
Disappearing/getting lost	Disappearance from supervision	Exploring alone Exploring unfamiliar territories

When children spend time in nature they will naturally construct adventures. They will engage in fantasy and imaginative dramatic play. When children are outdoors they will have the time to naturally make friends with the creatures that they discover. During time outdoors, children will explore the natural geography of a place and make maps and pathways. Given time in nature children create their own special places like dens and forts. With found natural materials children will create miniature representations of the world they are discovering. When outdoors, children love to gather found objects and hunt for treasure. The knowledge of these play motifs supports early learning teachers in designing time, space, and materials for children (Sobel, 2008).

Diane Kashin

Animal Allies

Special Places

Maps and Paths

Fantasy and Imagination

Adventure

Small Worlds

Hunting and Gathering

Figure 3.6 Play motifs.

Canadian Research

Canadian researchers have been contributing to research on outdoor play. For example, Herrington and Lesmeister (2006) compared 12 sample outdoor play centres at early learning centres and developed the "Seven Cs" for early learning teachers, designers, administrators, and families. The goal of the informational guide is to design outdoor spaces that support children's development and play that can be used in concert with existing standards and guidelines. The 7 Cs include the following:

1. **Character**—the overall feel and design of the outdoor space.
2. **Context**—the actual play space and the larger landscape that surrounds it.
3. **Connectivity**—the physical, cognitive, and visual connectivity of the space.
4. **Change**—how the space changes over time.
5. **Chance**—chances for the children to manipulate and create.
6. **Clarity**—the obstructions that may interfere with the view early learning teachers have of the space.
7. **Challenge**—the physical and cognitive challenges of the space.

Source: Adapted from Herrington and Lesmeister (2006).

CURIOUS?

The informational Guide to Young Children's Outdoor Play Spaces can be downloaded from: http://www.wstcoast.org/playspaces/outsidecriteria/7Cs.pdf

Dietze & Kim (2014) researched core elements of outdoor play environments that support children in having spaces that are intriguing and spark a sense of curiosity and wonder. Their assessment tool advocates for early learning teachers to examine the space in relation to play zones, play environmental elements, physical movement and risk-taking, experiential play, loose parts, the role of the early learning teacher, and involving parents and families in the outdoor play options.

Canadian researchers continue to recognize that, with safety being a key driver of play space design, children's free play opportunities with natural elements are declining. Taking the lead to reverse this trend, Brunelle, Herrington, Coghlan, and Brussoni (2016) conducted a survey with adults that focused on their own recollections of their childhood experiences. Of the 592 respondents, 69 percent felt that playgrounds today are too safe. When they reflected on their own childhoods, 59 percent of participants preferred natural play spaces. The authors concluded that children should have more challenging play opportunities with natural elements and access to unstructured play areas.

Canadian research on outdoor play is increasing. With the support from academic institutions and funding, greater opportunities for children and an expanded knowledge base for early learning students and teachers will be

Photo 3.7 Active play in the forest.

Diane Kashin

possible. For example, the Lawson Family Foundation is a major foundation and advocate for supporting Canadian research projects on outdoor play. The authors of this textbook have conducted research on staff attitudes toward outdoor play with funding from the Lawson Foundation. The research findings indicated that there is a desire among early learning teachers to have access to specialized training. The participants indicated that ideally, with more knowledge, children's experiences outside would be enhanced.

The Back to Nature Movement

Children learn more from what adults do than from what adults say. Children observe the adults in their lives as a way to learn about what is valued, sacred, and important. The values that children experience and see reflected in the lives of the adults around them "tend to be the attitudes and values they'll carry with them throughout their life" (Wilson, 2012, p. 51). Wilson (2012) identified that "if we want children to be sensitive to and interested in the world of nature, then that's the way we'll have to be" (p. 51). Citing Rachel Carson (see Featured Theorist Box 3.3), who encouraged adults to explore nature with children as partners in exploration, Wilson recommended that adults nurture their own sense of wonder rather than worry about amassing a large body of scientific knowledge. Adults benefit from developing a disposition and attitude that demonstrates to children caring and respect for the natural environment. Wilson suggested that

> [c]are and respect can be modelled through the gentle handling of plants and animals in the classroom and outdoors, establishing and maintaining outdoor habitats for wildlife, attending to the responsible disposal of trash, and recycling or reusing as many materials as possible. (p. 52)

BOX 3.3 Featured Theorist: Rachel Carson (1907–1964)

Rachel Carson was an American marine biologist and conservationist who is credited with advancing the global environmental movement. She was instrumental in advocating legislation that would eliminate the use of pesticides that were harmful to the environment. She also encouraged families to expose their children to nature, assuring them that even if they had limited knowledge of nature, they could help their children to appreciate it. For more information on Rachel Carson: http://www.rachelcarson.org/

The present generation is suffering from a lack of time spent outdoors, which in turn presents many health, academic, and psychological challenges for children. These challenges have the potential to become lifelong issues (ParticipACTION, 2015). The ParticipACTION Report Card (2015) emphasized the importance of outdoor play by stating: "The biggest risk is keeping kids indoors" (p. 1). Outdoor play influences healthy living and development.

In North America, growing interest in preserving the planet and getting children back to nature are, according to Frost (2009), being spurred on by the former Vice President of the United States Al Gore's (2006) book, *An Inconvenient Truth*, and his Academy Award-winning documentary by the same title. In addition, Frost stated that Richard Louv's (2005) best-selling book, *Last Child In the Woods: Saving Our Children from Nature-Deficit Disorder* has had an equal effect on stimulating the call to action. While Al Gore focused on building public awareness concerning global climate change, Louv, Charles, and others formed the Children & Nature Network (C&NN) in an effort to build an international movement to reconnect children and nature (Frost, 2009).

CURIOUS?

Want to know more about Children's Outdoor Bill of Rights (2005) and Ontario's Children's Outdoor Charter, if so, check out:
http://www.parks.ca.gov/?page_id=24952
http://www.childrensoutdoorcharter.ca/

A significant development that has occurred as a result of the back to nature movement has been the creation of the *2004 Children's Outdoor Bill of Rights* by the California Roundtable on Recreation, Parks, and Tourism and later adopted by many other states. Similarly, in 2013 the province of Ontario released the *Children's Outdoor Charter*. The Ontario *Children's Outdoor Charter* is a long-term initiative intended to:

1. Raise awareness of the important benefits for children of connecting to nature on a regular basis;
2. Invite all interested people and organizations to take part in building opportunities for children to connect with nature; and
3. Strongly advocate for direct personal experiences in nature to foster lifelong health and happiness, and the development of a strong conservation ethic.

CURIOUS?

Connecting Canadians to Nature can be found at: http://www.parks-parcs.ca/english/ConnectingCanadians-English_web.pdf

In 2014, the Canadian Parks Council released *Connecting Canadians to Nature* (Parks Canada, 2014). This document makes the case for supporting the nature movement as a way to invest in the well-being of all Canadians. From a national perspective, the Government of Canada has reinvested in ParticiPATION. This not-for-profit organization has been instrumental in campaigning publicly as a way to encourage parents and educators to get children outdoors and moving. At the time of writing this book, three provinces, British Columbia, New Brunswick, and Nova Scotia, have endorsed and are developing strategies to promote the importance of children playing and learning outdoors.

Biophilia Theory

There are many researchers and theories that support the movement to provide children with having access to nature and outdoor play (Sandseter, 2010; Parsons, 2011). Educators are now recognizing this movement as a societal need and are attempting to incorporate more opportunities for children to engage in environments that support them in playing, learning, and connecting with nature.

Photo 3.8 Discovering an affinity for worms.

Biophilia refers to the perspective that humans seek to connect with nature and other forms of life.

The perspective that humans seek to connect with nature and other forms of life is known as **biophilia**. The biophilia hypothesis suggests that there is an instinctive bond between human beings and other living systems. Edward O. Wilson (1984) introduced and popularized the hypothesis in his book *Biophilia*, in which he suggested that humans evolved as creatures deeply enmeshed with the intricacies of nature, and more importantly, that humans still have this affinity with nature ingrained in our genotype.

The biophilia theory suggests that children have an innate, genetically predisposed tendency to explore and bond with the natural world, known as *biophilia*—a love of nature (Wilson, 1984). Moore and Marcus (2008) identified that biophilia has been observed in children as young as two years of age. For children's natural inclination of biophilia to develop, they flourish best when they are given developmentally appropriate opportunities to learn about the natural world based on sound principles of child development and learning (Wilson, 2016).

PRACTICAL APPLICATIONS

Professional early learning standards serve the purpose of seeking to improve the quality of education for young children and to support early learning teachers by identifying benchmarks for children's' growth and development. Early learning teachers and students who have used research to inform their practice incorporate outdoor standards as part of their accountability practices. The standards that early learning professionals apply to practice may depend on their jurisdiction and the existing regulated standards (Banning & Sullivan, 2011). Banning and Sullivan (2011) identified seven standards of practice for outdoor learning as listed in Chapter 1. In this chapter, we feature the engagement and persistence standard of professional practice.

Engagement and persistence standards are important in the outdoor environment because they support healthy child development (Banning & Sullivan, 2011). Table 3.2 features Banning and Sullivan's (2011) engagement and persistence standards. When children are in outdoor environments, there is a greater willingness to engage in play, connect with others, and explore (Dietze & Kashin, 2016). They are more willing to use materials in unconventional ways and to take safe risks (Banning and Sullivan, 2011). The multi-sensory nature of the outdoors helps children focus (Taylor, Kuo, & Sullivan, 2001) and

Table 3.2 Standards for outdoor play and learning: engagement and persistence standard.

The child concentrates on a variety of appropriate tasks, activities, and projects, despite distractions or interruptions.

The child pursues increasingly complex tasks, projects, and activities, willingly working on them over a period of hours or days.

The child continues to attempt a difficult task, sustaining attention and working through attendant frustration, disappointment, difficulty, and obstacles.

The child purposefully chooses activities and interactions of interest, develops a plan, and follows through with increasing independence.

The child seeks and accepts help, information, tools, and materials from peers and adults when needed (Banning and Sullivan, 2011, p. 201).

Source: Banning and Sullivan, 2011, p. 201.

Diane Kashin

Photo 3.9 Children preparing food in forest school camp.

develop persistence by being engaged in activities that inspire them. Children may persevere with an activity because the freedom of learning outdoors allows them to be successful (Banning & Sullivan, 2011).

PRINCIPLES OF PRACTICE: SELF-ACTIVATED PLAY

Play helps children develop life-long skills. The absence of play on the other hand, "can result in delayed and incomplete development" (Nell, Drew, & Bush, 2013, p. 1). When early learning students and teachers incorporate the principle of self-activated play into practice, the possibilities for children to "experience and express wonder, curiosity, knowledge, creativity, and competence" expands (Nell, Drew, & Bush, 2013, p. 1). According to Nell et al. (2013), when play is spontaneous and the materials played with are open-ended, it is self-active play.

The idea of self-active play extends back to Froebel. It involves the manipulation of open-ended materials to create a physical construction, which is a visual representation of the play process (Nell et al., 2013). As illustrated in Figure 3.7, there are many other terms used by early learning teachers to describe this type of play, illustrated in the word cloud below.

Figure 3.7 Interchangeable words about play.

LEARNING IN PLACE: THE PLAYGROUND AS PLACE

Parsons (2011) makes a distinction between natural and constructed outdoor play places. Natural includes an element of vegetation, such as forests, fields, and wooded areas. These are places for natural play and if they are untouched by human impact are considered wild environments. We will explore the forest as place in Chapter 4 and consider the playground as place as it relates to those attached to early learning programs in Chapter 9. In this chapter we next look at the evolution of the playground. This is a place where neighbourhood children gather to play. Parsons (2011) referred to these as constructed environments.

Over the twentieth century, playgrounds grew in popularity and complexity, but the Great Depression and World War I halted the rapid development of the playground movement. With the advent of World War II, the metal equipment in playgrounds was sold to aid the war effort. During the war years, school children were allowed to take periods from their school day to gather scrap metal from nearby farms or businesses and place it in piles at the edge of schoolyards for the military to pick up. This was play for the children. Imagine those piles of junk! As they were being created, a simple but revolutionary type of playground was developing in Denmark often called the "junk playground" (Frost, 2015).

A Danish landscape architect first proposed the concept of a "junk playground" in 1936. These playgrounds became known as adventure playgrounds and in 1950, *McCall's* magazine sponsored the first adventure playground in Minneapolis, USA. Even though these playgrounds began appearing in other North American cities, their life span was short due to concerns about their junky appearance, the expansion

Photo 3.10 A community playground.

Photo 3.11 An adventure playground.

of safety regulations, fear of injury and liability, shortage of funding and play leaders, and lack of support from community leaders (Frost, 2015). Now, adventure playgrounds are beginning to appear once again as leaders seek ways to bring back the excitement and desire among children to engage in outdoor play.

Since the 1970s playground standards, safety regulations, and guidelines have become the norm. Do standards inhibit children's play? Do standards keep children safe? There aren't easy answers to these questions, and early years teachers and families must consider the implications of the lack of adventure and risk in the play of children.

PROGRAMMING

Early learning teachers enhance children's outdoor play experiences by planning and programming for experiences that are engaging and interesting. The terms "invitations" and "provocations" are used as ways to describe what traditionally have been called activities or learning centres. An invitation is the action of inviting. To be inviting is to request the presence and participation of children in a kind, courteous, and complimentary way. This may be done verbally, pictorially, or in printed form. A provocation is something that arrives as a surprise to children. It is something unexpected and generally displayed in a way that will trigger children's curiosity (Dietze & Kashin, 2016) and ultimately, their desire to explore it.

Photo 3.12 An experience for the senses.

Diane Kashin

From an outdoor play perspective, invitations and provocations refer to how the materials are presented in the environment. These are different from activities and learning centres. There is great attention to detail in the design or the aesthetics of the experience. From the perspective of the 'PEER Principle' of plan, engage, explore and reflect, an invitation to explore natural material is featured in Photo 3.12 and presented in Table 3.3. Consider how this experience also supports the standard of engagement and persistence.

Table 3.3 Plan, engage, explore, reflect—material rubbings.

PLAN	Make a plan of the materials that you will need to present that could include an array of flowers, potpourri, paper, and rocks for the children outside.
ENGAGE	Present the materials in an invitational way for children to engage with all their senses.
EXPLORE	Using the tools, children create by combining scents, colours, and textures. Using the paper and materials, the children create rubbings that they can touch, see, and smell.
REFLECT	Were the children engaged in the experience and did they display persistence as they explored? By reflecting on the length of time the children spent and the interactions between the children and the materials, further materials can be provided to build on the experience.

FAMILY SUPPORT AND ENGAGEMENT

Not all families or children come to early learning environments with the same comfort level with regard to outdoor and nature play. Some may be wary of play that is labelled as "risky play," while others may feel that there is an increased possibility of children developing illnesses from exposure to different weather conditions. Early learning teachers support and offer families research findings that outline the many benefits of outdoor play. How might you support families to recognize the importance of outdoor play?

Families want what is best for their children (Ontario Ministry of Education, 2014). When families understand the researched benefits of outdoor play to children's development, they are motivated to extend and expand the children's experiences at home.

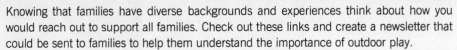

THINK ABOUT IT! READ ABOUT IT! WRITE ABOUT IT!

Knowing that families have diverse backgrounds and experiences think about how you would reach out to support all families. Check out these links and create a newsletter that could be sent to families to help them understand the importance of outdoor play.

http://eclkc.ohs.acf.hhs.gov/hslc/tta-system/ehsnrc/docs/ehs-ta-paper-14-outdoor-play.pdf

http://pediatrics.aappublications.org/content/129/1/e204.full

ACCESSIBILITY AND DESIGN

Many municipalities, communities, and early learning programs are interested in creating places for play and learning that support modelling healthy lifestyles. However, many of the play spaces restrict or eliminate children or adults who have mobility restrictions (Dietze, 2013). The United Nations *Convention on the Rights of the Child* (United Nations High Commission for Human Rights, 1989) contains a number of articles which focus on ensuring children have access to and experiences within their local communities. For example, Articles 31 states that:

> Every child has the right to rest and leisure, to engage in play and recreational activities appropriate to the age of the child and to participate freely in cultural life and the arts.

And Article 23 indicates that:

> A mentally or physically disabled child should enjoy a full and decent life, in conditions, which ensure dignity, promote self-reliance and facilitate the child's active participation in the community.

Although Canada ratified the UNCRC in 1991 and released the Canadian Standards Association (CSA) position on play spaces accessibility in 2007 (CSA, 2007), Canadian researchers, including Dietze (2013), Michalko (2009), and Titchkosky (2008), have suggested that there are many public play spaces in Canada where children or family members with mobility restrictions are excluded. Accessibility to play spaces contributes to children increasing their physical activity as well as their self-concept, which evolves from having the freedom to explore and discover. Children with restricted mobility who do not have equal access to play spaces, such as neighbourhood playgrounds, may feel isolated from peers and not engage in the same level of experimentation, exploration, or risk-taking (Dietze, 2013). Without these experiences, children's opportunities to develop networking skills, social groups, or community identity (Loukaitou-Sideris & Sideris, 2009; Dietze, 2013) are drastically reduced.

CURIOUS?

How would you incorporate technology and nature? Follow this link to learn more: http://naturalstart.org/feature-stories/bridging-gap-integrating-technology-and-environmental-education

Prellwitz & Skar (2007) defined accessibility as one's ability to approach, enter, and exit a playspace in a functional manner. Playground usability is described as the person being "able to move around, be in and use the environment on equal terms with others" (Tamm, 1999, p. 145).

Ronald Mace, a researcher and founder of the Centre for Universal Design at North Carolina State University, emphasized the importance of products and environments being designed so that they are usable by all people, without the need for adaptation or specialized designs. From an early leaning perspective, researchers are clearly identifying that there is a relationship between children's ability to interact with their early learning environments and their sense of worth (Sandseter, 2011). Examining spaces, creating policies, and implementing practices that support all children and adults in the environment are important in accommodating diverse needs (Dietze & Kim, 2014).

TIPS AND TOOLS FOR OUTDOOR PLAY

There are many ways that technology can be integrated to support learning about outdoor and nature play (Willis, Weiser, & Kirkwood, 2014). Using technology to support children's outdoor play experiences is an effective use of this tool. Conversely, if technology is used to replace outdoor learning experiences, there are numerous negative effects on children's development, and its use is not supported by the research (Plowman, McPake, & Stephen, 2012).

What if children were given cameras to take photos outside? The camera becomes a tool for self-active play. The photos taken can be viewed and considered in relationship to children's connection to place. The photos can be used to recall experiences and enhance language and social interactions. Children can be invited to make collaborative books with the photos that tell the story of their place in nature.

ON THE GROUND—PROFESSIONAL REFLECTIONS: "WHY I LOVE OUTDOOR PLAY"

What makes some early learning teachers and students passionate about outdoor play? Does passion come from experience? Do early learning teachers need to have a childhood spent outdoors to become passionate? Read the professional reflection featured in Box 3.4 as an early learning teacher reflects on her passion for outdoor education.

>> BOX 3.4   Why I Love Outdoor Play

I have loved the outdoors for as long as I can remember. My father has always been an outdoorsman (fishing, camping, and the like) so my family would go camping every summer throughout my childhood. My parents would also take my sister and me for long drives in the country on weekends (this was 30+ years ago so those "country" areas are now developed). My "happy place" has always been anywhere I am surrounded by nature (especially if I'm near a lake/river/creek with trees nearby). When I became a kindergarten teacher, I was excited to be able to share my love of nature with my students. My first school (Birchbank Public School in Brampton, ON) was 40 years old and so it had lots of mature trees (including huge weeping willows) in nearby parks. My teaching partner and I would spend extended amounts of time outside with our class as often as possible. We would often bring our snacks, water bottles and "Wonder Wagon" (a wagon that we fill with various things such as magnifying glasses, paper, pencils, crayons, books about nature, watercolour paints and brushes, blankets, plastic containers for the children to collect things in, etc.) and be outside for close to two hours every morning. The children often commented that they wanted to stay outside all day (because they were having too much fun exploring nature). This made me very happy because I have always felt the same way. Two years ago I started working at my current school (Springbrook Public School in Brampton, ON) and was ecstatic when I learned that there was a pond and forest nearby (within 5–10 minutes walking distance). We regularly go on morning nature walks and have lots of fun learning and exploring. In the forest, our children love to explore (e.g., climbing over/under or walking across logs, using big sticks to build forts, discovering moss and mushrooms, comparing the sizes of various sticks, counting and sorting leaves, etc.). At the pond, they enjoy counting the birds, tossing rocks in the water and seeing who can make the biggest splash, counting how many circles appear after their rock lands in the water, observing the cattails (which they call "hot dog plants"), crossing the creek by stepping on the big stones, and so much more. There are so many opportunities for learning when you take your class outside. Not just outside in the paved schoolyard. But venturing further to explore the neighbourhood and other nearby natural areas. I bring my iPad with me and come back (from our nature walks) with SO many pictures and anecdotal notes that touch on many curriculum expectations, including literacy and math. The children do lots of counting, measuring, comparing, estimating, sorting, creating letters of the alphabet, and so much more using natural "loose parts" from nature. They ask so many questions and share their observations with their classmates and teachers. There's definitely a focus on active learning through exploration, play, and inquiry. It's wonderful! I have always encouraged my students' families to get outdoors together. I recently sent home copies of the Wild Family Nature Club toolkit with each of our students (http://cwffcf.org/en/explore-our-work/connecting-with-nature/in-your-community/wild-family-natureclub/get-the-toolkit.html). I love hearing from parents that my passion for nature has inspired them to spend more time outdoors with their child. Or that their child insists that they go on family nature walks because we do in school. I love nature and sharing this passion with others.

Nevella Schepmyer
Kindergarten Teacher
Used with permission from Nevella Schepmyer.

CASE STUDIES

Early learning teachers who are passionate about outdoor play have a commitment to the children and themselves to include it in their practice on a daily basis. Some early learning teachers and students may have a desire to offer children positive and memorable experiences outdoors but require further development in moving beyond a supervisory role in the playground (McClintic & Petty, 2015). Read the scenario presented in Case Study 3.1 and reflect upon the questions featured below.

The early years team at Stuart Public School has been transforming the indoor learning environment for the past two years, slowly removing plastic, closed-ended toys and replacing them with more open-ended materials including natural found loose parts. They have changed the way they teach in that they are now less instructive and focused on a more progressive, constructivist approach. They have scheduled outdoor time during the first 15 minutes in the morning as children are being dropped off and the bus children are arriving. When children arrive, they enter a fenced in space off the side of the building adjacent to the school. The surface is paved. The children play on the small climber. There are not any additional toys or materials for the children or any other equipment. The team would like to do more outside and has been raising money to purchase new equipment and hire a consultant to help them decide how to use their funds. During this time, it is very busy with parents wanting to talk and the team has to keep an eye on the climber because it is not big enough for all the children and sometimes they fight for space. The team has to supervise very carefully. As soon as all the children have arrived they go indoors. In the morning the team has provided provocations for learning throughout the classroom and children have the freedom to play where they want. The next time they go outside is right after the children have had lunch. They usually stay outside for 30 minutes, sometimes longer depending on the weather. Sometimes the team takes balls and hoola hoops outside so that there is more for the children to do. The children are not very interested in playing with them though. All they want to do is be on the climber at the same time! The team is constantly intervening to stop the fighting. When the children go inside they are very tired. The early learning team finds that this is the best time to do quiet activities. Usually the children get more energetic after they have afternoon snack so the team sets up more provocations related to the children's interests and they usually schedule group meetings to discuss their ongoing project investigation. When the school bell rings, some of the children are picked up for the day, while the others go to the after school program in the gym.

1. What additional materials or equipment would you recommend to the team at Stuart Public School?
2. Why do you think that the team has to intervene with the children on the playground?
3. How could you change the schedule to enable the children to be outside longer?

An important first step for the team in the case study is that they are motivated to change. In this chapter, we emphasized the importance of early learning students and teachers moving beyond their current practice by drawing upon research to inform new knowledge and practice. Key features of using research to inform practice include:

- examining current research from a national and international perspective;
- determining how the research findings inform practice—what does it look like in programming and in facilitating children's outdoor play options; and
- considering how the research on outdoor play is influencing policies, practices, and opportunities for children to engage in healthier lifestyles.

Research, when used in practice, communicates to the users why the current state of outdoor play must be changed to be more active and intriguing. Research and practice can

BOX 3.5   **Take It Outside**

Consider some of the things that you do everyday indoors, such as reading or eating. Take these experiences outdoors! Bring a book and a snack to a place in nature. Instead of staying inside, go outside. What difference did it make to your day? What experiences that children have everyday can be taken outside?

work together so that early childhood students and professionals achieve a focused goal that promotes outdoor play as an important part of each day for children. When research and practice are carefully aligned, we can prioritize how to make the outdoor play environment supportive of children's needs and interests.

KEY TERMS

Pedagogy
Quantitative research
Qualitative research
Professional vision
Literature review
Peer-reviewed articles
Biophilia

Diane Kashin

Photo 3.13 Key terms.

Summary

- There has been a decline in children's access to and opportunities for outdoor play that is contributing to alarming rates among children of Type 2 diabetes, depression, being overweight, obesity, hyperactivity, and academic challenges.

- Research has an influence on practice. Examining research on how children learn and how outdoor play contributes to their learning is foundational to the roles of early learning teachers.

- Research is a concept that underpins most early learning program philosophies and methodologies. It is a way of thinking and developing context for practice.

- Early learning teachers are encouraged to understand and reflect upon their attitudes and dispositions as they relate to research and outdoor play programming. These two perspectives influence the depth and breadth of the outdoor experiences extended to children.

- There are two basic categories that are associated with research. They are: qualitative and qualitative. Quantitative research generally refers to data generated from descriptors or stories in response to specific questions asked (Hartas, 2015). Qualitative research focuses on answers to *why* questions that may evolve from their philosophy, vision, observations of children and environments, conversations with children and adults, or questions that evolve from interactions with colleagues, children, family, or community partners.

- Types of research that are being conducted on outdoor play include: outdoor play and risk-taking, outdoor play designs, outdoor play and children's health, outdoor play curriculum, staff attitudes, loose parts, and outdoor play and sustainability.

- In 2015, a cross-sectorial group on active outdoor play developed a *Position Statement on Active Outdoor Play* for Canada.

- Research principles include being ethical, purposeful, well designed, transparent, contextualized, imaginative and equitable.

- Action research is a cycle of planning, acting, observing, and reflecting.

- The province of Ontario has created a *Children's Outdoor Charter*. Its purpose is to raise awareness of the important benefits for children to connect to nature on a regular basis. The Canadian Parks Council has released a document entitled *Connecting Canadians to Nature*.

- Parsons (2011) makes a distinction between natural and constructed outdoor play places. Natural includes an element of vegetation, such as forests, fields, and wooded areas. These are places for natural play and if they are untouched by human impact are considered wild environments. Constructed environments include neighbourhood playgrounds.

- Early learning teachers enhance children's outdoor play experiences by planning and programming for experiences that children will find engaging and interesting.

- Accessibility to play spaces contributes to children increasing their physical activity as well as their self-concept, which evolves from having the freedom to explore and discover. Children with restricted mobility who do not have equal access to play spaces such as neighbourhood play grounds, may feel isolated from peers and not engage in the same level of experimentation, exploration, or risk-taking (Dietze, 2013).

QUIET REFLECTION

Sit spots are used in forest and nature school programs as a way to help children make connections to nature. The idea of a sit spot is for a child or an adult to find a place in nature to sit alone and quietly reflect. We encourage you to find a spot, sit and reflect on nature, and why it is important for us to help children and ourselves make our own connections.

COMMUNITY DIALOGUE

In every chapter, we will present professional narratives about outdoor play written by early learning teachers from across Canada. Reread Nevella's story featured in Box 3.4, then discuss with others the fundamental question of what makes Nevella passionate about outdoor play? What life experiences contributed to her passion? How do you think children react to adults who are passionate about outdoor play?

FOR FURTHER THOUGHT AND ACTION

Do you believe that children should have more opportunities to play outdoors? How can you act upon those beliefs? Some children do not have opportunities to play outside beyond a fenced-in playground. Sometimes there is a natural space such as a forest, meadow, or hillside just beyond their playground. What would you say if you had an opportunity to make a case for playing outside in natural spaces to educators?

RESOURCES

Find out more about what international advocates are doing to support outdoor play in nature by following this link to the Nature Pedagogy International Association: https://www.naturepedagogy.com/

CHAPTER 4

Loose Parts—Using Natural and Found Materials in Outdoor and Nature Play

There is no description, no image in any book that is capable of replacing the sight of real trees, and all of the life to be found around them in a real forest.

(Maria Montessori, 1870–1952)

LEARNING OUTCOMES

After exploring this chapter, you will be able to:

- Explain what is meant by loose parts.

- Discuss the relationship between loose parts and physical literacy.

- Describe the history of loose parts from their earliest proponents to the development of adventure playgrounds.

- Outline various theories connected to loose parts.

- Compare loose parts to fixed equipment.

- Explain the early learning teacher's role in providing children with loose parts in various play spaces.

CHILDHOOD MEMORIES

One of my fondest memories from my childhood was when we moved to a new neighbourhood. My older brother was not happy about moving away from his friends, but I was excited. After the movers came and the new appliances were delivered, we had so many boxes! My father asked if we would like to take some of the boxes outside. I will never forget the cardboard box city that we created and how much fun we had imagining we were in a real city. It was not long until other kids from the neighbourhood came by and asked to play. Before we knew it we had new friends! We played with those boxes for days and days until one day it rained and our city was ruined. We were not sad though because we had made so many new friends and we had learned about the possibilities of cardboard boxes!

CHAPTER PREVIEW

Loose parts are materials that are open-ended, variable, unstructured and can be used in multiple ways. Cardboard boxes are just one of the materials that can be described as loose parts. In 1971, Simon Nicholson, a landscape architect, coined the term loose parts. Nicholson (1971) maintained that children love to interact with variables in order to play, discover, invent, and experiment. He said:

> In any environment, both the degree of inventiveness and creativity, and the possibility of discovery, are directly proportional to the number and kind of variables in it. (p. 30)

A review of the literature related to loose parts reveals that there are a number of definitions for the term loose parts, however there is one that was found to be the most "all-encompassing" (Houser, Roach, Stone, Turner, & Kirk, 2016, p. 15). Sutton (2011) defined loose parts as:

> Any collection of fully movable elements that inspire a person to pick up, re-arrange or create new configurations, even realities, one piece or multiple pieces at a time. Loose parts require the hand and mind to work in concert; they are catalysts to inquiry. Loose parts are the flexible edge of an inviting open-ended interactive environment that allows participants to make an imprint of their intention. Experiences with loose parts provide a profound yet playful way for children to form associations between learning and pleasure. (p. 409)

The cardboard box city is an example of creativity that results from materials that are open-ended and variable. To be variable means that it is likely to change. Many cardboard boxes of various sizes strewn upon a lawn, mixed with a group of children, will have variable results as the children collectively use their imagination to create. Today, in early learning indoor environments, loose parts have become a common feature. These may include items such as shells, rocks, pinecones, glass gems, marbles, boxes, and other variable materials that are added to support children's creativity and imagination.

Loose parts are essential for outdoor play. They are not just materials that are for indoor learning environments (McClintic, 2014). Nicolson (1971) developed the theory of loose parts with the outdoor environment in mind.

THINK ABOUT IT! READ ABOUT IT! WRITE ABOUT IT!

What do you think about loose parts for outdoor play and learning? What kinds of loose parts do you think Nicolson (1971) had in mind when he wrote the article, *How Not to Cheat Children: The Theory of Loose Parts*? Write a list of materials that you think would be suitable for outdoor play. Find the article by searching the Internet. Read the article. Compare your list to the ones suggested in the article.

When children are playing with loose parts, they are engaged cognitively, socially, and emotionally, and are physically active. Houser et al. (2016) identified various research studies suggesting that children interact with unstructured, variable material in ways that involve active physical engagement, which in turn supports the development of **physical literacy**. The variables inherent in loose parts invite children to discovery on their own, leading to decision making and problem solving. Children become actively involved when playing with loose parts. The way in which the materials are used is dependent on the children's interests and imagination, not on a toy manufacturer, parent, or teacher. Think about it this way: children are active and the materials are passive until they are acted upon. When children engage in loose parts they are playing in many different ways. Consider Figure 4.1 and the types of play that evolve from engagement with loose parts.

Photo 4.1 Creating a cardboard city.

Physical literacy refers to the motivation, confidence, physical competence, knowledge, and understanding to be physically active for life (Houser et al., 2016).

Figure 4.1 Play and loose parts.

CURIOUS?

Are you curious about loose parts and how they connect to play and learning? Check out this toolkit for loose parts! http://creativestarlearning.co.uk/book-reviews/the-loose-parts-play-toolkit/

Photo 4.2 Loose parts and solitary play.

Physical play happens with loose parts (Houser et al., 2016). Constructive play occurs with various materials such as cloth, blocks, boards, boxes, etc., and a variety of tools. Dramatic play occurs when children build playhouses similar to the cardboard city described in the childhood memory that opens this chapter. Children use loose parts to create games with rules (McClintic & Petty, 2015). Loose parts can support collaborative group play or be used by one child engaged in solitary play, as depicted in Photo 4.2, or two children playing side by side in parallel play. The use of open-ended material can also lead to risky play, which will be discussed later in this chapter and in Chapter 6.

SETTING THE STAGE FOR OUTDOOR PLAY

When you think back to ancient times, children played with sticks, stones, and pinecones. These materials were available to play with outdoors in the absence of manufactured toys and equipment. In the middle of the eighteenth century, however, because of the influence of Friedrich Froebel, the stage was set to support and encourage children to use loose parts in their play. This was the beginning for the loose parts movement that we see now taking place. Friedrich Froebel was an early pioneer in the use of props to foster hands-on learning. Froebel saw a link between children using loose parts in their play and their cognitive and aesthetic skill development that contributed to their abilities to manipulate objects in various ways. As a result, he developed specially designed kits containing different forms of wooden, geometrically shaped modular parts (Sutton, 2011).

Froebel's work influenced Maria Montessori, the Italian doctor and educator who founded the Montessori approach to early learning. She noted as early as 1907 that young children would engage deeply when they had access to hand-sized loose parts that they could arrange and explore. She also created her own sets of learning props (Sutton, 2011). Sixty years later, in the era of adventure playgrounds, Nicholson (1971) spoke of the value of loose parts and kindled the movement that continues today.

Adventure playgrounds are spaces dedicated to children's play. Skilled playworkers support and facilitate the children's experiences in that space where the children have ownership in the design and development of what is in the playground (Teague, 2015).

In the 1970s children explored their outdoor environments in fields, streets, alleys, woods, creeks, and lakes. Children "were always outside messing around" (Keeler, 2017, p. 9). In these "glory days of play-freedom" the **adventure playgrounds** discussed in Chapter 2, with their loose parts and opportunities for challenge, risk and adventure were prevalent (Keeler, 2017, p. 10). During that time children would play in construction sites rather than in conventional playgrounds (Teague, 2015).

CURIOUS?

Are you curious about what it takes to be a playworker? Perhaps it is something to consider in addition to an early childhood education designation. Find out more here: https://popupadventureplaygrounds.wordpress.com/welcome/services/playworker-development-course/

Table 4.1 Principles of playwork.

One	Play is an innate impulse in all children.
Two	Play is a process that is freely chosen and personally directed. When children determine the content of their own play, it is intrinsically motivating.
Three	The role of playworkers is to support and facilitate the process of play.
Four	The play process takes precedence for playworkers who are advocates for play.
Five	The playworker supports all children in the creation of their play space.
Six	A playworker is a reflective practitioner who has up-to-date knowledge of the play process. Responses to children are based on knowledge and reflection.
Seven	Playworkers also recognize their own impact on the play space.
Eight	Playworkers intervene in children's play to extend their play, while balancing risk with the children's well-being and the developmental benefits of play.

Source: Adapted from Kilvington & Wood (2010). *Reflective playwork: For all who work with children.*

In 1943, after observing children playing, a teacher and landscape architect opened the first junk playground in Emdrup, Copenhagen. They used "wood, natural materials, rope, canvas, tires, bricks, nets, balls, abandoned furniture, wheels and other building materials" (Teague, 2015, p. 11). The first play leader or **playworker** for this first adventure playground was John Bertelsen. He felt that it was very important for children to be designers and constructors of their own spaces (Teague, 2015). Playworkers are very common in Europe now, but it is a relatively new profession that has been gaining prominence only since the 1980s (Kilvington & Wood, 2010). To understand what it means to be a playworker, consider these eight principles of playwork as adapted from Kilvington and Wood (2010) in Table 4.1.

Playworkers are professionals who facilitate children's play in adventure playgrounds, parks, and other settings, principally in the United Kingdom (Wilson, 2010).

When Marjorie Allen (also known as Lady Allen of Hurtwood) visited the playground in Emdrup, she returned to the United Kingdom and suggested that adventure playgrounds be built on bombed sites so that children could have a safe place to play. In 1948, she opened Britain's first junk playground. Drummond Abernethy followed in Lady Allen's steps and created more playgrounds for children in Britain. He "changed the name from junk playgrounds to adventure playgrounds to reflect a more positive image" (Teague, 2015, p. 12). Over time, adventure playgrounds were closed for lack of funding or concern over safety issues. However, there is now a global "play renaissance," where dedicated adults such as playworkers are working to improve the lives of children by "providing time, space and materials with which children can explore, roam, run free, and be" (Keeler, 2017, p. 9). With the resurgence of adventure playgrounds today in North America, early learning teachers and students can join this renaissance movement but will need to consider the value and importance of loose parts!

Diane Kashin

Photo 4.3 A pop-up adventure playground.

Loose Parts and Twenty-First Century Competencies

Loose parts offer children multiple opportunities to play, learn, and develop skills and competencies. Skills and competencies are terms often used interchangeably, but they are not the same. A skill is the ability to do something with expertise whereas competency is a broader concept. Part of being competent may actually comprise skills as well as attitudes and knowledge (Ontario Ministry of Education, 2016). There are specific competencies that have been considered important to success in the twenty-first century.

Loose parts support the development of twenty-first century competencies (Daly & Beloglovsky, 2014). These twenty-first century competencies support children's growth in the cognitive, interpersonal, and intrapersonal domains (Ontario Ministry of Education, 2016) as featured in Figure 4.2.

When children engage with loose parts they exercise their capacities across these domains and develop their abilities to think critically, communicate, collaborate, be creative, and innovate (Ontario Ministry of Education, 2016). Imagine that a group of children are playing with sticks, rocks, and baskets. Are they developing twenty-first century competencies? Table 4.2 illustrates the possibilities inherent in this loose parts play.

As open-ended, variable materials, loose parts encourage children to manipulate and experiment. Children are drawn to materials that can be moved and manipulated. When new, interesting, and unique items are added to the outdoor environment, children's curiosity will be piqued. Loose parts are springboards for child-led play (McClintic, 2014). It is up to the early learning teacher to provide loose parts that will spark children's curiosity and lead them to engage in unique and innovative experimentation. In considering the provision of loose parts, understanding that there are different types is important.

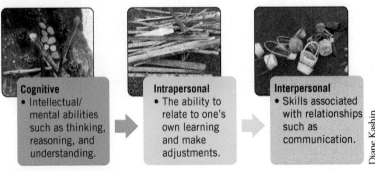

Cognitive
• Intellectual/mental abilities such as thinking, reasoning, and understanding.

Intrapersonal
• The ability to relate to one's own learning and make adjustments.

Interpersonal
• Skills associated with relationships such as communication.

Diane Kashin

Figure 4.2 Twenty-first century competencies across domains.

Source: Based on Ontario Ministry of Education (2016).

Table 4.2 Loose parts and twenty-first century competencies.

Critical Thinking	Ability to design, manage projects, solve problems, and make decisions (Fullan, 2013).	Using the baskets to transport the rocks, the children decide to design a 3D sculpture. After multiple attempts, they realize a stable foundation is necessary for the sculpture not to fall down.
Communication	Ability to communicate effectively and to listen (Fullan, 2013).	When the early learning teacher asks the children about the sculpture, they are able to describe the process involved. They listen to the teacher when she invites them to put a sign on their sculpture.
Collaboration	Ability to work with others and contribute to the learning of others (Fullan, 2013).	Each of the children contributes ideas about the transporting of the materials, the creation of the sculpture, and the signage.
Creativity and Innovation	Ability to pursue new ideas (Creativity) and achieve the realization of those ideas (Innovation) (Ontario Ministry of Education, 2014).	This is the first time that this group of children build a vertical structure rather than a horizontal one.

Source: Adapted from Ontario Ministry of Education (2016).

Types of Loose Parts

Loose parts can be categorized as manufactured, natural, and recycled. You can find loose parts at home, in thrift shops, and at garage sales. Early learning teachers and students consider sustainability practices when using loose parts. When loose parts are altered with glue and paint, will they continue to be used by the children? Or will they be sent home as an individual finished product? When these altered loose parts products arrive home what will happen to them? Early learning teachers and students benefit from viewing children as creators rather than consumers.

To support children in their loose parts play, reflect upon the types of loose parts and how children might use them. Figures 4.3, 4.4, and 4.5 provide examples of each type of loose parts.

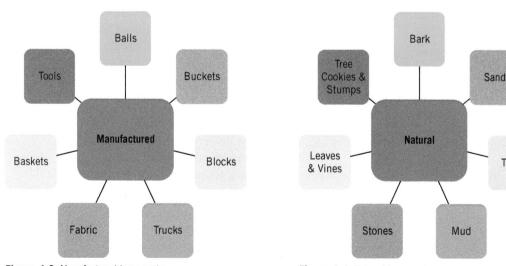

Figure 4.3 Manufactured loose parts.

Figure 4.4 Natural loose parts.

Figure 4.5 Recycled loose parts.

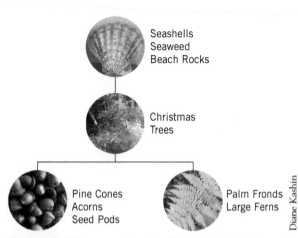

Figure 4.6 Adding seasonal and local materials to the playground.

Consider offering children combinations of loose parts such as natural pebbles with recycled cardboard tubes for a potential marble run. With branches, fabrics, and clips, the children may create a shelter or house. Tree cookies, which are slices of branches, can offer children opportunities to expand their play. Add recycled pots and pans to an area with soil, and a mud kitchen could evolve. The types of loose parts that are incorporated into the outdoor environment can depend on the season and the location where the play takes place (Neill, 2013). What the beach offers is different than the forest. If the play takes place within a fenced in playground, seasonal and local materials can be added as featured in Figure 4.6.

Loose parts can be purchased, and many early learning suppliers now feature loose parts in the catalogues. However, loose parts do not have to be costly. You may already have materials that can be re-purposed. Friends and community members can be asked to donate items that they don't need anymore. Local businesses may have leftover materials that they would be happy to donate. A carpentry workshop may have wood pieces. A restaurant could offer empty bottles or pails. A garage or local mechanic could spare steering wheels and tires. Imagine the possibilities (Saxby-Leichter & Law, 2015).

Pedagogy of place Inspired by the work of John Dewey, the pedagogy of place refers to learning in a particular place (Jayanandhan, 2009).

Natural loose parts can be gathered from the forest or local park. A good rule to follow is to collect only what has fallen to the ground. Taking branches or stripping bark from a tree is not environmentally acceptable, nor appropriate to model to children. When possible, children benefit from experiencing the loose parts from the place that is their point of origin. This way, children develop a connection to place, which supports the development of **pedagogy of place**.

Children's lives are shaped by the places they inhabit. When early learning students and teachers of young children recognize the significance of place-based education, experiences and opportunities for learning in and with nature will expand. Place-based education is the process of using the local community and environment as a starting point to learning in all areas of the curriculum. Emphasizing hands-on, real-world learning experiences, this pedagogical approach helps children

Photo 4.4 Playing with tires.

to make a stronger connection to the natural world in a way that will increase environmental stewardship.

Place "means more than a geographic location as it includes opportunities for seclusion, for exploring, for changing things about, for immediate encounters with the natural world, and for memorable moments" (Wilson, 2016, p. 140). According to David Sobel (2005), place-based education "creates a heightened commitment to serving as active and contributing citizens" (p. 7). Pelo (2009) believed that it is the role of the teacher to foster an ecological identity in children, one that shapes them as surely as their cultural and social identities. This ecological identity can be born in a particular place. It is our vision for young children that they will have the opportunities to develop an emotional connection to place. When loose parts stay in place and children have the opportunity to re-visit this place over time and seasons, the development of pedagogy of place is supported.

OUR VISION FOR OUTDOOR PLAY

Our vision for loose parts play is that early learning teachers and students see these materials as key materials for the outdoor environment. Loose parts belong outdoors! Nicholson (1971) envisioned loose parts as additions to outdoor environments. When thinking about loose parts, we encourage you to consider how to include large, moveable, and flexible materials for the outdoor environment (Neill, 2013).

It is our hope that early learning teachers will see outdoor play as a vital part of childhood and recognize the place loose parts can have to encourage diverse play opportunities. We want you to do your part to promote the use of loose parts outdoors. Loose parts may be obtained with a minimum of expense to no expense. They make a difference to the depth and breadth of play and peer connections. "It is surprising what large impacts even small amounts of loose parts can have" (Almon, 2017, p. 19). Children are especially drawn to natural materials such as acorns, stones, and wood pieces (Almon, 2017).

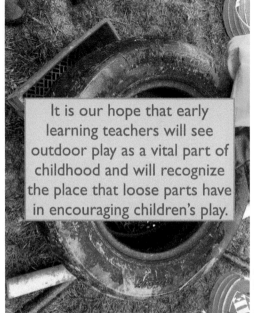

It is our hope that early learning teachers will see outdoor play as a vital part of childhood and will recognize the place that loose parts have in encouraging children's play.

Photo 4.5 Vision for loose parts.

Diane Kashin

POSITIONING OUTDOOR PLAY IN THE LIVES OF CHILDREN

There is something very exciting about discovery. When you find an object in nature and then find out something about that object, it is like going on an adventure. Being adventurous is all about opportunities for children to explore and test their own capacities, to manage risk, and to grow in their capacity, resourcefulness, and resilience (Solly, 2015). Adventurous play is imaginative and creative. Adventurous play can be risky but should not be hazardous.

Risk and hazards are different. A child cannot anticipate a hazard, as it is an unexpected occurrence. Children can anticipate risk. When children are given opportunities to take risks, they can assess risks to manage them. Risks are visible to children because they can anticipate them (Couchenour & Chrisman, 2016). For example, there is a pile of heavy, large rocks. The child chooses to pick one up, managing the weight to carry it over to the slide. It would be a hazard if the child picked up the rock and there was a piece of broken glass beside the rock that the child stepped on. Early learning teachers inspect

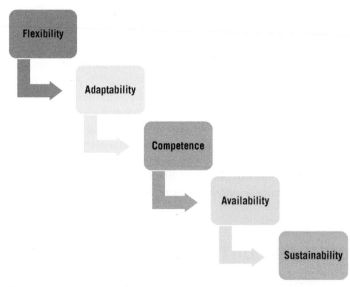

Figure 4.7 Key elements of loose parts.

materials such as loose parts and the related space to remove hazards so that children may pursue safe risk taking (Couchenour & Chrisman, 2016).

Jumping in a pile of leaves is not without risk—and that is part of the adventure—but it is a relatively safe risk. With the loose parts that nature offers, children can construct their own adventures. They can balance, jump, and scamper using their whole bodies in ways that support their kinaesthetic development (Sobel, 2008). When children find themselves in a woodsy playground such as a forest, the loose parts are already there.

The kinds of loose parts available to young children in the outdoor environment and the way their play is supported can significantly influence and impact their experiences. When open-ended loose parts are combined with other open-ended materials such as sand, water, or vegetation, the experience will be versatile and responsive to children (Maynard & Waters, 2014). Children will develop a sense of competence and capacity when engaging with these materials. Think about these five key elements featured in Figure 4.7 when choosing loose parts for the outdoor environment (Dietze & Kashin, 2017).

Flexibility refers to the versatility of an item. How many ways can it be used? How flexible is it? For instance, a piece of fabric can be used in the outdoor dramatic play area one way and used differently in the construction area.

Adaptability refers to how the item can be used and reused in different ways. For example, how would plumbing pipes be used if placed near the water area? How would these pipes be adapted if placed by an array of marbles and small balls?

Children's Competence relates to the ease with which children may use the loose parts. Early learning teachers consider whether children are able to manipulate the material on their own or require adult support. Early learning teachers think carefully about how

Michelle Thornhill

Photo 4.6 Moving rocks.

the material supports children's competence when choosing loose parts. For instance, can children move the large rocks placed in the playground from one area to the other? Are the rocks the right size for the children's strength and experience in using them? Are there supports such as wagons or dollies available if children require assistance in moving the rocks?

Availability refers to how easy it is for something to be gathered, replenished, repurposed, and reused. Is there limited access to the material? For instance, there may be pine trees close by where fallen pinecones are plentiful, but the small beach rocks used in the playground were donated by a family and gathered from a beach miles away. Inviting children to break off small pieces of pinecones to add to their clay creatures will consume the supply. However, the material is easily replenished. In contrast, inviting children to paint the rocks to take home as gifts to their families will consume a supply that is not easily replenished.

Sustainability refers to the durability of the materials. Can the material be left in the playground after the end of the day or does it have to be stored? Think about the difference between the durability of fabric cushions compared to that of plumbing pipes. Or compare the use of large cardboard boxes to tires. Fabric and cushions are not as durable as pipes and tires. The need to store these materials at the end of the day to avoid weather damage will affect the children's play. Early learning teachers consider how sustainability influences children's play from one day to the next and the extension of play episodes.

THINK ABOUT IT! READ ABOUT IT! WRITE ABOUT IT!

How would you add loose parts to a playground on a limited budget? Read this manual: http://www.abcee.org/sites/abcee.org/files/Loose%20parts%20manual.pdf and write out a list of items that you can obtain in your own community. How much money do you need to create your own loose parts play kit?

Loose parts are valuable to children because of their versatility. Think about a playground you have seen or have experienced. Does it have fixed equipment or loose parts? Tables 4.3 and 4.4, adapted from Dietze & Kashin (2017) compare the play value of fixed equipment such as slides and climbers to loose parts.

Table 4.3 Fixed equipment.

- ◾ Tends to focus on gross motor play such as climbing, spinning, and jumping.
- ◾ Limited opportunities for children to incorporate ideas into the usage of the equipment.
- ◾ Becomes boring over time as the thrill of trying new ideas is limited by the stationary nature of the equipment.
- ◾ Limits peer and social play because of the equipment's limited movement capacity.
- ◾ Low maintenance.
- ◾ Focuses on building children's physical competence.
- ◾ Limited need for children to think, ponder, and explore options.

Table 4.4 Loose parts.

- Provides opportunities for children to design and redesign the materials to support their play episode.
- Accommodates all types of play and children's skills.
- Supports children building, dismantling, manipulating, incorporating, and repurposing materials as required for the play experience.
- Encourages active, creative, and imaginative play with peers.
- Requires maintenance and storage.
- Increases skills and competence in social, emotional, physical, and cognitive domains.
- Uses thinking and problem-solving skills necessary to incorporate loose parts into the play episode.

When you compare the characteristics of fixed equipment with loose parts, it is evident that there are very different play values, activity options, and potential learning experiences extended to children with loose parts. Loose parts require children to use their thinking and problem-solving skills. They provide more opportunities than fixed equipment can to create novel, unique, and inspirational ways to use everyday objects. Loose parts also afford children the opportunity to take risks that challenge, stretch limits, and provide joy (Woods, 2016). A fall from a stable, fixed playground structure can be dangerous to children. Playing with loose parts can offer the benefits of safe risk (Neill, 2013). Chapter 6 will explore risky play in depth.

THEORETICAL FOUNDATION

Theorize is to form a theory or set of theories about something.

To look beyond thinking about loose parts as tangible things, early learning teachers and students are encouraged to **theorize**. In early learning, a theory is a group of ideas that help explain a certain topic about children's learning and development. Typically, a theory is developed through abstract thinking based on general principles independent of what is being explained or theorized. Theories provide early learning teachers and students with "ways of knowing" that influence thinking and make an impact on practice (Nolan & Raban, 2015, p. 5). We study major theorists such as Piaget, Vygotsky, and Bronfenbrenner to guide our work with young children, families, and communities as "they provide conceptual understandings on aspects that otherwise are difficult to comprehend" (Nolan & Raban, 2015, p. 6). To theorize is to think deeply about a particular topic related to your work to form a theoretical premise.

Loose Parts as a Theory

Praxis refers to the process in which theory is enacted into practice.

When Nicholson (1971) considered the use of loose parts in children's play, he was theorizing. With theoretical premises grounding your work with young children, you can act in an informed way to improve, enhance and change practice leading to **praxis**. Praxis involves theory and action coming to together to create a transformative process of change (Nolan & Rabin, 2015). Considering the work of the theorists featured throughout this textbook will help you with the theoretical foundation needed to use theories to inform and change practice. However, theorizing is not an act, which is the purview of only renowned theorists. Early learning students and teachers can theorize too. Reflect on the words in Figure 4.8. These are synonyms for the verb theorize.

Think about loose parts. Nicholson (1971) suggested that loose parts are materials that are combined, transported, and transformed. Speculate about loose parts.

Figure 4.8 Theorizing words.

Why are children drawn to these materials? Observe children engaged in loose parts play and submit an idea about children and loose parts. Waller, Ärlemalm-Hagsér, Sandseter, Lee-Hammond, Lekies, and Wyver (2017) suggested that children have a strong attraction to loose parts for adventure play. They have a strong attraction to a range of manufactured and recycled loose parts, as well as natural items such as flowers, berries, acorns, pinecones, seeds, rocks, and sticks.

The outdoor environment provides a backdrop for loose parts play that cannot be duplicated indoors. The outdoor environment has the potential to excite and motivate children, as it seems infinite in its possibilities for discovery. Every outdoor adventure will differ because of the variables—the array of sights, sounds, living creatures, weather patterns, and other aspects of nature are in constant flux (Waller et al., 2017). Are children drawn to the novelty of the outdoor environment because of how it can change from day to day? Ostroff (2016) suggested that beginning in infancy and throughout the lifespan, humans are motivated by newness, change, and excitement. Imagine going outside and coming upon a fallen branch after a thunderstorm. The ground is full of leaves, twigs, and pinecones. This change could be intriguing: upon discovering it, the first thing children might do is collect the treasures.

According to the biophilia theory, children have a natural urge to collect because they have an innate connection to the natural world. More than 30 years ago, Wilson (1984) developed the theory suggesting that children have a biological need to affiliate with nature. Nature affords children many opportunities to exercise their need to be connected to found materials. Specific features of loose parts influence the way children play because of the *affordances* that the materials offer children (Maxwell, Mitchell, & Evans, 2008).

Affordance theory was put forth by Gibson (2014), who suggested that environments and objects within them have values and meanings that are unique to the child using them. The 'affordances' of the space or object are all the things that it has the potential to do or be (Casey & Robertson, 2016). Some materials offer different affordances than others. Balls bounce, bricks balance, and sticks line up. It all depends on the user. Swiss psychologist Jean Piaget referred to physical knowledge as what children learn when they act on objects and materials to discover their characteristics, attributes, or affordances (Kamii, 2014).

Affordance theory refers to the idea that clues in the environment indicates possibilities for action (Gibson, 2014).

Jean Piaget has made significant contributions to helping early learning teachers understand the cognitive development of children. He was the first to develop a comprehensive stage theory of child development. As a constructivist theorist, Piaget believed that children construct their understanding of their world within their own thought processes. Playing with objects is an important part of children's cognitive development (Jarvis, Swiniarski, & Holland, 2016). Through schemas, assimilation, and accommodation children develop their thought processes.

Piaget's theories are important to consider as they reflect the affordances of materials. Children can discover much about the properties of objects when they have the opportunity to combine, transport, and transform them. Piaget believed that children learn from discovery and asserted that "each time one prematurely teaches a child something he could have discovered for himself, that child is kept from inventing it and consequently from understanding it completely" (Piaget, 1970, p. 715). It is through **schemas**, assimilation, and accommodation that the learning occurs. Figure 4.9 illustrates schemas, accommodation, and assimilation.

Schemas are recognized as repeated patterns in children's play behaviours (Nutbrown, 2011).

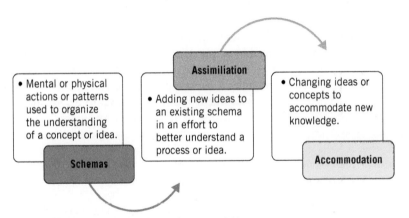

Figure 4.9 Schemas, assimilation, and accommodation.

Schema Play

Athey (1990) was instrumental in making the connection between play and schemas. These are integrated, coordinated behaviours through which children gain access to knowledge that is used to sort out ideas, feelings, and relationships. Schema theory is a lens through which to observe and consider the significance of children's actions and behaviours and how they relate to their thought processes (Maynard & Waters, 2014, p. 29). Athey (1990) suggested that schemas are at the core of the developing mind. Nutbrown (2011) indicated that educational experiences should be related to this core (Maynard & Waters, 2014). Imagine a child playing with tree cookies all day. From a list of schemas adapted from Nutbrown (2011), Table 4.5 illustrates the potential experiences that children may have as they engage in play with tree cookies.

Athey (1990) and Nutbrown (2011) continued to build upon the work Piaget and Cook (1952) conducted on schemas, assimilation, and accommodation with the theory of schema play. **Schema play** is a way children pursue their schemas, which are their

Schema play refers to patterns that children repeat in their play.

Table 4.5 Tree cookies by schema.

Transporting	Picking up and moving a basket of tree cookies. Dumping the basket of tree cookies.
Transforming	Painting the tree cookies to alter their colour.
Trajectory	Exploring the movement of the tree cookies by tossing them into the basket.
Rotating and Circulating	Turning and spinning the tree cookies.
Enclosing and Enveloping	Surrounding the tree cookies with other objects. Hiding the tree cookies under material.
Connecting	Stringing tree cookies together that have been drilled.
Disconnecting	Taking the string of tree cookies apart.
Positioning	Ordering the tree cookies by size. Lining up the smaller tree cookies. Stacking the larger tree cookies.

Source: Based on Nutbrown (2011). Threads of thinking: schemas and young children's learning. Sage

understandings of themselves and the world around them. Playing with the tree cookie to make it spin, the child is working through the concept of spinning (the rotating and circulating schema) and considering what actions are needed to produce this result. The schema is the spinning. The assimilation is the ability to spin the tree cookie. And the accommodation is the manner in which this new knowledge becomes evident in future play in the continued spinning of tree cookies and other materials.

Heuristic Play

In the early 1980s, the child psychologist Elinor Goldschmied, coined the term **heuristic play**. The word 'heuristic' comes from the Greek word 'heurisko', which means to discover or reach understanding (Goldschmied & Jackson, 1994). Heuristic play refers to the exploratory play of toddlers with objects. The child usually plays alone but is interested in what others may be doing with similar objects. The goal of the child is to discover what can be done with the object or objects. Often the objects are placed in baskets by adults and referred to as **treasure baskets**. These baskets can be used outside as easily as they can be used inside. For all ages, any activity which involves experimenting can be described as heuristic. It starts in toddlerhood and continues throughout the lifespan (Hughes, 2015).

Heuristic play is when one experiments with objects to discover possibilities.

Treasure baskets were inspired by the work of Elinor Goldschmeid and are popular in the UK to encourage children's curiosity with the use of non-commercial and non-plastic toys for infants and toddlers.

THINK ABOUT IT! READ ABOUT IT! WRITE ABOUT IT!

Why do you think the term "treasure baskets" was conceived? Do an Internet search using the key terms "treasure baskets for infants and toddlers". Search for websites and images. After reading and viewing what you find, create a list of items that you could provide in a basket. What would you call the basket?

Photo 4.7 Experimenting with materials.

Auld (2002) identified five principles of heuristic play, as illustrated in Figure 4.10, that can be easily related to outdoor play and nature pedagogy for children of all ages. When choosing materials for heuristic play, early learning teachers consider objects that have different properties and uses. Auld (2002) suggested offering objects such as wood, metal, wool, cardboard, and stone. To add interest, the objects can be light, heavy, small, and large. The objects can be from the kitchen, bathroom, laundry room, or bedroom, and objects that fit inside each other lend themselves to schema play. The adult's role in heuristic play is considered "hands-off" in relation to the children's play and involves observation and intervention only if necessary. The timing of heuristic play is important, as toddlers need to be well fed and rested to focus and discover. The play is set up in an area free of distractions. If there are multiple children involved in heuristic play at the same time, the materials should be plentiful (Auld, 2002).

When these principles are followed, infants and toddlers begin the process of exploring loose parts. It is a type of play that lends itself to being child-led and offers multiple opportunities for discoveries. At any age there is something very profound about **self-discovery**. Moustakas (1990) developed the methodology of heuristic research as a process of internal

Self-discovery refers to finding out about oneself and discovering on your own.

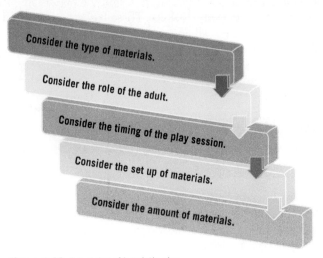

Consider the type of materials.

Consider the role of the adult.

Consider the timing of the play session.

Consider the set up of materials.

Consider the amount of materials.

Figure 4.10 Principles of heuristic play.

Table 4.6 Standards for outdoor play and learning: imagination, invention, and creativity standard.

1. The child demonstrates, appreciates, and enjoys a sense of humour.
2. The child engages in pretending, expressing feelings, and trying out new ideas and behaviours.
3. The child role plays with real or make-believe objects.
4. The child experiments and explores. The child tries out new ways of doing things by combining and using materials in new and original ways (Banning and Sullivan, 2011, p. 202).

searching to discover the nature and meaning of experience. The process is dynamic and creative and leads to self-discovery and self-knowledge. Discovery is important at any age.

PRACTICAL APPLICATIONS

Banning and Sullivan (2011) described imagination, invention, and creativity as the language of early childhood. As important learning tools for children, they are necessary parts of childhood but are increasingly becoming less valued (Banning & Sullivan, 2011). When early learning teachers consider whether they are providing outdoor experiences with materials that support imagination, invention, and creativity they can look for the following indicators listed in Table 4.6.

What loose parts would you provide to encourage children to demonstrate, appreciate, and enjoy humour? Using materials in unique ways may amuse children. Imagine the laughter that might ensue when children put buckets meant to collect natural materials on their heads? Rather than redirect this experience, encourage the humour because it shows children creatively expressing an idea. It is a sign that they have made a connection and that they understand something new (Banning & Sullivan, 2011).

Think about the loose parts that nature offers children. According to Banning & Sullivan (2011) "the materials of nature are flexible and ambiguous" (p. 84). This ambiguity provides children with a chance to use their imaginations. A fallen tree in the forest can be a space ship, a fairy house, or a castle. The leaves can be fairy blankets, the sticks magic wands, and the knobs on the tree can be the control panel for launching the rocket. Adding other loose parts to the play adds to the children's experiences and supports their opportunity to engage in pretend play with make-believe objects.

When children have the opportunity to combine materials and move them, they are exercising their creativity by using them in new and novel ways (Banning & Sullivan, 2011). Creativity will emerge when there are ample, variable materials in the environment that lend themselves to be combined, transported, and transformed. Early learning teachers provide children with loose parts so that they can direct their own learning in ways we could never imagine.

Photo 4.8 Expressing creativity with materials.

Michelle Thornhill

PRINCIPLES OF PRACTICE: CHILD-LED PRACTICE

Early learning teachers support children to become independent in their play, as this leads to them gaining competence and capacity. To achieve independence, children require ample opportunities to lead their own play. This is also referred to as child-directed or

Observer

Listener

Resource

Documenter

Facilitator

Thinker

Theorist

Encourager

Provocateur

Diane Kashin

Figure 4.11 The role of the early learning teacher in the provision of loose parts.

child-initiated play (Pyle & Danniels, 2017). It stands in contrast to adult- or teacher-led, directed, or initiated experiences, which by definition may not be play, as play is freely chosen (Lindon & Rouse, 2013). Children may use materials in ways not considered by the early learning teacher. For example, an early learning teacher puts out planks beside two tires under the assumption that the children will make an elevated walkway. Instead, two children work together to prop one tire on top of the other and create a ramp. Supporting the children in this child-led experience the early learning teacher suggests that the children try rolling something down the ramp and that they look for suitable loose parts. This is a child-led experience. There is richness in this experience—that is why it is important that the early learning teacher abandons the adult agenda and follows the children's lead.

Early learning teachers consider the value of the play experience and the importance of child-led initiatives before intervening. They also consider the value of learning from experience rather than taking a direct teaching approach. Imagine that beyond the playground is a forest full of deciduous and coniferous trees. Instead of taking children to the forest and pointing out the different types of trees and differences amongst the trees, the children can learn in an experiential and child-led way by having baskets and buckets available for them to collect and play with the different leaves and cones. If appropriate, early learning teachers may encourage children to look at the differences. Children benefit from being with early learning teachers who make the principles of child-led play as part of their practice. This does not mean that children are not supervised and supported or that "anything goes". With loose parts experiences, early learning teachers have many roles to play. Figure 4.11 depicts these important roles.

Early learning teachers have many roles to play in the provision of loose parts. Early learning teachers look for loose parts that are unique and diverse as depicted in Photo 4.9. By observing and listening, ideas emerge for gathering and offering further resources to facilitate play. By documenting and thinking, early learning teachers can come up with their own theories on how to enhance children's learning with loose parts. When children are engaging with loose parts, early learning teachers can encourage children and act as **provocateurs**.

Provocateurs foster self-direction in their role as facilitators rather directors in environments where learners become increasingly adept at problem-solving (Mezirow, 1997).

Diane Kashin

Photo 4.9 Unique and diverse loose parts.

LEARNING IN PLACE: THE SANDPIT AS PLACE

In the 1880s, a German political leader placed piles of sand in the public parks of Berlin where children played. When Dr. Marie Zakerzewska from the United States visited Berlin and saw the experiences children were having with sand, she was instrumental in the birth of sand gardens for children's play in North America (Frost, 2012). Think about the developmental benefits of sand play. What can children learn from a pile of sand?

Sand along with water is considered one of the most critical elements of the children's outdoor environment. Sand has great value for children's social and cognitive development (Olsen & Smith, 2017). Spend time observing children playing in sand, which is a variable material. Sand engages. When loose parts are added to sand, the sandpit becomes an important place for children to have rich, tactile experiences that lead to creative thinking (Olsen & Smith, 2017) and problem-solving skills. The sandpit is an important place in the lives of children. Think about the types of loose parts that may be added to the sand area. Examine Table 4.7 and think about the potential play that could evolve if children had exposure to sand and the loose parts identified.

Michelle Thornhill

Photo 4.10 In the sand.

PROGRAMMING

Many early learning teachers are recognizing how loose parts support children's outdoor play (Olsen & Smith, 2017). Children's creative expression with loose parts can be triggered through books. Reading outdoors adds the extra excitement of the elements. The wind, the sun, and the clouds add to the ambience of the experience. We offer this list of children's books that feature loose parts in Table 4.8 and a program plan based

Table 4.7 Loose parts and sand possibilities.

SAND

■ Fabric	■ Water jugs, boats, and sticks
■ Cardboard and staplers	■ Pine cones and sticks
■ Ribbons and sticks	■ Pylons and rope
■ Boxes and duct tape	■ Plumbing pipes and water jugs

Table 4.8 Children's books about loose parts.

Book Title	Description	Author	Illustrator
Not a Box	A celebration of the power of imagination featuring the cardboard box.	Antoinette Portis	Antoinette Portis
Not a Stick	Following the ideas of *Not a Box*, this book speaks to the versatility of the stick to spark the imagination.	Antoinette Portis	Antoinette Portis
Stick and Stone	With the main characters of the book being a stick, a stone, and a pinecone, children will have ideas to use these loose parts in imaginary and creative ways.	Beth Ferry	Tom Lichtenheld
Roxaboxen	Tells the story of how a group of neighbourhood children created their own community from loose parts.	Alice McLerran	Barbara Cooney

Table 4.9 Plan, engage, explore and reflect—using children's books.

PLAN	Read the book *Roxaboxen* to the children.
ENGAGE	Engage the children in a discussion of the materials that the children used in the book to create their community.
EXPLORE	Explore the environment to find similar materials and invite the children to create their own community in an appropriate space and place.
REFLECT	Were there signs in the children's play that the book influenced them? Did they come up with rules for the community? Did they assign roles for each other as members of the community? How can this experience be built upon to further support children's collaboration and sense of community?

on the principles of Plan, Engage, Explore, and Reflect in Table 4.9, where we have chosen one of those books to illustrate how it can be used to support loose parts play outdoors.

FAMILY SUPPORT AND ENGAGEMENT

Each season offers new possibilities for loose parts play. It is important for families to understand the benefits of all-season outdoor play. If families are uncomfortable with outdoor play because of seasonal change, it may be due to a number of reasons, such as having misinformation about the benefits of children playing in the rain or colder temperatures. By inviting family members to be part of and experience the outdoor environment in all seasons, family engagement can be encouraged. Early learning teachers need to support families and communities in understanding the importance of outdoor play. Research continues to indicate that there is a correlation between children's outdoor play and later success (Underwood & Killoran, 2012). When early learning teachers create opportunities for families to experience the outdoor play space throughout the seasons, the connections made will support the building of community.

Michelle Thornhill

Photo 4.11 In the mud.

Keeler (2016) wrote that natural playscapes are best designed when they "are successful for the preschoolers and families they serve" (p. vii). For example, in the summer planting rows of kale will create a forest; brussel sprouts, a jungle. Plant a multi-sensory garden that encourages children to collect plant material as loose parts. Use tree stumps as tables and drums. Add other loose instruments or music-making loose parts throughout the playscape. In the autumn, rake a pile of leaves and watch what happens. Use sticks and driftwood to create sculptures. In the winter, embrace the snow and ice. With shovels use the snow to cover things up. Collect pieces of ice and snow to build. In the spring, plant seeds and embrace the mud. When families are invited to engage in the experiences of the seasons they too will find the joy of outdoor play.

ACCESSIBILITY AND DESIGN

Loose parts are accessible materials for children. Open-ended materials can provide an entrance point for all learners. The key is to provide ample time to use these open-ended materials and to know the child. Children with exceptionalities "benefit from unlimited time to practice new skills. If they are rushed, or told to stop doing the same thing and try something new, they may become discouraged or frustrated, and may lose interest" (Mitchell, 2013, p. 15). Since loose parts offer so many possibilities, children may wish to use them over and over. This repetition is important because it allows them to experiment, persist, practice, and figure ideas out. With practice, they will "become more adept at handling the materials while discovering the materials' properties and varying how they use and combine them. Loose parts encourage creativity and innovation in all types of play, and at each child's developmental level" (Mitchell, 2013, p. 15). Children require time to fully engage with and experience the benefits of loose parts.

Loose parts add variety and novelty to the outdoor play environment and support an inclusive space. Some children will be tentative in their explorations. If loose parts are always available, these children will participate as their confidence grows. The wider the variety of materials, the more likely it is that different kinds of play will evolve. It is essential for children to feel inclusive in the environment, no matter what their abilities and needs are (Casey, 2011).

TIPS AND TOOLS FOR OUTDOOR PLAY

Given that some materials such as cardboard cannot be left outside everyday, storage is a requirement and its location crucial (Murray, 2011; McClintic & Petty, 2015). Do you think that if early learning teachers and children have to carry loose parts to the outdoor environment each day, the range of loose parts that is available will be limited? Ideally, several storage structures will be available in the play space to accommodate the loose parts for easy access. "The richness and quality of play are heavily influenced by the type and variety of equipment and materials that are available in the outdoor environment" (McClintic & Petty, 2015, p. 31). Early learning teachers benefit from thinking carefully about storage for loose parts and trying to blend storage facilities into the outdoor environment.

Storage for loose parts can be challenging. Consider what is already in the environment. If there is a chain-link fence, milk crates can be hung with S-hooks to store pots, pans, and dishes near the mud kitchen. Blocks, tools, buckets, dramatic play props, fabrics, and clothes can be kept in containers. Tarps can also be used to cover materials. A storage shed can be organized to house containers and larger loose parts that cannot be left outside.

ON THE GROUND—PROFESSIONAL REFLECTIONS: "WHY I LOVE OUTDOOR PLAY"

What makes some early learning teachers and students passionate about loose parts for outdoor play while some may feel these open-ended materials are dangerous? Do you believe that having a strong image of the child as capable and competent is essential? Read the professional reflection featured in Box 4.3, as an early learning teacher reflects on his passion for sticks as loose parts.

James and Nick run across the grass, chasing each other with sticks. Nick stops and holds his body still, while James slowly extends the point of his stick toward Nick's body. As he makes contact, he smiles and shouts "Tag! You're it!" and then runs away. As an educator, I have worked in many schools where objects like sticks are not permitted. Children in those environments were discouraged from picking sticks up because there was a sense of fear of children hurting one another. However, part of seeing the "strong image of the child" is viewing the children as being capable of setting their own boundaries and guidelines. Seeing this interaction between James and Nick is a reminder that children in our program are capable of playing a game like this without anyone getting hurt and that they do not need adults to define how to play.

Michael Bruce
Early Learning Teacher

CASE STUDIES

Read Case Study 4.1 and consider the questions below to critically reflect on the possibilities for the early learning teacher and the children involved.

CASE STUDY 4.1   The Migration of Loose Parts

Katriana and Mirella worked in a program that valued loose parts. Families, colleagues, and friends responded to the call for donations, resulting in buckets of tree cookies, branches, stones, rocks, and pinecones. There were containers of fabric and an assortment of pots, pans, and kitchen utensils. In addition to these smaller items, there were logs, stumps, planks, and crates. These materials were added to what Katriana and Mirella already had in the play space, which included sand buckets, shovels, blocks, toy trucks, and baskets. With all of the loose parts in the environment, Katriana and Mirella felt that the children's outdoor play had become chaotic. The loose parts were everywhere in the play space. Whatever could be moved had been moved and dumped. Mirella was feeling very frustrated and approached Katriana to suggest that all the loose parts be removed. Katriana was frustrated too but felt there was a solution to the issue.

1. Do you agree with Mirella and feel that the loose parts should be removed, or do you side with Katriana and feel that there are other solutions? What would be possible solutions?
2. Do all the loose parts have to be out at once? If the loose parts are not being used, how and where can they be stored?
3. How might the children be included to come up with solutions to the loose parts migration?

BOX 4.4   Take It Outside!

Take a large piece of fabric outside. How many ways can you use the fabric? Find something to cover then find something to wrap. Spread the fabric out smoothly on the ground and take a few minutes to reflect on the affordances of the fabric. What else could you add to enhance this loose parts experience?

KEY TERMS

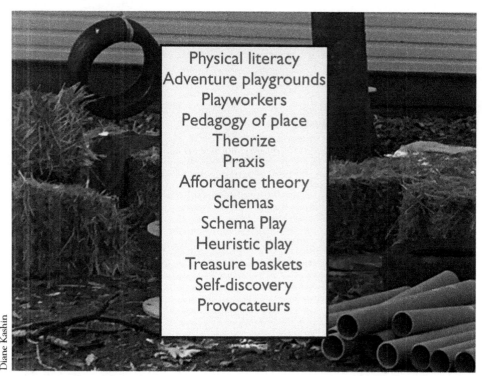

Physical literacy
Adventure playgrounds
Playworkers
Pedagogy of place
Theorize
Praxis
Affordance theory
Schemas
Schema Play
Heuristic play
Treasure baskets
Self-discovery
Provocateurs

Diane Kashin

Photo 4.12 Key terms.

Summary

- Loose parts are open-ended materials that are variable, unstructured, and able to be used in multiple ways. Simon Nicholson, a landscape architect, coined the term loose parts.

- When children play with loose parts, they are engaged cognitively, socially, and emotionally and are physically active. Being physically active supports the development of physical literacy. Loose parts also support constructive, dramatic games with rules and cooperative, parallel, and solitary play.

- Support for loose parts can be traced back to the eighteenth and nineteenth centuries, notably from theorists Froebel and Montessori. The advent of adventure playgrounds featured loose parts, and the development of a 'playworker' designation was identified for adults who support children in their experiences with loose parts.

- Loose parts support the development of twenty-first century competencies across cognitive, interpersonal, and intrapersonal domains. Twenty-first century competencies include critical thinking, communication, collaboration, creativity, problem solving, and innovation.

- Loose parts can be sorted into three categories; manufactured, recycled, and natural. Loose parts from each category can be combined to enhance children's play experience. Loose parts can be obtained from a variety of sources. The environment and the pedagogy of place are considered when acquiring loose parts.

- Schema play can be seen in children's experiences with loose parts. The concept of schema play was derived from the work of Jean Piaget's theories of schemas, assimilation, and accommodation. Loose parts support heuristic play, with treasure baskets being particularly useful to support self-discovery with toddlers.

- The key elements of loose parts include flexibility, adaptability, children's competence, availability, and sustainability. Loose parts have particular play advantages for children as compared to fixed equipment.

- Early learning teachers support child-led discovery and have important roles in enhancing and encouraging the play experience with loose parts.

- Since the 1800s, the sandpit has been providing children with an important place to play and is a basis for loose parts play.

- Loose parts experiences can be combined with language and literacy in various ways, such as by introducing children's books related to loose parts into the environment. Early learning teachers are encouraged to plan for these connections between loose parts and literacy development.

- Families can be encouraged to support their children's play with loose parts by offering opportunities to engage with loose parts throughout every season.

- Loose parts add variety and novely to the outdoor play environment and support an inclusive space. The wider the variety of materials, the more likely it is that different kinds of play will evolve. It is essential for children to feel inclusive in the environment, no matter what their abilities and needs are.

- Storage is an important consideration, yet often a challenge in the provision of loose parts.

QUIET REFLECTION

Spend some time with sand. It doesn't have to be a lot of sand, just enough to experience its sensory and soothing effects. Play with the sand, swirl it, move it, and write with it. Think about sand and sand play. What loose parts would you add to enhance your experience? Now imagine being at the beach. What loose parts would you be able to find to add? How could you duplicate this experience for children in their own playgrounds?

COMMUNITY DIALOGUE

With others, enter in a dialogue about loose parts. As a group, reflect upon these questions:
1. Where can you find loose parts?
2. How would you store loose parts in the outdoor environment?
3. What if you worked with someone who did not value loose parts? How could you help them see the light?

FOR FURTHER THOUGHT AND ACTION

Do an audit of your community and make a list of the places where loose parts can be found. Are there local thrift shops where materials can be recycled or "upcycled"? Are there local businesses that would offer children loose parts for outdoor play, such as tires and planks? Perhaps there is a place specifically for early learning teachers to access loose parts? If you have one of these places, such as The Creative Zone, in Mississauga, Ontario https://familydaycare.com/about-us/the-creative-zone/, pay a visit and determine which materials are best suited for outdoor play. If there is not a place for teachers to obtain these materials, what steps would have to be taken for your community to have their own recycling depot?

RESOURCES

There are many resources available online that support loose parts in the outdoor environment. Check out these resources:

https://www.fix.com/blog/get-children-playing-outside/

http://www.childcarequarterly.com/pdf/winter14_parts.pdf

http://www.playscotland.org/wp-content/uploads/loose-parts-play-toolkit.pdf

http://www.abcee.org/sites/abcee.org/files/Loose%20parts%20manual.pdf

The Relationship of Outdoor and Nature Play to Development, Health, Learning, and Thinking

LEARNING OUTCOMES

Look deep into nature, and then you will understand everything better.

Albert Einstein (1879–1955)

After exploring this chapter, you will be able to:

- Discuss the array of social, emotional, cognitive, communication, and physical development skills that children acquire from outdoor play.

- Outline strategies that early learning teachers may implement in outdoor play environments to support children's development of critical thinking, problem-solving, and reasoning skills.

- Explain how Vygotsky's perspectives on the zone of proximal development and Bruner's perspective on scaffolding support children's learning and development.

- Identify what is meant by play-based.

- Explain the value of all children having opportunities to engage in play in parks.

- Describe the varying roles that early learning teachers may exhibit during outdoor play.

CHILDHOOD MEMORIES

When I was a child, with my older sister and young brother, for two weeks we left our home in the country, where we had treehouses and places to hide, and lots of space, to a place where we played in the city parks. There, we experienced wading pools and swings; we spun around on the merry-go-rounds, and we sat under a tree to read our books while we waited for our aunt to come get us when she was finished work. We met children there every day that came to play with us, even though we didn't really know their families. We played differently in the park than when we were home—two people would be on the swing and the other would push them. Two would be on the merry-go-round and the other would try to make it go as fast as it could. We helped one another experience the thrill that we could have from the equipment in the park. Now, as an adult, when I look at my neighbourhood parks, I can see that all the fun equipment has been removed from them. There is, however, one park near me that has paths beside the park, and that is where I like to take children so that they can play on the great big rocks and then find places to hide.

The children and I like to do things in spaces there that we can't do at home.

CHAPTER PREVIEW

Understanding the importance of outdoor play to children's development is not a new area of study. As far back as the seventeenth and eighteenth centuries, the relationship between nature and children's development has been a topic of inquiry. Theorists such as Jean-Jacques Rousseau observed that education in outdoor environments provides children with opportunities to engage with and experience nature with their bodies and senses. Similarly, Johann Heinrich Pestalozzi determined that children from less-advantaged backgrounds made significant strides in learning in outdoor environments that allowed them to engage in arts and agricultural activities (Coe, 2016). In 1840, in his observations of children, Friedrich Froebel identified that outdoor play was an essential experience. When he created the concept of the kindergarten, its meaning referred to a child's garden. He perceived children's growth and development to be similar to a plant that required the right conditions to thrive. His principles were grounded in children learning in outdoor environments where they discovered and manipulated natural materials (Froebel, 1889). John Dewey also emphasized that children learn by seeing, experiencing, and doing. He maintained that children benefit from outdoor environments, including those with gardens (Dewey, 1962).

THINK ABOUT IT! READ ABOUT IT! WRITE ABOUT IT!

What do you think about children's development being compared to that of plants and gardens? If you embrace that perspective, what does programming look like for you and why? Make a drawing or a list that outlines what you believe plants require to be healthy and nourished. Then, do a list of what you think children require. Compare the lists. Find an article that discusses Froebel's principles about children learning in outdoor environments.

From a Canadian perspective, as outlined in Chapter 1, early learning students and teachers are guided by the Convention on the Rights of the Child (United Nations High Commission for Human Rights, 1989). Although all aspects of the United Nations Convention are important, Articles 3, 12, 19, 23, 30, and 31 are particularly relevant to children's outdoor play, development, and learning. Despite the compelling research and policies, over the years, children's access to outdoor environments has diminished. Across Canada, many children today experience the majority of their days primarily in indoor settings with limited time in outdoor environments (Coe, 2016). **Longitudinal studies** are confirming the importance of outdoor play to children's play and development (Cooper, 2016). For example, Cooper (2016) suggested that these studies are now confirming that the experiences that children have in their early years have a direct correlation to the economic, academic, and social status of communities. He identified that at the same time, "a substantial body of research indicates that outdoor play learning and play environment[s] with diverse natural elements" advanced and enriched "all of the **domains** relevant to development, health, and wellbeing of young children" (p. 85). Cooper (2016) further identified that despite such findings, there is limited emphasis placed on its importance in guidelines, regulations, or standards that are intended to enhance the quality of early learning programs.

Longitudinal studies A research design that includes observing the same children over long periods of time, often for more than five years.

Domains In early childhood development, it refers to cognitive, social/emotional, communication, language, and physical development.

Photo 5.1 Children learn about their environment through exploration.

Family Space Quinte, Inc.

Similar to Cooper (2016), Sobel (2008) argued that it is detrimental for children to be in environments that emphasize curriculum standards rather than experiential learning. When children are in environments that practice a pedagogical approach based on having first-hand outdoor and nature experience, they discover learning based on these lived experiences.

It is not uncommon for outdoor play to be associated with children's physical development. Although this is an important domain to which outdoor play contributes, the impact of outdoor play on children's overall development is far greater than just the physical. Think about what children may potentially gain from building a fort or creating a play with actions. Think about them creating meals or finding ice that is starting to melt in a bowl in the mud kitchen. How do those experiences add to children's overall development and learning? The research is accumulating on the benefits of interacting with nature, people, and places for children's overall development (Beyer et al., 2015). In this chapter we will highlight the concept that children require opportunities for and access to outdoor play because children adapt to the environments in which they are exposed to (Lee, Jordan, & Horsely, 2015). We encourage you to think about, observe, and discuss how both simple and complex experiences outdoors lead children to a variety of learning options and discoveries.

Early learning students and teachers who view and embrace the outdoors as a laboratory for children's overall development and learning will effectively be in a position to support and advocate for children to have access to outdoor play spaces. Accordingly, this requires early learning teachers not only to shift the discourse to why outdoor play is important in all kinds of weather and seasons, but also to ensure that children's voices in ideas, decisions, time, spaces, and places are prevalent in the program planning and implementation processes (Kernan & Devine, 2010).

SETTING THE STAGE FOR OUTDOOR PLAY

Environmental citizenship refers to children and adults as being integral to the environment. How we interact, engage with, care for, and protect the ecosystems will influence future living space (Dietze & Kashin, 2016).

Outdoor play is as important to children's development as nourishing food and healthy relationships (Seltenrich, 2015). Traditionally, educators have viewed outdoor play as contributing to children's social, emotional, cognitive, and physical development (Gundersen, Skar, O'Brien, Wold, & Follo, 2016). In recent years, physical literacy, inclusion, academic success (Swank, Cheung, Prikhidko, & Su, 2017), and **environmental citizenship** have become prevalent themes in the literature on the importance of outdoor play to children's development (Gleave & Cole-Hamilton, 2012). Now, research outlines the importance of children having opportunities to engage in outdoor play and interact with nature. Research suggests that children who have interactions with nature, green space, and play "develop higher levels of social cohesion and [a] sense of community" (Beyer et al., 2015, p. 253). As well, this interaction contributes to children having increased levels of physical activity, which in turn reduces unfavourable health conditions such as stress, obesity, mental fatigue, vitamin D deficiency, cardiovascular disease, sleep apnea

Table 5.1 How outdoor play contributes to children's development.

Physical	Cognitive
Skilled Actions with Objects	**Processes**
Throwing, striking, hanging, swinging, pushing, pulling, lifting, sliding, rocking, catching, building/constructing, hiding, manipulating, moulding, digging, planting, and using tools.	Observing, identifying, labelling, reasoning, matching, naming, conceptualizing, applying, and transferring.
Motor Skills	**Logical thinking**
Walking, running, jumping, hopping, galloping, skipping, crawling, climbing, rolling, balancing, and tumbling.	Classifying, seriating, developing spatial and temporal concepts, predicting, estimating, symbolizing, arranging, ordering, displaying, and developing vocabulary.
Social/Emotional	**Communication**
Self and Others	**Communication and Representation**
Initiating, taking turns, building self-concept, persevering, cooperating, tolerating, respecting, appreciating, sympathizing, emphasizing, controlling, taking responsibility, engaging in group participation, cooperative problem solving, responding to personal needs, sharing, pushing limits, joining in group management, making social connections, and cooperating.	Explaining, speaking, listening, reading, writing, dramatizing, representing pictorially, making models, moving, singing, dancing, music making, role-playing, rebuilding, mimicking, performing rhythmic movement, displaying creative self-expression, and engaging in fantasy play.
Sensory Awareness	**Investigation**
Touching, tasting, smelling, listening, looking, feeling, and seeing.	Questioning, exploring, perceiving, articulating, manipulating, initiating, adapting, collecting, experimenting, and group exploring.
Creative Problem Solving	**Critical Thinking**
Appreciating, building relationships, imagining, inventing, concluding, evaluating, risk-taking, rebuilding, reflecting, tinkering, and engaging in discovery.	Conceptualizing, generating ideas, implementing, synthesizing, reasoning, revising, reflecting, engaging, and risk-taking.

(Ogden, 2006), and diabetes. Beyer et al. (2015) concluded in their review of 25 studies examining the relationship of time outdoors to health benefits that when children have exposure to natural environments, there is a reduction in negative emotions such as anger, fatigue, and sadness and an increase in energy levels and attention span (Bowler, Buyung-Ali, Knight, & Pullin, 2010). As outlined in Tables 5.1 and 5.2, the developmental relationships for children and outdoor play are vast. As you review the tables, think about the array of outdoor play experiences that children require access to in order to gain these benefits.

Table 5.2 Benefits of outdoor play to development.

- Children who participate in outdoor play develop more varied patterns of play (Martensson, Boldmann, Soderstrom, Blennow, England, & Grahn, 2009).
- Children with more exposure to outdoor play have greater capacity for concentration and attention (Mayer, Frantz, Bruehlman-Senecal, & Dolliver, 2009).
- Children develop empathy, responsibility, mindfulness, environmental stewardship, and appreciation for nature (Cheng & Monroe, 2012; Howell, Dopko, Passmore, & Buro, 2012).
- Children who play together outdoors have more positive feelings towards their peers and adults, improved self-esteem, self-confidence, and connectedness to others (Maller, 2009; Moore, 1996).
- Children with exposure to nature have lower levels of anxiety and depression and higher levels of self-worth and esteem (Chawla, Keena, Pevec, & Stanley, 2014).
- Natural environments often increase children's engagement in free play, risk-taking, and building authentic relationships (Coe, 2016; Waters & Maynard, 2010).

As outlined in Figure 5.3, additional research findings illustrate the scope of the benefits exposure to the outdoors has on children's development.

Early learning students and teachers benefit from examining each of the domains and then thinking about the types of play, materials, and opportunities to which children are being exposed. How might the experiences be different from one season to another or from one type of weather to another? How do the spaces, places, and routines influence children's engagement? Why is understanding child development at the core of practice? As you explore this chapter, we encourage you to think about the different types of play experiences that children engage in. What might those experiences mean to their development? How might unique questioning expand children's options for learning? How might adults model options for play that offer children new development and learning opportunities?

>> BOX 5.1   Shedding Light on Outdoor Play—Points of Reflection

Why is outdoor play as important as nutritious food and relationships? What might children be missing in their development if they do not have exposure to outdoor play? Seltenrich (2015) observed that "'[P]ark prescriptions' are gaining popularity as researchers learn more about the benefits of spending time in nature" (p. 254). What does this tell you about the state of childhood today? How might exposure to parks improve children's health and development?

OUR VISION FOR OUTDOOR PLAY

Our vision is for children to be in environments that provide them with open access to the outdoors that includes a variety of places, experiences, and opportunities to engage in outdoor play daily. Ideally, early learning teachers have a passion for being outdoors and in role-modelling a sense of curiosity in their conversations with children. Statements such as "what if we do this" or "imagine if we do this" or "I wonder about this idea" are ways in which teachers support children in expanding their sense of wonder and ideas for exploration. Collectively and individually, children and adults will embrace the beauty of nature when it is a lived experience. This requires children to have opportunities to feel the wind blowing or the snow gently falling on one's cheek, and experience the sun shining brightly or splashing in the puddles in the rain—such opportunities are to be embraced.

THINK ABOUT IT! READ ABOUT IT! WRITE ABOUT IT!

When you think about the ideal play space for children, what image do you have? Why might that be important to play? In her informational guide to young children's outdoor play spaces Seven Cs, Susan Herrington (2007) identifies the importance of outdoor play space having charter, context, connectivity, change, chance, clarity, and challenge. Find the guide by searching Seven Cs. How does this inform your thoughts about outdoor space? Go to www.wstcoast.org/playspaces/outsidecriteria/7Cs.pdf

There is an increased body of research that supports the relationship between outdoor play and children's development (Szczytko & Stevenson, 2017). As more research is conducted, it is our vision that, increasingly, the research will be connected to practice. As early learning teachers connect research to practice, children ultimately will have increased access to and opportunities for a variety of outdoor play experiences that contribute to development and learning. Connecting research to practice and practice to research are essential foundational skills for early learning teachers (Dietze & Kashin, 2016). This is not an easy task. Early learning students and teachers benefit from examining new research in depth to determine what it means in the context of children, programming, staff, and environments. Some research may not necessarily be conducive to the program philosophy, the children that the program is serving, or practical requirements due to considerations such as space or staffing models.

To support children's development through outdoor play and nature, early learning teachers may need to move from their comfort zones and change practices to reflect research. Such change involves some element of risk and challenge as new ways are tested and refined into practice. For instance, early learning teachers with a high commitment to supporting children in having outdoor play experiences respond positively to new ways of thinking about and engaging in the outdoor experiences. Conversely, early learning teachers who are comfortable with their current practices may not have the same level of motivation or desire to change programming, materials, or options that would support children's outdoor play. There are many models that early learning teachers may use to guide them when transferring research to practice. Early learning teachers benefit from determining a model that works for their program and professional practice philosophy (Doan, 2013). As shown in Photo 5.2, it is our vision that outdoor play and nature experiences will continually evolve and that practices will be informed by research.

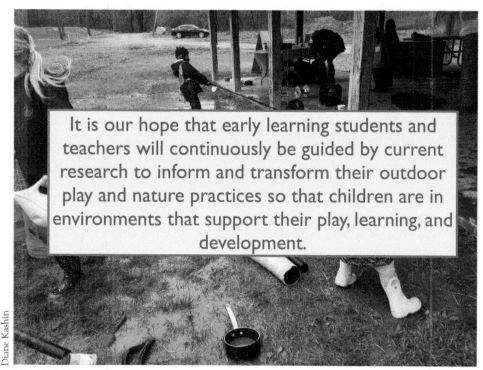

Photo 5.2 Vision statement.

POSITIONING OUTDOOR PLAY IN THE LIVES OF CHILDREN

Researchers, educators, health professionals, and others agree that having exposure to outdoors is essential to children's learning and development (Duque, Martins, & Clemente, 2016). This is especially important today as children experience living in urban environments, have **hurried childhoods**, and more technology in their daily lives (Villanueva et al., 2016). Children's free time is being replaced with structured and scheduled events, and the fear of a lack of neighbourhood safety is impeding their outdoor play (Seltenrich, 2015). If the pendulum does not swing back in favour of outdoor play, the impact on future societies will be profound. Szczytko & Stevenson (2017) contend that children who have "trees outside [their] classroom windows can improve attention and test scores" (p. 36). They also point to the work of researchers at North Carolina State University who determined that children who go outside during class time are more likely to develop environmental stewardship attitudes and behaviours.

Not all outdoor play space provides children with the same opportunities for exploration and learning. As early learning students and teachers think about how children may be exposed to a variety of outdoor play opportunities, it is beneficial to examine the places and spaces where children play. How might the space influence children's play? What are the possibilities, challenges, or impediments of the space? What does the space communicate to children?

> **Hurried childhoods** refers to children who have over-scheduled lives and high expectations placed upon them (Elkind, 2013).

THEORETICAL FOUNDATION

Curiosity, critical thinking, and problem solving are foundational to children's play, learning, and development, and all of these skills are necessary for children to develop the twenty-first century competencies that were introduced in Chapter 4. The environments to which children are exposed during the early years set the stage for their development of the social, emotional, cognitive, and physical skills that align with curiosity, critical thinking, and problem solving. Outdoor environments that provide space, materials, and options can provide children with enriched learning opportunities that are not achievable in indoor environments (Burdette & Whitaker, 2005). Outdoor environments stimulate children's "imaginations, inventiveness, and creativity" (Ernst, 2012, p. 9). Burdette & Whitaker (2005) suggested that:

> . . . a child is likely to encounter opportunities for decision making that stimulate problem solving and creative thinking because outdoor spaces are often more varied and less structured than indoor spaces. In addition, there are fewer constraints outdoors on children's gross motor movement and less restriction on their range of visual or gross motor exploration. Together these factors that do not prescribe or limit activity induce curiosity and the use of imagination. (p. 48)

Others such as Dietze and Kashin (2016) have argued that children who are exposed to outdoor play environments that offer them the freedom to play and are rich in experiences develop more flexible thinking, creativity, and problem-solving skills. Conversely, children with limited exposure to or time for outdoor exploration have reduced curiosity and risk-taking skills. It is beneficial for early learning teachers to view children's reasoning and problem-solving skills evolving from their outdoor play experiences in relation to cognitive and social-emotional development, as outlined in Figure 5.1.

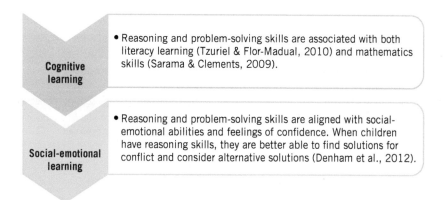

Cognitive learning	• Reasoning and problem-solving skills are associated with both literacy learning (Tzuriel & Flor-Madual, 2010) and mathematics skills (Sarama & Clements, 2009).
Social-emotional learning	• Reasoning and problem-solving skills are aligned with social-emotional abilities and feelings of confidence. When children have reasoning skills, they are better able to find solutions for conflict and consider alternative solutions (Denham et al., 2012).

Figure 5.1 How outdoor play supports children's cognitive, social, and emotional learning.

Early learning teachers are familiar with the practice of encouraging reasoning concepts and problem-solving skills with children, especially in the indoor environment (Seltenrich, 2015). Outdoor play environments offer many options for children to engage in new types of play and learning. Banning and Sullivan (2011) remind early learning teachers that "every moment of their day, children are occupied with trying to figure things out by applying various problem-solving skills and strategies" (p. 93). Critical thinking, problem solving, and reasoning are connected but each differ in meaning and the manner in which children execute such skills. Each will be examined.

Critical thinking is a self-guided, self-disciplined (Elder, 2007), and self-correcting mode of thinking about an idea, experience, or problem. It spans across multiple domains (Whittaker, 2014). The process requires "conceptualizing, applying, analyzing, synthesizing, and or evaluating information gathered from, or generated by, observation, experience, reflection, reasoning, or communication, as a guide to belief and action" (Scriven & Paul, 1987, n.p.). As identified by Lai (2011) and Galinsky (2010), children require many opportunities through their play to pursue knowledge and use self-control to:

- Understand the connections between ideas and experiences;
- Identify, construct, and evaluate ideas and possible solutions;
- Try to figure out what they did, why the idea may not have worked, and what they may wish to try next and why;
- Reflect upon what they know and believe about the experience; and
- Identify what is known, how to make to make use of information that may lead to problem solving, and determine other resources that may lead to solving the particular problem to be solved.

Think about children who are interested in making a hammock from rope and fabric. They think that they can position it between two trees. What types of critical thinking might the children be required to engage in to be successful in making the hammock? Why would children learn to think critically with this type of experience as opposed to a paper-based matching exercise that requires them to circle what is similar and what is different, using different markers? How is the learning different?

Children require opportunities to engage in critical thinking for many reasons, including its relationship to language and communication skills, creativity, and self-reflection. As children engage in the process of thinking critically and systematically, they also gain new language skills that support them in expressing their ideas and perspectives. Children

Table 5.3 Strategies for supporting children in developing critical thinking skills.

IDEAS	LINKS	DECISIONS
Thinking of ideas. Examining potential ways to solve problems and determining what strategy they will use to solve problems. Finding new ways to do things.	Making links and noticing patterns in their experiences. Making predictions. Tinkering with ideas and then testing them. Developing ideas around themes, sequences, cause and effect.	Making decisions about how to solve a problem. Be flexible and change strategy as needed. Reflect upon the result and determine if the intended results were achieved.

are able to think about their play and describe what they need to be able to do to create the hammock and describe why their first ideas required further development. This process supports children in being able to engage in effective discussions about their experiences (Lai, 2011). Discussions enhance their skills in analyzing ideas, actions, and solutions. As children think about new ideas or possible solutions, they are engaging in creative thoughts. Creativity is related to children's abilities to generate new ideas, evaluate the ideas, and select the ideas that will support what they are hoping to achieve. Self-reflection, as part of the critical thinking process, supports children in justifying their ideas, actions, and decisions. It therefore helps children to evaluate successes, mistakes, and new options.

As identified in the *Early Education Development Matters in the Early Years Foundation Stage* (EYFS) (Stewart & Moylett, 2012), learning to think critically begins in childhood. The outdoor play environments, when supported by adult interactions, foster children's critical thinking skills. As outlined in Table 5.3, adults encourage children to create ideas, make connections, and choose ways to do things.

Early learning students and teachers role-model critical thinking behaviours first by being curious; and second by being a thinker. As shown in Figure 5.2, early learning teachers make their thinking visible.

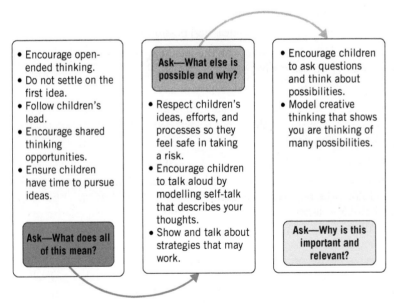

Figure 5.2 Ways to encourage critical thinking.

As you review Photo 5.3, think about what you see. Do all of the children appear to have the same level of competency? How might you support children in using critical thinking skills in determining how they can maintain their balance and have success walking down the plank? How might your curiosity and encouragement about how to walk down the plank advance children's thinking processes? Making connections is a vital part of the critical-thinking process. Early learning teachers use many strategies daily in their practice. They may be as simple as drawing attention to the sounds and experiences or posing a question to the children that requires them to think in different ways. Early learning teachers evaluate their outdoor

Photo 5.3 Children balancing on the plank.

environment regularly to view it as a discovery space. What are the opportunities from the children's perspective for new learning and discoveries to occur?

Children begin **problem solving** at birth as they try to figure out the world around them. Early learning programs that are rich in opportunities for play and learning require children to engage in problem solving naturally. Problem solving occurs as children experiment and investigate ideas or materials, when they select materials to use to execute their ideas, or when they participate with a peer. Have you heard children ask a peer, "how far can you throw the ball" or "what will happen if we put one more block on top?" These actions support children in developing their problem-solving skills.

Problem-solving opportunities are embedded in early learning programs. Children gain these skills through observation, interactions with adults and their peers, experimentation with the people, places, and things in their environments, and with opportunities to practice ideas, and make decisions and conclusions (Innis, 2012). Vygotsky (1978) found that children's abilities and strategies used for problem solving differed depending on the circumstances. He pointed out that when more than one child is trying to solve a problem or assist another child in solving a problem, the thinking is deeper than solving the problem by oneself. He suggested that this deeper learning and experience stretches children's thinking, known as zone of proximal development. Think about children trying to climb a tree to reach the tree house. When competent children assist other children either through role-modelling, verbal instructions, or physical support, those receiving the help move to a new phase of problem solving. This process as identified by Bruner (1966) is part of scaffolding learning, whereby children move from their current level of problem solving to more complex thinking and options to reach goals or solve problems. Some children are natural problem solvers; others may require assistance and coaching until they develop confidence in their abilities to problem solve.

As outlined in Figure 5.3, there are five important steps that support children in strengthening their problem-solving skills (Hemmeter, Santos, & Ostrosky, 2008). One of the most challenging elements for children in the problem-solving process is to be able to identify the problem. Similar to critical thinking, children benefit from hearing early learning students and teachers identify problems in their dialogue within the environment. This role-modelling supports children in developing the vocabulary necessary to express the problem. Think about children trying to move heavy stumps from one end of the play space to another. They have tried to tip them on the side to roll them.

Problem solving as related to early learning refers to the process that children and adults use to identify what is not working, determining the cause of the problem, and identifying, prioritizing, and testing ideas to reach a solution that supports the goal trying to be achieved.

Figure 5.3 Steps in supporting children in strengthening problem-solving skills.

They tipped them back and forth and finally used their arms and hands to push them over, while pushing their feet up against a different stump. Once they started rolling the stumps, they tried but soon realized that they could not get them up the three stairs. As the early learning teacher observed this, she asked if she could help. When the children answered yes, she had them verbalize what they were trying to do and what they perceived the problem to be. The children identified they would not be able to roll the stumps up the stairs. The teacher asked, "What other solutions have you thought about?" Then, she asked if they wanted her to record their solutions on the board so they could examine each and determine which might be a solution to their problem. Having children state possible solutions supports them in realizing there are options to the problem. This is how children develop **divergent thinking**.

After the children had brainstormed four possible solutions, the teacher asked them to identify which one might be the best solution and why they thought that. For example, Jeran thought that placing planks up the stairs to roll the stumps on would be the best idea. Thomas thought that using the planks was good but then added that maybe they could use the moving dolly and the planks. As the children moved to put the planks on the stairs and get the moving dolly, they had discussions about how they were going to push and pull the dolly up the planks. First, Thomas suggested they try the plank idea and dolly without the stumps to see if their idea was going to work. They soon discovered that the planks were not as wide as the dolly. Then, they had to return to problem solving to deal with that situation. As they thought about solutions, the early learning teacher listened for both their possible solutions and possible signs of frustration. Thomas wondered if they put the two planks together if they might be successful. Was the problem that the two planks had too much space between them? Again, the children tested their solution. As one problem was solved, others surfaced. Because these children were familiar with focusing their problem-solving strategies, they had the persistence to pursue their ideas. Although it is not unusual for children to act on their first idea or impulse, effective critical thinkers and problem solvers require **inhibitory control** (Diamond, 2006). This control supports children in managing their emotions, impulses, and related behaviours, resulting in their problem-solving skills being more focused.

As outlined by Gundersen et al. (2016), children's learning is often divided into the emotional, social, cognitive, and physical domains, but as illustrated above, children's play often requires them to use all of the developmental domains. Such processes and experiences support children in learning to value differing ideas and perspectives, flexibility in thinking and doing, and expanding their logical and creative-thinking processes. These abilities are related to critical thinking and reasoning skills.

Reasoning skills are the processes that are used to formulate one's views based on perceptions, facts, or a combination of the two (Lao, 2017). Previously, based on the work of Jean Piaget (1896–1980), it was determined, that there are four major stages of reasoning: sensorimotor stage (0–2 years old), preoperational (2–7 years old), concrete operational (7–11 years old) and formal operations (11 years old—adulthood) and that higher order

Divergent thinking refers to a free-flowing process of thought that generates ideas and explores possible solutions.

Inhibitory control refers to "the ability to ignore distractions and stay focused, and to resist making one response and instead make another" (Diamond, 2006, p. 76).

thinking was developed only by older children. However, research is now suggesting that this may not be the case. For example, Woodward (2009) suggested that children can reason and problem solve in infancy. As they gain more life experiences, children as early as three years of age may be making connections, formulating complex thoughts, and beginning to engage in logical thinking and reasoning (Whittaker, 2014).

Children develop reasoning skills during their early years and these are foundational for lifelong learning. As children engage in and experience outdoor environments, they must be places where they can learn concepts by doing. As part of that experiential learning, early learning teachers support the children by encouraging the use of critical thinking and problem-solving techniques. Early learning students and teachers role-model sound reasoning skills in dialogue with children. For example, think of children wishing to play hopscotch. Some children may offer that they can play hopscotch only if they have a hopscotch board made by drawing it on a sidewalk with sidewalk chalk. How might early learning teachers extend this thought process? What types of questions might you pose that

Photo 5.4 Children explore how to make the water splash.

will lead children to examine other possibilities? What types of misinformation might you need to address with the children? How might you explore with children other ways of making a hopscotch board? For example, how might sticks or masking tape be used?

As discussed earlier, scholars are now suggesting that there is evidence that challenges Piaget's (1930) claims that logical reasoning does not begin to develop until adolescence. Researchers including Gopnik et al. (2004); Hollister and McCullough (2010); and Cannon and Woodward (2012) have posited that there is sufficient evidence to suggest that logical thinking and reasoning begins during infancy and develops further during childhood (Whittaker, 2014). Reasoning and problem-solving skills require an understanding of causality, symbolic thinking, inductive and deductive reasoning, analogical reasoning, and reasoning with abstract ideas. Table 5.4 provides brief descriptors of each.

Table 5.4 Types of skills required for problem solving and reasoning.

Causality is the relation between one event or behaviour and another, in which the first influences the second and the second is dependent on the first. For example, an infant babbles "dada" and the adult responds "dada".	**Inductive reasoning** is a type of thinking that uses personal behavior or experiences, rather than facts or general rules, to draw conclusions or make decisions. For example, children will add water to mud because they have previously used it with sand to change the consistency.
Deductive reasoning is a type of thinking that uses facts or general rules to draw conclusions or make decisions. For example, if I put the larger blocks on the bottom, I will be able to build the tower taller.	**Analogical reasoning** is a type of thinking that identifies similarities between new and understood concepts and then uses those similarities to understand a new concept. For example, children use similar moulding techniques with clay and play dough.
Abstract reasoning is the ability to think about objects or ideas that are not physically present. For example, children may identify how they could use rocks for a game, despite them not being present in the play space.	**Symbolic thinking** is the ability to substitute a symbol for an object or idea. For example, a rock can be used for creating structures similar to building blocks.

Vygotsky (1978) identified the zone of proximal development as "the distance between the actual developmental level as determined by independent problem solving and the level of potential development as determined through problem solving under adult guidance, or in collaboration with more capable peers" (p. 86). He recommended that children's environments offer them opportunities to stretch their current knowledge and competences by offering materials and potential experiences that require new thinking, reasoning, and problem-solving skills. When children have the correct environment—peers, teachers, and materials that challenge them, they engage in achieving the task by combining what they know, with what they are trying to accomplish, while in some instances drawing upon the support and guidance from others.

Reciprocal teaching is a process that takes the form of dialogue between children and adults for the purpose of constructing the meaning of a particular idea, process, or experience.

Vygotsky's (1978) approach to zone of proximal development is evident in contemporary approaches that use **reciprocal teaching** and collaborative learning (McLeod, 2012) strategies with children. Reciprocal teaching draws upon children using summarizing, questioning, clarifying, and predicting skills; all of which are related to critical thinking, problem solving, and reasoning skills that help them bring meaning to new knowledge created (McLeod, 2012). Collaborative learning refers to groups of children working together to achieve a common goal. As part of the process in which children develop critical thinking, problem-solving and reasoning skills, early learning teachers

Family Space Quinte, Inc.

Photo 5.5 Children explore the rock together.

create safe outdoor play spaces that encourage children to express their diverse ideas and perspectives, as this leads to divergent thinking and acceptance of differing ideas and opinions.

PRACTICAL APPLICATIONS

The research that is emerging is clearly identifying the relationships of outdoor play to children's learning, health, wellness, and dispositions. Children require all kinds of spaces, places, and experiences for their development to flourish. Development is a complex process that should not be taken for granted. As outlined in the Theoretical Foundations section, some of the core skills that are essential for children to develop are critical thinking, problem solving, and reasoning. Banning and Sullivan (2011) identified the development of reasoning and problem solving as an important standard of practice, as outlined in Table 5.5.

Early learning teachers have key roles in supporting children in developing reasoning, critical thinking and problem-solving skills. This begins by supporting children in making sense of their world through observations, dialogue, materials, and opportunities that build on children's curiosity and interests (Ramani, 2012). When children have exposure to intriguing outdoor play environments, they "manipulate objects and interact with others, construct knowledge about the way the world works, and learn vital concepts such as cause and effect" (Whittaker, 2014, p. 84). Without intriguing places to play, the opportunity to build relationships, consider other's ideas, and negotiate is diminished.

Early learning teachers are instrumental in facilitating play. Their approach should scaffold children's learning while supporting them in understanding the difference between guessing and knowing (Whittaker, 2014). This may require the early learning teacher to encourage children to think in broader terms or expand the resources used to solve a problem. Early learning teachers may also support children in testing their ideas to determine next steps. "The ability to distinguish when there is and is not enough evidence to draw conclusions is fundamental to good problem solving" (Whittaker, 2014, p. 84). Children require outdoor environments that push them to have these experiences—ones that challenge them to explore new perspectives. Their abilities to problem solve during the early years influence their later academic success and social connections with others. Early learning teachers ensure that their practices are reflective of ways to support children in advancing their problem-solving, reasoning, and critical-thinking skills.

Table 5.5 Standards for outdoor play and learning: reasoning and problem-solving standard.

Standards for Outdoor Play and Learning: Reasoning and Problem-Solving Standard
1. The child explores and is able to identify meaningful issues.
2. The child approaches issues with more than one solution.
3. The child applies various strategies to resolve problems such as trial and error, comparing, sorting, and classifying.
4. The child engages in discussions and consults and collaborates with other children and adults to work through questions during investigations.

Source: (Banning and Sullivan, 2011, p. 202.)

PRINCIPLES OF PRACTICE: PLAY-BASED PRACTICE

Play-based pedagogy is not new to early childhood literature as a curriculum model. Vygotsky maintained that children's play is foundational to their overall development and that it is not distinct from academic work. There are many definitions used to describe play-based practice. We view it as being child-initiated or child-directed and self-motivated. The play is unstructured, imaginative, exploratory, active, and without defined goals initially. Philosophically, play-based programs value the role of experiences that lead children toward creating their knowledge and learning. When children are in play-based environments they are engaged in experimenting, discovering, creating, imagining, improvising, manipulating objects, and constructing, while gaining new understandings, ideas, and knowledge. Children are active participants in planning, executing, and reflecting upon their learning (Cutter-Mackenzie & Edwards, 2013). As identified by the Council of Ministers of Education, Canada (2017), "there is now evidence that neural pathways in children's brains are influenced and advanced in their development through exploration, thinking skills, problem solving, and language expression that occur during play" (p. 1). They reinforced that research is clearly identifying that play-based learning leads children to experience great social, emotional, and academic success.

Play-based programs that occur outdoors support children's curiosity cycles. Through experimentation, investigation, questioning, tinkering with ideas, and asking and solving questions, critical thinking, problem-solving and reasoning skills are enhanced (Council of Ministers of Education, Canada 2017). Play-based programming requires children to have flexible schedules that allow for them to have large blocks of time to engage in play. The outdoor play space has meaningful materials available that support children's ideas and areas of exploration.

CURIOUS?

Watch this video to see children playing in nature https://www.youtube.com/watch?v=Jkiij9dJfcw

LEARNING IN PLACE: THE PARK AS PLACE

The loss of connections to nature and the opportunities for children to play in unstructured spaces is increasingly becoming a concern (Gundersen et al., 2016). Despite their importance, many children could have exposure to parks but do not (Gundersen et al., 2016). Seltenrich (2015) found that research conducted over the past 10 years clearly identifies that "children have much to gain from time spent outdoors and much to lose from a lack of park access" (p. 22). Many levels of governments across Canada have parks designed to be public spaces, some of which are considered traditional with playground equipment and related accessories, and others in a more natural state with trails, trees, and various aspects of nature.

As Dietze (2013) stated, neighbourhood parks are generally intended to offer "children and families a place to play, meet other families, and participate in activities that support the establishment of healthy lifestyles" (p. 14). As the movement continues to highlight the benefits that nature and play have in children's learning, neighbourhood parks can be outdoor spaces that offer different learning experiences than are generally found within early learning fences. The word *park* has different connotations for children, families, and early learning teachers and students depending on lived experiences, family culture, demographics, and connections to nature (Szczytko & Stephenson, 2017).

Szczytko & Stephenson (2017) maintained that traditional parks, such as those that are primarily designed for playground equipment, are less desirable places for children than those that are more "wild". They described "wild" as being those parks that are "less human-maintained with native vegetation" (p. 36). Such wild areas are preferred by children because of the options that they provide for adventure, experimentation, and the feeling of freedom. Fjortoft (2004) asserted that children view natural beauty more for the wildness of the space than order. Parks with more varieties of nature stimulate children's curiosity and interest and provide greater options for exploration and learning. Parks that are maintained and manicured reduce the types of experiences or discoveries that may naturally occur in more wild parks. Imagine how place changes children's play. Gundersen et al. (2016) suggested that nature, such as that found in parks, provides many opportunities for play because of the "qualities of openness, diversity, alteration, exploration, creativity, anonymity and wilderness" (p. 117). These spaces do not have instructions for what must be; rather, they offer children options to change the play based on need, experience, and disposition (Chawla, 1991).

Think about children being in an early learning environment where they have access to some plants, trees, mud, and leaves. Then think of the neighbourhood park that has the grass mowed. Then, think about how the play might be different again when children have access to spaces not mowed, where they may hide in the grass or follow different paths that go up and down and around corners. They climb on slippery logs or rocks that have moss on them. How do the potential learning experiences change? Children require access to a variety of spaces and places so that they are encouraged to explore and embrace nature. Think about how the play differs in various parks. Early learning teachers are uniquely positioned to ensure that children visit parks and are given the freedom to explore them based on their needs and interests.

Gunderson et al. (2016) contended that for children to get the most benefit from parks and to experience nature, the role of the adult needs to be redefined. If adults control the play within the park, the opportunities for learning are reduced. If adults were to take a "more hands-off approach instead of organizing and planning specific activities, then more spontaneous, unstructured and self-directed children's play [could] generate a more emotional, sensuous and embodied engagement with nature" (p. 117). This approach is consistent with unstructured or play-based learning principles and practices.

Rebekka Bradshaw

Photo 5.6 Children engaging in play in the park.

PROGRAMMING

Although it is recognized that play-based programming is child-initiated, it is important to think about the roles of early learning teachers and students in the programming process. Research has increasingly recognized that early learning teachers have key roles in supporting children during their play outdoors. The roles that teachers play either advance or inhibit children's developmental opportunities. Adult interactions and engagement during outdoor play correlate with children's learning (Cutter-Mackenzie & Edwards, 2013). Siraj-Blatchford (2007) noted that children's play is enhanced when a sustained-shared thinking process is visible. That means that children and adults engage in discussions and document their ideas and learning in various ways. Similarly, co-constructing knowledge further enhances the depth and breadth of outdoor play engagement and learning (Gundersen et al., 2016).

Outdoor play requires preparation similar to that required for the indoor portion of the program. It requires planning, observation, and evaluation. Children require access to a variety of materials that will stimulate play types in an environment that offers safe but challenging risks. Effective outdoor programs fully engage children in active play activities and experiences. Versatile space, coupled with equipment and materials, supports children's sense of curiosity and need for exploration.

Developing the curriculum for outdoor play is influenced by the children's interests, followed by the values and priorities of the early learning setting. In the programming process, early learning teachers recognize that outdoor play benefits neither the educator nor children if it is always group-based, or if it is presented as a rigid play experience; rather, outdoor play offers a balance of skills, concepts, and games that promote active movement and the interest of the child.

The role of the early learning teacher is connected to programming, both in planning and in implementing it. Based on the perspective that play-based learning includes tenets of child-initiated actions, co-construction of knowledge and sustained-shared thinking, we present three key roles that early learning teachers engage in during outdoor play as outlined in Figure 5.4.

Programming that models these types of roles supports creating environments that invite children to experiment with experiencing fluidity in their play. Through programming,

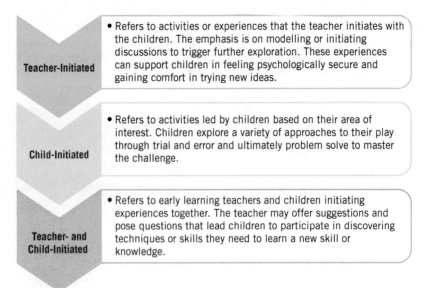

Teacher-Initiated
- Refers to activities or experiences that the teacher initiates with the children. The emphasis is on modelling or initiating discussions to trigger further exploration. These experiences can support children in feeling psychologically secure and gaining comfort in trying new ideas.

Child-Initiated
- Refers to activities led by children based on their area of interest. Children explore a variety of approaches to their play through trial and error and ultimately problem solve to master the challenge.

Teacher- and Child-Initiated
- Refers to early learning teachers and children initiating experiences together. The teacher may offer suggestions and pose questions that lead children to participate in discovering techniques or skills they need to learn a new skill or knowledge.

Figure 5.4 Key roles of early learning teachers.

Table 5.6 Plan, engage, explore, reflect—using a ladder in play.

PLAN	When four of the children saw a maintenance person with a ladder, they became intrigued about having one to use in their play space. Wanting to support children's interests, you make a list of benefits and challenges in placing the ladder in the play space. As part of this process, the children's physical literacy skills are assessed. Offering the experience can be done with confidence that it would provide children with risk-taking opportunities. Ensure that if the ladder becomes part of the play environment, children would be capable of using it and avoid sending mixed messages to them about a fear of falling.
ENGAGE	Present the ladder in the play space then, if children show any interest, engage in dialogue with them. Depending on the direction of the conversation, this may include having them create their rules for the use of the ladder in the play space, including rules for the role of the teacher.
EXPLORE	Support the children in exploring and using the ladder. Based on observations, determine if and when the children require teacher support. Document children's success and engage in dialogue with them about their experience.
REFLECT	Were the children engaged in the experience and did they display persistence as they explored? Which children participated in the experience? What were some of the conversations you heard either during the experience or as the children reflected on the experience? How did the experience support their development and learning? What other materials might you offer next time? Which role of the teacher was predominant during the experience?

facilitation, and guidance, children form their own hypotheses, predict what might happen, use the information, compare their findings, discover new strategies—and ultimately alter their mental structures to bring their personal meaning to their learning (Munroe & MacLellan-Mansell, 2014).

From an outdoor play perspective, early learning teachers examine their role. Early learning teachers can use the "PEER Principle" of plan, engage, explore, and reflect to determine which role best suits a situation. As seen in Photo 5.7, children have identified an interest in using a ladder to climb to the roof of the playhouse.

Table 5.6 illustrates the process that early learning teachers consider and their role in relation to children's interests in using ladders and the potential for their development and learning.

Photo 5.7 Children's play requires early learning teachers to exhibit different roles.

FAMILY SUPPORT AND ENGAGEMENT

For many families, the publicity associated with ensuring their children are ready for the school system has resulted in their desire to forfeit outdoor play for more academically based experiences (Gleave & Cole-Hamilton, 2012). As identified in Chapter 3, families generally want the best for their children (Ontario Ministry of Education, 2014). This means that it is beneficial for early learning teachers to create strategies that will support families in understanding the relationship of outdoor play to later academic performance. For example, if families are given information about how outdoor play experiences support children in developing skills such as social competence, problem solving, and creative thought processes, as well as in acquiring the foundational skills of mathematics, science, and language and literacy, some of the barriers to outdoor play may be reduced. Families require opportunities to interact with early learning teachers who have developed qualities that role-model the curiosity that can be found outdoors. As role models, early learning teachers facilitate discussions that help families expand their knowledge of how the outdoors provides a vast array of options for their children's development and learning.

ACCESSIBILITY AND DESIGN

The design of the outdoor play space influences how children use the environment to support their play. As outlined by Greenman (2005), one of the key roles of early learning teachers is to examine the outdoor play spaces to determine what the environment "says" to the children. What does the space communicate—is it organized? Is there room for children to move their loose parts to various parts of the play space? Where do they climb and where do they go for those places to pause? Where are the sheltered spaces that support children in creating a secret hideaway? The tone of the outdoor play space influences how children engage with the materials, their peers, and adults. There is a correlation between how the space is laid out and how children feel, how they use the space, and how they find their way around the space (Dietze & Kim, 2014; Dietze & Kashin, 2016). Dietze and Kashin (2016) and others stipulate that as part of the space considerations, children must be given the freedom to engage in **wayfinding** processes. Folz (1998) created eight design principles for wayfinding, two of which we have adapted in relation to children's outdoor play space.

> **Wayfinding** refers to the process children use to guide them through the physical space.

- Principle I—Create different identities for each area or location. This means that early learning teachers ensure that each area such as sand, water, or nature exploration has a unique perceptual identity. Generally, the space has some function and provides children with a recognizable point of reference in the larger space.

- Principle 2—Create sections of differing visual character. From a wayfinding perspective, this means that each section of the play space should have visual attributes that differ from the other spaces. Some of the spaces may have very defined borders, while others may offer specific types of natural characteristics, such as a place to pause built around a circle of tall sunflowers.

  Children look for spaces and places that offer them a sense of comfort. Wayfinding is connected to children's abilities to problem solve in asking where is the space, what they want to do in the space, and what is needed in the space. When children enter a space, they make a **cognitive map**, based on the information that their brain processes. The cognitive-mapping process assists children in developing an awareness and accumulation of spatial knowledge. This supports them in being able to visualize images, recall information, and then add changes as new experiences or perceptions occur. These combined processes contribute to children taking play into all kinds of unique directions and places.

> **Cognitive map** refers to the mental representation of one's physical or spatial space.

TIPS AND TOOLS FOR OUTDOOR PLAY

Across Canada, the winter months appear to be most challenging in ensuring that children have access to and opportunities for outdoor play. There are many benefits for children to be engaged in outdoor play during the winter months, including the reduction of the spread of germs and bacteria, increased vitamin D, and opportunities for use of larger muscles, problem solving, and imagination.

Think what would happen if large bubble wands and solutions were taken outdoors. What types of science principles might the children learn? For example, the bubbles outside are larger than if they are blown indoors and they last longer because of the temperatures.

Photo 5.8 Children will experience with materials and creativity when the environment is intriguing.

The bubbles become an activity that requires the children to be physically active and has great potential for more than one child to engage in the play by chasing the bubbles.

ON THE GROUND—PROFESSIONAL REFLECTIONS: "WHY I LOVE OUTDOOR PLAY"

Early learning teachers that consider children's development as it relates to outdoor play think reflectively. Outdoor play should be a right for all children. Read the professional reflection featured in Box 5.3 as an early learning teacher considers outdoor play from her own context.

❯❯ BOX 5.3   "Why I Love Outdoor Play"

We know that outdoor play is essential for healthy child development. There are physical, cognitive, social, and emotional benefits to spending time freely playing outside. Children with disabilities often face barriers to outdoor play. Spaces may be inaccessible or unsafe for them or there might not be enough adult support. Children with disabilities are often overlooked in designing truly inclusive outdoor experiences for children, yet they have the most to gain from outdoor play. Natural surfaces strengthen gross motor skills, and the sights and sounds of nature strengthen sensory processing, self-regulation, and attention skills. The freedom to play also strengthens confidence and self-esteem. I have seen children's joy at accomplishing what may have seemed impossible to some—an overnight canoe trip, building and cooking on a fire, fully participating in art, drama, music, and sports outside of the confines of a classroom or "therapy" space. Some children with special needs spend a lot of time following an adult's lead—in school, in therapy sessions, and during medical appointments. Time and space to play and to make their own choices are essential in strengthening children's resiliency. The skills and confidence built during summer experiences often are continued on into the school year. In the midst of winter, many children think back to these summer days and count down the days until their summer program begins again. Typically, developing children are also able to benefit from inclusive outdoor experiences—friendships develop naturally and quickly when children feel comfortable and are able to truly be themselves.

Karen Tegel
Early Learning Teacher

CASE STUDIES

Read Case Study 5.1 and consider the questions below to critically reflect on why a team approach to outdoor might be used to change current practice.

CASE STUDY 5.1   A Team Approach to Outdoor Play

The early years administrative team at the University Child Care Centre is interested in increasing the outdoor play portion of their program. They are very enthusiastic but have felt some resistance from their staff. They realize that the vision the administrative staff has will only be successful if there are early learning teachers who have a desire to champion this movement. Over the past four weeks, at each staff meeting the team has devoted 15 minutes to discuss the importance of outdoor play. This has sparked some great conversations among some of the teachers. As the teachers began to express more interest and the discussions related to children's development and programming became much more intense, the administrators indicated that they were willing to bring in a consultant to support any staff interested in examining outdoor play programing in more depth. They felt that teachers truly wanted to learn more about outdoor play.

As the discussions continued, the administrators observed that some of the teachers were starting to ask questions, and just as important, these staff members were engaging in new ways with the children outdoors. The administrators know that one of their challenges is that they rent their space from the university and, as a result, there are some restrictions about how the space can be transformed. Yet they are also confident that there are some areas that could be changed to support children's curiosity and desire to play and explore outdoors. As a way to further engage teachers, at the upcoming

meeting they are going to break the teachers into groups to determine the types of materials that the teachers would like to have available in the space. Each group has a budget of $700. In an effort to think "outside the box" they also provide each group with 40 photos of interesting natural and synthetic materials as a way to support the teachers in thinking about their children. What types of items may children not have been able to access that could spark their curiosity? Included in the photos are natural materials and children playing at the local park. This process further engages teachers in imagining what could be. At the conclusion of the group work with the teachers, the lists of materials were compared. What was particularly interesting is that groups began to discuss the importance of natural materials being brought to the space or children going to spaces that had natural materials. The other fascinating development was that one group made a suggestion that the child care centre acquire some of these materials and then have the consultant come work with them as a way to support them in facilitating children's play with the materials.

1. What types of photos might you include in the 40 photo packs and why?
2. Why do you think that the administrators have used this gradual approach to supporting early learning teachers in changing their practice?
3. What would you view as three of the most important aspects to facilitate children's outdoor play? Why?

We have emphasized throughout this chapter the relationship of outdoor play and nature to children's development, health, learning, and thinking. Yet, there are many early learning teachers, for a variety of reasons, who do not necessarily embrace the opportunities that outdoor play provides children with. As a result, many early learning programs are in the midst of making changes to their philosophies and practices.

Key components of this case study are the strategies used by the administrative staff to begin the process of preparing early learning teachers to make changes to their practice. Key advantages of consistently following the lead of children are:

■ Early learning teachers benefit from engaging in professional development and determining ways in which the new learning is transferred to practice;

- Early learning teachers and administrative staff benefit from exploring concepts together and determining what might work in their settings; and

- Learning and planning programs with positive co-workers increases the quality of the experiences for children and in transferring theory to practice.

Understanding how outdoor play and nature influences children's development is essential for early learning teachers. Combining the research on the vital role of outdoor play in children's development with an understanding of the various roles that early learning teachers play in facilitating the array of opportunities for and with children is crucial. When early learning teachers embrace outdoor play, they are in essence contributing to the overall health of children, families, and communities.

BOX 5.4 | **Take It Outside!**

Take a large blanket outside. How many ways might children use this material? What might happen if you add sticks and rope? Is there a natural place where these materials could be set that might trigger the children to make tents or secret places? What else could you add to push the children to experience new ideas or concepts? What might children learn from having blankets and sticks in their play space?

KEY TERMS

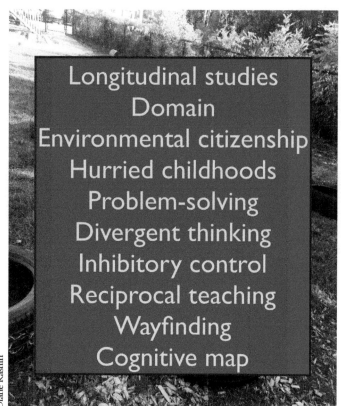

Photo 5.9 Key terms.

Summary

- Longitudinal studies confirm the importance of outdoor play to children's development.
- Research identifies that it is detrimental for children to be in environments that emphasize curriculum standards rather than experiential play.
- Research suggests that children who have interactions with nature, green space, and play develop higher levels of social connections, community, and environmental stewardship.
- Outdoor play influences an array of social, cognitive, emotional, and physical development skills.
- Children benefit from outdoor play in a variety of ways, including development of patterns of play, greater capacity for concentration and attention, lower anxiety, improved self-esteem and confidence, and more positive feeling towards their peers.
- Early learning teachers with a high commitment to supporting children in having outdoor play experiences respond positively to new ways of thinking about and engaging in the outdoor experiences.
- Children who are exposed to outdoor play environments that offer them the freedom to play and are rich in experiences develop flexible thinking, creativity, and problem-solving skills. Conversely, children with limited exposure to or time for outdoor exploration have reduced curiosity and risk-taking skills.
- Critical thinking is a self-guided, self-disciplined, and self-corrected mode of thinking about an idea, experience, or problem.
- Problem solving related to early learning refers to the process that children and adults use to identify what is not working, determining the cause of the problem, identifying, prioritizing, and testing ideas to reach a solution that supports the goal trying to be achieved.
- Reasoning skills refers to the processes that are used to formulate one's views based on perceptions, facts, or a combination of the two.
- Lev Vygotsky introduced the notion of "zone of proximal development," which became prevalent in developmental and educational theories.
- Play-based pedagogy is not new to early childhood literature as a curriculum model. The play is unstructured, imaginative, exploratory, active, and without defined goals initially.
- Research conducted over the past 10 years clearly identifies that "children have much to gain from time spent outdoors and much to lose from a lack of park access" (Seltenrich, 2015, p. 22).
- "Wild" play places are those parks that are less maintained by people and have native vegetation. Such wild areas are preferred by children because of the options that they provide for adventure, experimentation, and the feeling of freedom.
- Research has increasingly recognized that early learning teachers have key roles in supporting children during their play outdoors. The roles that teachers play either advance or inhibit children's play and experiences outdoors.
- Outdoor play requires preparation similar to that for the indoor portion of the program. It requires planning, observation, and evaluation. Children require access to a variety of materials that will stimulate play types in an environment that offers safe but challenging risks.

- The development of the curriculum for outdoor play is influenced by the children's interests, followed by the values and priorities of the early learning setting.

- It is beneficial for early learning teachers to create strategies that will support families in understanding the relationship of outdoor play to later academic performance.

- One of the key roles of early learning teachers is to examine the outdoor play spaces to determine what the environment "says" to the children.

- When children enter a space, they make a cognitive map, based on the information that their brain processes. The cognitive-mapping process assists children in developing an awareness and accumulation of spatial knowledge.

- Early learning teachers benefit from engaging in professional development and determining ways in which the new learning is transferred to practice.

- Early learning teachers and administrative staff benefit from exploring concepts together and determining what might work in their settings.

- Learning and planning programs with positive co-workers increases the quality of the experiences for children and in transferring theory to practice.

QUIET REFLECTION

Spend some time in a park space. Look at the materials that are on the ground. Touch and smell the materials. What do you feel and smell? What materials can you combine together? What new words might children be exposed to from where you are? What are you thinking about, dreaming about, or tinkering with? What parts of the experience would you want to share with children and why?

COMMUNITY DIALOGUE

Think about how outdoor play is foundational to development, health, learning, and thinking, and discuss why there is a need to become advocates for children to have access to and opportunities for outdoor play.
1. How do you promote this discussion with families and in our communities?
2. How would you support families in making the connections between outdoor play and children's learning?
3. What happens if the pendulum does not swing back in favour of outdoor play? How will this affect our society 20 years from now?

FOR FURTHER THOUGHT AND ACTION

After reading this chapter, ask yourself why do we struggle with providing children with opportunities to engage in outdoor play and nature? What do you think the barriers are? Do you envision that you will bring passion to children's outdoor play? What causes you the biggest concern? How do you view playing in all kinds of weather and in all seasons? How do you support families in understanding the importance of outdoor play to children's development, learning, health, and environmental stewardship?

RESOURCES

Find out more about what EcoKids Earth Day Canada are doing to support children in their efforts to strengthen their connection to nature and environmental stewardship https://ecokids.ca/play/earthplay.

Read *A world without play: A literature review* at http://www.playengland.org.uk/media/371031/a-world-without-play-literature-review-2012.pdf

Outdoor Play That Involves Challenge, Adventure, and Risk

Instead of keeping him mewed up in a stuffy room, take him out into a meadow every day; let him run about, let him struggle and fall again and again, the oftener the better; he will learn all the sooner to pick himself up. The delights of liberty will make up for many bruises. My pupil will hurt himself oftener than yours, but he will always be merry; your pupils may receive fewer injuries, but they are always thwarted, constrained, and sad. I doubt whether they are any better off.

(Jean-Jacques Rousseau, 1712–1778)

LEARNING OUTCOMES

After exploring this chapter, you will be able to:

- Define risky play and describe your position on the risky play continuum.

- Discuss the differences between risks and hazards.

- Explain the developmental benefits to children when they are able to engage in risky play.

- Outline Sandseter's (2007) six categories of risky play.

- Explain how risk-benefit assessments can be used in early learning settings.

- Discuss ways to support families in understanding the benefits and need for children to engage in risky play.

CHILDHOOD MEMORIES

The first time I went camping with my family I must have been about three years old. For years, we went back to the same campground where all of the sites were nestled within a majestic and old forest. When I was five, my cousins came along too and when they introduced me to whittling it became my favourite past time. I found it very relaxing to peel away the bark from the sticks. Sometimes I would make the perfect stick for roasting marshmallows, and other times I would spend hours creating the smoothest stick possible and paint it in rainbow colours. I never thought of the activity as dangerous at the time but now I don't know if I would give a child that age a knife to whittle with! It has gotten me thinking about risk in children's play!

CHAPTER PREVIEW

Children require environments that allow them to engage in play that is adventurous, challenging, and even risky. Risky play helps children learn about their world; test out what is and is not possible; learn about making mistakes; and discover new things about their space, place, and environment (Dietze, Pye, & Yochoff, 2013). Risky play can be defined as a thrilling and exciting experience that involves a risk of injury, but more importantly offers children opportunities for challenge, testing limits, exploring boundaries, and learning about managing risk (McFarland & Laird, 2017). This chapter will explore the concept of risky play and its relationship to children's learning and development and identify the differences between risk and hazard in children's play.

Sandseter (2011) suggested that the concept of risky play might seem at odds with an early learning teacher's desire to keep children safe. In this chapter, we recognize the significant role of adults in supporting this kind of play. While there is a growing debate about the use of the term risky play, we suggest that early learning students and teachers consider it as an opportunity for children to recognize and assess risk for themselves. With support, adults can teach children safe ways of doing things and develop a positive attitude towards this type of play. For example, children can learn safe ways of whittling with sticks. We have decided that in this chapter to use the term risky play and accept that there are other words, such as adventurous and challenging, that are also being used to describe risky play.

Much of the current research on children's outdoor play clearly suggests that instead of trying to remove all risk in children's play to create a safe environment, it is important for early learning teachers to promote the creation of an environment that is "safe enough for children to act on, transform, seek out challenges and take risks" (Tovey, 2017, p. 179). Did you use a knife as a young child? Did you ever try whittling? Imagine the skills that children develop from this experience. Not only is whittling wood a pleasant pasttime, it is something that has spanned generations and is often a family tradition. Whittling supports children in learning safety skills, while exploring their creativity. This experience contributes to their problem-solving and critical thinking skills.

Photo 6.1 Risky play supports children's development and well-being.

The thought of young children using knives to whittle may be alarming to some, as there is an element of risk in the experience. Similarly, there is risk associated with climbing a tree or balancing on a plank, as there is a possibility that a child may fall. How about a child wandering through the forest on her own? This too is risky, as there is a chance the child may get lost. Did you have any of these experiences when you were a child? Did you climb up the slide instead of going down? Did you swing so fast that it made you dizzy? All of these experiences can be labelled as risky play. How did they make you feel? Did you feel a sense of excitement, exhilaration, and adventure? Did you feel a sense of freedom? Were you scared?

Children in over-regulated environments have significantly fewer opportunities to master the challenges that are found in more active play spaces (Frost, Wortham, & Reifel, 2012). Children require environments that challenge them. Children have a right to these types of environments. The opportunity to experience adventurous, challenging, and even risky play is important to children's development and overall well-being (Brussoni et al., 2015). Early learning teachers can influence the types of challenges that children may embark on during their outdoor playtime.

Jean-Jacques Rousseau understood the benefits of risky play when he wrote about the fictional character Emile in the book by the same name in 1889. Rousseau wrote the book from the perspective of Emile's teacher, and it reveals his **treatise** on education. Rousseau's ideas have had a great influence on the development of modern educational and political thought. *Emile* was a ground-breaking book that suggested children were capable of being able to make informed decisions about choices in their play, particularly their natural play (Solly, 2015). Rousseau's philosophy stressed the importance of play as an instrument for the development of the senses, the exercise of judgment through sensory experience, and contact with things. He believed that children should learn in the natural world. Rousseau's work influenced Pestalozzi and Froebel (Elkind, 2015).

Consider the epigraph that opens this chapter. Why was Rousseau advocating for Emile to fall often? Rousseau understood that when children have the opportunity to take risks, they would learn how to manage risk. He suggested that they would have a sense of liberation. Rousseau believed that having these self-initiated experiences in nature perpetuated a child's inborn goodness (Elkind, 2012). Risk-taking play has a positive influence on children. This positive perspective stands in contrast to what Rousseau believed was the commonly held position of other educators in his time. In our time, has this changed?

Treatise A body of work dealing formally and systematically with a particular subject.

THINK ABOUT IT! READ ABOUT IT! WRITE ABOUT IT!

If Rousseau proposed a new image of the child, he was responding to the conventional view of children at that time in history. What do you think that view was? Do some research online to find out more and read Rousseau's own words in *Emile* and then write your own view of the child.

Search the Internet by using these words Emile by Rousseau.

"Risk in our society is generally associated with something negative, if you mention the term risk most people associate risk only with negative thoughts and consequences" (Eager & Little, 2011, p. 6). However, risky play is now aligned with generating many positive outcomes for children. It is time for early learning students and teachers to reframe their perceptions that risk is something to be avoided. "Risk is not necessarily a danger that needs to be avoided, but rather something that needs to be managed" (Sandseter, 2011, p. 261). Children flourish in outdoor play environments that promote, support, and encourage risk, while at the same time being mindful of children's safety.

How do you feel about risk in children's play? Does it make you nervous, anxious, and stressed? Perhaps you feel excited when children have opportunities for risky play and you are comfortable and at ease with providing these experiences for children. As you think about how you feel about children's risky play, think of a number between 1 and 10 and place yourself on the continuum of risky play as depicted in Figure 6.1, with "1" representing the least comfortable and "10" indicating a high comfort level. Photo 6.2 shows a risky play continuum from a workshop provided by Forest School Canada. You can see that with this group of educators, their comfort level varied and went from one end of the continuum to the other. The educators in this workshop placed their flags according to

Photo 6.2 A risky play continuum.

Figure 6.1 The continuum of risky play representing comfort levels.

how they felt about risky play. If they were secure about providing children with these types of experiences they hung their flags to the right side of the line. As you read through this chapter and explore risk-taking play and all its benefits and important considerations, that number may change. You will be asked to revisit the continuum of risky play later in the chapter.

Risky play as depicted in Figure 6.2 involves adventure and challenge. Sandseter (2010) used the term "scaryfunny" to describe the intense exhilaration that comes as a result of engaging in risky situations. Coster and Gleeve (2008) indicated that children engaging in risky play experienced feelings such as fun, enjoyment, excitement, thrill, pride, and achievement. These feelings are thought to account for why children pursue this type of play. The play can be both fun and scary at the same time. Sandseter (2010) referred to various bodies of research to suggest that the expression of these exciting feelings can take the form of smiling, laughing, shrieking, screaming, yelling loudly, or dancing.

When children are engaged in challenging play, it is usually something that they have created themselves and it involves excitement and adventure. A **challenge** that presents itself in children's play is something obvious. The child can determine their ability and decide whether to take that risk. It is different than a **hazard**, which is something unseen or not obvious to children that may result in injury. Children require challenge in their play in order to move forward in their development. Early learning teachers provide support and encourage challenging play, especially for children who may exhibit signs of behaviour that would suggest they are reluctant (Solly, 2015) to engage in it. **Adventurous play** refers to children being adventurous by taking opportunities to explore and test their own capacities, to manage risk, and to grow in their capacity, resourcefulness, and resilience. Adventurous play is imaginative and creative. Adventurous play can be risky but not necessarily hazardous.

Recall that in Chapter 4, we discussed the difference between risk and hazard in relation to loose parts. The British Columbia Injury Research and Prevention Unit (2015) described risky play as a thrilling and exciting form of play that involves a risk of physical injury. Early learning teachers understand that all children's play can involve a risk of injury.

Challenge refers to play that involves excitement and adventure. A challenge is obvious to the child where they can determine their ability and decide whether to take that risk (Solly, 2015).

Hazard refers to something that is inherently dangerous that needs to be removed.

Adventurous play refers opportunities for children to explore and test their own capacities which may involve risk.

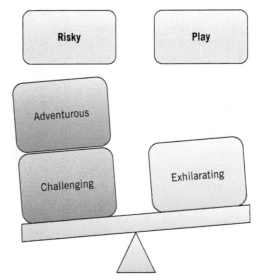

Figure 6.2 Risky play.

For example, children fall and bump their heads, just like adults do on occasion. Risky play involves children recognizing and evaluating the challenge and deciding on the course of action that they will take. A hazard, in contrast, is a source of harm that is not obvious to the children, and therefore the potential for injury is not apparent. When risk is equated with hazards, the benefits of this type of play is diminished (British Columbia Injury Research and Prevention Unit, 2015).

There are many benefits to children engaging in risky play. Table 6.1 lists some of these, as adapted from the British Columbia Injury Research and Prevention Unit (2015).

Photo 6.3 Risky play is freely chosen.

Children need to practice risky play in order to learn to manage risk in their lives. Practice helps them to learn to navigate risk to avoid injury (British Columbia Injury Research and Prevention Unit, 2015). Imagine how children feel once they have mastered the use of a hammer as seen in Photo 6.3. Knowing how to hold the hammer and use the tool to produce a desired result contributes to a child's sense of efficacy. **Self-efficacy** is a salient factor in children's development. Self-efficacy refers to children's estimation of their ability to be successful (Gardner, 2011). According to Bandura (1997), self-efficacy develops through experiential play and learning, is influenced by encouragement and feedback from others, and is related to numerous interpersonal outcomes for children.

Self-efficacy is the belief in one's capacity to perform a task or manage a situation.

CURIOUS?

Do you want to read more about efficacy and the importance of high efficacy on health and development? Follow this link: http://www.aboutkidshealth.ca/En/HealthAZ/FamilyandPeerRelations/life-skills/Pages/Self-efficacy-children.aspx

Table 6.1 Benefits of risky play.

Developmental Benefits of Risky Play

Physical, motor, and kinaesthetic competence.

Spatial orientation skills.

Environmental competence and literacy.

Self-worth and efficacy.

Cognitive and social development, including making predictions, engaging with peers, examining differing perspectives, and formulating plans.

Reduction of fear through natural and gradual exposure.

Risk perception and management skills.

Language development.

Other Benefits of Risky Play

Promotion of physical activity.

Reduction of mental illness and learning difficulties.

Promotion of independence.

Photo 6.4 Risky play in all seasons.

Children require play opportunities that involve taking risks. This is different from early learning teachers requiring children to complete a task that may involve managing risk. The latter is not risky play. In order for an experience to be considered play, the experience must include a measure of inner control, the ability to bend or invent reality, and a strong internally based motivation for playing. If there are specific requirements for an experience set by early learning teachers or families, then it becomes work, not play (Dietze & Kashin, 2018). In order to be classified as play, the experience needs to be freely chosen (Saracho, 2013).

During all seasons, outdoor play environments can provide children with challenging opportunities as shown in Photo 6.4. Twenty years ago, Fromberg and Bergen (1998) attested that "the purpose of play settings is to provide exciting places for children to congregate, play together, and be motivated to return because the challenge meets their level of competency" (p. 322). Fromberg and Bergen suggested that early learning students and teachers could differentiate between what is developmentally challenging and what is unnecessary risk. They used the example of a swing that has heavily worn hooks. Children swinging are not able to recognize or evaluate this problem; therefore, it is a hazard. On the other hand, swinging as high as possible is risky and challenging play.

Gill (2007) identified four arguments in support of risky play in childhood as shown in Figure 6.3. Encounters with certain types of risk help children learn how to identify

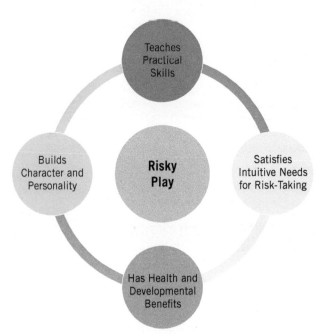

Figure 6.3 Four arguments to support risky play.

actions, problem solve, and make decisions about next steps. Undergoing these processes is how children learn to manage risks (Waite, Huggins, & Wickett, 2014). Since children have an intuitive sense for risk-taking, early learning teachers are encouraged to offer these opportunities to children in a controlled environment so that they will not seek to embark on risks that could result in hazards elsewhere. Children who do not have the opportunities to fulfill their desire for risk, adventure, or challenge in a safe way may create greater risks and hazards. Outdoor play always involves some risk, but the risks are greatly outweighed by the health and developmental benefits. Finally, children build character and personality by learning to examine the circumstances and project the possibility of adventure or injury.

SETTING THE STAGE FOR OUTDOOR PLAY

The research is making the case that children need to have opportunities to take chances and try new things in their play (Niehues et al., 2013; Brussoni et al., 2015; ParticipACTION, 2015). However, in practice, early learning teachers may encounter opposition to this idea from their own beliefs, families, or colleagues. Children are positively or negatively influenced by the language and communication strategies early learning teachers use with them, especially as it relates to risky play opportunities. As well, how early learning teachers interpret and express themselves influences the overall language that is used as a community of professionals. Early learning teachers benefit from being conscious of their choice of words used in the company of children, families, and colleagues. Ideally, their verbal communication and body language is encouraging and supportive of outdoor play and children's desires to engage in play that involves risk-taking. The more positive the environments, the more likely children will be motivated to want to play and learn outside (Dietze & Kashin, 2017).

As identified at the beginning of this chapter, the terminology that we use matters. Consider the following scenario. An early learning teacher has set up an obstacle course in the outdoor playground. As families bring their children to the program in the morning, the teacher indicates that the children will have an opportunity to engage in risky play. What might families be thinking? How might different families interpret this experience? Why? Voce (2016) argued that risky play is an ambiguous, contradictory term, open to misinterpretation. He has consistently recommended the use of the word adventurous rather than risky. Voce stated that while the words risky and adventurous are synonymous, the latter word has a more positive meaning in early learning environments. According to Voce, the word adventurous more aptly captures the essence of children at play. In adventurous play children want to push boundaries, test limits, and take some risks but they are pursuing fun and excitement. Risky play, on the other hand, evokes reckless endangerment.

Allsup (2016) wrote that risk management is a bizarre phrase to use in relation to children because it is a concept that was originally developed for the insurance industry. Allsup recommended minimizing risk rather than managing risk because children may be confused about the correct meaning. Risky means dangerous so children may interpret that it is okay to take chances. It is too risky to use the word "risk" when communicating with children about challenging activities. Emphasizing the word "risk" shows that there is more of a focus on what could go wrong than how to prepare children to be both independent and safe in challenging situations. Rather than using this term, Allsup suggested that early learning teachers use the words adventure, preparation, and trust.

THINK ABOUT IT! READ ABOUT IT! WRITE ABOUT IT!

Voce (2016), Sandseter (2016), Allsup (2016) and Gill (2016) have all written blogs about the language that is used and why terms are important to consider. Read the blogs here:

Adrian Voce (2016): https://policyforplay.com/2016/06/08/the-trouble-with-risky-play/?fb_action_ids=10154040579166609&fb_action_types=news.publishes

Ellen Sandseter (2016): https://ellenbeatehansensandseter.com/2016/06/14/risky-play-adventurous-play-challenging-play/

Kim Allsup (2016): https://childrengrowing.com/2016/06/08/please-dont-say-you-allow-your-child-to-take-risks/

Tim Gill (2016): https://rethinkingchildhood.com/2016/06/15/risk-uncertainty-adverse-outcomes-play/

What words do you think are best to use with families, other early learning teachers, and children? Are they the same words or different ones?

Gill (2016) supported the use of the term risky play and suggested that the acceptance of risk is not just a detail: it is the single most important step to help get those who are anxious about risky play to consider its importance. Using the word 'risk' is of value precisely because it faces head-on the possibility of adverse outcomes. Avoiding the word 'risky' and instead using 'adventurous' or 'challenging' implies to families that children will have adventures and nothing will go wrong.

Sandseter (2016) responded to the debate about terminology from the Norwegian context. In Norway, there is no problem using the term risky play in the common language, and she suggested the disagreement about the terminology might be a result of different cultures and languages. While risky play and risk-taking have both positive and negative associations, Sandseter suggested that we shouldn't cover what we mean with softer words to emphasize only the positive. Rather, the use of the term should also include the possibility of a negative outcome, since the fear of this outcome is the reason we have all the restrictions and surplus safety regulations in the first place.

Being aware of the discussions, controversy, and thinking around the terms risky, adventurous, and challenging builds knowledge that influences early learning teachers' philosophy and practice during outdoor play. As professionals, early learning teachers choose words carefully to meet the needs of the intended audience and context.

With the evidence-based research available to support the importance of children engaging in outdoor risky play, early learning teachers may wish to review the programming options extended to the children. The research on the negative impact on children's development if they do not engage in risky play is plentiful and far reaching. A Canadian study documented preschool children's use of play equipment in 16 centres and found that play equipment was used only 13% of the time and only 3% of the time used as intended

Rebekka Bradshaw

Photo 6.5 Climbing to great heights.

(Brussoni, Olsen, Pike, & Sleet, 2012). In another study, in the United States, child care providers expressed concerns that overly strict standards had rendered outdoor play areas unchallenging and uninteresting to children, thus hampering their physical activity. Furthermore, Brussoni et al. (2012) noted that some children used equipment in unsafe ways to create and maintain a sense of challenge.

Concerns from families regarding children's safety are one of the most significant influences on children's access to adventurous, challenging, and risky play (Niehues, Bundy, Broom, & Tranter, 2015). Research, on the other hand, has found that parents recognize that restricting their children's play in the early years has the potential for putting them at increased risk once they are older. This potential may be due to not having built up their confidence through the practice of risky play during childhood (Brussoni et al., 2012). In one British study, focus groups were conducted with 93 children aged 7 to 11 years living in urban and rural areas. The results showed that the children wanted the opportunities to assess risk for themselves (Brussoni et al., 2012).

> Taking risks allowed them to display courage and physical skills to themselves and their peers. Interestingly, while they viewed minor injuries as a way to show that risks had been taken, there was an understanding that too many injuries indicated carelessness or clumsiness, which was perceived in derogatory ways. Thus, they appeared to have their own regulatory system for maintaining risks and injuries at a manageable level. (Brussoni et al., 2012, p. 3140)

From this research a connection can be made between risk-taking and **self-regulation** (Kleppe, Melhuish, & Sandseter, 2017). Children use self-regulation when responding to other children and adults in their environment. Children's level of self-regulation skills influences how they respond to the people and the materials within the environment. They learn to self-regulate as they engage in risky play. They learn to regulate anxiety or discouragement. Children who do not learn to self-regulate "will move away from, rather than engage in, challenging learning activities" (Florez, 2011, p. 47). Self-regulation relates significantly to children's risky play opportunities. When children are able to replace the feelings of being unable to do something, they build their confidence required to embark on play experiences that have risk embedded in them. This contributes to them replacing feelings of anxiety and lack of competence with confidence (Florez, 2011).

Self-regulation refers to the complicated processes that allow children to respond to their environment appropriately (Florez, 2011).

There are further benefits to risky play. When children experience what Sandseter (2010) called scaryfunny feelings, there is a shift back and forth between negative and positive emotions, which ultimately push their limits and strengthen their physical and emotional skills. Risky play is unpredictable play. Without access to this type of play, children miss out on self-determined challenges that promote self-management and well-being (Niehues et al., 2013). When children take physical risks in play, they learn about the capabilities of their bodies while managing risk to avoid injury. They build self-confidence, self-awareness, perseverance, and independence (Cevher-Kalburan & Ivrendi, 2016).

Risky play helps children to develop perceptual-motor and spatial-orientation abilities. It helps them to master social skills, such as conflict resolution, when interacting with others. Children also learn to balance their emotions and deal with fears and phobias while they take risks in their play (Cevher-Kalburan & Ivrendi, 2016). Consider this example: Charlie and Sabrina are playing with a set of outdoor blocks. As the two children work together, adding block after block, the structure begins to sway. Charlie tells Sabrina not to add another block, but she proceeds to pull a bucket over to the structure and climb on top of it with a block. At first, when the early learning teacher observes the interaction, she wonders what Charlie will do since he appears hesitant and concerned. However, seconds later he also approaches the structure, and while Sabrina adds the block he straightens the others to stop the swaying. The children are problem-solving while working together and, at the same time, they are working through scientific principles of weight, height, and balance in addition to mathematical concepts of spatial-orientation.

Intrinsically motivated refers to play undertaken for its own sake rather than for any external goal or reward (Lester & Russell, 2008).

Charlie and Sabrina were **intrinsically motivated** to engage in this risk-taking play. It was self-directed play that was freely chosen and directed by the children. They made predictions about the stability of their structure and the impact of adding another block. They did this without the need of reward or extrinsic motivation. Intrinsic motivation offers children independence, autonomy, and self-confidence. Carlton and Winsler (1998) suggested more than 20 years ago that children need challenge. Early learning teachers can be motivational role models who demonstrate persistence and a preference for challenge. Children's self-efficacy increases when they have challenging tasks that allow them to feel competent. By providing Charlie and Sabrina with time, the large blocks in their outdoor environment, and space to accept the challenges that these materials afforded, they were able to use intrinsic motivation to engage in risk-taking that ideally, led to feelings of competence and confidence.

The importance of risky play can be traced back more than 20 years in the research. Valentine (1997) found that children perceived themselves as competent at negotiating their own safety. Children felt that they, and not their parents, were primarily responsible for their own safety. Children learn risk-management strategies as a result of risky play experiences (Brussoni et al., 2012). Observational studies of children at play found that they appeared to be aware of potential dangers and adjusted their activities accordingly (Brussoni et al., 2012). Sandseter and Kennair (2011) theorized that children's engagement in risky play reduces fears. Children require sufficient risky play opportunities, as this is how they learn to cope with fear-inducing situations. Otherwise, they will maintain their fears, which may translate into anxiety disorders.

As noted earlier in this section, while children's risk-taking and play has been studied since the 1970s, there is still limited consensus on definitions. Research, however, does suggest that risk-taking includes curiosity, exploration, deep concentration, fear, and excitement. "Children explore their surroundings and their capabilities through trial and error, and their behavior involves a balancing act between exhilaration and fear, as the child either masters the challenge or withdraws because of fear" (Kleppe et al., 2017, p. 371). Early learning students and teachers have a responsibility to understand the complexities of risk-taking in play and to determine how their philosophical perspective is transferred to children's outdoor play environments.

≫ BOX 6.1   Shedding Light on Outdoor Play—Points of Reflection

Children learn through all types of play, including risky play (Gray, 2014). By exploring their environments, testing out ideas, and challenging themselves, they learn about the world around them. It is important to recognize the value of risky play, as well as the immense benefits it can bring to children. Find a video about risky play online or view this one: https://www.youtube.com/watch?v=Jkiij9dJfcw What are children learning? What risks are the children taking? How do you think the adults involved are managing and minimizing the risks?

OUR VISION FOR OUTDOOR PLAY

"Children have a natural propensity toward risky play" (Brussoni et al., 2012, p. 3134). Early learning teachers have a responsibility to offer experiences for children to exercise this natural propensity. It is our vision that early learning teachers will think carefully about how they make provisions for children to have access to environments that encourage them to engage in experiences that involve risk, adventure, and challenge. Risky play helps children learn about their world; test out what is and is not possible; learn about making mistakes; and discover new things about themselves, their space, place, and environment (Dietze & Kashin, 2017).

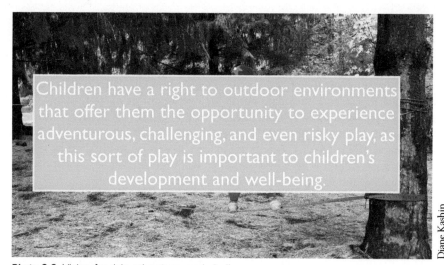

Children have a right to outdoor environments that offer them the opportunity to experience adventurous, challenging, and even risky play, as this sort of play is important to children's development and well-being.

Diane Kashin

Photo 6.6 Vision for risk, adventure, and challenge.

Risk-taking contributes to children's in-depth problem-solving and critical-thinking skills. Children in over-regulated environments and environments with limited materials have significantly fewer opportunities to master the challenges that active play spaces provide. Children have a right to environments that offer them the opportunity to experience adventurous, challenging, and even risky play as this sort of play is important to children's development and overall well-being (Dietze & Kashin, 2017).

POSITIONING OUTDOOR PLAY IN THE LIVES OF CHILDREN

Children require opportunities to take risk, but at what age do early learning teachers provide these risky, adventurous, and challenging play environments? Generally, the focus of the research on risk-taking in play has been with children from the age of four and upwards. What about children under four years of age? Kleppe et al. (2017) conducted an observational study with children from five early learning programs. The intent of the study was to explore the occurrence and characteristics of risky play for children under four years of age. The study found that one-year-old children show less risky play than older children. Since children of this age are learning to walk, risky play can be seen in relation to motor development. They are testing their surroundings and their bodies in relationship to their surroundings. This type of play involves uncertainty and exploration—bodily, emotional, perceptional, or environmental. There could be positive or negative consequences.

Today the toddlers worked together to set up crates with wood planks in the forest area of our Nature Classroom. They were super excited to climb on, walk all the way across, and then jump off the structure that they built. Occasionally they would say "Help please!", but for the most part they wanted to do it on their own. This shows tremendous growth on their part, as they continue to discover safe risk-taking.

The children took turns using the interesting apparatus that they worked hard to create. Later, they decided to take a break and sit on a raised log. The children transformed this simple seat into a train. They raised their arm saying "Choo....choo!"

Others explored a makeshift ramp for their cars and trucks. This worked for a while, and then they walked up and down the ramp. Some were brave enough to run down. This was so much fun!

Children of all ages encounter risks in their surroundings. When children are not permitted to play in physical and active ways, they are more likely than active children to develop health problems, including becoming overweight or obese (Marano, 2011). Children may develop anxiety or fears later on in life (Sandseter, 2011). "Judging risk requires the application, first, of common sense and then some calculation of risk versus benefit" (Marano, 2011, p. 426). Adults are doing a disservice to children by trying to eliminate risk (Gill, 2012). Without risk, children will become over dependent on adults for decision-making and problem-solving (Marano, 2011).

Early learning teachers can support children's opportunities to manage risk by being intentional in their teaching. Examine Case Study 6.1, which illustrates an experience with a group of toddlers that was documented and shared with families by early learning teachers Toni and Grace. Working in a program that supports outdoor play, Toni and Grace felt it was important to engage with families so that they could gain new information about and understand the importance of risky play in the lives of their children. Toni and Grace see themselves as significant role models in encouraging children to explore the possibilities that exist in their environments. Look at the photos that follow and consider the questions below. These children are learning about risk and how to manage it!

1. How would you describe the facial expression of the adult in the first photo?

2. Look at the proximity of the adults in the photos to the children. What difference does this make for the children?

Photo 6.7 Toddlers and risky play.

Karen Eilersen

3. If you were their teacher, what would you do next to continue to support children's opportunities for risk-taking?

Early learning teachers have a role to play to ensure children have access to challenging and adventurous play, while building in strategies to keep them safe. Early learning teachers recognize that an environment without challenging and adventurous play reduces children's opportunities to develop to their fullest. In Figure 6.4, Dietze and Kashin (2017) have illustrated the various aspects of this important role.

Dietze and Kashin (2017) suggested that early learning teachers focus on safety to ensure that there is a balance maintained between the risks and benefits of outdoor play. With policies and procedures in place and the completion of **risk assessments** done on a regular basis, early learning teachers support children's opportunities to take risks (Dietze & Kashin, 2017).

Risk assessments are done in early learning outdoor environments to eliminate hazards and identify measures to manage risk.

Risk assessments include descriptions of the potential risks and the possible benefits. Take, for example, tree climbing. When children are climbing trees, the benefits include the fun and pleasure derived from the experience. The children may feel empowered and show increased competence across multiple domains, including cognitive, social, emotional, and physical. While climbing the tree, they may employ their imagination as they pretend and engage in adventure. After detailing the benefits involved in the experience, early learning teachers assess the risks. What are the potential risks? These could include a branch breaking while the children are climbing or playing on it. Once the benefits and risks are listed, action can be taken to manage the risk. Is the branch loose and can it be removed before the children begin to climb? There needs to be ongoing monitoring of the area as there may be changes to the tree because of weather. Even with the removal of the branch, there may still be risk involved. However, children need opportunities where they can be adventurous and feel challenged. They require time to test themselves and extend their own abilities. Providing risky play for children gives them a chance to learn how to assess and manage risk for themselves (Ball, Gill, & Spiegal, 2012).

Taking a leadership position, early learning teachers lead by example to support children's opportunities for risky play. This begins by providing children with outdoor environments that are rich with opportunities, while working toward managing the risk. Taking first aid training and having first aid kits, policies, and procedures in place can

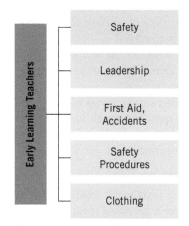

Figure 6.4 The role of the early learning teacher in risky play.

CURIOUS?

Are you wondering what a risk-benefit form looks like and what should be included when filling out the form? Follow this link to learn more: http://www.playengland.org.uk/resource/risk-benefit-assessment-form/

address minor and more serious accidents. Daily checks of equipment help to reduce or eliminate hazards. Everyone in the outdoor play environment, children and adults alike, require clothing that is suitable for the weather and risky play. For children and adults to become successful in managing risks, they need practice. When early learning teachers understand the benefits of risky play to children's development, they develop dispositions to create outdoor play environments that are safe and open to children experiencing adventure and challenge.

THEORETICAL FOUNDATION

Adventure, risk, and challenge are not new concepts. Consider what Margaret McMillan (1930) suggested as quoted by Solly (2015), about her ideal outside play area:

> A little children's garden must offer every kind of inducement to muscular play and action. It must be planned with an eye to real safety whilst encouraging children to play bravely and adventurously. Rough stones, narrow curved paths, jumping-off places and a grassy stretch to lie on. (p. 10)

Take a moment to reflect on McMillan's choice of words and remember that she verbalized these words more than many years ago. Think about the play areas that you have observed. Do they reflect muscular play, action options, and a stretch of grass to lie down on? Does the space encourage children to play bravely and safely?

Since the turn of the last century, advocates of active play have continued to voice concern for the welfare of children whose childhood lacks play opportunities, especially active outdoor play. Think back to your own childhood—how would you characterize your childhood? Would you consider it an indoor childhood or an outdoor childhood? Did you have many hours of unstructured play outside? Did you take risks? Do you remember what it was like to engage in risky play? Now think about the children you know today. Do they have these same opportunities?

Ellen Sandseter (2011) is one of the leading theorists today providing research on risky play. She continues to advocate for children to have these experiences. Her body of work serves as a treatise for risky play.

Sandseter (2007) identified six categories of risky play. These categories support early learning teachers in viewing spaces where children play. Think about why it is important to accommodate each of these risky play types into children's environments. How might they look in early learning programs?

- Rough and Tumble: Wrestling. Fencing with sticks. Play fighting.
- High Speed: Swinging at high speed. Sliding and sledging at high speed. Running uncontrollably at high speed. Bicycling at high speed. Skating and skiing at high speed.
- Great Heights: Climbing and jumping from still or flexible surfaces. Balancing on high objects. Hanging and swinging at great heights.

>> BOX 6.2 | Featured Theorist—Ellen Sandseter

Ellen Sandseter is one of the leading authorities on risky play. Sandseter (2011) identified how the risk perceived by early learning teachers influences children's opportunity for risky play. Teacher attitudes, tolerance to risk, and management of risky play influence children's opportunities. According to Sandseter, Norwegian early learning teachers have a more positive attitude towards risky play than educators in most other countries. A survey among Norwegian educators identified that they are generally positive about thrilling and risky kinds of play and that they rarely interfere in or restrict this type of play.

- Dangerous Tools: Cutting tools: knives, saws, and axes. Strangling tools: ropes, etc. Other tools: hammers, nails, etc.
- Dangerous Elements: Cliffs. Deep water or icy water. Fire pits; and
- Exploration: Go exploring alone. Playing alone in unfamiliar environments.

Photo 6.8 is a collage of images depicting the categories of risky play as suggested by Sandseter (2011). Can you identify which category is primarily demonstrated in each photo?

Photo 6.8 Collage of risky play categories.

Sources: Top Left, Gill Robertson; Top Middle, Michelle Thornhill; Top Right, Cathy Wilkowski; Bottom Left, Cathy Wilkowski; Bottom Middle, Gill Robertson; Bottom Right, Laurel Fynes

PRACTICAL APPLICATIONS

The elements—earth, water, air, and fire—have potential for children to experience challenging, adventurous, and risky play. Knight (2011) situated risk and adventure in outdoor play within the four elements. Every day in the outdoor environment weather can change, as can the opportunities provided to support children in learning about the elements and experiencing thrilling adventures. Imagine standing, arms stretched with the wind blowing. You know that you won't blow away: think of how exciting it is to feel the strength of the gusts of the winds and to imagine flying. Imagine being outside, participating in a risky play workshop with other educators during the month of May and experiencing sunshine, wind, rain, and hail—all in one day! Now think about the exhilaration that you would feel. Should children today have this experience? Early learning teachers use these elements to support children in having various types of play experiences that support risky play.

From the four elements comes much adventure. With earth comes an opportunity for digging, sliding, rolling, and running. Tactile play is one of the earliest ways in which young children learn about their environment and world around them. Tactile experiences provide children with comfort, knowledge, stimulation, and pleasure. Many early learning programs offer children sand rather than mud, even though mud has so much play potential. It is malleable. It comes in a variety of colours and textures. It encourages digging. It can be used for art and construction. Mud provides opportunities for slipping and sliding as featured in Photo 6.9. If the risk of children putting mud in their mouths or hurting themselves while playing with mud is managed, the experience can be joyful (Knight, 2011).

With water, children can feel the pelting of the rain, or have the sensation of spraying water or being sprayed. Children can wade into shallow water or feel water as it runs from an outdoor tap. Using gutters, they can create water flow, experiencing cause and effect. Playing in water can be soothing and fun. It can also be dangerous if the water is too deep. However, playing in the rain can be magical. Children are drawn to play in sprinklers and to spray water as they explore the flow of water. Puddles provide never-ending potential for inquiry as they change over seasons and with the placement of the sun. Running water gives children a chance to discover how they can change its direction, as it ebbs and flows, such as by making gullies and water holes (Knight, 2011). Shallow water and beaches make for endless discoveries. When early learning teachers consider the element of water, they determine strategies to manage the risk in order to provide all the benefits that water can bring to children's play.

With the wind, children experience playing with kites and flags. Light and dark are also qualities of air. Light experiences at night are thrilling for children as they feel the power of lighting up the darkness. The air and the wind produce sounds, and with instruments made by children, they can manipulate and produce various sounds (Knight, 2011).

There are many benefits to outdoor experiences that include fire. Many early learning teachers around the world have developed strategies to manage the risk so that children's lives may be enriched with this exciting element. However, fire lighting with children is done with caution and careful planning. There are also many points to consider (Knight, 2011), including the ages and stages of development of the children involved, as well as their prior experience with fire. There is still great benefit from watching flames and eating food cooked on a fire. Despite the danger, there are numerous benefits to children, including observing the flames, eating food cooked around the fire, and experiencing the sense of community with peers that evolves by

Nevella Schepmyer

Photo 6.9 Playing in the mud.

socializing around a fire. With experience and confidence and low adult-child ratios, early learning teachers can involve children more fully (Knight, 2011).

THINK ABOUT IT! READ ABOUT IT! WRITE ABOUT IT!

What do you think should be in a risk-assessment form? Put these words into a search engine "risk assessment template for early childhood". Read and review a few of the images that come up. Design your own risk-assessment form and use it!

Outdoor experiences that involve fire require early learning teachers to implement risk-assessment processes that involve the identification of risk or hazard and to make decisions about precautions. How will the risk be managed? Waite, Higgins and Wickett (2014) suggested the following four steps to prepare for risky play:

1. Develop a policy framework for outdoor play that lists the benefits for children. The policy should also indicate how the outdoor learning environment and early learning teaching team will support children's opportunities for outdoor play;

2. Create a written risk/benefit analysis of the environment and for each experience offered to children;

3. Carry out regular inspections of the outdoor environment, as well as recurring reviews of risky play activities; and

4. Ensure that the members of the early learning teaching team are involved in the development of the policy and regular inspections/reviews so that they are well prepared to engage in "in-the-moment interventions" during outdoor play experiences. These are referred to as "dynamic risk assessments" (Waite, Higgins, & Wickett, 2014, p. 79).

Early learning teachers learn to minimize and manage risk by conducting risk/benefit assessments, which identify benefits and levels of hazard. Prior to taking children into an outdoor environment, early learning teachers scan the area that children would be playing in to examine it for potential risks, such as fallen logs or branches. Early learning teachers document the risk-benefit assessment as part of due diligence. They identify levels of hazard and ways to minimize harm to the children. The information is documented and shared with administrators and families. This professional practice helps to identify potential injury and determine strategies that support children in risky play without danger.

Children are active learners who get to know their world through their bodies as they test 'what will happen if?' As children learn, they act and interact with others and the environment (Banning & Sullivan, 2011). Remember as a child, when you wanted to learn to pump your legs so that you could swing higher and higher? This goal indicates that you, like most children, had a desire to self-direct the play. The pumping process is an example of how children become internally motivated and develop independence and self-confidence. Table 6.2 illustrates the standard of risk-taking, responsibility, and confidence.

When children have opportunities to take risks that are appropriate and commensurate with their level of independence, they begin a process of taking responsibility in their self-directed play. Applying strategies such as trial and error, children take responsibility for their learning and develop confidence in their abilities. When children reach this standard, their play, learning, and health are enhanced (Banning & Sullivan, 2011).

Table 6.2 Risk-taking, responsibility, and confidence standard.

Standards for Outdoor Play and Learning: Risk-Taking, Responsibility, and Confidence Standard
1. The child chooses appropriate physical, social, and cognitive challenges.
2. The child sets goals and follows through on plans with increasing independence.
3. The child communicates ideas and opinions in interactions with others, including peers and adults.
4. The child expresses delight and satisfaction when solving problems or completing tasks.

Source: Banning and Sullivan, 2011, p. 202.

PRINCIPLES OF PRACTICE: HEALTH-BASED PRACTICE

Children's health is a focus of professional practice. As a principle of practice, early learning teachers recognize the

> Numerous developmental and health advantages have also been linked to children's need for outdoor risky play as a means to learn through experience. Societal trends limiting children's access to outdoor risky play opportunities combined with a culturally dominant excessive focus on safety can pose a threat to healthy child development. (Brussoni, Olsen, Pike, & Sleet, 2012, p. 3142)

Brussoni et al. (2015) emphasized that "children's development, learning, mental health, and physical health, including physical activity, and healthy weights" are associated with risky play opportunities (p. 6423). Despite the health benefits of risky play, child injury prevention programs suggest limiting risky play because of the possibility of injury (Brussoni et al., 2015). Early learning students and teachers who understand the health benefits of risky play can become advocates for health-based practice to support children's opportunities for adventure, challenge, and risk.

Families have concerns for children's safety and do not want to appear neglectful of their children so they may wish early learning teachers to increase supervision. Extensive supervision will diminish children's independence and engagement in risky play (Brussoni et al., 2015). Early learning teachers play a key role in sharing with families the health benefits of risky play and the adverse consequences from a lack of risky outdoor play experiences (Brussoni et al., 2015). Early learning teachers can become part of the discussion and part of the solution.

LEARNING IN PLACE: THE HILLTOP AS PLACE

In Chapter 7, there are detailed accounts of outdoor play spaces and programs designed to support outdoor play such as forest schools and nature preschools. In this chapter, the natural playground is introduced. There are many benefits of **natural playgrounds** as compared to traditional playgrounds with manufactured slides, swings, and climbers (Zamani, 2016). Natural playgrounds are now often favoured in various community settings over traditional playgrounds. One feature of a natural playground could be a sloping or grassy hill. These can also be found in spaces and places beyond the playground.

Imagine what children would do when they approach a hilltop. Have they climbed up the hill to get to the top? What will they do at the top? Will they slide down and feel the softness of the grass in the summer or the slippery feel of the snow beneath them? How will

Natural playgrounds are areas for children to play. They have natural elements such as sand, water, living plants, and sloping hills.

the experience change from one season to the next? After the rain, the hillside may become muddy and wet. The hilltop as place becomes a space where children can experience the elements of the wind, rain, snow, sun, or fog and use their motor abilities to feel the exhilaration that comes from a hill. Do the benefits of the hill outweigh those of a fixed slide, which is a piece of equipment that is both expensive and limited in its creative play options? How do children's risk and challenge in play change on the hilltop compared to on a slide? How does this influence their social, emotional, cognitive, and physical development?

CURIOUS?

Learn more about the possibilities of rainbow math sticks by following this link: http://creativestarlearning.co.uk/maths-outdoors/rainbow-maths-sticks/.

PROGRAMMING

As early learning students and teachers expand their knowledge about outdoor risky play, they program with intention to support children's access to this type of play. The use of tools is considered a risky play category (Sandseter, 2011). Dangerous tools such as knives and saws are introduced by having adults model how to use them safely. This will be part of the planning process as per the "PEER" principle.

Whittling is a wonderful experience for children and a way for them to connect with a skill passed down from our ancestors. In this experience children are whittling the ends from sticks that they have gathered to create a manipulative math material. See Photo 6.10 for a picture of these sticks. These can be used to play dominos or to create geometric shapes. To begin the process of whittling, children can use industrial strength vegetable peelers rather than knives but they still must exercise caution, as these too can be dangerous. Teachers introduce this activity with small groups of children so that established safety practices with children may be monitored. The rainbow math stick experience is described in Table 6.3.

Photo 6.10 Rainbow math sticks.

Diane Kashin

Table 6.3 Rainbow math sticks.

PLAN	Begin with a risk/benefit assessment. Make sure that the materials and tools are provided and the group size is small enough to demonstrate to children the proper use of the peeler. Gather the sticks with the children. Look for greener sticks that have fallen to the ground or access sticks that have been purposefully pruned from a tree. Do not cut branches from a tree if it will harm the further growth of the tree.
ENGAGE	Have the children line the sticks up so that they are relatively the same length and thickness. Using garden sheers help the children trim the sticks to the same size. Ensure that the children are seated and whittling away from their body. Once the ends of the sticks have been cleared of bark, the children can paint the ends.
EXPLORE	The children can sort the sticks by colour or use them in construction projects. The children can create geometric shapes or play a game of dominos.
REFLECT	Did the benefits of this experience outweigh the risks? How did the children respond to the whittling? Did you start with a vegetable peeler or with knives? What mathematical concepts were explored with the sticks? Will you continue to offer this experience to the children to increase you math stick collection?

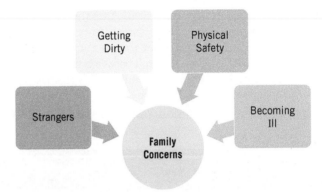

Figure 6.5 Family concerns.

FAMILY SUPPORT AND ENGAGEMENT

Concerns and worries of families "are individual due to their uniqueness and the uniqueness of each child" (Solly, 2015, p. 106). As illustrated in Figure 6.5, stranger danger, getting dirty, becoming ill, and physical safety are four concerns that families may have (Solly, 2015).

Worries about strangers or "stranger danger" can be high on the list of concerns a family may have so it is important that they know the procedures that are put into place in early learning programs. These may include visitor check-in rules, badges, door security, and so forth. Families may also have practical concerns about children getting dirty. A way to address this concern is to have a washer and dryer on site so that children's clothing may be sent home clean. Another way is to ensure children have multiple sets of clothing available. If families are concerned about their children's safety, they may transfer their apprehension to children through their verbal communication or body language. Early learning teachers help to alleviate these concerns by sharing policies and procedures in place intended to help keep children safe. Early learning teachers use a variety of strategies to learn about family values, cultures, and practices that either positively or negatively influence children's outdoor play experiences (Solly, 2015). Families might also be concerned that children will become ill when they play outside during cold or rainy weather and they get wet. Early learning teachers must confront their own perceptions about the implications of weather on children's health, as these will limit children's experiences and the opportunity to engage families in discussions about the benefits of outdoor play across seasons (Copeland, Kendeigh, Saelens, Kalkwarf, & Sherman, 2012).

ACCESSIBILITY AND DESIGN

Children will naturally seek to engage in risky play. Certain features of the outdoor play environment will influence children's play (Sandseter, 2009). The affordance theory introduced in Chapter 4 can be applied to risky play experiences. While Gibson (1982) constructed the theory of affordances, Heft (1988) elaborated on the theory to include a taxonomy of different types of play that invite children to engage in risk-taking (Sandseter, 2009). As outlined in Figure 6.6, early learning teachers can create these invitations in the outdoor play environment. When designing outdoor playgrounds, look for these features of affordances.

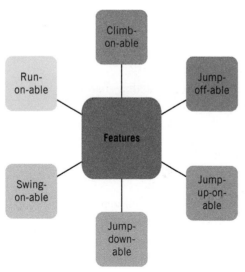

Figure 6.6 Affordance features in the outdoor playground.

TIPS AND TOOLS FOR OUTDOOR PLAY

There are many strategies that early learning teachers may use to begin the dialogue with colleagues, families, and children on risk-taking. Here is a list of our top 10 ideas (Dietze, 2016). Use these tips to increase the experiences that children have to outdoor risky play and to help families understand the benefits.

1. Support families in encouraging children to take risks. Provide families with information about the relationship of risk-taking to child development and learning in newsletters and on websites.

2. Invite families to engage in outdoor risky play times with children and teachers. This allows early learning teachers to highlight the types of play that are supporting risk-taking opportunities.

3. Create pedagogical documentation that visually shows children engaged in risk-taking play. Include key points on how the play in the photos supports risk-taking.

4. Examine your own philosophy on and feelings about risk-taking. As a group, early learning teachers take inventory of the personal feelings of the team and then collectively develop strategies that will balance positions and roles during outdoor experiences so that children's risk-taking adventures will be encouraged and supported.

5. Engage in observing children's skills and then create opportunities for them to advance in their risk-taking. Scaffolding experiences supports children's success in their risk-taking play.

6. Create challenging environments for children by providing a range of heavy loose parts such as ropes and rocks, differing terrain, and materials that support children in creating large structures.

7. Become conscious of your verbal and body language with children during the outdoor exploration. Early learning teachers reduce their natural instinct to say "No!" or

"That is dangerous". They determine if the act is dangerous or if children are being overprotected.

8. Examine procedures and practices at least every six months to ensure that they are addressing hazards and risks appropriately.

9. Engage in professional development that shares current research on children and risk-taking.

10. Reflect upon the following:

- How do adults help children make decisions about the risks they wish to take?
- How do adults support children in helping children learn from their risks, especially with those that are not successful?
- How do you offer children support for some of their explorations without reducing their enthusiasm for their potential idea?
- How do you communicate with families about the value of children's risk-taking and how often do you have such communication?
- How do you continue to develop your knowledge and comfort for risk-taking?

Remember the number you chose at the beginning of the chapter that represented where you felt along the continuum of risky play that is outlined in Figure 6.1? Revisit the continuum now that the chapter has come to the end. Would you change that number now? Are you more comfortable with risky play now that you have gained more knowledge about its importance to children's development? Your comfort level will also increase the more experience you have. Read in the section that follows the professional reflection of a very seasoned teacher. Where do you think she would place herself along the continuum?

ON THE GROUND—PROFESSIONAL REFLECTIONS: "WHY I LOVE OUTDOOR PLAY"

>> **BOX 6.3** **Why I Love Outdoor Play**

The outdoor environment offers a multitude of opportunities for children to challenge themselves, to test their personal limits, and to realize their own capabilities. Through developing these skills, children become competent self-risk assessors, a vital life skill. Scrambling onto rocks, jumping, climbing as high as you dare into a tree, chasing waves into the sea, jumping over waves are happy childhood memories so often lacking today as children are carefully guarded and prevented from participating in any activities considered by adults to be too risky. It is vital that children develop a risk-taking disposition. Research shows that physical risk-takers outdoors are also risk-takers indoors, where they will seek and accept challenge in areas such as numeracy, literacy, and science as well as social and emotional situations. Outdoors, children are faced with various levels of risk where they can choose the level of risk they are prepared to undertake. Some will delight in their ability to climb a tree onto the lowest limbs, while others will celebrate climbing onto the higher branches. Children set their own expectations and challenge outdoors.

Niki Buchan
Senior Educational Consultant
Natural Learning Early Childhood Consultancy
Australia

CASE STUDIES

Read Case Study 6.2 and take a look at Photo 6.11 to answer the questions.

≫ CASE STUDY 6.2 | The Rocky Playground

George has taken a new position as an early learning teacher at a brand new program a few miles from where he lives. George is very excited about his new position. He felt his values aligned with the philosophy of the program and was so impressed with the innovative design of the outdoor playground. However, George was worried about the rocks that surrounded the play space. He kept thinking that children would fall and get hurt. When he asked about the playground in his interview, he was told that there was a detailed policy framework for risky play and that the teachers filled out risk-benefit assessments on a regular basis. George was given a form. How do you think he should fill out the following parts listed in the questions below?

Photo 6.11 The rocky playground.

On the form that George was given, the following parts were ones he was not sure how to fill out. Based on what you can see in Photo 6.11, how would you complete the following components?

1. How will the children benefit from playing in this area?
2. What are the possible hazards or risks?
3. What measures can be put into place to reduce the risk or hazard?

≫ BOX 6.4 | Take It Outside!

When was the last time you climbed a tree? Find a tree in your neighbourhood. Look for the best climbing tree in your yard, the local park, or forest. As you climb the tree, think carefully about what you are learning and what you are practicing as you go from limb to limb. What are the risks and what are the benefits for children when they climb trees?

KEY TERMS

Treatise
Challenge
Hazard
Adventurous play
Self-efficacy
Self-regulation
Intrinsically motivated
Risk assessments
Natural playgrounds

Diane Kashin

Photo 6.12 Key terms.

Summary

■ Children require environments that support their opportunities for risky play. Jean-Jacques Rousseau understood this when he wrote the book *Emile* more than 100 years ago.

■ A challenge is something obvious to children and is different than a hazard, which is something unseen or not obvious and can result in injury.

■ Adventurous play refers to play where children explore and test their own capacities to manage risk and to grow in capacity, resourcefulness, and resilience. Adventurous play can be risky but it does not have to be hazardous.

■ There are many benefits to risky play for children, including the gaining of physical and motor competence, spatial orientation skills, environmental competence and literacy, self-worth and efficacy, cognitive and social development, and reduction of fear and risk-management skills. Risky play promotes physical activity, reduces mental illness and learning difficulties, and promotes independence.

■ Early learning teachers benefit from being conscious of their choice of words used in the company of children, families, and colleagues. Being aware of the discussions, controversy, and thinking around the terms risky, adventurous, and challenging builds knowledge that influences both philosophy and practice during outdoor play.

■ There is a connection between risk-taking and self-regulation. Children use self-regulation when responding to other children, adults, and materials in their environment. They learn to self-regulate as they engage in risky play. They learn to regulate anxiety or discouragement. When children are able to replace the feelings of being unable to do something, they build their confidence in being able to take risk. This contributes to them replacing feelings of anxiety and lack of competence with confidence.

■ Risky play helps children develop perceptual-motor and spatial-orientation abilities. It contributes to them mastering social skills when interacting with others and conflict resolution. Children also learn to balance their emotions and deal with fears and phobias while they take risks in their play.

■ Children who are intrinsically motivated to play and take risks develop independence and autonomy. Children's self-efficacy increases when they have challenging tasks that allow them to feel competent.

■ There is evidence-based research that suggests children learn risk management strategies as a result of risky play experiences. Observational studies of children at play found that they appeared to be aware of potential dangers and adjusted their activities accordingly.

■ Risk-taking includes curiosity, exploration, deep concentration, fear, and excitement. Early learning students and teachers have a responsibility to understand the complexities of risk-taking in play and to determine how their philosophical perspective is transferred to children's outdoor play environments.

■ Early learning teachers' focus on safety to ensure that there is a balance maintained between the risks and benefits of outdoor, risky, and challenging play. With policies and procedures in place and the completion of risk-benefits assessments done on a regular basis, early learning teachers support children's opportunities to take risks. Risk assessments include descriptions of potential risk but also should list the possible benefits.

■ One of the leading theorists today providing research on risky play is Ellen Sandseter, who identified six categories of risky play. They include rough and tumble play, playing at high speed, playing from great heights, using dangerous tools, and playing with dangerous elements and exploration.

■ The elements—earth, water, air, and fire—have potential for children to experience challenging, adventurous, and risky play. Some research has situated risk and adventure in outdoor play within the four elements. Early learning teachers use these elements to support children in having various types of play experiences and environments that support risky play.

■ Children are active learners who get to know their world through their bodies, testing 'what will happen if?' As children learn, they act and interact with others and the environment. When children have opportunities to take risks that are appropriate and commensurate with their level of independence, they begin the process of taking responsibility in their self-directed play. Applying strategies such as trial and error, children take responsibility for their learning and develop confidence in their abilities.

- Families have concerns for children's safety and do not want to appear neglectful of their children so they may wish early learning teachers to increase supervision. Extensive supervision will diminish children's independence and access to risky play. Early learning teachers play a key role in sharing with families the health benefits of risky play and the adverse consequences from a lack of risky outdoor play experiences. Early learning teachers can become part of the discussion and part of the solution.

- The hilltop as place is often a feature of natural playgrounds. Here, children have opportunities to climb, slide, and experience changes because of the elements of the wind, rain, snow, sun, or fog. Children use their motor abilities to feel the exhilaration that comes from a hill.

- Concerns and worries expressed by families are of an individual nature because they are unique to each child. There are many strategies that early learning teachers may use to begin the dialogue with colleagues, families, and children on risk-taking.

QUIET REFLECTION

Spend some time whittling and thinking. First, find a green stick with bark; using a knife or a vegetable peeler remove the bark from the stick. As you remove the bark, think about how a child would feel when offered experiences that provide opportunities to develop mastery and confidence.

COMMUNITY DIALOGUE

With others, enter in a dialogue about taking risks in play. Go back to the continuum of risky play and compare your numbers. How many in your group changed the way they felt about risky play? Discuss the reasons why some might have a greater comfort level than others. How might you help families feel comfortable with risky play?

FOR FURTHER THOUGHT AND ACTION

Are there any organizations in your community that are supporting challenging, adventurous, and risky play for children? You might be able to attend a pop-up adventure playground to see how children respond to risky play. Are there workshops available for early learning teachers? Attend a workshop to get involved and network with others who understand the importance of risky play. How are they taking action to support the risky play movement? What can you do?

RESOURCES

A newsletter from the British Columbia Injury Research and Prevention Unit detailing the benefits of risky play and making suggestions for moving forward can be found here:

http://www.injuryresearch.bc.ca/wp-content/uploads/2015/02/Injury-Insight-February-2015.pdf

An online tool to help families gain the confidence to allow their children to engage in outdoor play even if there are risks is available at:

https://outsideplay.ca

CHAPTER 7

Nature–Based Early Learning Places and Spaces

"Let it lie", the vigorous youngster exclaims to his father, who is about to roll a piece of wood out of the boy's way – "let it lie, I can get over it." With difficulty, indeed, the boy gets over it the first time; but he has accomplished the feat by his own strength. Strength and courage have grown in him. He returns, gets over the obstacle a second time, and soon he learns to clear it easily. If activity brought joy to the child, work now gives delight to the boy. Hence, the daring and venturesome feats of boyhood; the explorations of caves and ravines; the climbing of trees and mountains; the searching of the heights and depths; the roaming through fields and forests.

(Friedrich Froebel, 1782–1852)

LEARNING OUTCOMES

After exploring this chapter, you will be able to:

- Explain the importance of children having access to natural spaces in their lives.

- Discuss how Froebel's values and beliefs about outdoor play have influenced current perspectives on outdoor places and spaces.

- Describe various movements historically that have changed children's exposure to outdoor play spaces and places.

- Outline the characteristics of natural playgrounds, outdoor classrooms, ecoschools, forest kindergartens, and nature preschools.

- Discuss the types of roles that early learning teachers have in assisting children to interpret, reflect, and extend their thinking by applying their previous learning to their next discovery.

- Explain the significance of children developing a sense of place and place-based learning.

CHILDHOOD MEMORIES

I hear my mommy tell me that I have to work hard in kindergarten if I want to get ahead. I am not sure what she means, but I keep very busy every day. I spend time every morning in the math centre and then I go to the book nook to read. Then, I work at the writing centre. I get to fill in sheets that my teacher gives me, and I try very hard to colour and print nicely. I love getting stickers from my teacher when she tells me I did a good job! I don't like going outside. I don't like the fence; it makes me feel like I am in a cage. And there is nothing to do outside. I like having my crayons and sheets to work on. I like my stickers.

CHAPTER PREVIEW

Where are children playing today? Where are children learning today? The child, whose memory leads this chapter, is spending most of the day indoors engaged in experiences associated with work rather than play. The classroom depicted in the story is designed around learning centres. When there is time to play, the fenced in almost empty space leaves much to be desired by the children. Children flourish in space where they can run free in the field, slide down the hill, or play in the garden.

Children's outdoor play and learning requires connections to special places and spaces in nature. Natural places stimulate curiosity, exploration, and discovery. Natural places are "responsively alive". Children's curiosity is heightened when they have opportunities to have experiences in these places. These environments contribute to children feeling connected to a larger universe of living things. The memories of these places and spaces form a "reservoir of calm" from which they can draw from (Chawla, 2012, p. 50). Early learning students and teachers have the ability to offer children access to natural spaces and places. Outdoor play spaces can range from relatively natural or wild to well-maintained or developed spaces, such as grassy mowed areas, landscaped park settings, paved areas, or playgrounds. The spaces and places for outdoor play and learning abound. The question to be answered is are they being used to their full potential?

According to Miller, Tichota and White (2009) natural outdoor settings have been under-utilized in early childhood education. Ernst (2014) suggested that although natural outdoor settings hold "endless possibilities for learning in all curricular domains," early learning teachers might not recognize the potential opportunities for learning in these spaces (p. 736). Early learning teachers may "lack the foundational experiences necessary to see the affordances in natural outdoor settings" (Ernst, 2014, p. 736). If early learning students and teachers have not had their own experiences in natural outdoor settings, it may be difficult for them to recognize the potential these spaces and places hold for children.

"The importance of natural spaces in education is not a new idea, as educational theorists such as Froebel, Dewey, Montessori, Steiner, Rousseau, and Malaguzzi all emphasized the role of experiences in nature for young children's development and well-being" (Ernst, 2014, p. 735). Friedrich Froebel, whose words introduce this chapter, and whom we learned about in Chapter 2, was an advocate for outdoor play in nature. He created the first kindergarten and inspired the kindergarten movement (Sobel, 2016). Now, many of Froebel's ideas and perspectives are embedded in early learning programming today.

In 1837, Froebel opened his school, which later became known as kindergarten (Muelle, 2013). In his school, Froebel (1974) "emphasized play, which started with simple activities and later progressed to more complex games. He felt that children should learn through play" (Muelle, 2013, p. 87). Froebel's influence was widespread and spurred what has become known as the kindergarten movement. His work has had significant influence on early learning settings today (Elkind, 2015). This chapter will include an exploration of the spaces and places where children presently play. Examining Froebel's ideas and how they influenced the kindergarten movement in the 1800s reveals an alignment with current day outdoor play and nature movements. More than 100 years ago, Merrill (1916) described a kindergarten curriculum inspired by Froebel as including nature interests. Table 7.1 provides an overview of the curriculum components.

The kindergarten movement began with the spread of kindergartens throughout Germany and, eventually, into North America. Following the societal impacts of industrialization, social activists supported the growth of kindergarten. Recognizing the importance of play and learning in the early years, free kindergartens became very popular (Muelle, 2013). Today, we refer to Froebel's work once again for inspiration as other movements to support

Photo 7.1 Terra Nova Nature School, Richmond, B.C.

advancing children's outdoor play are taking form. The planting of flowers and vegetables for children to experience gardening continues to be evident today as depicted in Photo 7.1.

When the kindergarten movement came to North America in the 1850s, it brought with it Froebel's emphasis on the importance of nature (Frost & Sutterby, 2017). The first kindergarten in North America was established in Wisconsin, in the United States. In Canada, the first kindergarten was opened in 1870 in Charlottetown, Prince Edward Island. By the end of the 1870s, there were kindergartens in some larger towns and cities. In 1883, the Toronto School Board established a kindergarten program (Prochner, 2015). At the same time that the concept of kindergarten was spreading, there was also a desire for preserving natural spaces (Frost & Sutterby, 2017). During the 1840s, social reformers realized that the unplanned growth of cities had negative consequences for children. Large cities such as Boston and New York were very crowded and the streets were dangerous due to heavy traffic. This resulted in the first major public park project in Central Park in New York City (Frost & Sutterby, 2017). By the 1880s, social reformers became increasingly concerned about the needs of children living in these congested urban environments.

Outdoor play was seen as a way to meet children's needs. During the 1880s, there was a growth of the German-style sand gardens, as featured in Chapter 4 (Frost & Sutterby, 2017). Another movement, known as the **playground movement** soon followed.

Playground movement began as an answer to the crowded cities and long work days of parents that characterized realities of the industrial revolution. The movement sought to help poor, immigrant, and homeless children. The belief was that supervised play would improve the overall well-being of children (Bachrach, 2012).

Table 7.1 Nature interests in kindergarten.

1. Observing the sun, the moon, the stars, the sky, the clouds, rain, and snow. Observing shadows, indoors and outdoors. Observing the seasons.

2. Caring for animals, such as a cat or a rabbit. Imitating sounds of animals. Observing life in the aquarium.

3. Caring for caterpillars, its cocoon, the butterfly or moth.

4. Planting flower and vegetable seeds in the springtime; planting in the fall; watering plants.

5. Naming plants, flowers, fruits and grains, and leaves and grasses. Use them for decoration and in pictures. Sorting and arranging seeds, shells, and pebbles.

6. Observing nests and other animal habitats. Learning names of natural objects such as acorns, cones, mosses, etc. The children handle and play with these natural objects to learn their names, colours, and uses.

7. Take walks and go on excursions.

Source: Based on Merrill, J. 1916. The kindergarten of today. In *Paradise of Childhood* by Edward Wiebe.

The playground movement included the installation of manufactured play equipment in public spaces. By the 1920s, with various forms of political and financial support, cities began including parks and playgrounds in city planning (Frost & Sutterby, 2017). Yet although the playground movement was gaining ground in cities, this movement did not take place in rural areas. This absence was due in part to the open spaces, farm animals, and natural materials that children already had to play with (Frost & Sutterby, 2017). Now, there is a movement in many early learning centres that are integrating outdoor play and nature-based principles and practices into their programming (Sobel, 2016).

Recall that in Chapter 2 we introduced social movements. A social movement is characterized by a group of people who get together to advance their shared ideas intended to bring about change. The kindergarten movement changed the face of early childhood play and learning. What will be the impact of present-day movements?

Over time, the Froebelian influence on early learning dissipated somewhat with the advent of a new psychological theory known as *behaviourism*. Behaviourists such as Thorndike and Watson warned teachers against motherly love in the classroom. They felt the emphasis should be on learning objectives. Even though John Dewey and his theory of progressive education stood in opposition to the tenets of behaviourism, education as a social reform movement was diminishing, and the behavioural emphasis began to dominate (Muelle, 2013). The goals of kindergarten were to help children become acclimatized to the routines of school and the social environment of the school. The emphasis was less on nature and more on academics (Muelle, 2013). The surge of academic kindergartens made way for current-day movements. Examining history helps early learning students and teachers understand how the past has contributed to the present and to think about the future.

In the early 1890s, as kindergartens became part of public schools, nursery schools were also becoming common. Some nursery schools were private and served children of the elite, whereas others were free and served disadvantaged children. At the same time, as a result of industrialization and urbanization, day nurseries that provided child care grew in numbers. In Canada, these programs were relatively stagnant until the onset of the Second World War. As more two-parent families entered the workforce during the war years and particularly after the 1960s, when more women entered the workforce, there was a demand for more full-time daycare to be available for families (Prochner, 2015). At their inception, nursery schools and child care and kindergarten programs generally focused on either custodial care or academic skills. The 1960s also popularized the theories of Jean Piaget and the belief in children's self-activity (Muelle, 2013). Similar to Froebel, Piaget believed children learn from experience. Piaget believed that children should learn through play that is creative and imaginative (Elkind, 2015). Piaget's research continues to have an influence on early learning.

CURIOUS?

For more information about playground safety standards see: http://www.parachutecanada.org/injury-topics/item/playground-standards-in-canada-lt

In the 1950s, another movement took hold. Playground equipment was excessively tall, placed on hard surfaces like concrete, and allowed for high speed. Citizens became concerned about children's safety, and the safe playground movement began. Unsafe playground equipment was removed and guidelines developed. In recent years, in many jurisdictions, there have been high rates of playground injury litigation amongst school age children resulting in more regulations (Frost & Sutterby, 2017). As regulations became more extensive, there was concern that playgrounds no longer met children's needs (Frost & Sutterby, 2017). The Canadian Standards Association (CSA) has a set of safety standards for children's play spaces and equipment designed to minimize risk and injury. In 1990, the CSA published a guide entitled *Children's Playspaces and Equipment* that was updated in 1998, 2003, and 2007. The standards include detailed specifications for the following features of playgrounds as specified by Fuselli and Yanchar (2012).

- Layout
- Access (getting on and off equipment)
- Surfacing material
- Equipment strength
- Performance requirements
- Installation requirements
- Inspection and maintenance
- Design specifications for each piece of play equipment

Photo 7.2 Playgrounds representing standards.

In an effort to comply with these standards, play spaces began to phase out swings, teeter-totters, and merry-go-rounds resulting in more sterile but safe equipment. In response, critics argued that the new standards failed to consider the loss in developmental benefits afforded by the older equipment because of their opportunities for risk-taking (Brussoni et al., 2014). Photo 7.2 shows a playground adhering to standards.

While the CSA standards are voluntary, in practice many jurisdictions have insisted on adherence in the interest of minimizing injury and litigation (Fuselli & Yanchar, 2012). Yet, having a strong focus on safety can result in negative impacts on child development. Today, we are seeing a growing debate over the standards because of how limited play spaces have become. Play equipment with minimal imaginative play options limits children's play. Consider the questions depicted in Photos 7.3 and 7.4 while examining the playground images.

Are these playspaces inhibiting children's access to spaces and places that support their development and provide connections to nature?

Photo 7.3 The influence of standards on playgrounds.

Are these spaces having an impact on children's exposure to outdoor play?

Diane Kashin

Photo 7.4 Playgrounds and outdoor play.

Today, for many reasons including the allure of technology, children are less active and less connected to nature. This lack of outdoor play and access to nature is sparking a new outdoor play movement. Many child advocates are attempting to educate society on the importance of reconnecting children with nature. Forest and nature schools are considered an important part of this movement (Sobel, 2016).

Sobel (2016) makes a distinction between forest kindergartens and nature preschools. **Nature preschools** are native to North America and have emerged from the **environmental education** movement. Environmental education aligns with a number of early learning philosophical frameworks. More than 25 years ago, Wilson (1994) maintained that environmental education in early learning programs includes children having the opportunities to:

- Develop a sense of wonder and be able to act upon their curiosity;
- Become aware of the beauty of their surroundings;
- Experience many options to touch, feel, taste, smell, and see the environment from different perspectives; and
- Identify and respect all people and creatures that the environment is shared with.

Incorporating environmental education into the framework of early learning programs "is a holistic concept that encompasses knowledge of the natural work as well as emotions, dispositions, and skills" (North American Association for Environmental Education, 2010, p. 2). Nature preschools emerged from these ideals. They may not necessarily take place exclusively outdoors. These programs have "beautifully designed indoor environments" (Sobel, 2016, p. 36) and many opportunities to connect with nature and with domestic and wild animals on a daily basis. Nature preschools follow a more traditional readiness path with emphasis on literacy and numeracy (Sobel, 2016).

Forest kindergartens have their roots in Europe, surfacing in the Scandinavian countries. Forest kindergartens emphasize minimizing indoor facilities and being out in all weather (Sobel, 2016). With the surge of forest kindergartens and nature preschools in Canada, there is a return to the nature interests that were inspired by Froebel's kindergarten and the growth of the kindergarten movement. Although "Froebel's vision waxed and waned throughout the twentieth century" it did re-emerge in Sweden in the 1950s and 1960s (Sobel, 2016, p. 31). By 2008, there were 180 nature-based nursery schools in Sweden.

Nature preschools make a commitment to having children outdoors every day to connect with the natural world. Indoors and outdoors they have a commitment to developmentally appropriate curricula (Sobel, 2016).

Environmental education refers to a process that supports individuals to explore environmental issues, engage in problem solving, and take action to improve the environment.

Forest kindergartens focus on learning with "no paper, no crayons just the great outdoors" with less focus than nature preschools on indoor experiences (Sobel, 2016, p. 38).

According to Sobel (2016) these programs are "even more nature-based than Froebel's original kindergarten" (p. 33). In these Swedish nature schools, the forest and its raw materials are the primary learning sources (Sobel, 2016). Froebel's kindergarten emphasized the use of a set of toys that he called "gifts". These gifts focused on children's mathematical and science learning. Today, sticks, pebbles, and pinecones as well as other conventional and often plastic math manipulatives replace Froebel's gifts. These modern versions of Froebel's gifts can be found in a variety of early learning programs including forest and nature-based programs (Sobel, 2016).

Today, there are thousands of forest school programs throughout Europe, Australia, and New Zealand and they are "cropping up in many Asian countries" (Sobel, 2016, p. 1). Photo 7.5 was taken at a forest school in Switzerland. In North America, nature-based early learning programs surfaced "around the time of the original Earth Day in 1970" (Sobel, 2016, p. 1). In recent years, across Canada there has been a growing interest in outdoor play for children in the early years that includes both the forest school movement and nature-based programming for young children.

Photo 7.5 Forest school in Switzerland.

Forest kindergartens have a variety of names, depending on their country of origin. For example, in Sweden, they are called Rain or Shine Schools (Sobel, 2016). In Germany, they are called Waldkindergarten (Fritz, Smyrni, & Roberts, 2014). In Australia you can find Bush Kinder, an adaption of the Scandinavian forest schools (Davis & Elliott, 2014). There are a variety of other types of outdoor play places for children. These include eco-schools and outdoor schools, adventure playgrounds, pop-ups, outdoor classrooms, play gardens, and edible gardens. Early learning students and teachers can learn from these outdoor places and spaces for play and learning to enhance the experiences they give to children in their own contexts.

CURIOUS?

Do you want to know more about Forest and Nature Schools in Canada? http://childnature
.ca/wp-content/uploads/2017/10/FSC-Guide-1.pdf

SETTING THE STAGE FOR OUTDOOR PLAY

Not all the programs featured in this chapter take place outdoors exclusively; however, they all encourage children to use the outdoor environment. Although there has been in recent years a surge in programs that emphasize outdoor play, as outlined throughout this text, this is not a new phenomenon. Rudolph Steiner, who founded the Waldorf approach

Figure 7.1 Features of a Waldorf outdoor environment.
Photo Sources: Michelle Thornhill and Diane Kashin.

to education in 1919, believed that the outdoors was the best place for learning to occur. Steiner promoted outdoor play in all seasons, regardless of the weather. Steiner suggested that the outdoor environment be equipped with a covered area to escape the elements when playing outside. He "encouraged all children to use the outdoor environment and provided spaces that were as natural as possible" (Constable, 2017, p. 4). The features of a Waldorf outdoor environment as adapted from Constable (2017) are featured in Figure 7.1.

According to Constable (2017) Steiner's approach "is probably the closest historic model we have to our current outdoor classrooms and Forest Schools" (p. 4). Forest and nature schools are programs that have regular and sustained access to the same natural space (Andrachuk et al., 2014). Many other early learning programs may have access to natural space that is used regularly by the children and early learning teachers.

Forest and Nature Schools

When children have access to the same natural space on a regular basis, they are "provided with opportunities to build an on-going relationship with the land, to a dedicated educator, to one another, and to themselves through this educational approach" (Andrachuk et al., 2014, p. 12). Forest and nature schools can operate on a full- or part-time basis and can take place in a variety of different outdoor areas that are not necessarily forests. Children who attend these programs can spend all day or half a day "in local woodlands and green spaces, in various urban and near-urban parks, natural spaces adjacent to or on school grounds, or natural playgrounds and outdoor classrooms" (Andrachuk et al., 2014, p.12). The programs follow an emergent, experiential, inquiry-based, play-based, and place-based learning approach (MacEachren, 2013). In Canada, many early learning teachers who work in forest and nature schools often receive their training through a practitioner's course offered by the Child and Nature Alliance of Canada. Others may acquire their knowledge and skills from professional learning options that integrate a variety of perspectives into outdoor play pedagogy and programming approaches.

The guiding principles from the Forest and Nature School in Canada: A Head, Heart, Hands Approach to Outdoor Learning (Andrachuk et al., 2014) are listed in Table 7.2. Many of these approaches are transferable to a variety of outdoor play pedagogies and environments.

Table 7.2 Principles of forest and nature schools.

Takes place in a variety of spaces, including local forests, creeks, meadows, prairie grasses, mountains, shorelines, tundra, natural playgrounds, and outdoor classrooms.

Is a long-term process of regular and repeated sessions in the same natural space.

Is rooted in building an on-going relationship to place and on principles of place-based education.

Is rooted in and supports building engaged, healthy, vibrant, and diverse communities.

Aims to promote the holistic development of children and youth.

Views children and youth as competent and capable learners.

Supports children and youth, with a supportive and knowledgeable educator, to identify, co-manage, and navigate risk. Opportunities to experience risk are seen as an integral part of learning and healthy development.

Requires qualified Forest and Nature School practitioners who are rooted in and committed to FNS pedagogical theory and practical skills.

Requires that educators play the role of facilitator rather than expert.

Uses loose, natural materials to support open-ended experiences.

The process is as valued as the outcome.

Requires that educators utilize emergent, experiential, inquiry-based, play-based, and place-based learning approaches.

Source: Based on Andrachuk et al. (2014) *Forest and nature school in Canada: A head, heart, hands approach to outdoor learning.*

As you will note, these principles can be implemented in a variety of outdoor play environments. Early learning students and teachers can take inspiration from these principles and examine their local contexts for spaces such as forests, creeks, meadows, prairie grasses, mountains, and shorelines to determine if and how they may adapt some of the principles in practice. They may also look to their own playground space to consider how these principles can be embedded. In this textbook and in this chapter in particular, value is placed on children's access to spaces that offer the affordances available outdoors.

Think about how spaces and places influence children's outdoor play experiences. For example, taking children on a repeated basis to the same natural space helps them to identify with and develop a sense of place (Pelo, 2013). A **sense of place** refers to a special space that provides children with an emotional connection. This connection supports their affective development (Hashemnezhad, Heidari, & Hoseini, 2013). The growth of place-based education in relation to the forest kindergarten and nature preschool movement is significant (Sobel, 2016).

> **Sense of place** is the emotional connection that happens when a space gets under the skin. A regional sense of place can lead to a broader consciousness for the world (Sobel, 2008).

Expanding children's access to outdoor spaces and places supports their engagement with community. Early learning settings can be vibrant members of that community, expanding diversity and supporting children's healthy development. This supports children's holistic development and situates them as capable, competent, risk-taking members of their community. Early learning teachers can help children build their confidence and ability to manage risk in their outdoor play (Ontario Ministry of Education, 2014).

There is a thread that runs through each of the chapters in this text that promotes children having access to outdoor play environments. Adults who promote experiences that are emergent, inquiry and place-based utilize loose parts as essential materials for children's play. Examine the photos on the following page that were taken in a forest school.

Photo 7.6 Resting in the forest—Discovery Child Care Centre.

Photo 7.7 Whittling in the forest—Discovery Child Care Centre.

Photo 7.8 Observing tracks in the forest—Discovery Child Care Centre.

In Photo 7.6 children can be seen resting in the forest. How does this experience support their holistic development across multiple domains? In Photo 7.7, a child is whittling. How does this support children's opportunity for risk-taking? In Photo 7.8, children are observing animal tracks in the snow. How might the early learning teacher use this experience to begin an inquiry born in place? The forest can become an outdoor classroom of learning. How might similar experiences be found in other outdoor play environments? For example, how might early learning teachers create opportunities to sleep outdoors in their play spaces? What resources might be presented to the children to use to examine animal tracks in their play space or their neighbourhood? Where might there be special spots that children may adopt as theirs? Where might these spots be found in urban settings? How might they differ in more rural areas?

Outdoor Classrooms

The outdoor environment can become a classroom when it is a place where children learn. It can be formally designed or can be any outdoor play space. It is impossible for any two outdoor classrooms to be the same and every day the environment can change because of the elements. Many outdoor classrooms in school settings are located in yards or fields (Constable, 2017). Outdoor classrooms can duplicate the indoor classroom with seating and teaching platforms. Creating a classroom design outdoors that has a teaching platform and seating reflects an environment that does not support self-directed play. In early learning settings, play is the vehicle for children to learn (Dietze & Kashin, 2018).

In this textbook, we view outdoor classrooms from a broader perspective. Rather than focus on a space that is designed as a classroom, we look at all spaces as potential places for children to play and learn. While the term 'outdoor classroom' is familiar in school settings (Constable, 2017), it can be limiting from the perspective of early learning (Maynard & Waters, 2007). Siraj-Blatchford, Sylva, Laugharne, Milton, and Charles (2006) suggested that the term would benefit from further "consideration, clarification and revision" (p. 81). The outdoor classroom can be considered anywhere outside that children play, explore, discover, and learn. Natural playgrounds are places and spaces for learning as well as playing.

Natural Playgrounds

Across Canada, early learning programs are guided by provincial regulations. The regulations vary from province to province, including the regulations related to outdoor play spaces. Although traditional playgrounds that utilize structures such as slides, monkey bars, and swing sets continue to be widely used, there is a growing interest in natural playgrounds (Coe, Flynn, Wolff, Scott, & Durham, 2014). Jennings (2014) stated, "a movement has begun to naturalize children's playgrounds" (p. 2). Richard Louv's book *Last Child in the Woods* (2005) is cited as one of the many reasons why there is an emerging trend to incorporate natural elements into the spaces where children play (Coe et al., 2014). When children play on manufactured equipment, their play is more predictable and less creative than what is possible in natural playgrounds. Children spend five times as much time engaged in play experiences in natural playgrounds as they do in a traditional playground (Weintrub, 2010). The role for early learning students and teachers includes continuously creating or accessing outdoor spaces that allow for children to get the most play value and opportunities from their environments.

Keeler (2016) recommended creating safe spaces for play that offer endless possibilities. Logs, stumps, branches, wood chips, trees, shrubs, scrap lumber, tires, and giant wood spools are excellent, cost-efficient additions to naturalize playgrounds. Adding water pumps and hoses rather than standing water (pools or ponds) are preferable so that children don't fall into the water. Sand and water provide opportunities for loose parts play (Kuh, Ponte, & Chau, 2013). The affordances of children's spaces impact their engagement with that place.

Nedovic and Morrissey (2013) cited research that found children with increased exposure to natural play spaces have greater motor coordination and concentration than children who played daily in spaces that had less natural features such as plants. Franklin (2008) observed that children's pretend play was richer with access to natural features and materials such as trees, grass, twigs, and pebbles than in traditional play spaces. The presence of greenery and trees increases creativity in children's play. The different colours of nature, the trees, and the variations in topography intrigue children. The outdoors is a place where children go to make sense of their world (Nedovic & Morrissey, 2013).

Photo 7.9 Natural playground—Discovery Child Care Centre.

Nedovic and Morrissey (2013) concluded from studying the redevelopment of a play space used by three- to four-year-olds that children want spaces where nature such as plants, trees, flowers, water, animals, and insects abound. One of the key findings of the study was the effect that the natural features and materials have on the depth of children's dramatic play. As well, an unexpected finding of the study was that green, natural garden growth has a soothing effect on children. The researchers suggested that natural materials and organic growth appeared to help children slow down and focus on their play, rather than move from one experience to another in short periods of time.

Natural playgrounds offer children certain affordances not found in traditional playgrounds that generally only feature fixed equipment like slides and swings. Drown and Christensen (2014) researched the question of whether natural playgrounds provided more dramatic play affordances than manufactured equipment-based playgrounds. Look at Photo 7.9. Note that at the far left side is a section with tall grass. What might children do in that space? What affordances will it provide? For example, Mykah and Molly waded through the grass one morning to find ladybugs, grasshoppers, and spiders. Soon after that discovery, Mykah pretended that she was a ladybug and spoke to Molly in character. Molly responded in character as a grasshopper and began to jump in the tall grass. Griffen, who was playing nearby under the tree, crawled into the grass. Mykah suggested that he be a spider and the play episode continued for the morning with all three children staying in character as they role-played. How did the tall grass support and encourage the experience? How would it be different if the children were in a manufactured, equipment-based playground?

The advantages of natural playgrounds are that they are multipurpose and open spaces for children to play in. "In an open play space, children can engage in a range of gross motor activities skills such as running, jumping, crawling, and rolling" (Spencer & Wright, 2014, p. 29). When adding manipulative equipment such as balls, beanbags, and hoops into open spaces, more play options evolve. Loose parts support children in partaking in construction play, which contributes to both their gross and fine motor skills. Adding props or costumes encourages role-play and fantasy play (Spencer & Wright, 2014). With trees, shrubs, grasses, nonpoisonous flowering plants, vines, topographic variation (i.e., mounds, terraces, slopes), and safe ground surfaces, natural playgrounds become a welcoming and beautiful environment that provides children with variety and interest. Risk, challenge, and adventure can be supported with open-ended components. Logs, balance beams, and stumps that challenge children's physical, social, and cognitive abilities can encourage them to create their own challenge or obstacle course and engage in increasingly more difficult and complex activities (Spencer & Wright, 2014). Figure 7.2 provides examples adapted from Spencer and Wright (2014) of what can be featured in a natural playground.

When children use tricycles, scooters, wagons, and push toys, they can experience speed, cooperate with others, and engage in role-play. These experiences help children develop large muscles as they negotiate pathways. Adding pathways with a slight slope provides children with additional challenges and affordances (Dietze, 2013; Spencer & Wright, 2014). With manipulative equipment such as balls, ribbons, ropes, and hula-hoops children can practice their "object control skills, such as throwing, rolling, bowling, kicking, and batting" (Spencer & Wright, 2014, p. 30).

Wheeled Toys · Manipulative Equipment · Sand Play Area

Water Play Feature · Music and Movement · Balance Beams and Stepping Stones

Play Houses and other Structures

Figure 7.2 Features in natural playgrounds.

Photo Sources: Michelle Thornhill, Diane Kashin, and Karen Eilerson.

Sand areas can be either raised or ground level. Spencer and Wright (2014) described the affordances of sand in natural playgrounds:

> Elevated sand tables may make sand play accessible to children who have special needs. At a raised sand area children can sit or stand around the containers to play with the sand. In lower sand areas, children use their bodies to develop nonlocomotor skills, such as bending and squatting as they dig and play in the sand. Dirt or soil digging areas afford children a different tactile experience and the chance to discover insects and earthworms. (p. 31)

In a natural playground, water play features can be permanent, such as a waterfall, or temporary and portable such as a hose, wading pool, or water table. Water offers children opportunities to learn many scientific principles through play. Think about how children learn about these principles when they engage in play that enables them to experience how water moves and changes, what objects sink or float, and how water impacts or changes other materials such as dirt, clay, and sand (Spencer & Wright, 2014).

When children use balance beams and stepping-stones, they are practising their stability skills to balance, bend, turn, and transfer weight. Large tree logs serve as excellent balance beams, and smooth stones or tree stumps are great opportunities to practice balancing while

| Flower and Vegetable Gardens | Loose Parts | Trees for climbing |
| Climbing and Rolling Mounds | Decks or Stages | Decorative Elements |

Figure 7.3 Additional features in natural playgrounds.

Photo Sources: Michelle Thornhill and Diane Kashin.

incorporating natural elements into the playground (Spencer & Wright, 2014). Playhouses and other structures, such as gazebos, offer children a chance to socialize and communicate. Music areas with chimes, drums, rain sticks, and other instruments give children opportunities to explore natural sounds in their environment. Pots, pans, and aluminum garbage can lids hung on a fence are an inexpensive alternative to purchased instruments (Spencer & Wright, 2014). Figure 7.3 illustrates additional features recommended by Spencer and Wright (2014) that can be added to natural playgrounds.

By providing children with opportunities to be involved in growing vegetables, herbs and flowers, they experience the life cycle of plants in the garden. Not only do gardens have an aesthetic appeal, children experience a variety of textures and smells to explore and discover (Spencer & Wright, 2014). Loose parts material such as pinecones, milk crates, blocks, stumps, logs, and branches promote constructive play that can be enhanced with found natural materials (Spencer & Wright, 2014).

If the natural play space has good climbing trees, children have opportunities to climb, balance, and transfer weight. Climbing trees offers children experiences that requires them to calculate and manage risk, to possess greater control over their large muscles, and to engage in a variety of problem-solving scenarios. Not all natural spaces come with climbing trees. Large tree trunks and rocks give children a similar experience and sense of adventure (Spencer & Wright, 2014). Climbing and rolling mounds support children in developing stability skills such as balancing, rolling, and stopping. They develop locomotor skills such as running, galloping, and skipping (Spencer & Wright, 2014). Imagine the joy and excitement children would feel running down a hill!

Raised decks or stages become gathering or welcoming places for children. Children read stories together, act out stories, sing, or dance. Large pallets can be used to create interesting gathering places in different parts of the play space. Some days the gathering places may be located in one place and then moved to other areas. Early learning teachers change the gathering places periodically as a way to support children in observing various parts of their play space (Spencer & Wright, 2014). According to Spencer and Wright (2014)

> A high-quality outdoor play space includes decorative elements, such as banners, wind chimes, wind socks, statues, flags, cultural artifacts, or decorative objects (e.g., wreaths, fence weavings, murals, weather vanes, pinwheels, whimsical signs, garlands, or sculptures) which add visual and auditory interest and appeal. (p. 33)

Keeler (2008) suggested using the local talent in the community to personalize the play space and to make it welcoming and unique. Local mechanics, farmers, construction workers, and gardeners intriguing materials and experiences to the space. Whatever elements are added to playgrounds to naturalize and encourage children's play opportunities, the materials should be sustainable and ecologically focused (Davis, 2010).

Eco-Schools

As identified earlier in the chapter, programs with an ecological focus are often called eco-schools. Eco-Schools is a global program for Education for Sustainable Development that encourages children and youth to engage in and with their environment. "Eco-Schools runs in kindergarten, primary, secondary, and third level education institutions across five continents" (Andreou, 2017, p. 39). There is a seven-step process for schools to become an Eco-School (Andreou, 2017). Figure 7.4 lists the seven steps. How might these steps be used to support early learning programs in further advancing their practices toward being more ecologically focused?

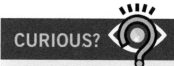

CURIOUS?

Do you want to know more about the seven steps to becoming an Eco-School? Follow this link: http://www.ecoschools.global/seven-steps/.

Form an Eco Committee

Carry out an Environmental Review

Create an Action Plan

Monitor and Evaluate

Engage in Curriculum Work

Inform and Involve

Produce an Eco Code

Figure 7.4 Seven steps to become an Eco-School.

Early learning settings can adapt the seven-step process in their environments either to advance their eco practices or to become an eco-school. While eco-schools are generally located in school settings, early learning students and teachers can reflect on the process and determine how similar processes could be applied to early learning environments. Forming an Eco Committee is the first step of the process. The Eco Committee reflects the school's population and includes administration, caretaking staff, educators, and students. Upon completion of an environmental review that identifies issues, an action plan is created that includes measurable goals for change. The achievement of the goals is monitored and evaluated while the environmental efforts are integrated into the curriculum of the school. The Eco Committee ensures that the whole school knows of the school's ecological work by informing and involving. Finally, an Eco Code is created. This is a statement that represents the school's commitment to the environment.

Early learning teachers can take inspiration from the process of becoming an eco-school and work in their own way to become more ecologically focused. Read Case Study 7.1, which tells the story of Karen, a director of an early learning program. She describes her centre's journey to becoming ecologically focused. Karen has been committed to learning more about creating healthy outdoor environments for children. Consider the questions that follow. As you read Chapter 8, you will learn additional information about the principles and practices of environmental sustainability as they relate to children's outdoor play and learning experiences.

≫ CASE STUDY 7.1 | Becoming Environmentally Aware

I opened my centre in 1998. In my early days as an early learning teacher, I attended a conference on pesticides and their negative effects on children's health. This awakened the environmentalist inside of me, and I vowed to create a healthy environment for the children, families, and staff. We have environmental policies that focus on the children practicing the three Rs (reduce, re-use, recycle), water conservation, and composting in the child-care setting. We also intentionally provide children with hands-on learning experiences so that they can learn the habits of being environmentally aware. Our hope is to instill life-long habits and environmental stewardship in the children.

In 2006, I attended a forum on nature education for young children. It really changed my thinking and focus! I realized that I needed to teach children to love the earth before I could ask them to save it! While we always spent lots of time outside, our new focus has been connecting children with nature. Our programs are immersed in nature

and follow an emergent curriculum philosophy. The majority of our day is spent outside in our outdoor classroom. I believe that there is almost no bad weather, just bad clothing. I believe that being outdoors in beautiful natural environments is an essential experience for all children. We have been working on transforming and naturalizing our playgrounds. We have added lots of loose parts and created new areas for play, including a sound garden, a mud kitchen, a messy materials space, an organic garden, and a pollinator peace garden.

1. What steps do you think the director took on this journey to ensure that the early learning team, the families, and the children were a part of the process?
2. What does the director mean when she says that if children do not love the earth, they can't be asked to save it?
3. What do you imagine is in a sound garden?

The spaces created in the place where children play make a difference to their lives every day. Samuelsson and Kaga (2008) suggested that we "urgently require new kinds of education to help prevent further degradation of our planet." These new kinds of education "must begin in early childhood, as the values, attitudes, behaviours and skills acquired in this period may have a long-lasting impact in later life" (p. 9). Does this statement motivate you to consider being ecologically aware in the outdoor spaces that you create for children? What else would the ideal space for children to play and learn have?

Adventure Playgrounds as Places to Play

Adventure playgrounds are places for children to play in ways that support their health, creativity, and learning. Recall that adventure playgrounds were introduced in Chapter 2 and discussed further in Chapter 4 in relationship to loose parts. In this chapter, we look at adventure playgrounds as spaces and places for **open-ended play**. Open-ended play is the term used to describe the type of play that the adventure play movement is seeking to restore. Adventure playgrounds align with the "burgeoning maker movement" and the "growing desire to foster innovation and creativity in children." The **maker movement** refers to the "growing number of people" engaged in creating artifacts and then "using physical and digital forums to share their processes and products with others" (Halverson & Sheridan, 2014, p. 496). The maker movement has spread from industry to education and is aligned with the theories of constructivism which emphasis a hands on approach to learning (Halverson & Sheridan, 2014). Early learning students and teachers who encourage and invite children to make things are supporting the maker movement. With the open-ended materials in adventure playgrounds they are "incubators for future innovators" (Mills, 2017, p. 58). In addition, there are other benefits to adventure playgrounds for children.

In adventure playgrounds children feel empowered, as they are able to be creative, experiment, and take risks in their play space (Staempfli, 2009). For children to have the ability to create their own play environment, they require opportunities to engage in thinking, experimenting, and doing things that lead them to experience high levels of learning.

Open-ended play allows children to express themselves in play freely and creatively. Their play is not bound by preset limitations (Frost, Brown, Sutterby, & Thornton, 2004).

Maker movement refers to those who creatively design and build projects for both play and function (Martin, 2015).

Pop-up Adventure Play Spaces

As a way to introduce children to the unique features that are embedded in adventure playgrounds, there is a growing movement of pop-up playgrounds. Pop-up adventure playgrounds are designed to demonstrate that adding adventure play to existing outdoor environments can be possible in many different places (Leichter-Saxby & Law, 2017).

Adventure play spaces offer children challenge and risk. In the United Kingdom, as a way to support children in accessing adventure play spaces, various government agencies invest in **play rangers** who "travel to open spaces of housing projects with small kits of loose parts" (Leichter-Saxby & Law, 2017, p. 23). There is a difference between play rangers and playworkers (as described in Chapter Two) associated with adventure playgrounds. The practice of playworkers was only brought to North America in 2010, so it is a relatively new idea here (Leichter-Saxby & Law, 2017).

Play rangers are playworkers who move from community to community supporting outdoor play rather than staying at one adventure playground.

CURIOUS?

To learn more about the registered charity, Pop-Up Adventure Play from the UK, see: https://popupadventureplaygrounds.wordpress.com/pop-ups-canada-tour-2017/

Small pop-ups can be started anywhere in a community; they can take shape in any appropriate space where relationships are formed and connections are made to support a shared belief in play (Leichter-Saxby & Law, 2017). The pop-up adventure play movement demonstrates that outdoor spaces can be modified for children to be able to experience open-ended play and that this can occur in everyday places. For example, in

Diane Kashin

Photo 7.10 Pop-up adventure play.

2017 the United Kingdom-based Pop-Up Adventure Play groups conducted a Canada-wide tour, popping up in cities across the country. Photo 7.10 is a collage of photos taken at two of the stops on the tour.

Also taking hold in recent years is the garden movement, which seeks to bring the garden back to the lives of children, just as Froebel recommended all those years ago.

Gardens for Play and Food

Gardens as place provide children with multiple play and learning experiences. Nimmo and Hallett (2008) described a garden as a place where young children work and play. Food gardens allow children to observe and take part in the wonders of growing food. According to Nimmo and Hallett, gardens offer children opportunities to:

- Play and inquire;
- Take safe risks;
- Develop diverse relationships;
- Develop community;

- Invite and uncover diversity; and
- Widen social views.

Gardening has become increasingly popular as a context for learning. Research on school gardens shows the importance of gardens as places for nutrition and ecological learning and the development of environmental stewardship (Vandermaas-Peeler & McClain, 2015). The garden is also a place for scientific and mathematical learning (Vandermaas-Peeler & McClain, 2015). Imagine the learning possibilities for children when they experiment and explore with the materials shown in in Photo 7.11.

A longitudinal case study conducted by Vandermaas-Peeler, and McClain (2015) of children's interactions with an early learning teacher in a garden suggested "the potential of a richly provisioned garden as an environment in which learning can be fostered through a holistic and integrated approach" (p. 24). "A preschool garden affords myriad opportunities for young children to develop mathematical and scientific thinking, ecological awareness and positive affective responses to the natural world" (Vandermaas-Peeler & McClain, 2015, p. 24). Playing in gardens that yield food provides opportunities for children to develop one of their hundred languages, the language of food (Edwards, Forman, & Gandini, 2012).

Photo 7.11 Gardening with children—Discovery Child Care Centre.

Karen Eilersen

>> **BOX 7.1**   **Shedding Light on Outdoor Play—Points of Reflection**

In the infant-toddler and preschool centres of Reggio Emilia, Italy, the presence of gardens in the outdoor environment is considered to be highly important. Children get to take care of the garden, to plant seeds, and to watch them grow. The children get the opportunity to understand the life cycle of a plant and see how it is nourished by time and care and influenced by environmental conditions such as sun, rain, and temperature. In helping to prepare a meal, the children see how food goes from garden to table, while learning the languages of food (Cavallini & Tedeschi, 2008).

Farm to table is a phrase you may have heard often. Have you ever heard of **farm-to-preschool**? As an area of research, there have been numerous studies about farm-to-school programs that unite local farmers with schools. "Fewer studies still have focused on examining farm-to-school programs in preschools settings" (Carbone et al., 2016, p. 178). The farm as a space and place for learning can focus on food and healthy eating. Making connections with local farms to purchase fresh produce was found to save money for early learning settings. Having access to fresh produce encourages children to eat more fruits and vegetables (Carbone et al., 2016). Additional benefits include the opportunity for children to make community connections (Carbone et al., 2016). Expanding children's horizons in the community by connecting them to spaces and places supports our vision for children. There are many benefits of early learning programs being connected with local farms and gardens. Figure 7.5, outlines a sampling of the benefits.

Farm-to-preschool is an expansion of the farm-to-school model, which links children to nearby farms (Institute for Agriculture and Trade Policy, 2011).

When children have an opportunity to engage in the cycle of food development—from seeds to harvest—they will be exposed to new food and become aware of the different types of foods that are grown in their communities.

The Process of Harvesting

Introduction of New Foods

Awareness of Regional Foods

Figure 7.5 The benefits of edible gardening with children.
Photos Source: Diane Kashin.

OUR VISION FOR OUTDOOR PLAY

We foresee a time when there will be a merging of approaches and pedagogy in early learning so that inspiration can be derived from multiple sources. Early learning teachers do not have to be pedagogically centric and adhere to the philosophy of only one approach. Take inspiration from the many social movements influencing the world of early learning today. What can you draw from the forest kindergarten and nature preschool movement? What can you glean from the environmental education, natural playground, and adventure play movements? Early learning teachers look to the spaces and places where children play all over the world to find inspiration for their own backyard. Read our vision for outdoor play spaces and places in Photo 7.12. What aspects of our vision aligns with your values and beliefs? What aspects might you develop further or change and why?

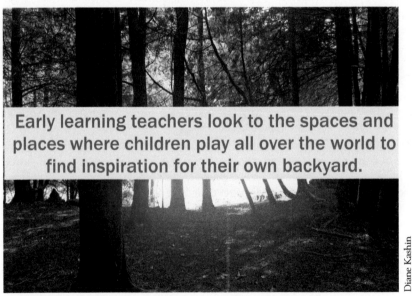

Early learning teachers look to the spaces and places where children play all over the world to find inspiration for their own backyard.

Diane Kashin

Photo 7.12 Vision statement.

POSITIONING OUTDOOR PLAY IN THE LIVES OF CHILDREN

According to Brillante and Mankiw (2015) "most children are born ready and eager to explore their physical world" (p. 3). Gandy (2007) suggested that children start developing their sense of place during the early years. When children explore and manipulate materials in their environment, they are trying to understand the world around them. "Developing this sense of place lets children know that they belong in the physical world around them and in the social and cultural world they share with others" (Brillante & Mankiw, 2015, p. 3). There is a strong connection between developing a sense of place and forming a sense of belonging. As featured in Figure 7.6, developing a sense of belonging in place is different than being in a space (Brillante & Mankiw, 2015).

Developing sense of place is linked to a sense of **belonging**. A sense of belonging relates to a sense of connectedness. Along with well-being, engagement, and expression, a sense of belonging is foundational to learning and development (Ontario Ministry of Education, 2014).

There is an emotional connection with place (Pelo, 2013). Vergeront (2013) described place as where we feel at home, whereas space would be our address. Early learning teachers can be "place-makers" for children (Brillante & Mankiw, 2015, p. 5). Experiences with nature and explorations in the outdoor environment support children in developing relationships with people and places. Brillante and Mankiw (2015) described the importance of a sense of place for children:

> It is important for early childhood educators to understand that early geography experiences, such as actively exploring spaces and manipulating objects in the environment, help children develop cognitive skills and begin to understand the world around them. These experiences are the foundation for understanding our sense of place. Thus, our sense of place relies on both the experiences we have had and the thoroughness of our education. (p. 9)

According to the National Council for the Social Studies (2010), ideally, early learning teachers program with a commitment and responsibility to engendering a sense of place with children. This fosters the formation of children's deep attachments to people and places.

Ralph (1976) stated that one's attitude and connectedness towards place can be divided into **authentic** and **inauthentic**. He described an authentic attitude towards place as something:

> Understood to be a direct and genuine experience of the entire complex of the identity of places—not mediated and distorted through a series of quite arbitrary social and intellectual fashions about how the experience should be, nor following stereotyped conventions. (p. 64)

Children develop a sense of place with nature and the environment from their direct experiences and the opportunities they have to exercise their sense of curiosity. Ralph (1976) described an inauthentic sense of place as the feelings and attitudes that

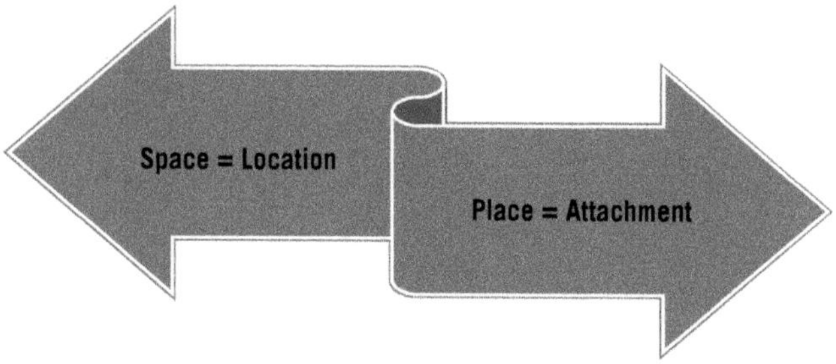

Belonging refers to a sense of connectedness to others and of being valued. It relates to forming relationships with others and making contributions as part of a group, a community, and the natural world (Ontario Ministry of Education, 2014).

Authentic refers to genuine experience.

Inauthentic refers to an experience that is not genuine or lacking reality or sincerity.

Space = Location

Place = Attachment

Figure 7.6 Space and place.

develop when individuals are in environments where stereotypes, rules, and the "taken-for-granted truism" (Hung, 2014) are evident. Ralph further identified that an inauthentic attitude refers to one in which individuals do not have a sense of place nor an appreciation of the place or their identity. From an early learning perspective, early learning teachers ensure that children have choices for expressing their sense of place and in making meaning in it. This requires children to have time, space, and options to explore the open and secret places within the spaces. Such connections are necessary for children to develop a sense of place and caring attitudes toward their environments.

THEORETICAL FOUNDATION

Friedrich Froebel's influence on the mission of contemporary outdoor play and nature movements to change the spaces and places where children play cannot be underestimated. As outlined in Figure 7.7, the distinct features of a Froebel kindergarten are listed. These features are evident in a variety of early learning play spaces today (Sobel, 2016).

The Froebel approach is a way of thinking about children and childhood based on a set of principles. First, the space and teachers within the space are inherently respectful of children and see them as powerful and curious learners with an innate urge to learn. Another key feature is connectedness, as all learning should be meaningful, holistic, and connected to the children's experiences. Play, conversation, and first-hand experiences are central to learning. Creativity is also fundamental with play, imagination, and symbolic representation important features of creativity (Tovey, 2016).

The Froebelian approach emphasizes that children benefit from the freedom to move about and make self-activated choices. The outdoor natural world is essential so that children can "appreciate its wonders and begin to understand the interrelationship between all living things" (Tovey, 2016, p. 3). Relationships are positive, close, and trusting. The role of the early learning teacher is to build on children's positive strengths "extending what they can already do, rather than what they are not yet able to do" (Tovey, 2016, p. 3).

Figure 7.7 Key features of the Froebelian approach.
Source: Tovey (2016).

Early learning teachers influenced by the Froebelian approach facilitate and guide children, creating a democratic and respectful kindergarten community which is closely connected to the wider community of people and places (Tovey, 2016).

Sobel (2016), a well-known writer and researcher in education, is often credited with the development of the philosophy of place-based education. He recognized how Froebel's values are influencing the current movements to get children outside to play. Reflecting on the "academification" and "indoor-ification" of preschool, Sobel (2016) cited forest kindergartens and nature preschools as a "well-needed corrective" (pp. 34 and 35). An advocate for the nature-based early childhood movement, Sobel sees this early bonding to the environment as fundamental for children's well-being and the future of the planet.

》》 BOX 7.2   Featured Theorist—David Sobel

David Sobel is an academic who works at Antioch University, New England in United States. He has written extensively on the topic of children and place. His book *Children's Special Places* examined the role of forts, dens, and bush houses in the lives of children. He described the role these spaces play in children's evolving sense of self and place. In *Childhood and Nature: Design Principles for Educators* (2008) Sobel defined children's play motifs, which are described in Chapter 3. His work has contributed to the movement promoting place-based education.

Sobel (2004) suggested that place-based education involves using the local community and environment as a starting point for children to learn across the curriculum. According to Sobel, hands-on real-world learning increases academic achievement and helps children to develop stronger ties to their communities. These experiences help children develop an appreciation for the natural world and in creating a heightened commitment to serving as active and contributing citizens. Early learning students and teachers recognize even the youngest learner as citizens with rights (Dietze & Kashin, 2016). Understanding place-based education is important to increasing children's exposure and experience with outdoor play and nature pedagogy.

PRACTICAL APPLICATIONS

What can early learning teachers do to bring theory into practice so as to support children's play in spaces and places that are rich in possibility? Whether it is the playground, the forest, or the beach, children require opportunities to have a connection with their environment and early learning outdoor play space. Their "bodies and their senses are tools for discovery, investigation, and understanding" (Banning & Sullivan, 2011, p. 141). One of the roles of early learning teachers is to assist children to interpret, to make sense of their experiences, and to help to extend their thinking by applying what they learn to the next discovery (Banning & Sullivan, 2011). Examine Table 7.3 for examples of how reflection and interpretation may be stimulated from previous outdoor play experiences.

Table 7.3 Standards for outdoor play and learning: reflection, interpretation, and application standard.

Standards for Outdoor Play and Learning: Reflection, Interpretation, and Application Standard
1. The child relates past experience to new situations, generating ideas, increasing understanding, and making predictions.
2. The child speculates and demonstrates a beginning understanding of motivation of intentions and what others are thinking.
3. The child uses play, representation, and discussion to process information and apply ideas.

Source: Banning & Sullivan (2011), *Lens on outdoor learning*. p. 202.

Photo 7.13 Exploring a log and its inhabitants.

Early learning teachers create opportunities for children to make meaning from their experiences by observing, listening closely, and encouraging them to further explore their ideas. Children will want to discuss what they are seeing and experiencing. What do you think the child in Photo 7.13 is seeing? Given the opportunity, children may want to draw, paint, or make representations (Banning & Sullivan, 2011). Such experiences support deeper engagement with place in a variety of ways and with various tools.

PRINCIPLES OF PRACTICE: PLAY-BASED PRACTICE

Place-based education seeks to connect children with their immediate environment and surroundings (Gruenewald & Smith, 2014). The unique characteristics of specific places are important to the learning and the teaching that occurs there. In place-based education, there is a close connection with experiential learning, contextual learning, problem-based learning, constructivism, outdoor education, indigenous education, environmental and ecological education, bioregional education, democratic education, multicultural education, community-based education, and critical pedagogy (Gruenewald, 2003). Place-based education requires the examination of the spaces where children explore and make discoveries as the primary source for learning. Children gain knowledge from their immediate world or their place and then learning opportunities can be expanded outward (Sobel, 2008).

Every place is unique with play and learning possibilities. For example, consider the beach as a place. What pedagogy can be born from this place? Some early learning teachers can access local beaches as places for children to experience and discover. Reflect upon your beach experiences as a child. What emotions do your memories evoke? The beach as place offers children distinctive opportunities that can have lasting emotional connections. Examine Photo 7.14 and think about what possibilities could occur after experiencing play and learning at the beach as place.

The beach offers many possibilities for learning. Imagine collecting and counting rocks or sorting according to colour, shape, or texture. The beach as place affords opportunities for math, science, language, art, and construction play, as depicted in Figure 7.8.

Photo 7.14 The beach as place.

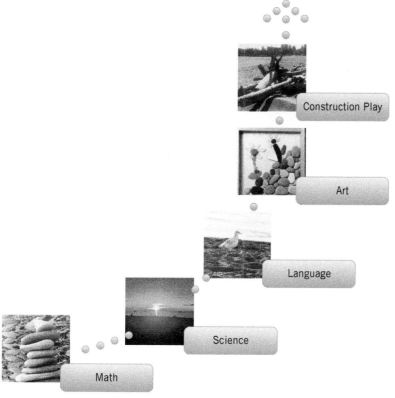

Figure 7.8 The beach as place.

Photos Source: Diane Kashin.

How many rocks can you balance? What are the best rocks for stacking? As children use the materials found at the beach, they engage in math experiences. As the sun goes down, they are observing the science of the sunset. Children can engage with the animals found on the beach by learning new names and creating stories about birds and fish. Rocks and beach glass offer endless possibilities to create transient art, and the driftwood washed up on shore offers opportunities for construction play. Now let's go from the beach to the forest. Do you have childhood memories of being in the forest? Let's consider the forest as place.

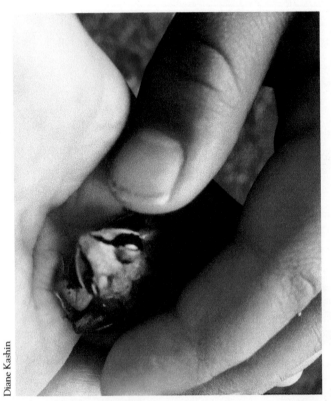

Diane Kashin

Photo 7.15 Caring for a frog.

Place meaning   refers to the emotional connection one attaches to a place.

LEARNING IN PLACE: THE FOREST AS PLACE

Place-based education promotes a relationship with the natural environment for and with children (Lloyd & Gray, 2014). In the forest as place, children will engage with the trees, wildflowers, and frogs. What can the children learn from these experiences? Rafferty (2013) cited examples of how children can learn empathy by handling frogs, wildflowers, and trees. In the forest as place, children develop their ecological identity and learn ecological literacy. Look closely at Photo 7.15 to see how the frog found at a forest school is being handled. What do you see? When children have sustained and continued experiences in the forest, they demonstrate more caring behaviours towards the environment and the animals and insects that they may encounter, than do children in more traditional settings who lack such exposure (Rafferty, 2013).

Cumming and Nash (2015) discovered that not only do children develop a sense of place from their experiences learning in the forest, they also form an emotional attachment to place that contributes to **place meaning**. Place meaning can help to explain why people may be drawn to particular places. What meaning does the forest hold for you? Is it a place to experience peacefulness? Is it a place to experience wonder? Place meaning helps to support the development of place identity and to promote a sense of belonging (Cumming & Nash, 2015).

PROGRAMMING

Small worlds are representations of the world created by children. They contribute to children's imaginative play, language, and social development. The creation of small worlds is a concrete endeavour that helps children to grasp abstract ideas. The many invitations for discovering and creating small worlds are around every corner in the forest. Peering inside the hollow of a tree stump rewards children with a miraculous miniature forest of plants, fungus, and aromas. Using loose parts or newly discovered materials from nature, children descend into fantasy utilizing an artistic, visual language to represent unique understandings of their world. When children create a small world, they use an object to communicate a thought or idea in a meaningful way. They also

Table 7.4 Small worlds and clay creatures.

PLAN	Children are given a small amount of clay and offered a collection of loose parts or invited to find woodland material to create a small creature that they would find in the forest. All that is needed is clay, rocks, pinecones, feathers, sticks, etc.
ENGAGE	As children create their clay creatures, early learning teachers engage in conversation about the personalities, characteristics, and names for each creation. Looking for common characteristics, the children can bring their creatures together to begin to develop a small community or world.
EXPLORE	Children are invited to peek inside the stump of a tree or a rotten log to find homes for the creatures. Loose parts and items found in the woodland can be used to build their own small world.
REFLECT	As the children create their small world to represent a house, hotel, fort, or whatever they choose, early learning teachers document their unfolding narratives and take photos of the creations. Even when the small world is dismantled, the children can examine the documentation and decide to recreate, build onto, or change their representations.

demonstrate the ability to understand the symbolism necessary for manipulating the many symbols they utilize in reading and writing and for mastering the art and language of mathematics. In Table 7.4 the invitation to create clay creatures is illustrated.

Sobel (2004) suggested that when children have an opportunity to play in a woodsy and natural space, they will shape small worlds, as this activity is one of the seven play motifs. As described in Chapter 3, according to Sobel, children love to create miniature worlds. Through creating miniature representations of ecosystems, or neighbourhoods, children conceptually grasp the bigger picture, which provides them with a concrete vehicle for understanding abstract ideas.

FAMILY SUPPORT AND ENGAGEMENT

Families can be the best resources for information about the spaces and places where children can play in the community. What local destinations are in close proximity? What local destinations can be accessed? Early learning teachers share local destinations and their attributers with families. Villanueva et al. (2016) indicated that poor proximity to green spaces has been associated with behavioural problems such as hyperactivity/inattention in children. They found that proximity is important for children and families when deciding whether or not to use neighbourhood green spaces. Children and their families are more likely to use spaces and services located within walking distance of their homes. Proximity to destinations becomes increasingly important as children age, as it is more likely that the place will continue to be part of their lives and have meaning for them (Villanueva et al., 2016).

Early learning teachers have an important role to play in supporting families and children in learning that the benefits of playing and interacting with outdoor spaces and places outweighs the risks (Villanueva et al., 2016). Inviting families to be part of outdoor play excursions support children in having continued access to unique spaces with invaluable play opportunities.

ACCESSIBILITY AND DESIGN

According to Brillante and Mankiw (2015), the outdoor environment plays a role in children's development, including in the attachment stage. When accessible, the space reflects the idea that all children are valued. Their differing abilities and ways of learning are understood and respected. All children and adults require access to inclusive play spaces (Spencer & Wright, 2014). When designing outdoor play spaces, it is important that the surfacing of the play areas and the paths surrounding are accessible. The width of the path and the surface texture is designed to support members of society who require mobility devices such as walkers and wheelchairs (Dietze, 2014; Spencer & Wright, 2014).

All children benefit from outdoor play. Casey (2007) suggested play spaces include lower and higher climbing areas. If children feel anxious or overwhelmed by a busy play space, adding natural features such as shrubs, plants, and trees that provide them with more sheltered and intimate spaces may help them to feel less anxious. An effective outdoor environment supports diverse play behaviours rather than highlighting differences of children in a negative way (Casey, 2007).

TIPS AND TOOLS FOR OUTDOOR PLAY

Landscape architects who specialize in children's outdoor play spaces may be hired to design early learning outdoor play spaces. Changes to outdoor play spaces that will intrigue children do not need to be elaborate. Simple additions to spaces will enhance the places where children play. Early learning students and teachers are encouraged to let the landscape beyond the fence speak to the children. For example, an open field will invite children to run through the field. Sloping hills encourage rolling and sliding. Places where water gathers offer opportunities for puddle play. No matter what the outdoor play elements are, they have some play value. We offer nine tips to facilitate possibilities outdoors.

1. Get to know the area on your own before bringing children to a particular place.
2. Find someone with knowledge of nature or utilize a nature app or identification book to learn about and identify the plants and animals in that place.
3. Assess the place for risky play and hazards. See Chapter 6 for more on risk assessments. Hazards such as broken glass can be removed or plants such as poison ivy can be fenced off.
4. Ensure children have the appropriate clothing. If possible, maintain a supply of extra clothing so that children have the right clothing for the space and the weather.
5. Let the children learn their boundaries and discover the place on their own the first time they go to the space.
6. Decide on a consistent schedule for going out to visit the place. Make sure there is sufficient time to walk there and play there. Consider going there on a regular basis, such as every Wednesday or Friday. You could have "Woodsy Wednesdays" or "Forest Friday" or any name relevant to the place.
7. Communicate with families about the space through posters, newsletters, emails, and social media posts and provide information about dressing for the weather and the conditions of the place and the play.
8. Let the children play and explore. Create invitations that support children's learning and inquiry. Chapter 9 will offer some of these tips and tools. When the moment is appropriate, seize on opportunities to share the names and identities of the plants and animals in the place.
9. Push through initial feelings of nervousness and reluctance displayed by some early learning students and teachers. Recognize that these feelings are not unusual. Just go outside, engage in the special places, reflect upon your dispositions, and think about how you may develop or deepen your passion and love for outdoor play!

ON THE GROUND—PROFESSIONAL REFLECTIONS: "WHY I LOVE OUTDOOR PLAY"

> ## BOX 7.3   Why I Love Outdoor Play
>
> The forest is most magical! The moment we enter our 'Forest Door' and place on our forest hat, that is when the transformation begins. Children who can't speak for fear of being wrong suddenly find their voice, and those that can't sit still find comfort and calm at their 'sit-spot'. Trees have a way with us. From the moment the children enter the forest, it's almost like they flip a switch. Communication, risk-taking, team building, engineering, exploration, and positive social relationships become natural. It never ceases to amaze me what children can do when you remove the barriers of the classroom! The forest is the ultimate adventure playground. I couldn't plan a play space better than what the forest can naturally provide. There are trees to climb, hills to roll and run up or down, and sticks to challenge an alien to a duel
>
> or build an amazing teepee. There are bushes to hide in, a stream to catch frogs and water striders, felled logs to search for salamanders—all provoking our sense of wonder. My students exercise their vestibular, proprioceptive, social, emotional, cognitive, biological, and prosocial development every day in the forest. There is no classroom with walls that could duplicate this learning! In short the forest is the ultimate classroom. The forest and children's self-regulation are like peas and carrots. They are best served together.
>
> **Gail Molennar**
> **Early Learning Teacher**
> Used with permission from Gail Molenaar, Early childhood Educator (RECE).

CASE STUDIES

Read Case Study 7.2 that describes how an early learning program transformed their play space. This case study is from the perspective of Heather, who is the director of the program. Heather has been working in the early learning sector for many years and has come to realize that collaboration with families and teachers is the key to success. Read about how she was able to create a shared vision for the space being transformed. After you are finished reading the case study, look at Photo 7.16 before answering the questions.

Photo 7.16 Transforming space–sunflower school.

We are located in a commercial building. When we moved into the space, the playground was pavement. We were perplexed as to what to do with this space. We wanted a natural playground for our children with loose parts and gardens. We had restrictions: we could not dig up the asphalt and we could not install anything to the surface. Not knowing what to do, we decided to wait to see how the children used the space with only loose parts. We watched for 18 months as children rolled tires, spools, and balls down the natural incline of our space. In the spring, after many days of rain, I watched the rain water run into a sewer just outside playground. At that moment I knew what needed to be done—a water feature! This water feature would be the focal point of the space. We were ready to start planning for our space. The whole early learning team worked together on the plan, and we included the children's suggestions. The teachers wanted gardens, and the children wanted an outdoor pool. We secured some funding from our municipality for outdoor artificial grass and received funds for a professional to create for us a blueprint for the water feature. A local garden centre helped create the water feature concept. I then contacted five landscape companies for a quote to install the water feature and all them said that we needed to dig up the asphalt. Instead, I went back to the garden centre and they suggested purchasing recycled rubber garden edging, black pond tarp, and many bags of stones. The rubber edging was glued to the pavement from the location of the water source (outdoor tap) to the sewer seven metres away. The width of the feature was two metres. The edging was reinforced with landscape glue. The black pond tarp was also glued in place and then the stones were placed into the body of the water feature. This construction took about three hours, and I was overjoyed when I turned on the water for the first time and it flowed

to the sewer. From there we went on to create the entire outdoor space, over a two day-weekend with the help of families and friends. It truly was a collaborative effort. We built large planter boxes and decks for our toddlers to climb on and sit upon for picnics; we installed sun sails for shade and added artificial grass to various spots on the playground; we even provided a boat for our pirates. Over the past two years we have become very creative with our outdoor space—we have now added branches (which we cemented into a planter box) and ivy (which has grown around the branches) to give the appearance of a large tree that gives off shade, vegetable gardens, a bean plant teepee for shelter and shade, and 35 milk crates which are used to build everything from a fire truck to a submarine. The water feature is now officially called "The River." The river is used every day by the children. They build bridges across it with the many different building materials we have been able to collect, jump over it to escape the crocodiles, float boats on it, and play with the stones. We have been able to stop the water from running into the sewer with a dam, and we release the water when the fun is finished. This play space was created with a vision for something different for the children. We believe you should not be limited to the physical space and that if you are a creative thinker you can create your own beautiful outdoor play space.

1. Notice the upper left quadrant of Photo 7.16 to see the beginning of the transformation. What do you think were steps taken by the Director to engage families and friends in helping with the transformation of this space?
2. What elements were included in the outdoor play space?
3. What might children do in this space?
4. What else could be added to this space?

>> BOX 7.4 | **Take It Outside!**

Find a spot in nature close to your home or work. Take time over the course of a month to visit that same spot. Each time you go there, look closely to notice details and changes. After you have visited frequently, see if you can conjure up an image and the feel of the spot when you are not there. You have made a connection to place! Think about how you can give children this same emotional connection.

KEY TERMS

There are a number of key words used in this chapter on spaces and places. Photo 7.17 depicts these significant terms.

Playground movement
Nature preschools
Environmental education
Forest kindergartens
Sense of place
Open-ended play
Maker movement
Play rangers
Farm-to-preschool
Belonging
Authentic
Inauthentic
Place meaning

Photo 7.17 Key terms.

Summary

- Natural outdoor settings have been under-utilized in early childhood education. Early learning teachers may lack experience with the affordances of these settings. Educational theorists such as Froebel, Dewey, Montessori, Steiner, Rousseau, and Malaguzzi all emphasized the role of experiences in nature in young children's development and well-being.

- The kindergarten movement brought with it Froebel's emphasis on the importance of nature. As social reformers became concerned about the needs of children living in urban environments, the playground movement began. The playground movement included the installation of manufactured play equipment in public spaces.

- The playground movement evolved into a safe playground movement. Guidelines were established and playground equipment was removed. The Canadian Standards Association (CSA) set standards for children's play spaces and equipment that were designed to minimize risk and injury. As learning centres and schools began to comply with these standards, playgrounds changed from having swings, teeter totters, and merry-go-rounds, to ones that were sterile but safe. These playgrounds may not consider the developmental benefits of children's risk-taking.

■ Today, children are less active and less connected to nature. Their lack of opportunity to play outdoors and access to nature is sparking a new outdoor play movement. Forest and nature schools are part of this movement.

■ There is a growing movement to naturalize playgrounds. Early learning students and teachers have a role to play by consistently creating spaces that allow for children to get the most play value and opportunity from their outdoor environments.

■ Programs with an ecological focus are often called eco-schools. Early learning settings can learn from the seven-step process of becoming an eco-school or in becoming more ecologically aware.

■ Adventure playgrounds are spaces totally dedicated to children that support their health, creativity, and learning. Pop-up adventure play spaces are designed to demonstrate that adding adventure play to existing outdoor environments can be possible in many different places.

■ Gardens as place provide children with multiple play and learning experiences. Food gardens allow children to observe and take part in the wonders of growing food. Playing in gardens that yield food provides opportunities for children to develop one of their hundred languages—the language of food.

■ Developing sense of place is linked to a sense of belonging. A sense of belonging relates to a sense of connectedness. Early learning teachers can be "place-makers" for children. Experiences with nature and explorations in the outdoor environment support children in developing relationships with people and places.

■ David Sobel, an environmental educator and advocate, recognized how Froebel's values are influencing the current movements to get children outside to play. Sobel sees early bonding to the environment as fundamental, suggesting that place-based education is a crucial starting point for children to learn about their environment including, people, place, and things within their environment.

■ Early learning teachers help children to interpret, make sense of their experiences, and extend their thinking by applying what they learn to the next discovery.

■ The unique characteristics of specific places are important to the learning and the teaching that occurs there. Every place is unique with play and learning possibilities.

■ The beach offers many possibilities for learning. The beach as place affords opportunities for math, science, language, art, and construction play. In the forest as place, children will engage with the trees, wildflowers, and frogs. When children have sustained and continued experiences in the forest, they demonstrate more caring behaviours towards the environment and the animals and insects that they may encounter, than do children in more traditional settings who lack such exposure.

■ Not only do children develop a sense of place from their experiences learning in the forest, they also form an emotional attachment to place that contributes to place meaning. Place meaning can help to explain why people may be drawn to particular places. Small worlds are representations of the world created by children. They contribute to children's imaginative play, language, and social development. When children have an opportunity to play in a woodsy and natural space, they will shape small worlds, as this activity is one of the seven play motifs.

■ Families can be the best resources for information about the spaces and places where children can play in the community. . Early learning teachers share local destinations and their attributes with families. Early learning teachers have an important role to play in supporting families and children in learning that the benefits of playing and interacting with outdoor spaces and places outweigh the risks.

- The outdoor environment plays a role in children's development, including in the attachment stage. When accessible, the space reflects the idea that all children are valued. Their differing abilities and ways of learning are understood and respected. When designing outdoor play spaces, it is important to consider accessibility because all children benefit from outdoor play.

QUIET REFLECTION

Spend time thinking about your childhood memories of place and space. Think about the feelings that you associate with indoor and outdoor spaces. Is there a particular place to which you feel the most emotionally connected? List the factors that contributed to these feelings, while considering the people who shared this space and the things that happened in this place.

COMMUNITY DIALOGUE

With others, enter in a dialogue about the places of your childhood. Describe them in detail to each other and then draw a diagram of what you remember. What was significant about this place to you? After each of your group has shared their childhood spaces, discuss ways that you could bring some of the spirit of these places to children.

FOR FURTHER THOUGHT AND ACTION

The Canadian Parks Council has published a *Nature Playbook*. This book is a strategy to connect children with nature in Canada. It is meant to guide and inspire actions that all Canadians can take to make sure that present and future generations make connections to nature. You can find the Nature Playbook and related communication tools at the following site: http://www.parks-parcs.ca/english/nature-playbook.php

RESOURCES

The following resource will provide more information on accessible play spaces:

https://www.rickhansen.com/Our-Work/School-Program/Accessible-Play-Spaces

To support children in developing a sense of place, this resource will be helpful:

https://www.naeyc.org/system/files/YC0715_Brillante.pdf

To learn about how to manage places where children engage in nature, read this set of guidelines:

https://naturelearning.org/nature-play-and-learning-places-creating-and-managing-places-where-children-engage-nature

CHAPTER 8

Sustainability and First Nations—Teachings

To waste, to destroy our natural resources, to skin and exhaust the land instead of using it so as to increase its usefulness, will result in undermining in the days of our children the very prosperity which we ought by right to hand down to them amplified and developed.

Theodore Roosevelt (1858–1919)

LEARNING OUTCOMES

After exploring this chapter, you will be able to:

- Describe the complexity of environmental sustainability as it relates to early learning programs.

- Discuss how Indigenous values support environmental sustainability practices.

- Outline ways in which early learning teachers can support children in becoming stewards of the environment.

- Outline Urie Bronfenbrenner's ecological theory.

- Describe what is meant by holistic experiences.

CHILDHOOD MEMORIES

When we were young, our dad would take us for walks in the woods. We had one particular route that we loved to go on. On this route the tree branches were tall enough for us to slip under, which meant we could run ahead, hide, and then yell "Boo!" as our dad approached our location. Our dad knew lots about the woods. He could tell when it was going to rain because of the ways in which the leaves were blowing. He knew what kind of a winter we would have because of the amount of food that the squirrels gathered in the fall. He helped us learn all the names of the different bugs, such as spiders, and he taught us how to extract the spruce gum from the trees just at the right time. He showed us where animals lived—those that burrowed holes in the ground for safety and those that found open space to sleep. Even though he gave us the freedom to smell, feel, and connect with the beauty of the woods, we learned early to look for seedlings and honour them. He taught us how to lift branches so that we did not hurt the trees, and he modelled where and how to protect the moss or forest floor. I love thinking of those memories and most of all, realize that my dad instilled in us the importance of taking care of the environment so that it will be available for the next generation.

CHAPTER PREVIEW

Young children are curious, inquisitive, and active (North American Association for Environmental Education (NAAEE), 2010). Adult role models influence children's desire to explore, discover, and care for their environments. For example, when children have opportunities to have sticks from the forest floor, they may choose to use them to make marks in the mud, make music on the rocks, create frames for nature collages, or incorporate them in superhero play. Natural experiences provide children with a combination of "rich sensory stimuli, as well as the opportunity for sensory integration processes critical to development in early childhood" (Ernst, 2014, p. 739). These experiences contribute to children developing an appreciation of how outdoor environments provide options for new experiences and discovery (Ernst, 2014).

Hedefalk, Almqvist, and Ostman (2015) identified that "today, children are born into a world where climate change, poverty, pollution, C02 emissions and loss of biological diversity are major global issues" (p. 975). As climate and environmental changes occur, there is a growing body of contemporary literature that suggests **environmental sustainability** is an emerging concept in early learning programs. For example, Redman (2013) identified that "achieving a sustainable future requires that individuals adopt sustainable behaviours, which are often learned and cemented at a young age" (p. 1). For children to become stewards of the environment, they require opportunities to engage in explorations with nature in multiple ways. The array of experiences that they have contributes to their building of knowledge and skills related to their environment and their ability to care for it (Redman, 2013). Children who are exposed to and encouraged to practice sustainability concepts have the potential to advance changing attitudes, values, and behaviours toward sustainable practices (Kellert, 2005). They will become our best ambassadors for the care of all aspects of the environment (Edwards & Cutter-Mackenzie, 2011).

Environmental education is not new (Hedefalk, Almqvist, & Ostman, 2015). Similarly, traditional ecological knowledge and wisdom is not new but is now becoming a major focus in literature associated with early learning programs and outdoor play (Turner, Ignace, & Ignace, 2000; Haas & Ashman, 2014). Based on a variety of research available on the evolution of environmental education, Dietze & Kashin (2016) documented the progression of environmental education in early learning programs (see Figure 8.1 and Table 8.1). As you will note, the focus of the recommendations for the current decade is for early learning teachers to engage with children, families, and communities to collectively determine the types of environmental practices that will be pursued.

> Environmental sustainability refers to the caring practices that are used to contribute to sustaining a quality environment on a long-term basis.

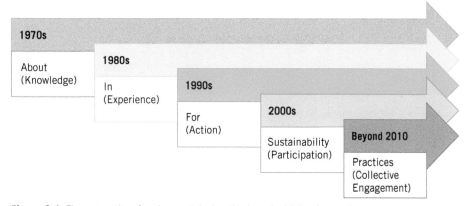

Figure 8.1 The progression of environmental education in early childhood education programs.

Table 8.1 The evolution of environmental education.

Knowledge Transfer (1970s)	Experience (1980s)
Early learning programs were encouraged to provide children with information on such topics as where water comes from through exposure to science books and charts.	Children were encouraged to participate in experiences and learning in their natural environment. However, outdoor play was being scaled back in favour of experiences oriented towards academic preparation.
Action (1990s)	**Participation (2000s)**
Early learning programs began taking action with the children. They were encouraged to plant trees, recycle paper, and contribute to reducing food waste. Discussions occurred about the types of actions that could support keeping the environment healthy. This was a forerunner to sustainability.	Children and early learning teachers increased outdoor play and the use of loose parts.

Collective Engagement (Beyond 2010)

Children, families, and early learning teachers are being encouraged to collectively move toward increasing experiences in natural environments, view the beauty of the earth, and develop practices that reduce negative footprints to the environment.

Increased engagement on learning about how Indigenous ways of knowing and the environment can benefit and influence practices by all citizens.

Child-orientated perspective refers to adults empowering children to make choices, have freedom to play, and encouraging them to use their preferred approach to experimenting with new ideas and concepts in their play.

Environmental pedagogy refers to the access, opportunities, and experiences extended to children in their natural environments—from the forest, to under the trees, to exploring bugs or ponds.

Ecosystem refers to the interaction among a community of living organisms in conjunction with nonliving components of the environment.

As outlined by Engdahl (2015), early learning teachers who adopt a **child-orientated perspective** use children's day-to-day living experiences, including in their places and spaces that are safe, enticing, and special for children, to learn about their environment and sustainability practices. As identified by Keeler (2008), "beauty and surprise should be the bases of every child's environment—every direction a child looks at should be filled with materials and structures that inspire curiosity and delight" (p. 51). Early learning teachers and families collectively connect and embrace outdoor play opportunities that enhance children's desire to play and engage with their environment. Dietze & Kashin (2016) suggested that early learning teachers develop an environmental pedagogy. They described **environmental pedagogy** as strategies that are used to support young children in learning about and experiencing how natural environments function, and particularly how children and adults can embrace sustainable practices and care for the **ecosystems** that are encountered.

Early learning teachers think about environmental sustainability as a pedagogy in broad terms, drawing on literature from a variety of resources. This will support early learning teachers in creating strategies, environments, and experiences that contribute to children developing skills and knowledge that are foundational to, and fundamental in, sustaining and improving their natural and social environments (Haas & Ashman, 2014). For example, children in early learning programs require experiences to get their feet wet,

THINK ABOUT IT! READ ABOUT IT! WRITE ABOUT IT!

Indigenous wholistic theory is based on the principles of whole, ecological, cyclical, and relational. The Medicine Wheel, Four Directions, and Circles are interconnected to the nature and the environment. Read Kathy Absolon's article on Indigenous Wholistic Theory at https://fncaringsociety.com/sites/default/files/online-journal/vol5num2/Absolon_pp74.pdf

What does this mean for you when working with children? What aspects of the article inform your practice as you think about children and nature?

Figure 8.2 Elements of a pedagogy of environmental sustainability.

Environmental
Stewardship

Social
Awareness
and Progress

Socio-
Economic
Processes

Sustainability

Indigenous knowledges refers to the ideas, cultural knowledges, values, belief systems, and worldviews of local peoples related to their environments. Indigenous knowledges are transferred from Elders to the younger generation.

Elders refer to individuals who have gained recognition as custodians of knowledge, and who have permission to share knowledge and beliefs.

Coming-to-know refers to connecting with people who connect with and support the exploration of new learning. This may include engaging in a journey or process together, and a reflective process that contributes to deep thinking.

slide on ice, run on grass, follow insects, hold a worm, and climb a tree (NAAEE, 2010). Such experiences connect children to their sense of place and characteristics of their lived environment. As outlined in Figure 8.2, a pedagogy of environmental sustainability includes environmental stewardship, social awareness and progress, social-economic processes, and sustainability practices. Aspects of these elements will be discussed throughout the chapter. As well, we will draw upon traditional ecological literature. The term Indigenous is used throughout the chapter.

As outlined earlier in Table 8.1, there is an increased awareness occurring in many sectors about how we as a society benefit from learning about **Indigenous knowledges** and pedagogies in environmental programs (Sutherland & Swayze, 2012). Sutherland & Swayze (2012) identified that Indigenous cultures and practices are based on a reverence for the natural world. They identified that **Elders** have a significant role in "shar [ing] traditional cultural teachings, exposing students to a worldview that recognizes the intrinsic value and interdependence of all living things" (p. 89). Lefleur (2014) described "Elders are seen as those who have accumulated knowledge, who have answers, or who know how to do things according to tradition" (p. 28). Their connections to their peoples and the land are foundational to the knowledge and values that they share.

Indigenous philosophies provide an additional framework that can guide early learning programs in reconnecting children with nature and creating environments that model respect and responsibility to the environment and to the living parts of the environment. Sutherland & Swayze (2012) suggested that Indigenous knowledges and pedagogies are based on a framework that incorporates the interactions and interconnections among Elders, language, culture, and experimental learning. They identified that learning about science and the environment requires a holistic approach that supports children in **coming-to-know** by having as illustrated in Photo 8.1, experiences that are culturally relevant and related to social and ecological justice, and ecological literacy.

Michelle Taylor-Leonhardi

Photo 8.1 Children require experiences that are culturally relevant.

Photo 8.2 Ways in which children learn about their environments.

Professional learning refers to engaging in activities or experiences with others that help to improve knowledge about and skills in working with children.

Inquiry-led pedagogy refers to the play and learning process that occurs in environments designed for children to experience a sense of wonder and opportunities to investigate their questions, ideas, and theories.

Building on the premise that children are engaged learners, Engdahl (2015) identified that they "have the right to be involved in issues that concern life here, now and in the future" (p. 363). She suggested that early learning teachers benefit from determining how they bring together children, families, and communities to develop cultural identities within a social and ecological framework (Engdahl, 2015).

For many early learning teachers, incorporating environmental practices into programming may be a new experience (Ernst, 2014). Like any change, changing programming strategies is most successful when early learning teachers use a gradual process to incorporate new knowledge into practice. Implementing changes to practice can be fragile. A sustained investment of time and **professional learning** for any change to be long term (Nicholson, Baurer, & Woolley, 2016) is necessary. Think about children in early learning programs. How might you introduce them to sustainable practices? How might you bring storytelling about the land and conservation into their environments? Examine Photo 8.2. What types of materials might be placed in children's environments to stimulate discussions about their environment? How might the materials placed in the environment stretch children's knowledge about their environment? Drawing on the understanding of Indigenous learners' ways of learning, Delpit (1995) asserted that to be effective role models for children, adults, including early learning teachers, must *really know* the children. Early learning teachers observe and make the connections with children and families to gain insight into what knowledge they bring to the setting, and "how their cultural practices, values and beliefs shape them as learners, and, as producers of knowledge" (Delpit, 1995, p. 183). Early learning teachers respect the fact that children and families have their own ways of learning, understanding of their world, lived experiences, and ways in which they connect and communicate with each other (Santoro, Reid, Crawford, & Simpson, 2011).

There are many definitions used to describe sustainability and sustainable development. One of the most popular definitions, despite being more than 25 years old, was documented by the World Commission on Environment and Development in 1987, in what became known as the Brundtland Report. The Commission defined sustainable development as "meet[ing] the needs of the present without compromising the ability of future generations to meet their own needs" (WCED, 1987, p. 43). Drawing on the work of Brundtland (1988), Hedefalk, Almqvist and Ostman (2014) defined sustainable development as "development that meets the needs of the present without compromising the ability of future generations to meet their own needs" (p. 975). Sustainable practices within early learning programs focus on supporting children in learning about their natural environment, as well as society and culture (Hedefalk, Almqvist, & Ostman, 2015).

Early learning teachers are encouraged to review and adopt a definition of sustainability and sustainability practices to guide their practice. Understanding the context of various definitions is fundamental for early learning teachers in creating a framework that guides them in why and how they embed sustainability practices into their programming decisions and modelling processes. Ideally, early learning teachers provide children with the opportunities to learn about their natural world, emphasize how to foster caring for others and their environment, and be responsible citizens with a genuine concern for the world they live in. Modelling a culture of **inquiry-led pedagogy** is an ideal approach that contributes to children discovering new knowledge about their environments.

Children benefit from environments where they experience a sense of wonder, curiosity, and concern for their natural world (Dietze & Kashin, 2016). Further information on inquiry-led pedagogy will be presented in-depth in Chapter 9.

Environmental Sustainability

The environmental conditions and continuous changes that children today will experience are significantly different from what children of 20 years ago experienced (Hedefalk, Almqvist, & Ostman, 2015). The increased concerns related to climate change, water quality and water shortages, treatments of environments, food security, and consumption of goods cross disciplines and are topics of concern in the fields of health, political science, and education (Dyment et al., 2014). Hedefalk, Almqvist and Ostman (2014) articulated that there is a strong need to "educate children to learn how to act in a sustainable way" (p. 975), from a very young age. Yet, Dyment et al. (2014) suggested that although the timing is right to embed sustainability actions into early learning programs, early learning teachers have limited exposure to the types of sustainability content or pedagogical processes that could support early learning programming. They determined that early learning teachers have an obligation to gain the knowledge, skills, and programing strategies that make sustainability transparent in their daily programs.

The terms *reduce, reuse,* and *recycle* are now ingrained in many Canadian communities and cultures. As outlined in Figure 8.3, the 7 Rs of sustainable practices are interconnected (Hedefalk, Almqvist, & Ostman, 2014). These are concepts that could be effective in guiding early learning teachers in sustainable practices.

UNESCO (2005) identified three integrated sustainable pillars that influence each other. The sustainable pillars are social-cultural, economic, and environmental. The pillars are positioned to interrelate to the 7 Rs and are viewed as foundational for sustainable development. Kahriman-Ozturk, Olgan, and Guler (2012) documented the pillars from an overall

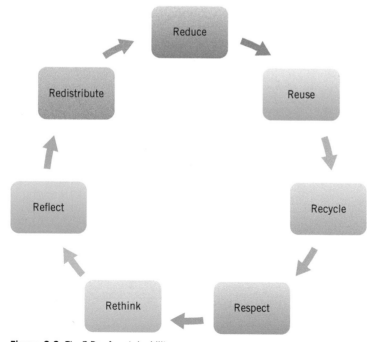

Figure 8.3 The 7 Rs of sustainability.

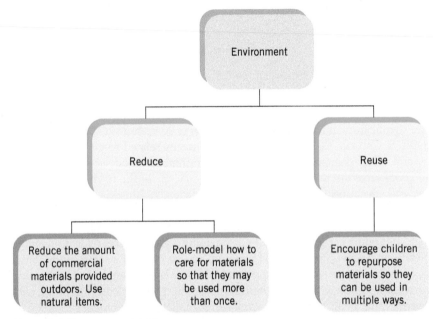

Figure 8.4 The environmental pillar.

societal perspective. As outlined in Figures 8.4, 8.5, and 8.6, Dietze and Kashin (2016) added to the descriptors to illustrate how the three pillars could support early learning practices.

As part of sustainable practices, early learning teachers discuss with the children the use of natural items in their play. They engage in discussions about ethical considerations in using the materials, collecting materials, and determining what may and may not be removed from the outdoor space. For example, early learning teachers and children may discuss picking wild flowers. Should they pick them for the classroom or let the flowers live out their natural life cycle? Similarly, if there are insects that children are interested in exploring, should they create a habitat while they explore them and then return them to the natural environment,

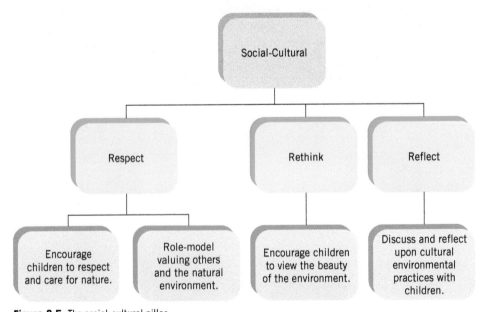

Figure 8.5 The social-cultural pillar.

```
                    ┌─────────────┐
                    │  Economical │
                    └─────────────┘
                           │
             ┌─────────────┴─────────────┐
      ┌─────────────┐            ┌─────────────┐
      │   Recycle   │            │ Redistribute│
      └─────────────┘            └─────────────┘
             │                          │
   ┌──────────────────┐      ┌──────────────────┐
   │ Support children │      │ Encourage children│
   │ in learning how to│     │ to examine ways in │
   │ sort waste and   │      │ which they can share│
   │ use materials in │      │ natural materials  │
   │ multiple ways.   │      │ with others.       │
   └──────────────────┘      └──────────────────┘
```

Figure 8.6 The economic pillar.

or do the early learning teachers use other strategies to support children in learning about the insects? Many of these decisions are influenced by the early learning teacher's perspective on learning about and caring for the environment (NAAEE, 2010).

Examine the environmental pillar. What might be modelled to support the concepts of reduce and reuse in outdoor environments? Think about when children are engaged in using leaves, branches, or pine cones that have fallen to the ground. How might children begin to understand that tree cookies and tree stumps have been repurposed from trees that were previously growing in the forest or their neighbourhood? Then think about how more natural products, such as tables made from wood rather than plastic support and model environmental practices.

Photo 8.3 Early learning teachers influence children's experiences.

The social-cultural pillar is strongly influenced by children's role models. For example, reflect back to Chapter 4 on loose parts. Think about how loose parts influence children engaging in discoveries together. As well, think about how children learn many aspects of risk-taking play from the observations they make of their peers. Imagine what happens when children are exposed to new aspects of nature, such as viewing frogs in ponds, and how collective discussions contribute to them gaining new knowledge about the frogs. Later in the chapter you will read about fire pits and their importance to children's development. Early learning teachers promote and focus on respecting nature and encouraging participation, **emancipation**, equality, and fairness amongst individuals and groups of children and adults.

Emancipation refers to children having a sense of freedom and the ability to explore and discover without boundaries set by adults.

From an early learning programming perspective, the economic pillar encompasses the lifecycle of all measureable goods and services consumed within the program, including the promotion of recycling and reducing waste (McNichol, Davis, & O'Brien, 2011). For example, the more time children spend outdoors, the less electricity is used indoors (McNichol et al., 2011). Children may be provided with a variety of alternative surfaces for drawing on outdoors such as the fences or rocks, rather than paper sources. For many families who emphasize environmentally sustainable practices, they may prefer to be given a digital photo of the children's creation on the fence or rocks rather than art work on paper that they will be required to recycle (McNicol et al., 2011).

In the document, *Pathways to Stewardship: A Framework for Children and Youth* (2016), the authors provide a framework for stewardship **benchmarks** for young children. As outlined in Table 8.2, Dietze and Kashin (2016) adapted the framework to combine and align it with outdoor play experiences and environmental stewardship. Many of the stewardship

Benchmarks refer to processes used to measure or judge the quality or level of a practice in comparison to an established practice.

Table 8.2 A framework for stewardship.

Stewardship Principle	Benchmark	Possible Experience
Children develop an appreciation for play in green spaces as they: ■ Experience outdoor play in a variety of green spaces and soil conditions. ■ Are encouraged to use their sense of curiosity and wonderment in their play. ■ Are given time and opportunities to experience imaginative play and exploration in the space. ■ Experience outdoor play in all kinds of weather and in all seasons.	■ Children are given access to the outdoor space on a regular basis. ■ Children are given time to engage in the exploration of the space.	■ Children collect items in the space. They touch, smell, and observe items, such as worms and bugs, butterflies, and leaves. ■ Children are given the freedom to climb, jump, run, and experience. ■ Children hear positive and affirming language from role models. ■ Children lead the ideas, experiences, and discoveries.
Children develop positive experiences with plants, animals, and insects to help them to understand life cycles and the needs of other living things. Children: ■ Are encouraged to develop and exhibit respect for all living things. ■ Gain support from adults through the use of a variety of "what and why" questions that help to develop an awareness of life cycles and needs of other living creatures.	■ Children are in environments where they are encouraged to engage with animals and plants on a regular basis throughout the seasons.	■ Children engage in feeding the birds. ■ Children adopt a tree and plant gardens. ■ Children go on animal hunts to see or hear birds, squirrels, worms, and related creatures.
Children engage in connecting with the environment through their senses as they: ■ Are encouraged to use their five senses and imagination to explore and make connections with their outdoor environments. ■ Experience the smells, tastes, sights, temperatures, sounds, and beauty of the outdoor spaces.	■ The outdoor environment provides children with the opportunity to use a variety of their senses daily.	■ Children use natural items such as pine cones, rocks, and fallen leaves in their play. ■ Children engage in sound walks, rainy-day excursions, and community discoveries. ■ Sensory gardens are planted and cared for. ■ Children document their discoveries with cameras and through art.
Children develop a sense of awe and wonderment of their outdoor play spaces and places as they: ■ Determine the types of outdoor play experiences that they will engage in based on space, materials, and peers. ■ Are encouraged to explore natural aspects of their environment such as shadows, puddles, snow, ice, blooming flowers, and natural climbing areas.	■ The outdoor play space is accessible to children in all kinds of weather and for long durations. ■ Adults support children's explorations of the environment.	■ Children have intriguing spaces to explore. ■ Curiosity triggers from the environment are displayed in various outdoor play areas. ■ Documentation is developed with the children and displayed outdoors. ■ Environmental literacy ideas such as words, explorations, and stories are displayed in the outdoor environment. ■ Children lead the ideas, experiences, and discoveries.

principles can be achieved through an inquiry-based and emergent approach to programming rather than teacher-planned activities.

SETTING THE STAGE FOR OUTDOOR PLAY

The research on environments, sustainability practices, natural play spaces, early learning programming models, and roles of early learning teachers are at the crossroads (Ernst, 2014). As outlined in a policy document by UNESCO (2005), "early childhood education for sustainability is much more than environmental education. It should be broader than simply taking children outdoors to discover the beauty of nature and speaking about the natural environment" (p. 12). Ideally, there will be some major shifts to the experiences and the attitudes associated with the consumptions of products that children are exposed to (McNichol et al., 2011). The shifts will depend on how early learning teachers role-model sustainability. How adults practise and role-model attention to the environment will become the drivers of change for the next generation. For example, if planting gardens and trees were to become a standard in early learning programs, children would have the opportunity to learn about the importance of sun, rain, wind, and growth processes in a natural environment. Early learning teachers may wish to rethink how water play is presented to children so that sustainable practices are evident and discussed. A change in practice may include supporting children to continue to have this sensory experience while extending discussions about exposing them to new knowledge and problem solving about water conservation. Early learning teachers may adjust their thinking about children having access to lots of loose parts, even though they may look messy in the play space. They balance the messy look with the play value that children gain from loose parts.

Early learning teachers are required to embrace making changes that support children in having new environmental experiences and in developing an appreciation for the outdoor environments. This may begin by early learning teachers developing a deep understanding of the research and the types of strategies that are effective in promoting learning, innovation in thinking, and responsible environmental modelling (Ferrerira & Davis, 2015; Dyment et al., 2014; Haas & Ashman, 2014).

THINK ABOUT IT! READ ABOUT IT! WRITE ABOUT IT!

What does your vision for environmental sustainability looks like? Do you have it clearly defined? Put "environmental sustainability in early childhood education programs" into a search engine. Read and review a few of the articles. Create a design that depicts how you would describe your image for practice. Share with your peers. What are the differences and what are the similarities?

CURIOUS?

Do you want to know more about what your curriculum framework says about environmental expectations? Search for the curriculum framework for your province/territory and see if environmental sustainability is identified. Is it evident? What does this tell you about our desire to influence the next generation?

Photo 8.4 Children benefit from having role models to support them in learning about the environment.

As outlined by Ernst (2014), early childhood is the most critical time for children to develop a "sense of respect and an ethic of care for the natural environment" (p. 738). The attitudes developed early in life become foundational for many of the lifelong attitudes and values that are and will be exhibited about our environment (Hedefalk, Almqvist, & Ostman, 2015). Within the Australian early learning curriculum framework, there are a number of identified outcomes specific to environmental expectations. For example, "educators [are] to foster children's capacity to understand and respect the natural environment and the interdependence between people, plants, animals and the land" (DEEWR, 2009, p. 14). As shown in Photo 8.4, children are required to have opportunities to "interact in relation to others and the natural world with care, empathy and respect" (DEEWR, 2009, p. 14). As well, children are encouraged to "become socially responsible and show respect for the environment" (DEEWR, 2009, p. 29). How might these types of outcomes be adapted for all early learning programs?

Developing children's and adult's dispositions so that they feel empowered to think critically and be fully connected with their outdoor surroundings requires attention (Ernst, 2014). Dyment et al. (2014) suggested that one of the challenges in repositioning early learning programs towards an emphasis on environments is in part the attitudes that early learning teachers have toward their current practice. In their study, Dyment et al. found that "many early childhood educators think that they are already implementing education for sustainability, because the early education field has traditionally considered playing in nature to be a fundamental plank of early childhood education" (p. 672). As more nature-based programs develop, it is important to recognize that playing in nature is only a beginning step toward addressing the contemporary environmental issues associated with the environmental, social, and economic domains (Dyment et al., 2014). Environmental sustainability is more than playing in nature.

Photo 8.5 Children learn about their environment by engaging with its elements.

There are many ways to develop positive dispositions about the environment, starting with the early learning teacher. Ernst (2014) identified that the beginning point toward refiguring dispositions is by reducing the perceptions that access to natural outdoor play settings, such as large parks or forests, is required. In Table 8.3, Ernst outlined some of the barriers that need to be addressed and recommendations to manage the barriers.

Ernst (2014) suggested that there are misconceptions that environmental pedagogy can occur only in nature-based programs. She identified that some early learning teachers who do not work in nature-based programs have perceived that they need access to natural parks and forest settings in order to fully embrace environmental education. This is not correct. These perspectives reinforce the need for early learning teachers to discuss the barriers and determine ways in which they can embrace and bring environmental pedagogy to the children's outdoor environments that are available to them. Breaking down the barriers is necessary so that dispositions do not remain static. As with any change process, it is important to acknowledge and support early learning teachers' existing practices, while challenging them to build new knowledge and confidence about environmental pedagogy (Dyment et al., 2014).

Table 8.3 Recommendations for overcoming barriers in outdoor play spaces.

Barriers to Outdoor Play	Recommendations to Address Barriers
■ Lack of walking access to natural space	■ Examine spaces and places near the early learning program that may provide children with different environmental experiences outside the fence. ■ Plan field trips to open spaces.
■ Lack of time	■ Rethink why there is a perceived lack of time in the early learning program routine. ■ Discuss how the schedule may be changed to support children's outdoor playtime and experiences. ■ Examine how and why the indoor programming experiences could occur outdoors.
■ Weather conditions and parental attitudes toward weather conditions	■ Create weather condition that address outdoor play programming and weather conditions. ■ Provide families with up to date research on what children learn and experience when they are outdoors in all kinds of weather. ■ Offer families information on why outdoor play environments are healthier for children than indoor environments.
■ Safety concerns	■ Discuss with families policies and practices on supervision strategies, staff and children ratios, risk assessment procedures, and the importance of children engaging in risky play. ■ Provide pedagogical documentation that illustrates children engaged in play and how they are learning to manage risks.
■ Lack of supervision	■ Provide families with information on supervision strategies, including completing head-counts, staff-specific responsibility for particular children, rules and regulations, and strategies used to prepare children for the play experiences.

Edwards and Cutter-Mackenzie (2011) suggested early learning teachers revisit their planning processes and pedagogical interactions by consciously including three types of play as outlined in Figure 8.7.

Concepts such as **biodiversity** can be embedded into play through exploratory and discovery experiences. As outlined by Edwards and Cutter-Mackenzie (2011), biodiversity topics connect "strongly with the lives of young children and teachers and is suitable for integrating into the early childhood curriculum" (p. 54). When you examine the definitions of biodiversity and **ecological biodiversity**, what are some ideas that you envision early learning teachers could introduce to children? How and why might you engage children in the three types of play outlined in Figure 8.7?

Biodiversity refers to the variety of life such as plants, animals, birds, and snakes. Biodiversity includes **ecological biodiversity**. This refers to ecosystems, natural communities, and habitats and how they interact with each other and the environment (National Wildlife Federation, Tolme (2017).

Open-ended play involves early learning teachers providing children with materials to create their own play and to make meaning of experiences or concepts.

Modelled play refers to early learning teachers showing or illustrating to children how to approach a particular experience as a way to illustrate environmental concepts prior to the children using the material.

Purposefully framed play refers to early learning teachers providing children with opportunities to use materials while role-modelling particular attributes or approaches when using the materials.

Figure 8.7 Three types of play that support environmental concepts.

Edwards & Cutter-Mackenzie (2011) identified that contemporary research on environmental education would suggest that early learning programs develop new programming strategies. They advocated that programming strategies include play-based and child-centred principles, with a focus on environmental issues. Such approaches would include a combination of open-ended, modelled, and purposefully framed play. They described open-ended play as requiring early learning teachers to provide "children with materials related to particular concepts derived from environmental education and allowing children to use the materials to create their own understandings of the concepts" (p. 54). This means that children require access to a variety of materials and the freedom to explore those materials.

Modelled play refers to "teachers 'showing' children how to use the materials to illustrate environmental education concepts prior to allowing the children to use the materials themselves" (Edwards & Cutter-Mackenzie, 2011, p. 54). Purposefully framed play is best described as play that "involves teachers providing children with opportunities to use the materials as well as participating in modeled-play experiences" (Edwards & Cutter-Mackenzie, 2011, p. 54). Encouraging early learning teachers to explore how and what these three types of play look like may require some re-visioning practices. Table 8.4 illustrates how early learning teachers may set the stage for outdoor play that incorporates these three types of play into opportunities for environmental exploration, using the example of an interest in bees.

This approach evolves from an environmental and social framework whereby children and adults engage in testing their ideas and perceptions. Adult role models offer children environments where they can connect with their environment and what is in their environments. For example, when children develop a thinking process about the importance of honeybees, it causes them to question or think differently about why we should preserve and nurture their existence. Rather than having a fear about bees, children become engaged in understanding their importance to the environment. They learn about the types of flowers that bees are attracted to within the environment. This learning contributes to them developing a higher potential to react differently to what they

Table 8.4 Three types of play that support environmental experiences.

Modelled play	Open-ended play	Purposefully framed play
The early learning teacher prepared a table outdoors with materials used for creating a bee hotel. The materials included books about bee hotels, compasses, milk cartons, bamboo canes of varying lengths, and wooden frames. After the children observed the materials, she engaged in a discussion about why bee hotels are important for our plants and food. She indicated that those who wanted to make a bee hotel should observe her constructing one before they began. Throughout the process, she discussed why the bamboo canes had to be fixed firmly and why the nest entrance must face south or east for the bees to be attracted to the house. As she discussed the location of south and east, she introduced children to the compass and how it could be used. She then worked with them to mark the sun's location.	The early learning teacher placed the same materials that were available for making the bee hotels on a different table and in a different location outdoors. Children who had been engaged in the dialogue with the early learning teacher about creating a bee hotel were drawn to the table area. There, they engaged in discussions that focused both on why bees have hotels and the children's ideas on how to make a hotel. Some children were attracted to the compass and experimented with where in the play space they could find south and east according to the compass. Over a three-day period, three bee hotels were built and positioned within the play space.	A few days later, the children continued to express an interest in bee hotels. The early learning teacher expanded the dialogue with the children to discuss processes such as what it means when we say bees are pollinators. She showed them photos that illustrated how bees pollinate plants. They discussed the positions of the bees' bodies when pollinating plants. Then she presented a book on the kinds of plants in their area that bees are attracted to. Then, she invited children who wanted to go for a walk to see if they could find bees pollinating plants to join her. They took cameras so that they could capture what they observed.

see and take steps to protect living and non-living things in their environment. These actions influence social change, cultural practices, and environmental sustainability practices. Such play processes can challenge early learning teachers to examine their current practice and encourage them to move toward pedagogy that gives children a sense of place and conditions within that space (Edwards & Cutter-Mackenzie, 2011). Intentional teaching moves toward creating an integrated environmental philosophy and approach in which differing play types serve children well in their engagement with the environment (Edwards & Cutter-Mackenzie, 2011).

THINK ABOUT IT! READ ABOUT IT! WRITE ABOUT IT!

The National Wildlife Federation identifies that biodiversity is more than just species and that it is vital for people and the health of the ecosystems. Read about why wild habitats are essential and how you can create one with children. Go to https://www.nwf.org/Wildlife/Wildlife-Conservation/Biodiversity.aspx

Now brainstorm what types of learning children could acquire by being engaged in building a wild habitat. What are children missing in environmental pedagogy if they don't gain these kinds of experiences during their early years?

As outlined in Figure 8.8, changing current practices to further enhance environmental sustainability requires early learning teachers to prepare for outdoor play and programming in very different ways. Children require outdoor play environments that offer them opportunities to create and advance experiential, multi-sensory, and project-based learning (Dietze & Kashin, 2016). The tenets of sustainability require **systems thinking**, whereby learning occurs by examining interactive and multi-layered perspectives. Systems thinking aligns with **eco-literacy**. Eco-literacy in children's outdoor play environments involves them in exploring; gaining a sense of belonging to a particular place in the world by watching and observing season, weather, plants, and animals; and by learning about life cycles of the natural world (Haas & Ashman, 2014).

Systems thinking is a holistic approach that focuses on how systems or parts thereof interrelate and work within the context of larger systems.

Eco-literacy refers to individuals, such as early learning teachers, using principles of ecology as foundational for nurturing healthy environments for children and families (Haas & Ashman, 2014).

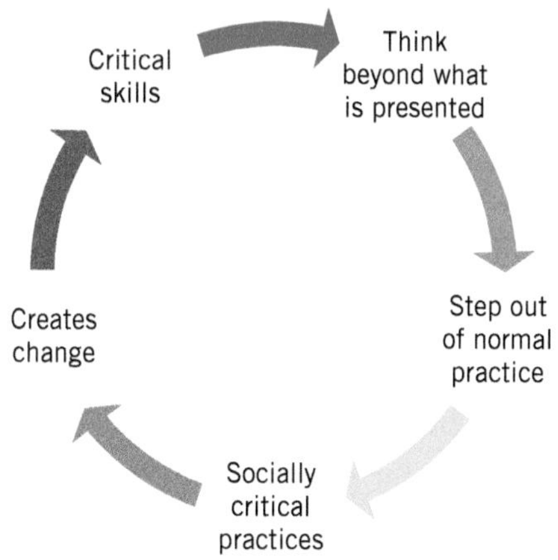

Figure 8.8 Change processes to increase environmental experiences with children.

>> BOX 8.1   Shedding Light on Outdoor Play—Points of Reflection

The Medicine Wheel

The Medicine Wheel is widely adopted/accepted as a language for (or way of) speaking about the principle of balance in Indigenous communities. It is a useful tool used to express cultural concepts and describe cultural knowledge and values that reflect commonly held principles. The teachings of the Medicine Wheel offer a model for inclusion of all children. When used to guide early learning programs, the Medicine Wheel builds on holistic practices. It begins with the individual child in the centre, and expands to include cultural views and practices related to the mental, spiritual, emotional, and physical development of the child, the family, and the community. What aspects of the Medicine Wheel are transferable to a variety of early learning programs? Why might you want to learn further about the concept of the Medicine Wheel?

Michelle Taylor-Leonhardi

Photo 8.6 Children connect and engage with their environment in many different ways.

OUR VISION FOR OUTDOOR PLAY

The value of learning how to support children in developing appreciation for the environment has never been greater in early learning programs. Children's role models influence their experience with nature, their depth and breadth of becoming stewards of the environment and in becoming empowered to advocate for the environment.

Our vision is that children will have role models who help them connect and broaden their understanding of how nature, the environment, and people interrelate (Boyle, 2008). This means more than learning to care for the trees or the ponds or animal habitats. It requires developing partnerships among families, community leaders, children and early learning programs so that collectively they can create a **macroclimate** to continuously embrace new sustainable strategies that will benefit future generations.

Macroclimate refers to the overall climate or feelings toward sustainable practices within the early learning community.

Our vision is that children have adult role models in early learning programs who help them to understand how nature, the environment, and people are interconnected.

Diane Kashin

Photo 8.7 Vision statement.

POSITIONING OUTDOOR PLAY IN THE LIVES OF CHILDREN

Understanding the relationship of environmental pedagogy to play is more than offering children natural materials to use in their outdoor play. In a literature review conducted by Hedefalk, Almqvist, and Ostman (2015), early learning programs appear to be showing a greater interest in sustainable development now than they did five years ago. Despite this finding, there is limited research to draw upon to determine the positions that Canadian early learning programs have taken on environmental pedagogy. With access to more research, early learning teachers may gain insight into and new knowledge about environmental pedagogy specific to the early years, rather than relying predominantly on environmental education research (Davis, 2009; Hedefalk, Almqvist, & Ostman, 2015). As illustrated in Photo 8.8, children may use repurposed natural materials in many ways in their play.

Leggett and Newman (2017) identified the need for a new definition of play that is reflective of "sociocultural approaches that recognize and value the role of the educator in order to counter any misconceptions that play is aimless. . . and should predominantly be promoted indoors" (p. 30). They believe

Michelle Taylor-Leonhardi

Photo 8.8 Many natural materials support children's play and their learning.

that any definition of play related to early childhood education must clearly embed the role of the educator. They suggested that the definition should be that:

> Play is intentional and involves children acting with purpose and goal for personal learning as they actively explore, discover, imagine and interact with objects, people and their natural world. Educators have a role in play and can foster children's holistic development by intentionally sustaining children's thinking and involvement in play-based learning environments. (p. 30)

Leggett and Newman (2017) identified that this definition acknowledges both the cognitive and sociocultural aspects of learning and development. These are necessary in supporting the advancement of environmental pedagogy in early learning programs.

Hedefalk, Almqvist, and Ostman (2015), suggested that early learning teachers have differing views and understandings of how to implement environmental pedagogy. Their findings identified that a large group of early learning teachers felt they needed to "educate children about the environment" (p. 981), drawing from themes such as nature and science. For example, early learning teachers would set up learning opportunities such as having children brainstorm and record what they knew about worms. Another example was the use of storytelling to explain environmental issues, especially if they did not have a breadth of knowledge from which to draw upon. Hedefalk, Almqvist, and Ostman identified that "some teachers cannot differentiate the environment from nature" (p. 981). Similarly, Arlemalm-Hagser and Sandberg (2011) suggested that there was also a large percentage of teachers that did not encourage children to act for social improvement as they had not embedded such concepts into their practice.

Hedefalk, Almqvist, and Ostman (2015) identified that early learning teachers generally position environmental pedagogy as providing experiences that would "affect children's behaviours to act for sustainable development" (p. 981). This means that the focus is on teachers directing children in how they should act in relation to the environment.

The final approach to environmental pedagogy that Hedefalk, Almqvist, and Ostman (2015) outlined was a "strategy to educate children to think critically . . . by **problematizing** the connection between the environment and society" (p. 982). For example, children exposed to the importance of separating recycled wastes should be able to express what happens to the environment if the wastes are not recycled, such as how plastic bags in streams damage the quality of life for fish.

Problematizing refers to identifying something as an issue or to make something into an issue.

Each approach outlined above neglects to identify how to support children in developing skills and knowledge about the environment through their play (Smirnova & Riabkova, 2016). As outlined by Leggett and Newman (2017), if we believe the contemporary views of children as being competent and capable and that they learn best in environments that encourage play, exploration, and discovery, as illustrated in Photo 8.9, early learning teachers benefit from conceptualizing how to incorporate environmental pedagogy into children's daily experiences.

Family Space Quinte, Inc.

Photo 8.9 Early learning teachers incorporate environmental pedagogy into their practice.

THEORETICAL FOUNDATION

Early learning teachers examine many perspectives and contrasting theories in their quest to understand their personal values and beliefs about how children develop and how play influences that development (Dietze & Kashin, 2016). For many early learning teachers, **ecological theory** as presented by Urie Bronfenbrenner (1979) has merit, especially when combined with aspects of a **social concept construct**. He used the term ecological theory as a way to emphasize how the environment, places of being, settings, and the institutions in which children gain their lived experiences, potentially affect their development. Bronfenbrenner identified that there are multiple ecologies within the five systems that he identified as the microsystem, mesosystem, exosystem, macrosystem, and chronosystem. His perspectives align with much of the research that outlines the barriers and challenges of children being exposed to outdoor play and to programming that supports environmental pedagogy.

Ecological theory refers to the belief that development is influenced and affected by five environmental systems.

Social concept construct refers to the development of jointly constructed understandings of the world that form the basis for shared understandings and assumptions about what is reality.

»» BOX 8.2 Featured Theorist: Urie Bronfenbrenner (1917–2005)

Urie Bronfenbrenner was a leading theorist on the ecological theory. He identified that children are influenced not only by their lived experiences within a family setting, but also by the larger community, including but not limited to extended family, neighbours, media, and culture (Bronfenbrenner, 1979).

Bronfenbrenner (1979) labelled the first layer of influence as the *microsystem*. This refers to where children live, including their home, early learning programs, and the neighbourhood. For example, a parent and early learning teacher may express their positions on children having access to and opportunities for outdoor play during the winter months. The early learning teacher may share that information with the director of the program, who in turn shares it with the governing board. These interactions may influence the depth and breadth of policies created on outdoor play.

The second layer is the *mesosystem*. The mesosytem provides the connections among people in the microsystem. For example, when there are large numbers of families advocating for children to have multiple experiences and time for outdoor play daily, there is an increased opportunity to positively influence children's lived experiences. Ideally, this results in children having more access to outdoor play environments that offer them a variety of play and discovery opportunities.

The third layer is identified as the *ecosystem*. This refers to the institutions or people who are directly connected to children but influence their life experiences (Dietze & Kashin, 2016). For example, early learning teachers may share information with families about how outdoor play contributes to more than just physical development. When families understand the relationship of outdoor play to children's later academic success and connectedness to the environment, the family may have the desire to advance the opportunities for environmental experiences (Ernst, 2014).

The fourth layer is identified as the macrosystem. This system focuses on the beliefs, values and "ideologies of families, communities, cultures, local traditions, and country norms" (Dietze & Kashin, 2016, p. 29). This layer influences children's exposure to outdoor play, how environmental experiences are shared and experienced, and how children learn about their environments. For example, families who value the environment role-model principles and behaviours that reflect environmental stewardship, social awareness and progress, socio-economic concepts, and sustainability. If children have fewer opportunities to experience outdoor play or engagement with the various attributes of their environment (Dyment et al., 2014), their connections with their environments are reduced.

The final layer is identified as the chronsystem. This system focuses on environmental events and the transitions that occur of life processes. For example, early learning teachers support children in examining the timing and process of leaves changing and they discuss what happens when they find a bird dead.

Think about Bronfenbrenner's ecological theory and compare it with the Indigenous information below. Are there similarities? How do they align and how could both perspectives advance children's programming related to the environment?

THINK ABOUT IT! READ ABOUT IT! WRITE ABOUT IT!

Many Aboriginal organizations and communities have adopted the 7 Grandfather teachings. These guiding principles are viewed as a moral stepping stone and cultural foundation. They share the same concepts of abiding by a moral respect for all living things. Go to http://ojibweresources.weebly.com/ojibwe-teachings--the-7-grandfathers.html.

Read about them and then think about the role of early learning teachers. How do they align with the work we do with children? How do they align with environmental sustainability? How are your perspectives similar or different to your colleagues?

Photo 8.10 Children's various abilities are viewed as gifts.

Not all Indigenous communities or cultures within them are alike. Communities may differ in historical and cultural values, aspirations, expectations, or practices. Battiste and Henderson (2009) identified that Indigenous peoples characterize learning as sacred, holistic, and a lifelong responsibility. From an Indigenous viewpoint, every child, such as the child in Photo 8.10, is unique in his or her learning journey and knowledge construction.

Values and approaches that inform socialization in many Indigenous families include: a recognition of children's varying abilities as gifts; a holistic view of child development; promotion of skills for living on the land; respect for a child's spiritual life and contributions to the cultural life of the community; transmission of a child's ancestral language; and building upon strengths more than compensating for weakness (Anderson & Ball, 2011).

PRACTICAL APPLICATIONS

Early learning teachers draw upon their knowledge and research from a variety of theories, perspectives, and approaches to determine ways in which they effectively plan and facilitate programs that support children in developing flexible thinking and resiliency skills. This begins with the relationship **rapport** that is developed between and among children, families, early learning teachers, and the community. Positive relationships are foundational to **flexible thinking**, resiliency, and human development (McCelland, 1987) and how children embrace play.

As outlined in the theoretical foundations section, providing children with opportunities to play in various outdoor environments, with peers, adults, families, or on their own is one of the most powerful ways for them to engage with and embrace their environments. As outlined in Table 8.5, flexibility and resilience is an important standard of practice.

Rapport refers to the interaction and depth of caring and concern expressed between two or more people.

Flexible thinking refers to the process of children being able to think about something in a new way.

Table 8.5 Standards for outdoor play and learning: flexibility and resilience standard.

1. The child demonstrates a sense of optimism, ownership, and a realistic sense of personal control.

2. The child is willing to attempt tasks that previously were difficult.

3. The child shows a growing ability to control impulses, accepting and adjusting to unplanned, unwanted, and unexpected events or outcomes

4. The child demonstrates comfort with open-ended questions and problems (2011, p. 203).

Source: Based on Banning and Sullivan (2011). *Lens on Outdoor Learning.*

CURIOUS?

Do you want to know more about children's resiliency and play? Search for Stuart Shanker in your search engine. What does he say about resiliency, self-regulation skills, and executive functioning skills? How do these areas of development influence how you support children in their outdoor environment?

Outdoor environments are classrooms full of learning options. Trees with branches attached and branches that have fallen offer unique opportunities for children to develop skills in balance and, weight and concepts of movement. When children create villages from sand, at times they will have the correct consistency of water and sand; at other times, the sand will not mold in ways that they are able to get the anticipated results. Think about children trying to make a fort with tree branches near an area where the location is covered with leaves, but there is ledge under the ground cover that prevents them from placing the tree branches securely into the ground. Now think about the type of rapport and relationships that adults would exhibit that would offer children support and encourage them in trying, testing, retesting, and rethinking their strategies. As identified earlier, children require time in outdoor environments to effectively engage in experiences that contribute to developing cognitive flexibility. Cognitive flexibility involves flexible thinking and **set shifting**.

Bora Kim

Photo 8.11 Children require experiences that contribute to them developing flexible thinking skills.

Set shifting refers to the process of children letting go of an old way of doing something and adapting new ways and practices.

THINK ABOUT IT! READ ABOUT IT! WRITE ABOUT IT!

There are many perspectives on the importance of flexible thinking. Read about how to enhance flexible thinking skills. Enter "flexible thinking" into a search engine. Read about it and then think about your flexible thinking skills. Would it be beneficial to expand your flexibility processes? Go to https://www.psychologytoday.com/blog/in-practice/201409/become-more-flexible-thinker

How does this concept transfer to your relationships and role-modelling with children?

Flexible thinking evolves from children having the time, materials, and supports to revisit play experiences so that they can retry and refine their strategies to reach their goals. Similarly, set shifting is achieved when children have a variety of experiences from which to draw upon. Children with adult role models, who exhibit encouragement and a sense of curiosity and wonder, are more likely to want to embrace new play experiences. Imagine children learning to skate. Generally, they begin by using a chair on the ice for balance. Then, they progress to holding onto an adult. Gradually, they learn to balance and support their bodies on their own. Children with flexible thinking skills are better able to make the transitions to these processes than children who have more rigid thinking skills. The set shifting process helps them to "unlearn" the need for a chair to support them in being able to effectively manoeuver their bodies on skates. Children who are rigid in their thinking have difficulty moving beyond the more basic ways of doing things and in having the confidence to try new tasks or opportunities.

Resiliency skills refer to children's abilities to manage the challenges that they face and their ability to bounce back, retry, and work toward achieving goals.

Thinking processes are related to children's abilities to develop **resiliency skills**. Children learn resiliency skills from many outdoor play experiences and these are linked to their comfort and abilities to engage in risk-taking. For example, imagine a group of children with the desire to build a treehouse in the early learning space. The early learning teacher took the opportunity to discuss with them why they wanted to build the house, how they might do it, and what materials they would require. Then, as the children began the process, they decided that they wanted to climb up four of the branches to see where in the tree, they would build the house. Three of the children got up to the space with ease. The fourth child, Andrew struggled with finding the right place to put his feet so that he felt secure to stretch his arms to the next branch. He did not feel secure. He decided to abandon his involvement with the others. Then, the next day he tried again. He began by watching the other children as they climbed the tree. He tried again. This time he slipped and the branch scratched his face. He had a few tears. The teacher reassured him that scratches happen and that they would heal. Then she asked how she could help him. He asked that she come near him as he climbed just in case he slipped again. She did so and used encouraging words as he had success getting to the first branch and then the second. He sat on the second branch for at least five minutes, then he started to manoeuvre his body to get to the next branch. He did not give up, but rather took the time to work through how he could achieve his goals. Developing the confidence to pursue such play options is a process, one that is strongly influenced by adults and the opportunities in the environment. The more that children are exposed to healthy relationships and role models, the stronger their opportunities are to develop inner strength, thinking skills, confidence, and the desire to learn new things and participate with others (Pearson & Kordich, 2017).

Turner & Berkes (2006) identified practices and strategies for sustainable living as they relate to traditional ecological knowledge and wisdom. Their model focuses on the importance of philosophy, worldview, communication, and exchange of knowledge, practices, and strategies for sustainability living. Time is necessary for ecological knowledge and wisdom to be developed and be embedded as beliefs and living practices. This is of particular importance for the outdoor play portion of early learning programs. The time allocated to outdoor play influences the depth and level that children mess about and embrace exploration (Ernst, 2012). If children have access to only short periods of time outdoors and frequent interruptions to their play, looking closely at the environment and taking advantage of play possibilities is negatively influenced.

Quick play refers to children's play that is short in duration and limited in scope (Dietze & Kashin, 2016).

Dietze & Kashin (2016) identified this as **quick play**, which limits children's abilities to become deeply involved in experiences. Pressoir (2008) suggested that children benefit from being surrounded by adults who create processes and environments that emphasize the following:

- **Learning to know**—acquiring support materials such as magnifying glasses that assist in exploration and developing new knowledge;

- **Learning to be**—feeling comfortable with supporting individuals in working toward achieving outcomes;

- **Learning to live together**—participating and co-operating with other people in all human development;

- **Learning to do**—reacting creatively and responsibly in all environments; and

- **Learning to transform oneself and society**—developing respect for the environment, social solidarity, and practices of non-discrimination.

Photo 8.12 Children learn by exploring.

PRINCIPLES OF PRACTICE: HOLISTIC-BASED PRACTICE

Holistic-based practices in some academic fields such as sociology and education refer to providing children with opportunities in all aspects of a particular area of interest or concept and supporting them in recognizing that the whole concept is interdependent on its parts (Schoonover-Shoffner, 2013). Some suggest holistic is different from *wholistic* in that wholistic refers to considering the interaction between the mind, body, and spirit (Schoonover-Shoffner, 2013).

Holistic-based practices include children finding meaning and purpose from their interactions with family, extended family, peers, community, and the natural world through experiential learning. Experiential learning supports children in developing a holistic way of thinking. This means that similar to flexible and set shifting, as children gain more experiences and learning to draw from, they integrate layers of learning into their thinking processes.

The Australian Department of Education, Employment and Workplace Relations (DEEWR) as part of the Early Years Learning Framework (EYLF) (2009) identified that holistic approaches to teaching and learning acknowledge that there is a connectedness of mind, body, and spirit. Early learning teachers understand the importance of the connections and reciprocal relationships among children, families, and communities. As outlined in the EYLF document, early learning teachers foster children's capacity to experience and gain an understanding of and respect for the natural environment as well as the interdependence among plants, animals, people and land. Similar to beliefs and values of Indigenous communities, holistic environments promote children's learning by ensuring that the environment supports learning as being organic, emergent, and experiential.

Early learning teachers, children, families, and communities connect to share learning and new knowledge. Learning in nature and from nature encourages children to care for and connect with their pedagogy of place, space, and internal spirit (Ernst, 2014). For example, children make earth connections when they have opportunities to think about and engage in experimentation that leads toward solving environmental concerns. This can be as simple as helping children learn about how ladybugs will eat aphids so that the leaves on trees are not damaged. Or it can be watching the geese fly south in the fall and return in the spring.

Holistic-based experiences connect children to their inner beings. One of the most successful ways of supporting children in connecting their inner beings to their external environment is through storytelling that occurs verbally rather than from a predetermined book. Storytelling captures children's imaginations. Storytelling supports children in understanding their culture and knowledge about the past and the present. **Talking circles**, rooted in Indigenous communities in Canada (Umbreit, 2003), are effective in supporting children and early learning teachers in have meaningful conversations that connect their ideas with people and experiences.

Talking circles refers to a process that encourages dialogue and co-creation of learning content. The people within the circle listen to the person speaking, and opportunities for speaking are rotated amongst the group.

LEARNING IN PLACE: THE FIRE PIT AS PLACE

As you examined in Chapter 6, when children have fire pit experiences, they develop skills to problem solve, take risks, and build confidence in being able to handle risky situations. Early learning teachers use the experience of the fire pit as a place for storytelling, communication, and making connections. It is a place for children and adults to discuss environmental conditions such as the relationship of wind conditions to a fire spreading; how meteorologists can predict the weather from the wind and the clouds; and how the smoke from the fire rises and falls. They learn about boundaries and a sense of place and how to manage within the boundaries. These skills support children in developing self-regulation skills. The fire pit is a place of conversation about nature, environmental elements, and safety. For example, children learn about the purpose of a fire blanket, what heatproof gloves are, and why a clean water supply is necessary. It is a place for children to gather information about ways to start a fire, how to extinguish a fire, and how to operate a fire extinguisher. The fire pit is a place that children learn about occupations such as the role of firefighters. An important component of children's experiences with storytelling around the fire is that the story is repeated to deepen learning (O'Brien, 2009).

Generally when there is a fire pit, children may experience baking bannock, toasting sandwiches, or using a kettle to make cedar tea. Such activities support children in gathering sticks fallen from trees to use for toasting (greenwood versus dried wood) and whittling the end of the stick so that they may use it for toasting. Fire pits bring together children, families, and early learning teachers through conversation and experiences that facilitate a feeling of connectedness to people, place, and the environment. Campfires are places where stories are told and wisdom is shared with the younger generation, who, in turn, become storytellers for the next generation (Dietze & Kashin, 2016).

Early learning teachers discuss with the children the temperatures that they will feel near the fire or on their fingers when they have toasted their food. This brings a sense of community engagement to the environment. "Fire is intriguing and magical to children" (Phillips, 2016, p. 47). Fire can be explored safely with children by using proper precautions and in implementing risk/benefit assessments. Early learning teachers can model respect by using the technique of "leave no trace" so that no harm is done to the environment (Phillips, 2016).

PROGRAMMING

There are many types of experiences and materials that may be offered outdoors that support children in learning about their environment. For example, many neighbourhoods have ponds. The learning and experiences that children gain when their early

Table 8.6 Plan, engage, explore, reflect—adopting a pond.

PLAN	Begin by developing an invitation for children to explore the photos and books about different things they may find around a pond. You might have photos of flat rocks, hard mud, grass, moss, debris, and bugs.
ENGAGE	Invite the children to go to the pond. Encourage them to take photos of what they see. Have them feel many of the natural items that they found. Discuss what and how they can safely remove debris from the area.
EXPLORE	When the children return from their walk, download and print the photos and have them classify what they saw. How many photos were similar or different? Classify the debris from the perspective of how to dispose of it. Engage in discussion about what happens when ponds are not cared for.
REFLECT	Did the children gain a sense of how to care for a pond? Did they build their knowledge about ponds and caring for the environment? If children visit and care for the pond on a regular basis, will this support them in becoming stewards of the environment? What types of dialogue occurred with the children about the pond? Does the dialogue change over time?

learning programs adopt the pond is significant. Children may be encouraged to visit the pond regularly to ensure that debris is removed so that the natural habitat can flourish. This is a beginning point for children to learn about water, animal habitats, plants, and the cycles of life that revolve around a pond. Through this type of exposure children connect science to their environment, especially if the early learning teachers have encouraged them to look at their environments with a new lens. This may include having the children observe, photograph, and discuss all of the natural environmental attributes that they see around the pond, such as in Photo 8.13. Table 8.6 illustrates how early learning teachers could support children in becoming intrigued by the neighbourhood pond.

Beverlie Dietze

Photo 8.13 A neighbourhood pond.

FAMILY SUPPORT AND ENGAGEMENT

Adapting to living sustainably requires children in early learning programs to have role models, including families and early learning teachers, who embrace natural environments and emphasize ways in which lifestyles and practices can have minimal impact on society (Dyment et al., 2014). Supporting families in understanding the importance of children being outdoors is a great beginning. Having unique experiences and options to explore adds to the depth of learning assimilated into children's body of knowledge.

Elliott (2014) suggested that "early childhood education for sustainability is a transformative and empowering process actively engaged in by children, families and educators who share an ecocentric worldview" (p. 15). To achieve this, explicit policies are required that communicate to families how outdoor play environments support children in learning about environments and sustainability practices.

Early learning teachers involve families in the development and implementation of policies that promote environmental sustainability. This may include discussing the policies, practices, and philosophy that focus on environmental pedagogy. Aspects of the children's involvement in environmental pedagogy may be shared with families in a variety of ways including, but not limited to, pedagogical documentation or news bulletins. As outlined in Figure 8.9, engaging families in an environmental agenda requires family and early learning program partnerships.

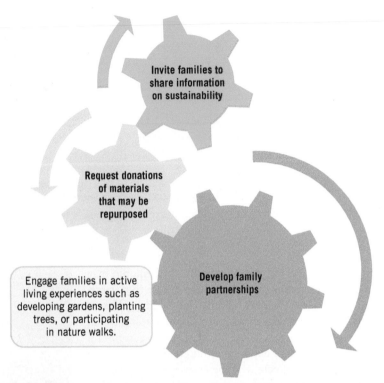

Figure 8.9 Family and early learning programming partnerships.

ACCESSIBILITY AND DESIGN

Early learning teachers encourage all children to have access to various outdoor environments. Differing environments help children learn about the similarities and differences of their surroundings. With access comes responsibility. Children are encouraged to care for and respect their environment. Early learning teachers role-model how and why they do not destroy plants or shelters for birds, invertebrates, or other animals that live in them. They introduce children to the space and support them in learning how to be gentle with the living creatures and how to return them to their space. They help children explore under a rock or log, and teach them how important it is to always return what they have explored back to its original place. Children learn to identify what must remain in the space and what can be removed, such as broken branches or pine cones. In their program design, early learning teachers ensure that children are immersed in environments that honour the living and non-living elements of the outdoor space.

TIPS AND TOOLS FOR OUTDOOR PLAY

There are many ways to support children in becoming stewards of the environment. Here are 10 tips that can support children in appreciating and embracing their outdoor environments.

1. Introduce children to a variety of flora and fauna. This may include having children create and care for gardens and plants. Support children in learning how to observe the plants and animals in their environment.

2. Offer children natural materials in their environments such as rocks, pebbles, sticks, pine cones, and twigs.

3. Support children in being co-constructors of knowledge about the natural world.

4. Encourage children to repurpose materials and use them for a variety of purposes such as cardboard cylinders for rolling and speed experiences, boxes for construction, and wood pieces or newly fallen snow for canvas.

5. Provide the juices from beets and carrots as a way for children to experience the use natural dyes in their creative work.

6. Invite Elders and other community resource people to support children in learning about their environment.

7. Champion environmental education for young children by viewing outdoor play and the environment as essential ingredients to early learning programs.

8. Encourage families to participate in updating environmental policies that address items such as water and energy conservation, plants that attract butterflies and honey bees, waste reduction strategies, and noise pollution.

9. Invite children, families, and early learning teachers to design outdoor spaces that will allow for the implementation of composting, collecting rain, and growing vegetables.

10. Develop resources that early learning teachers may share with children and families that enhance their learning about topics that support environmental pedagogy principles.

Early learning teachers have a responsibility to clarify their knowledge, skills, and perspectives on environmental pedagogy (Dyment et al., 2014). Early learning teachers and families observe children in action to deepen their understanding of how to effectively implement environmental pedagogy in their daily practice (Hedefalk et al., 2015).

ON THE GROUND—PROFESSIONAL REFLECTIONS: "WHY I LOVE OUTDOOR PLAY"

BOX 8.3   Why I Love Outdoor Play

When thinking about outdoors and loose parts it always brings me back to my childhood. As a Member of Curve Lake First Nation, I grew up on reserve. My fondest memories are playing outside with sticks and stones, running through the woods playing hide and seek, swimming, camping on Fox Island, climbing trees, and building forts. Nature was a part of who I was; it was integrated into everyday life for me. It was landmarks. "If you go past the big apple tree then you have gone too far," mom would tell us when we would be playing outside, making dandelion chain bracelets or necklaces. My brothers and I would be outside playing with our friends from morning 'til night. It is these kind of memories we must instill in our children. As educators we need to get our children outside learning and exploring. Children are naturally drawn to nature. The smells, sounds, and different textures that come with being outside only make you want to explore the how's, the what's, the who's and the why's. These are all things that children just want to do

naturally. What better place to allow them to do just that than outdoors. My daughter has a strong connection to Mother Earth. She understands at the young age of seven that we must take care of her. She loves to play outdoors in her natural environment for hours at a time during the summer months. She loves all the seasons. The rocks and sticks are alive in her play, they take meaning and a purpose, whether she is building "Pride Rock" or building a fire for a campsite for all her animals. Children are a sacred gift from our creator. They flourish on Mother Earth. We must enjoy the wonder of childhood and provide the children with endless possibilities of what to do with "sticks and stones".

Miigwech,
Michelle Taylor-Leonhardi
Coordinator of Oshkiigmong Early Learning Centre
Used with permission from Miigwech, Michelle Taylor-Leonhardi, Coordinator of Oshkiigmong Early Learning Centre.

CASE STUDIES

Early learning teachers benefit from looking closely at the outdoor space in a variety of ways including what is in the space and the ways in which children use the space. When analyzed and reflected upon, this information influences the types of invitations and programming experiences that early learning teachers incorporate into the environment. Martina was excited to join her new early learning program, especially because of the reputation it had in the community and the incredible early learning teachers that work there.

As you read Case Study 8.1 you will gain insight into what Martina learned when she took the time to look closely at the materials in the environment and then worked with her colleagues to add more natural materials to the environment. Consider the questions that follow the case study. How might you incorporate some of your learning from previous chapters into your responses?

》 CASE STUDY 8.1 | **Exploring Ways to Bring More Nature-Based Experiences into the Environment**

I am a new early learning teacher at a centre that has a great reputation for quality programming. Yesterday I examined and took inventory of our outdoor play space. It was a real eye-opener for me because I realized that of the 20 materials/experiences available to the children, they were all made of plastic. That shocked me. When I looked at the space, I realized that there were no sticks, no pine cones, no rocks, no mud, no leaves, and no plants. I was shaken by this discovery because I realized that without intrigue and opportunities to explore natural items and ideas, the children would not be connecting with nature—other than the fresh air, the weather, and the flat ground. I began thinking about the following questions. As a facilitator of children's learning, what are the important considerations in regard to resources that will offer children options for learning and testing of theories and agendas? What changes need to be made to embrace children's opportunities in the outdoors? What new curiosity items could be put in the environment now and how can the plastic items be replaced with more natural products?

Think about your role as a teacher. What types of natural materials would you suggest be placed in the environment immediately?

1. How would you engage families in changing the space?
2. How would you expand the environmental pedagogy in the program?
3. What would you envision to be your gap in knowledge and how would you gain that knowledge?

This chapter clearly identifies the relationship of role-modelling and its connectedness to environments and behaviours. The beliefs and practices of early learning teachers are among the major influences on children being exposed to outdoor environments and in becoming engaged with the vast learning options that can occur outdoors. If early learning teachers lack the knowledge, time, and opportunities to gain experience in nature and develop advocacy skills with children, opportunities to change the current outdoor practices are diminished (Ernst, 2014).

》 BOX 8.4 | **Take It Outside!**

When was the last time you sat around a fire pit? Look at a space for having a fire pit. What cautions about the environment would you take into consideration? What materials would you have available for safety? What would you do around the fire? What kinds of conversations would you have with children around a fire pit? When would you not have a fire pit available and why?

KEY TERMS

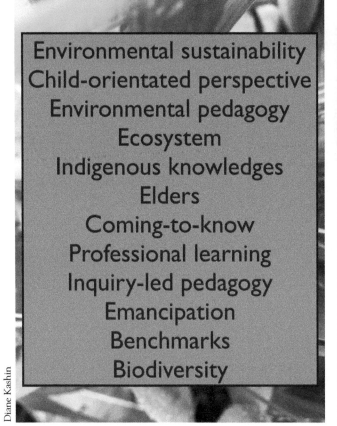

Environmental sustainability
Child-orientated perspective
Environmental pedagogy
Ecosystem
Indigenous knowledges
Elders
Coming-to-know
Professional learning
Inquiry-led pedagogy
Emancipation
Benchmarks
Biodiversity

Systems thinking
Eco-literacy
Macroclimate
Problematizing
Ecological theory
Social concept construct
Rapport
Flexible thinking
Set shifting
Resiliency skills
Quick play
Talking circles

Diane Kashin

Photo 8.14 Key terms.

Summary

- Environmental sustainability is an emerging concept in early learning programs.

- Environmental pedagogy refers to the access, opportunities, and experiences extended to children in their natural environments.

- Environmental sustainability includes environmental stewardship, social awareness and progress, social-economic processes, and sustainability practices.

- Incorporating environmental practices into programming may be a new experience for early learning teachers.

- The World Commission on Environment and Development, "The Brundtland Report," (1988) defined sustainable development as "meeting the needs of the present without compromising the ability of future generations to meet their own needs" (p. 43).

- Inquiry-led pedagogy supports children in understanding culture through role modeling and practices.

- The 7 Rs of sustainable practice are reduce, reuse, recycle, respect, rethink, reflect, and redistribute.

- Early childhood is the most critical time for children to develop a sense of respect and connection to the environment.

- Research suggests that early learning teachers incorporate open-ended play, modelled play and purposefully framed play into their practice.

- During a process of change, early learning teachers will experience stepping out of normal practice as they examine socially critical practice, create change, engage in critical skills, and think beyond what is presented.

- Eco-literacy refers to individuals using principles of ecology for nurturing healthy environments.

- Early learning teachers have differing views and understandings of how to implement environmental pedagogy.

- Urie Bronfenbrenner (1979) created the ecological theory that emphasizes the importance of environment, places of being, settings, and the institutions in which children gain their lived experiences.

- Indigenous views on learning characterize it as sacred, holistic, and a lifelong responsibility.

- Environmental stewardship evolves from the rapport amongst children, families, and early learning teachers. Positive relationships support flexible thinking.

- Flexibility and resilience are important standards for early learning teachers to embed in their outdoor play environment.

- A model for traditional ecological knowledge and wisdom includes a philosophy, a worldview, communication, and an exchange of knowledge, practices, and strategies for sustainability living.

- Research has suggested that children benefit from being in environments that support them in learning to know, to be, to live together, to do, and to transform oneself and society.

- Holistic-based principles include ways in which children find meaning, identity, and purpose through their interactions with family, peers, community, and their natural world through experiential learning.

- The fire pit provides children with a variety of learning opportunities that support environmental stewardship, community learning, and scientific principles.

- Policies support early learning teachers in advancing environmental practices with children and families.

- Early learning teachers support children in learning how to care for living things in their environment.

QUIET REFLECTION

Spend some time in a garden. Look at the types of bugs that you see on the ground and on the plants. Are there honeybees on the plants? Are there particular colours that they seem to be attracted to? How do they position their bodies on the plants? What would you suggest the children know prior to observing honeybees on the plants?

COMMUNITY DIALOGUE

When you think about children, the environment, environmental sustainability, and outdoor play, highlight what you would envision to be steps in advocating for children to become stewards of the environment.

1. What strategies would you use to discuss environmental sustainability with families?
2. What do you envision environmental sustainability to look like in early learning programs?
3. What happens when early learning teachers have opposing views on the importance of outdoor play and on ways to support children in exploring their environment to its fullest?

FOR FURTHER THOUGHT AND ACTION

Throughout the chapter there was an emphasis on the importance of early learning teachers having a thorough knowledge about and application of environmental practices. What do you believe the barriers may be? What role will you take in promoting new programming ideas that include environmental pedagogy with your colleagues, children, and families? How will you support families? How will you continue to examine information from the Indigenous cultures to inform your practice?

RESOURCES

Find out more about children's curiosity and environmental inquiry by going to https://www.naturalcuriosity.ca/aboutus.php?m=b

Read about Founded in Culture: Strategies To Promote Early Learning Among First Nations Children In Ontario. Go to: http://www.beststart.org/resources/hlthy_chld_dev/pdf/FC_K13A.pdf

CHAPTER 9
Programming from a Four-Season Perspective

Work consists of whatever a body is obliged to do. Play consists of whatever a body is not obliged to do.

Mark Twain (1835–1910)

LEARNING OUTCOMES

After exploring this chapter, you will be able to:

■ Explain the importance of children experiencing outdoor play over four seasons.

■ Discuss the terms emergent curriculum, negotiated curriculum, pedagogy, programming, intentionality, outcomes, invitations, provocations, and how they are related.

■ Describe how children can connect to nature with an inquiry stance, ecopedagogy, and the principles of mentoring.

■ Outline schema play as it relates to outdoor play.

■ Discuss how the scientific method can be applied to outdoor play.

■ Explain how to engage families in supporting outdoor play.

CHILDHOOD MEMORIES

I learned a lot from my grandmother, who was a very wise woman. She had a large vegetable and herb garden behind her house. I loved being outside with her in the garden. She would tell me about the medicinal qualities of each type of herb and plant. She would describe the recipes that she had to make sauces, soups, pesto, and teas from the herbs and plants. We would cook together too. My favourite was making basil pesto in the mortar and pestle. When I had a cold she would take Echinacea and steep it in hot water and then strain out the leaves, petals, and roots and serve me tea in a fancy teacup. It always made me feel better.

CHAPTER PREVIEW

Four-season outdoor play is important to children living in Canada. Children benefit from playing outside every day and every month of the year. We live in a country where children can witness the changes in the weather over the course of a day, week, month, and year, which supports their play options and learning. Seasonal play is rich with opportunities. The fall season offers children leaves to jump in and the discovery of frost on the rooftops and ice forming on puddles. Winter gives children the wonder of how ice cracks, and how they move their bodies to glide on it, or how the snowflakes feel and taste as they gently fall. Spring provides mud for pies and sliding. Summer has a bounty of natural materials to discover and explore. Each season offers unique and different possibilities for play and learning. What are your favourite experiences in each of the seasons? As an adult, do you like dipping your feet in the water in the summer and sliding on the ice that forms beneath your feet in the winter? What were your favourite experiences as a child— are they similar now or different? Did you like making snow forts in the winter, climbing trees in the summer, or feeling the crunch of the leaves on the ground in the fall? Did you experience and enjoy the downpour of April showers and exploring the smells and beauty of the May flowers in the spring?

Seasonal play offers children different aspects of exploration, thinking, tinkering, and discovery, all of which are foundational to their learning. Think about the winter—what scientific principles do children learn that are different from those in other seasons? Children can learn about temperature as they watch as water freezes and becomes ice. As the ice melts, they might hear the sounds of the ice cracking and the water dripping on the ground. In the winter, the snow can become a canvas that they may use for creative experiences. In the spring, when the signs of rebirth and renewal abound, the children can hear and see the birds return, the buds on the trees transform into leaves, and the sounds

Photo 9.1 Outdoor play across the seasons.

of insects such as frogs or crickets. Early learning teachers who embrace outdoor play view each season with enthusiasm because of the different play and learning affordances. Early learning students and teachers recognize that seasonal play is vital to children's life and lived experiences, even if they may themselves prefer to stay indoors to avoid inclement weather or getting dirty (Copeland, Sherman, Kendeigh, Kalkwarf, & Saelens, 2012).

Think about what children can experience in the rain. What might they learn? What different and similar concepts do children learn when they are exposed to mist or light and heavy rain? Think about science, math, and language—what might they experience? What would children experience if umbrellas, buckets, and barrels were added to the play environment with the rain? What observations might children make when using these materials? They might see that the rain comes from the sky, and that as the rain starts, the sky becomes dark. How might this lead them to think about their own theories about what causes the wet weather? They can listen to the sounds of the raindrops falling on the umbrella and consider how this human invention shielding them from getting wet works. Measuring the levels of rain in the buckets and barrels supports children in using their math skills as they reflect on water conservation. The collected water can then be used to nourish newly planted vegetables. As this example shows, when surrounded by early learning teachers who embrace outdoor play in all kinds of weather, children have multiple opportunities for experiences and learning that can never be duplicated indoors.

Observing fruits and vegetables grow helps children to understand that seeds germinate and plants may either grow in soil or water. As the harvesting season approaches, children can help pick or dig the fruit and vegetables from the garden. If the harvest is used for snack and lunch, they learn about food production and consumption. These are sources of wonder for children. In this chapter, the focus will be seasonal affordances for play, wonder, and learning. This requires early learning teachers to examine their philosophical perspectives on seasonal programming and determine how they support and encourage children in engaging in play year-round through the materials and invitations that they extend to children. It is our hope that these invitations for play will support early learning students and teachers in facilitating children's access to outdoor play and learning in all seasons.

Research suggests that children's opportunities for physically active outdoor play varies depending on the season (Carson, Spence, Cutumisu, Boule, & Edwards, 2010). Being outdoors is an important predictor of children's physical activity levels as well as other indicators of healthy development. Carson et al. (2010) studied children in a Canadian city where winter is characterized by extremely cold temperatures and wind chills. They determined that children had lower levels of physical activity in the winter as compared to the other seasons. This may be due in part to extreme weather conditions, but more likely stems from early learning teachers reducing the access to and amount of time children engage in outdoor play during the winter months (Ergler, Kearns, & Witten, 2016). As identified in Table 9.1, early learning teachers engage in a weather assessment process when determining whether it is safe for children and teachers to engage in outdoor play.

Children require first-hand experiences in the natural world. When children play in and with nature all year they engage their senses. According to Ernst (2014), research on brain development suggested that play during the early years should be devoted to imaginative, multisensory, and playful learning. Multisensory, child-directed, and open-ended play experiences are not replaced by formal instruction in academic areas. It was Comenius, a pioneer in early learning, who suggested that the more senses involved, the more effective the learning (Elkind, 2015). As the seasons change, nature creates invitations that support children in their play, resulting in them learning in multisensory ways. For example, think about how hard it is for children to resist jumping in a puddle. In the winter, the puddle becomes a provocation that invites a response from the children

Table 9.1 Weather assessment process.

When the temperatures are cold,* are the children at risk?
What is the risk of frostbite?

- Have indoor breaks if children say they are feeling cold.
- Ensure that children are dressed warmly at all times with insulated boots, winter weight coats, mittens, and something to warm their necks.

When there are extreme weather alerts, are the children at risk?
Are thunderstorms predicted?

- Assess how quickly children and early learning teachers can be moved to safety.
- Remain calm and address children's fears in an understanding way.

When the temperatures are hot, are the children at risk?
Is the extreme heat at a level where children may become quickly dehydrated?

- Determine if shaded areas outdoors provide children with the correct protection so that they can continue to play outside.
- Follow the guidelines from the Canadian Pediatrics Society for protecting children and ensure children are well hydrated and have access to water to drink and to play with.
- Suspend outdoor activity and remain inside during a heat alert.

*(i.e. lower than -25 degrees celsius with the wind chill factor)

to crack the ice. In addition to nature's invitations, ideally, early learning students and teachers provide planned environments that intentionally invite children to experience and explore with all their senses across seasons.

SETTING THE STAGE FOR OUTDOOR PLAY

Intentionally inviting children to play involves experiential learning. In this chapter we refer to experiences rather than activities. An **experience** is different than an **activity**. According to Watts (2013), an experience implies a deeper level of potential learning. An activity implies a limited provision for children. An activity is provided for children. For children to observe, wonder, and learn about the changing nature of the world around them they need experience. "They cannot learn about seasons purely from pictures, worksheets or photographs" (Watts, p. 4). First-hand experiences that are invitational and that take advantage of all the wonders each season holds can be intriguing for children in their quest for exploration and connections to their environment. An effective way to experience seasonal learning is to visit the same place during different months to experience pedagogy of place.

What can children learn from the changes that occur over the seasons? In Chapter 7 we encouraged early learning students and teachers to support children in developing a sense of place with sustained and regular visits to that same space. How does this place change across the seasons? Witt (2017) suggested that "stories can connect people and places so offer creative possibilities to stimulate children's engagement with the outdoors" (p. 59). Witt identified a series of questions that have been adapted in Table 9.2 to include a four seasons column. This is intended to encourage early learning students and teachers to think about the possibilities of play and learning in place across seasons and in varying weather conditions.

When children have the opportunity to explore and investigate the outdoor environment, with initial encouragement from adults, they use their senses to observe, notice, discover, and activate their curiosity about seasonal changes. Over time, they

Experience refers to an action that is open ended and encourages children to act upon their emerging interests. It is sustainable over time.

Activity refers to an action that occurs once and is predetermined by adults rather than flowing from children's interests.

Table 9.2 Telling stories of place in four seasons.

What stories can we find in this place?	*In four seasons*
What is in this place?	*In four seasons*
What does this place invite us to do?	*In four seasons*
Who (human and non-human) lives here?	*In four seasons*
Who relies on this place?	*In four seasons*
How can we be attentive to this place?	*In four seasons*
What does this place know?	*In four seasons*

embed these skills into their daily ways of knowing. Creating and documenting stories of place based on the observations, questions and wonderings of children deepens their relationship with the outdoor world (Witt, 2017). Think about a place from your childhood. How did it change over four seasons? What happened to the birds, insects, and animals that lived in that place when the winter came? How did the trees change? When children learn to know place across the seasons, their stories of place can provide early learning teachers with information that contributes to an emerging path for curriculum.

Curriculum is emergent when it evolves, diverging along new paths as children make choices and connections with their lived experiences. Curriculum options are always fluid so that new possibilities may be weaved in as seasonal changes evolve. Early learning teachers plan for children's experiences in place. According to Jones (2012), the planning process is made day-to-day in response to observations and reflections on children's interests. "The curriculum was set down only after it had taken place, not laid out in advance except in broad terms" (p. 66). Jones called this **emergent curriculum**. Place provides many possibilities for emerging interests. For example, when a group of children discovered that the trees, logs, and stumps in the forest were covered with incredible looking fungi they became fascinated by these formations. If you were the early learning teacher, how would you plan for the children's emerging interests in fungi?

An emergent curriculum is a **negotiated curriculum**. Forman and Fyfe (2012) suggested that the curriculum that emerges in early learning settings is grounded in the theories of social constructivism and is created or negotiated within a community of learners that includes teachers, children, families, and community. "The curriculum is not child-centred or teacher-directed" (Forman & Fyfe, 2012, p. 246). Curriculum emerges from children's experiences. However, the early learning teacher plays an important role in framing the path taken by planning for opportunities and experiences based on knowledge they have gained about the children from their observations, pedagogical documentation, and dialogue with families. The teacher includes the children's voices. In a negotiated curriculum, children express their interests, and follow-up experiences are proposed and negotiated with the children, other teachers, and in many instances with families.

Emergent curriculum refers to an approach that emerges from the interests of the learner and is co-constructed.

Negotiated curriculum means that curriculum does not just emerge from the child or from the teacher but is negotiated. It is "child initiated but teacher framed" (Hill, Stremmel, & Fu, 2005, p. 16).

Diane Kashin

Photo 9.2 Fungi in the forest.

What emerges from a negotiated curriculum is "teacher-provoked and then child-engaged" (Forman & Fyfe, 2012, p. 248). The early learning teacher acts as a provocateur—a concept introduced in Chapter 4 that uses the 'PEER Principle' (Plan, Engage, Explore, and Reflect)—to plan for experiences rich in possibilities for children's exploration, while documenting and reflecting on next steps. Building on Chapter 4, here we explore how curriculum emerges through negotiation during outdoor play experiences and with the pedagogy of nature.

Pedagogy is a term often used but often misunderstood (Colwell & Pollard, 2015). Pedagogy is not the same as curriculum. Curriculum is the content of the potential experiences that children may engage in and what we facilitate. Pedagogy is about how we teach it. Pedagogy is how learning happens (Ontario Ministry of Education, 2014). While pedagogy is your approach to teaching, curriculum refers to the contents of your teaching. Curriculum answers the question "what to teach," and pedagogy answers the question "how to teach it." Consider this example of two different early learning teachers who both wanted to teach children about deciduous and coniferous trees.

> **Pedagogy** is an encompassing term that relates to the approach an early learning teacher takes in facilitating teaching and learning opportunities.

CURIOUS?

Do you want to learn more about intentionality in teaching? This article may satisfy your curiosity: http://www.earlychildhoodaustralia.org.au/nqsplp/wp-content/uploads/2012/05/EYLFPLP_E-Newsletter_No4.pdf

Alex's philosophy about learning is based on children learning from observation and by being told the right answer. She takes a group of children to a nearby park with a small enclave of diverse trees. Alex has the children gather in front of a tree, and she points and identifies the type and name of the tree. The children repeat the tree type and name of the tree and then they move on to the next tree. Laurel has a different pedagogical approach to teaching, as she does not believe that children learn from being told. She takes children out to a wooded area nearby and invites the children to examine the trees closely by touching the bark; smelling the leaves and needles; and collecting pine cones, acorns, leaves, and branches that have fallen to the forest floor. Photos are taken for documentation. As the children sort through their forest treasures they begin to make their own theories about why some trees lose their leaves and others don't. Their ideas are expressed and notes of their conversations are recorded.

Photo 9.3 Examining deciduous and coniferous trees.

In the first example, children are given the answers. In the second example, children are supported in arriving at the right answer without being given the answer. The thinking that occurs during the process of theory building is aligned with the preferred way in which children learn. Rather than memorizing the right answer, the children have been challenged to speculate, make predictions, and create theories. This skill serves them better in later problem solving and critical thinking than any soon-to-be-forgotten answer from an early learning teacher (Dietze & Kashin, 2017). The term **programming** incorporates both pedagogy and curriculum. Programming requires planning. If you think about planning as a way to provoke occasions of discovery with children and adults, then you are co-constructing curriculum with children rather than imposing ideas (Walton, 2013). In this chapter we use the term programming to describe the process of preparing environments to support children in their play and learning.

Planning and programming for children's outdoor play experiences involves **intentionality**. Intentionality in play and teaching refers to when one acts with knowledge and purpose to ensure that young children learn while they are playing outdoors and that they have optimal experiences that will support their development. This is necessary to provide the foundation for later school success. According to Epstein (2014), intentional teaching does not happen by chance, as it involves being thoughtful and purposeful in planning. Educators from Reggio Emilia speak of the environment as the third teacher. For children, the outdoor environment is the ultimate teacher. Often programming is not necessary, as children will lead the play. Insightful early learning teachers seize the opportunity to support children's play experiences and their learning by observing and offering resources if and when necessary. At other times, experiences may be planned as a way to trigger children's curiosity or support their exploratory options.

Early learning teachers often program according to outcomes. Whether responding to a spontaneous experience that emerges outdoors or planning something purposeful for children's time in the outdoors, intentional teaching means to act with specific outcomes in mind for all domains of children's development and learning. Epstein (2014) refers to these as academic domains as outlined in Figure 9.1 (literacy, mathematics, science, and social studies), as well as what have traditionally been considered early learning domains as outlined in Figure 9.2 (social and emotional, cognitive, language, physical, and creative development). An additional consideration for early learning teachers is the current perspective of STEAM areas as outlined in Figure 9.3, which include science, technology, engineering, arts, and math. Learning to become an intentional teacher requires consideration of what is meant by theory and how theory is applied. This is foundational for being able to examine what happens in practice. This means that early learning teachers develop a thorough understanding of the theory of how play, child development, and outdoor environments influence how children execute outdoor play experiences in the academic and developmental domains and STEAM areas.

As outlined in Figure 9.4, provocations differ from invitations. Early learning teachers set out invitations to learning that may provoke a response and become provocations. A **provocation** is an invitation that has been responded to because it could not be ignored; that is, it provoked a response. An invitation that has been ignored is an opportunity for reflection (Kashin, 2017). **Invitations** are ways of creating experiences for children in the

Programming involves a process of developing curriculum (Dietze & Kashin, 2016).

Intentionality refers to being purposeful in planning experiences for children.

Karen Eilersen

Photo 9.4 Investigative play leads to new learning.

Outcomes refer to what you hope the child will be able to know or do at the conclusion of the experience.

Provocations arrive as a surprise to children. They are something unexpected and generally displayed in a way that will trigger children's curiosity and engagement.

Invitations involve the action of inviting. To be inviting is to request the presence and participation of children.

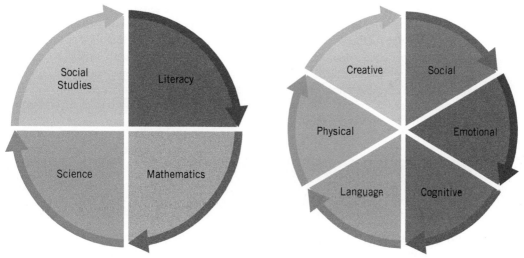

Figure 9.1 Academic domains.

Figure 9.2 Learning domains.

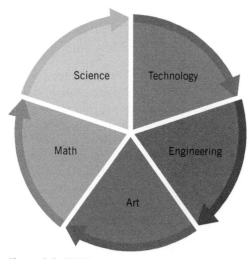

Figure 9.3 STEAM areas.

outdoor environment with which they will want to engage. The difference between invitations and provocations are depicted in Figure 9.4. They are set up intentionally. While Epstein (2014) suggested that intentional teaching begins with outcomes in mind, these do not have to be set prior to the invitation. They can be identified after the experience has occurred.

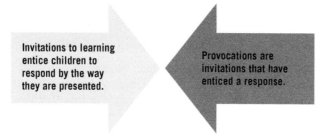

Figure 9.4 Invitations and provocations.

Outcomes related to outdoor experiences may be a requirement set by a workplace or a jurisdiction and related to a provincial framework for early learning. Outcomes are different from goals. Goals are broad and long term. Goals are not intended to be reached after one experience. Goals can be accompanied by outcomes. Both should be written with a measurable action verb. Outcomes can be measured after one experience. If these are set before an experience, early learning teachers may not see developing interests and emerging ideas, as they will be focused on assessing the goals and outcomes (Dietze & Kashin, 2017).

THINK ABOUT IT! READ ABOUT IT! WRITE ABOUT IT!

Do you think writing outcomes should come after an experience? Some call this backward planning or backward design. Read this article http://edglossary.org/backward-design/ and then write an experience with a backward design.

Photo 9.5 An outdoor experiencing meeting multiple outcomes.

Writing outcomes prior to the experience may be a practice that has to be abandoned. Setting strict expectations and overplanning may impact the ability to embrace the spontaneity of nature, which allows for early learning teachers to respond to the children's inquiries and interests (Porto, 2017). Photo 9.5 shows an outdoor invitation. The broad goal was that children would engage with each other and the materials to support the cognitive and social domain related to mathematics, language, and art. Using action verbs such as engaging, creating, designing, sorting, and composing, outcomes can be written for this experience. These are measurable after the experience.

THINK ABOUT IT! READ ABOUT IT! WRITE ABOUT IT!

Mud is an excellent source of learning for children (Rupiper, 2016). What barriers do you think might prevent an early learning teacher from providing children with invitations to explore mud in their play and learning journey? Did you know that there is an international mud day? Read about this day designed to celebrate mud https://www.daysoftheyear.com/days/international-mud-day/

According to Colyer, Reimer, Watters, and Watts (2017), an inquiry-led pedagogy is non-linear and fluid. Expectations for learning put forth by provincial curriculum frameworks can be uncovered through a process that involves the following:

- Observe and listen to children's learning;
- Notice, name, and document the learning;
- Map the learning onto a curriculum framework; and
- Negotiate next steps in learning (p. 58).

It is the role of the early learning teacher "to create opportunities for children to discover, dig deeper and construct new knowledge" (Colyer et al., 2017, p. 59). From a four-season perspective, opportunities can be framed as invitations and offered for children to learn about the cyclical and diverse wonders of nature. Each season brings different experiences for children (Watts, 2013).

>> **BOX 9.1** **Shedding Light on Outdoor Play—Points of Reflection**

You probably have heard the saying, "April showers bring May flowers". Have you also considered that spring rain also brings mud? Since the dawn of time, children have loved playing in the mud. There are many benefits to messy, muddy, and dirty play. Children can express their creativity, enhance their fine motor skills, and practice their social skills, as they cooperate, negotiate, communicate, and share with others. Emergent math and science skills are practiced as children compare, solve problems, test theories, measure, and count. Mud is also a moldable art medium that can be sculpted or used to paint. Mud play is also inclusive, as all children can play at their own developmental level (Rupiper, 2016).

In this chapter, theory will be applied to practice, as consideration is paid to invitations to experience outdoor play and nature pedagogy across seasons. The focus will be to set the stage for programming that takes full advantage of changes throughout the different seasons of the year. This is programming with intention while being open to the emerging interests of the children and the changes in the weather.

OUR VISION FOR OUTDOOR PLAY

Emergent curriculum allows for the twists and turns of children's interests as the natural world changes around them. A traditional curriculum has preset learning units or themes that teachers follow without the input of children as they encounter wonders about the world. This type of curriculum does not support children's interests or opportunities to influence their play or their curiosity. When early learning teachers respond to children's wonder, questions, and ideas about the seasons, they are co-constructing with the children. Co-construction is framed theoretically on the premise of social constructivism. Nature is unpredictable and creates the conditions for an emergent curriculum. Children can lead their own inquiries to discover the known and unknown, and this can lead to group learning (Porto, 2017). Recognizing that this unfolding of curriculum has a theoretical basis is key to developing programming that is intentional and planned, while at the same time allowing for the emerging interests, wonders, inquiries, and ideas of the children. It is our vision that early learning teachers will embrace theory and consider applications to practice as they co-construct an unfolding curriculum with children. It is our vision that early learning teachers will embrace the seasonally variant landscapes that are gifts to children's play, learning, and development. These variations provide ample opportunities for programming.

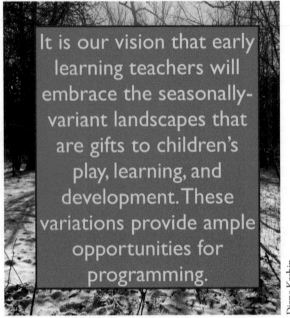

It is our vision that early learning teachers will embrace the seasonally-variant landscapes that are gifts to children's play, learning, and development. These variations provide ample opportunities for programming.

Diane Kashin

Photo 9.6 Vision statement.

When early learning teachers and students support children in embracing their interests and explorations, they embrace the unpredictability of nature and where the children take their learning. Reflect upon this question as you read Case Study 9.1 about Carmen's experience.

>> CASE STUDY 9.1 | **Learning Beyond the Tall Grass**

Carmen, an early learning teacher, knew the land that was beyond the playground. She took the children there often throughout the various seasons, as she was very familiar with the unique attributes of the space during the different times of the year. In the spring, water collected just beyond the tall grass after it rained. Sitting at their gathering place in the playground, Carmen suggested to the children that they explore the area because the rain had brought them something special. Knowing the importance of children learning together in a social construct, Carmen invited the children to make predictions about what they would find. She recorded their ideas and they set forth into the space behind the playground so that children could wander, examine, and perhaps discover a small river that flows through the area.

Carmen incorporated theory into her practice and embraced the offerings of nature to children as a way to extend their lived experiences in both play and in learning about their local space and environment. She listened intently to the children's ideas; she was open to their questions; and she supported their inquisitive minds by asking

Karen Eilerson

Photo 9.7 Looking for signs of the season.

questions that led them to engage in deeper thinking, while supporting a community of learners and culture of inquiry.

1. How might Carmen document the children's experiences?
2. In what ways could Carmen engage the families in the children's experiences?
3. What affordances might this space offer to children's play and learning in different seasons?

POSITIONING OUTDOOR PLAY IN THE LIVES OF CHILDREN

Children learn when they are curious and have a chance to make sense of their wonderings about the world around them (Colyer et al., 2017). Children are natural problem solvers. They are also natural scientists, engineers, artists, and mathematicians—they are constantly wondering about everything, then experimenting and answering their own questions. Inquiry-led pedagogy is a way to enhance children's experiences with nature play and for children to begin to make connections to various learning domains while building relationships with the environment and each other. This process is needed for, and foundational to, later academic experiences. How does seasonal play support this? Embracing an inquiry-led pedagogy requires children to have access to early learning teachers who have a commitment and conviction to the process to the point that it becomes a **stance** (Colyer, Reimer, Watters, & Watts, 2017).

The outdoor environment is rich for inquiry learning and **service learning**. Service learning benefits the world. While it is in wide use in primary, secondary, and higher education settings (Waterman, 2014), it is a newer approach that is expanding to early learning environments (Vandermaas-Peeler, McClain, & Fair, 2017). Vandermaas-Peeler and colleagues (2017) proposed environmental stewardship as a form of service learning with children. Affording young children with opportunities to develop positive relationships with nature supports their stewardship. This form of service learning can have an influence on a local and global scale due in part to the opportunities extended to children to reflect upon their experiences, interactions with peers, and ways their early learning teachers have facilitated opportunities for their ideas, explorations and discoveries to be achieved. Documentation of children's ongoing experiences help to demonstrate and make transparent their respect for and value of the natural world. For example, evidence of their environmental stewardship could be made transparent through documentation of planting, nurturing plants, growing, and eating their foods. Recycling, picking up trash, and mindful meditation in natural outdoor environments (Vandermass-Peeler et al., 2017) are other important aspects of service learning and environmental stewardship.

This type of curriculum is sometimes referred to as **ecopedagogy**, which has gained recognition as a framework for practice (Haas & Ashman, 2014). The purpose of ecopedagogy is for children to develop an ecological identity that promotes the image of children as citizens of the planet. Ecopedagogy evolved from the work of Freire (1967) and his work on critical pedagogy. The approach supports early learning teachers in challenging the beliefs and practices that have dominated current practices. With the support of early learning teachers, children can create ideas about and reflect upon ways in which they can support the natural world. In Figure 9.5, Dietze & Kashin (2017) demonstrated the relationship between ecopedagogy and ecological identity.

Jardine (2010) stated that the term ecopedagogy refers to the blending of the two terms ecology and pedagogy. He suggested that ecopedagogy is a curricular theory that helps us to think about learning from a position of place and previous learning. In Chapter 7 we examined the impact of place on the learner. In this chapter we look at the influence of place on the learning. The place has to be "perceived, sensed, understood, and interpreted by the people who are within it, surrounded by it" (Hung, 2014, p. 1390). Hung (2014) indicated that the sense of place is constructed through the experiences of the individuals who are in the place. From an early learning perspective, children will have different experiences of one place, due in part to the materials, role models, and feelings that evolve from being in the space. They also may have different experiences in the same space at different times (Hung, 2014). It is the role the early learning teacher to support the learner and the learning in place through a process of inquiry.

Stance involves standing up for something that you believe strongly in.

Service learning is an approach to education that involves learners in a wide range of experiences that are a benefit to a community (Waterman, 2014).

Ecopedagogy attempts to engage children to fully participate and better their societies (Misiaszek, 2015).

- Ecopedagogy
- Is nature based.
- Is influenced by decisions and choices related to outdoor play.
- Is based on Freire's work.
- Emphasizes the importance of helping children understand and respect the natural environment.

- Ecological Identity
- Refers to children building relationships with nature and the creatures that live there.
- Requires children to engage in ethical thinking that is aligned with respect and development of relationships among people and environment.

Figure 9.5 Ecopedagogy and ecological literacy.

Ecopedagogy aligns with the positions of Dewey, Froebel, and Gardner on programming strategies and experiences extended to children. Dewey (1916) argued that if curriculum and experiences are not built on natural contexts, children's experiences in nature become fragmented and artificial. Similarly, Froebel (1889) advocated for children to have experiential play in nature. He suggested that play in nature was fundamental for their development and that the outdoor environment and activities should be as carefully planned and implemented as those indoors; moreover, both should focus on the interaction with the natural world. Building on Dewey and Frobel's work, Gardner (2008) proposed that children require opportunities to develop **naturalistic intelligence**. This means that children benefit from experiences that help them learn to discriminate among living things as well as to acquire a sensitivity to other features of their environment and natural world.

Naturalistic intelligence refers to the ability to see patterns in nature and in making connections to the various attributes found in nature.

Photo 9.8 Developing sensitivity to the environment.

THEORETICAL FOUNDATION

Throughout history, there has been an "ancient way of passing on, from one generation to the next, knowledge of and connection to nature" (Young, Haas, & McGown, 2010, p. xxvii). This ancient form of **mentoring** originated from our ancestors, who were hunters and gathers. It was a way of passing on knowledge. Mentoring is often used in early learning and refers to a reciprocal relationship in a work environment where a more experienced educator supports the work of someone less experienced, referred to as a protégé (Dietze & Kashin, 2016).

Young, Haas, and McGown (2010) referred to the process of supporting children in realizing their full potential and to benefit their community as *Coyote Mentoring*. Using resources such as games, questioning, storytelling, and music making, children engage in core routines that support their connection to nature. This type of mentoring gently guides children in reaching their full potential. In the previous centuries, this connection happened naturally, as families depended on nature to survive. Elders taught children how to hunt, trap, fish, and gather what they needed, at the same time as how to care for the natural world.

Learning from others and experiencing nature with others is essential for children. Families, community elders, and early learning teachers can share adventures in nature with children. Carson (1956) recommended that this sharing "includes nature in storm as well as calm by night as well a day, and is based on having fun together rather than on teaching" (p. 10). Through experience, knowledge is transferred and an appreciation for nature will be developed.

The three essential elements to Coyote Mentoring involve a cyclical pattern of visits to nature, explorations of nature, and relationship building in nature, as depicted in Figure 9.6. Imagine what children can learn through this process when they visit the same location from season to season. Photo 9.9 depicts the same place from fall, to winter, to spring, and then to summer. Imagine the possibilities for play and learning!

Mentoring refers to a way of passing on knowledge so as to share it with others.

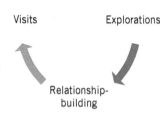

Visits   Explorations

Relationship-building

Figure 9.6 The process of Coyote Mentoring.

CURIOUS?

Are you curious about Coyote Mentoring and want to learn more? Follow this link: http://coyotesguide.com/

Early learning students and teachers benefit from the process of mentoring that focuses on questions before answers in their practice. A mentor builds on children's curiosity by formulating questions that provoke new ways of thinking for the children. The questioning process is often described as planting seeds or ideas for children to explore, rather than giving them the answers to their questions. The idea is for the early learning teacher to prepare the ground for the seed before planting it. According to Young et al. (2010), there are three levels of questioning, as listed below in Table 9.3.

Diane Kashin

Photo 9.9 Swan lake from season to season.

Table 9.3 Three levels of questioning.

Level	Type	Purpose	Example
Level One	Confidence Builder	Start with "Confidence Builder" questions, as they permit children to demonstrate what they already know.	"Tell me about what you found?"
Level Two	Edge Questions	Once there is confidence, an "Edge" question requires more searching, not only to build knowledge but also to offer opportunities that build sensory awareness and experience.	"Where do you think the frog's home is?"
Level Three	Beyond the Edge Questions	Next, "Beyond the Edge" questions remind learners to look beyond the obvious. They keep the learners thirsty to seek out answers on their own.	"Does the frog live in the same place in the winter?"

Early learning students and teachers may find that Levels One and Two questions fit better with the younger child. Using questions to build confidence and to support continued thinking and theorizing can build children's nature connection. The idea is to encourage children to look closely in nature and notice details, while wondering about their findings and developing their ecological identity.

PRACTICAL APPLICATIONS

Across Canada, children benefit from experiencing the four seasons, since this serves to build their connections to nature. We are a four-season country, even though in some areas seasonal changes may be more subtle than in others. As a way to offer children experiences for outdoor play throughout the year, Fishbaugh (2011) recommended that the coming of the seasons should be celebrated with children. When children notice the leaves of the trees are beginning to change colour and drop to the ground, this is a time to celebrate the end of the summer and the arrival of fall. When the first snow falls, it is a time to say hello to the affordances of winter with the play possibilities inherent in snow and ice. When the snow and ice melt at the end of winter, children can look for signs of new life and celebrate the arrival of spring. As the weather gets warmer, and the flora and fauna lusher, it is time to welcome the sun and the summer. Celebrate the end of one season and the arrival of another by introducing children to books focusing on the different seasons and by creating follow-up invitations that are intended to expand children's curiosity, play, and exploration, while continuing their learning (Table 9.4).

As these children's books demonstrate, each season offers affordances for outdoor play that are unique to that time of year. Within Canada there are variations and commonalities in the seasons. The first official day of autumn is September 22nd. The flowers in the garden are still vibrant, while at the same time trees are becoming colourful. Days can be

Table 9.4 Books and invitations to celebrate the seasons.

Season	Book	Invitation
Fall	Fall has arrived and the *Leafman* is on the move, travelling where the wind will take him. This book by Lois Elhert (2005) is a wonderful way to celebrate the season.	Children can be invited to create their own leaf people using a variety of leaves that they have collected themselves.
Winter	*Snow Rabbit, Spring Rabbit* by Il Sung Na (2011) is a book about changing seasons.	Children can be invited to pretend to be animals going to sleep in the winter and then waking up after months of hibernation.
Spring	Written by Nikki McClure (2010) *Mama, Is it Summer Yet?* is a book about the end of spring.	Invite children to find signs that the weather is getting warmer and think of ways to celebrate.
Summer	*Summer Wonders* written by Bob Raczka (2014) celebrates the arrival of the season in rhyme.	Invite children to be the flat rock skimmers and the sidewalk chalkers described in the book.

warm but at the same time shorter and cooler than summer. Fall can be a time for rain, wind, snow, and sun. It is a time to harvest fruits and vegetables. Winter officially arrives on December 21st, even though for weeks beforehand many parts of the country may experience days with colder temperatures, snow and ice, and darkness late in the day. Adults may not feel as enthusiastic about going outdoors in the winter; however, children benefit from the play opportunities associated with the winter season. Even though the weather is colder, if children have space to move and invitations within the space that intrigue and spark their play, they will naturally move their bodies and stay warm (Watts, 2013).

When the snow starts to melt and spring is in the air, weather can be unstable. Officially, spring starts on March 21st even though it is not unusual to experience warmer weather earlier and even snow after, right into April. There will be an increase in daylight hours. This is caused by the "axis of the earth increasing its tilt towards the sun" (Watts, 2013, p. 79). There is more light and more warmth, which increases new growth. In the spring, with buds on trees and plants swelling, the evolution of the trees and plants continue to grow and flourish into the summer. Officially summer arrives on June 21st and with the warmer

Photo 9.10 Keep moving to stay warm in the winter.

Photo 9.11 The lazy days of summer.

Table 9.5 Seasonal discoveries.

Fall	■ Leaves and fruits from trees that fall to the ground ■ Squirrels collecting nuts ■ Wild berries, fruits, and vegetables to be harvested ■ Decaying wood and fungus ■ Spiders and webs
Winter	■ Ice and frost on plants ■ Moss and lichen on trees ■ Pine needles and pine cones on the ground ■ Animal tracks in the snow ■ Cloud patterns in the sky
Spring	■ Buds sprouting ■ Birds chirping ■ Squirrels scampering ■ Insects emerging ■ Toads spawning ■ Caterpillars ■ Butterfly eggs on milkweed ■ Spring bulbs blooming ■ Wildflowers and weeds appearing
Summer	■ Insects and wildlife ■ Grasses, plants, shrubs, and trees ■ Effect of the sunlight as it reflects and creates shadows ■ Twigs, sticks, acorns, pinecones, and other materials that have fallen to the forest floor ■ Leaves eaten by caterpillars or insects ■ Effect of dry spells upon flowers and plants ■ Aromas of flowers ■ Bees, butterflies, wasps, and dragonflies

Source: Adapted from Watt, 2013.

weather and the sun shining, the season has a relaxing feel (Watts, 2013). Table 9.5 lists some of the seasonal discoveries that children can make.

In all seasons, children can be offered clipboards for recording or drawing their findings. They can be offered magnifying glasses or sheets. Having buckets, pails, and baskets will encourage collecting. Reference books, field guides, or photographs to identify plants and wildlife will help children to learn about what they find. Gardening tools, shovels, pots, pans, and kitchen utensils will encourage exploration. Cameras are excellent tools to inspire children to look closer and notice details.

In addition to the unique affordances of each season, there are play experiences that can continue throughout the year. The invitations that early learning teachers provide to children encourage self-directed play. Early learning teachers are not play directors; rather they become researchers that observe, record, and document how children respond. Reflecting upon and examining the documentation will open the path of an emerging curriculum.

Intentionally providing invitations in outdoor places and spaces that support self-directed play reflects an early learning teacher's understanding about how children learn and develop. Children learn through heightened curiosity and opportunities for discovery. From birth, babies begin the learning process, which is based on and reinforced by experiences. The process requires children to be active learners. As identified by Watts (2013)

Learning is not a passive process of knowledge acquisition with measurable and predictable outcomes. It is a process that draws on past experiences so that the learner can understand and evaluate the present before taking action to shape the future and thereby acquire new knowledge. (p. 17)

The role of the early learning teacher is to support active and self-directed learning while providing opportunities to extend and expand the experiences. Figure 9.7 illustrates how children learn in their outdoor environment. As you examine the figure, consider how to expand and extend children's opportunities for these experiences across seasons.

When toddlers play in a mud kitchen in the spring, they explore the texture of the dirt while filling the empty pot with mud. They discover that the pot becomes heavier and when half of the contents are emptied into another container, they begin to connect prior knowledge about weight distribution with the new experience. Taking both pots by the handles, children may try to climb up onto a platform. They are taking a risk because one or more of them may fall due to their difficulty in balancing. They may put one pot down and try again. This time there may be success, leading one or more of the children to climb down to retrieve the remaining pots. The children remain engaged in this experience. The early learning teacher observed the children's play closely and reflected on each of their strengths in using their creativity and critical thinking skills. Now imagine the mud kitchen in the summer. The toddler may now have access to water. How will the experience change? In autumn, leaves may be added to the mixtures, and in the winter, they may explore how the frozen concoction of leaves, dirt, and water has changed and how the ice skim on the platform changes their strategies for climbing there.

In this chapter, we focus on infants and toddlers who learn from their whole bodies and all their senses. They are physical thinkers, and through investigations with their senses they secure knowledge of the physical characteristics of objects and materials in their environment. This knowledge can be evoked at a later date (Atherton & Nutbrown, 2016). Infants and toddlers often repeat behaviours as they explore and discover the world

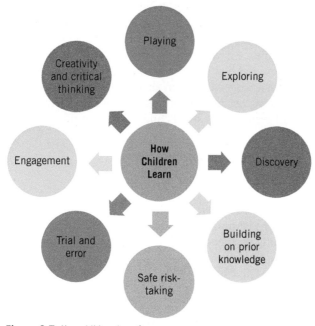

Figure 9.7 How children learn?

around them, including how their environments may change from one season to the next. These repeated behaviours are patterns or **schemas**. Piaget and Cook (1952) suggested that when children repeat actions they are able to transfer their knowledge into similar situations. Grimmer (2017) proposed that through repeated actions, children are investigating "whether what they think happens will happen again" (p. 12). Through exploration children are able to generalize about objects while categorizing and classifying their properties to make assumptions about what will happen (Grimmer, 2017).

As children engage in schematic play, they experiment with what they can do unaided or independently. They are experimenting like scientists. Early learning teachers observe, support, extend, and expand on children's schema play as appropriate. Theorists have identified a number of schemas that can be observed in children's play. These schemas do not occur in isolation from each other, as they often are linked and connected. For instance, children could be positioning with tree cookies in lines as they build a border and enclose a patch of grass (Grimmer, 2017). Nutbrown (2011) suggested the following:

- Connecting/Disconnecting—joining, connecting, disconnecting objects together
- Positioning—putting objects in lines, rows or positioning by size
- Enclosing—climbing into things or enclosing by building borders
- Enveloping—hiding or being covered up; wrapping or covering objects
- Transporting—moving things from one place to another
- Orientation—seeing things from different perspectives
- Rotation—spinning or rotating objects; interest in circular movements
- Trajectory—moving objects in space by throwing or bouncing; an interest in running water
- Transforming—exploring and seeing changes in objects and materials

Let's consider schema play across seasons as a strategy for early learning teachers to support children making sense of their world. Table 9.6 features the categories of schema play and suggested ways to support children from one season to the next.

Over 20 years ago, Gopnik (1996) suggested that adults view children as scientists. Developments in neuroscience have led to important discoveries about how much infants and young children know and how they learn. During their early years, children can use the same methods that scientists use to learn about the world (Gopnik, Meltzoff, & Kuhl, 2000). When early learning teachers adopt the principles of science-based learning into their practice, they can expand and extend children's play in their outdoor environment.

PRINCIPLES OF PRACTICE: SCIENCE-BASED PRACTICE

Early learning students and teachers use the process of scientific inquiry to support intentionality in outdoor planning and programming. Take the example of Jeremy and Honey, two early learning teachers who thought about ways to extend and expand on the experiences that the children had with a towering and majestic maple tree that they began to visit in the early fall. The children loved looking up to see how tall the tree was and would link arms to hug it to see how big it was around. In conversations, they would refer to the tree as "our tree". Over time, Jeremy and Honey suggested that the children adopt the tree. They created a plan to visit the tree every week, in every season, to observe

---

Schemas as defined by Athey (2007) are patterns of repeated behaviours.

Table 9.6 Schemas by season.

Schemas	Fall	Winter	Spring	Summer
Connecting/ Disconnecting	Scattering the leaf pile or knocking down sand structures; lifting pinecones on a pulley system.	Smashing ice with hammers and rocks; extracting toys and loose parts that have been frozen in a container.	Clearing out the walking path in the forest from fallen debris.	Connecting troughs and tubes to create a water course and/or a mudslide.
Positioning	Lining up leaves from largest to smallest; grouping them by colour, etc.	Stacking snowballs into a snowperson; stringing ropes between trees to help support navigation.	Creating a walking path/bridge by placing large wood cookies and planks in the muck.	Building a lookout tower using logs, boards, fabric pieces, and ropes.
Enclosing	Sitting in a pile of leaves.	Digging a hole out of the snow and sitting inside.	Jumping and sitting in puddles.	Sitting in tires; walking through tall grasses; being surrounded.
Enveloping/ Containing	Filling containers with leaves, rocks, and pine cones.	Winding tree trunks with yarn and fabric strips to "keep them warm."	Gathering branches to create a fort/den and hiding in it.	Creating a house out of large cardboard boxes and using in it dramatic play.
Transporting	Moving tree cookies, rocks, pumpkins, and gourds in a wagon.	Carrying ice chunks in a pail to move them and listen to the sounds they make.	Lifting soil into a wheelbarrow and pushing it to fill the garden beds.	Moving water in buckets, through hoses and clear tubing.
Orientating	Finding one's way out of a maze (corn field, hay bales).	Weaving fabric and branches through the fence.	Finding treasures hiding under rocks.	Climbing trees or milk crates to get the best view.
Rotating	Spinning self and falling into a pile of leaves; spinning on a tire swing.	Rolling self and/or large tubes down a snowy hill; hanging birdseed balls from trees.	Stirring up water and mud in the mud kitchen.	Painting with a swinging pendulum hanging from a tree.
Following a Trajectory	Rolling wood cookies down a hill.	Tobogganing, skating, and playing hockey.	Collecting and creating ribbon sticks to swirl through the air; blowing bubbles with solution made from melted snow.	Splashing water with scoops and throwing it at the wall, creating water representations.
Transforming	Cutting open a pumpkin and cooking the seeds for snack.	Putting containers outdoors and creating ice, spraying ice with coloured water/ liquid, painting ice with brushes or turkey basters.	Visiting the same place and noticing how long it takes for the leaves on the trees to appear; making froth and bubbles in water pockets found in the forest.	Pounding flowers and grasses with a mallet; creating natural art patterns.

seasonal changes and to care for the tree. Using scientific inquiry as their strategy to build on the children's learning, the early learning teachers and children collected more data to interpret and analyze. They assumed the role of teacher as researcher and supported the children to be researchers as well. This is the scientific method. It begins with observation. Figure 9.8 illustrates the steps involved in the scientific method.

The tree inquiry spanned across the four seasons. The children observed the changes in the tree and classified what they noticed by season. They would wonder, predict, and create their own theories (hypothesize) about what the impact of the coming season would be on the tree. They would inspect the tree closely during their visits to notice changes in the leaves, the coverings on the trunk of the tree, the wildlife, the sky, the temperature, and the flowers and plants that surrounded the tree. They kept a record of their wonderings in a science journal. The children constantly looked through the journal as part of their strategies to test out their theories and build upon new ideas and wonderments. The children drew conclusions about the seasons and communicated their findings to others, including their families.

Jeremy and Honey had not planned to adopt the tree or that the children would care about it. The experience led the children to gift the tree with special rocks or clay creatures. They worried about the tree after a severe storm. When they visited the tree, they picked up trash and swept around the bark. The children had made a connection to place. They became attached to the place where their tree lived. This is the beginning action of environmental stewardship and sustainability.

LEARNING IN PLACE: THE POND AS PLACE

In Chapter 8, the suggestion was made to adopt a pond. The pond as place offers children significant opportunities to make connections to the environment. How does the pond change over the seasons? What can children discover at the pond from one season

Observation

Classification

Wonder,
Prediction,
Hypothesis

Experiment,
Test,
Exploration

Drawing
Conclusions

Communication
of Ideas

Figure 9.8 The scientific method.

Diane Kashin

Photo 9.12 Learning at the pond.

to the next? When children have the opportunity to visit a pond over the course of the year, their experiences will change; they will develop new knowledge about ponds, water, and vegetation, and their connection to place will intensify.

In the fall, the children engaged in pond dipping experiences while noticing the leaves floating on the surface. In the winter, the pond freezes, and when the ice melts in the spring, pond plants, fish, and animals return. Children can engage in scientific inquiry when they observe and classify what they see over the year. The learning can be enhanced with books about ponds such as *In the Small, Small Pond* by Denise Fleming (1993) and Frank Serafina's *Looking Closely Around the Pond* (2010). Taking an inventory of the pond, vegetation and animal life over the seasons supports math, science, language and literacy, while enhancing environmental stewardship. What are some examples of what the children may notice from one season to the next? For example, they can count and record the number of geese at the pond when they visit. They can reflect on how the number of geese changes over the seasons and why. When early learning teachers focus on programming for outdoor play and learning, the possibilities are endless.

THINK ABOUT IT! READ ABOUT IT! WRITE ABOUT IT!

What experiences could you plan for using a local pond as a place for learning? What materials would you bring for the children to engage with the pond? A list of experiences and equipment can be found by following this link: https://naturefamilies.org/tag/inquiry-project/. Now find a pond closest to you and plan an experience for children based on the current season. Reflect on how this experience would support children's curiosity and the supplies needed to spark their curiosity. Will the list change over the year?

PROGRAMMING

Early learning teachers plan invitations for children for outdoor and nature play. These do not have to be elaborate plans since nature inspires children. Nature invites observation, exploration, and experimentation. Nature offers surprises and opportunities for challenge. "In many instances, as children interact with the natural world, it's nature that will do the teaching" (Wilson, 2016, p. 26). No matter what the age, nature can foster children's imagination and creativity. Early learning teachers may find programming for outdoor play children under the age of three more challenging than programming for older children. For infants and toddlers, natural loose parts are inviting. They captivate the children in part because of their open-ended properties. However, choking is a concern if the parts are small because young children tend to put objects into their mouths. The provision of natural loose parts for infants and toddlers is always contingent on whether or not choking could be hazard. Therefore, early learning teachers test the products for this possibility (Beloglovsky & Daly, 2016). Following the PEER Principle of Plan, Engage, Explore, and Reflect, Table 9.7 illustrates an invitation utilizing natural found materials safe for infants and toddlers to use when supervised.

Table 9.7 Plan, engage, explore, reflect—banging on natural loose parts.

PLAN	Infants and toddlers love to bang on objects to make music (Beloglovsky & Daly, 2016). Plan an invitation that supports this desire; their agility and skills will increase while they explore the potential of sticks, rocks, large tree slabs, and pieces of bark.
ENGAGE	Present the materials in an invitational way so that they are accessible to the children. Ensure there are enough sticks, rocks, and large tree slabs for multiple children to engage in a banging experience.
EXPLORE	Using the sticks or the rocks to bang the tree slabs, they are exploring the cause of their actions. The sounds that the sticks and rocks make as they meet the tree slab intensify with force. Toddlers may create rhythmic patterns by banging with these loose parts. This exploration of creating rhythmic patterns supports children later as they explore reading and writing (Beloglovsky & Daly, 2016).
REFLECT	Did the children engage with the loose parts? Reflect on the different ways that the children explored them. Did the children experiment with loud and soft banging? Did they create rhythmic patterns? How can this experience be extended from season to season?

Diane Kashin

Photo 9.13 An invitation to bang on natural loose parts.

FAMILY SUPPORT AND ENGAGEMENT

Early learning teachers have a responsibility to engage families in their outdoor play and learning experiences. Through engagement, families can be supported in continuing the opportunities and interests that children have for outdoor play. When planning for experiences, determining how to share them with families is important. In Chapter 11, documentation will be examined. In this chapter, we ask you to consider how digital documentation can be used to support families in learning about their children's outdoor play and how they may encourage further engagement and experiences. Natural loose parts are easy to find. By providing digital images of their children's experiences with these materials and documenting the benefits for learning and development, the hope is that families will be encouraged to get outdoors with their children in the evenings, weekends, and holidays throughout the year.

Watts (2013) suggested that when early learning teachers venture out on a walk with the children, they make a map and send it home with the children. This may inspire families to use the map with their children to repeat the journey. The children can take a lead role in the outing, as they describe and discuss what they have previously observed. A documentation panel can be created that is featured in an area accessible to families so that they can see images of local places to visit in all seasons. Families can be encouraged to share their own photos of their experiences in these places and to bring in any materials that they found. The children may use these materials in their play. In this way, families can extend the experiences that children have for outdoor play in and with nature.

ACCESSIBILITY AND DESIGN

Outdoor spaces can be designed to support all season play. Keeler (2016) proposed that by adding seasonal plants, natural spaces for children could change in each season. With thought and preparation, children can enjoy the late harvest vegetables of autumn. In the winter, with the right clothing, children can continue to play with sand and even water. In the spring, the garden can be tended to as the sprouts rise up. In the summer, children seek shady spots designed to shield the sun. These spots become places to hide and engage in pretend play. Bulbs can be planted that bloom in spring, offering a variety of colour, texture, and smells. Pots of lavender and herbs can be added in the summer to attract butterflies and other insects. In the fall, the flowerpot garden is prepped for the coming of frost (Watts, 2013). With careful consideration and preparation, outdoor spaces for children can be engaging all year.

TIPS AND TOOLS FOR OUTDOOR PLAY

Early learning teachers who recognize that play comes from the children provide intentional invitations to play, such as taking children to an open field where they can direct their own play. Adults take cues from children about entering play and not imposing themselves into the play. Intentionality with the provision of tools, materials, and supplies will encourage the children to engage in self-directed play. Here are some tips for what can be added to the outdoor environment:

- Photos of nature artists such as Robert Bateman and Georgia O'Keefe.
- A composter to encourage environmental awareness and sustainability.
- Magnifying glasses and magnifying sheets.
- Cameras to zoom into nature to encourage the children to notice details.
- Buckets and nets to practise pond dipping.
- Gardening tools, potting soil, and containers.
- Natural clay for creating creatures, embellishing trees, or pounding with sticks.
- Bird baths and butterfly gardens to entice visitors for the children to observe and wonder about.

Even the youngest learners can find wonder in nature. No matter what the age of the learner, outdoor play is foundational for learning, development, and wellness.

ON THE GROUND—PROFESSIONAL REFLECTIONS: "WHY I LOVE OUTDOOR PLAY"

>> **BOX 9.3** **Why I Love Outdoor Play**

As an infant teacher, I love outdoor play. Having the very youngest of children in my care gives me a wonderful and important opportunity to share the outdoors with them. I know that sometimes I am the first one they get to feel the grass with. It is amazing to watch infants when they are outside exploring for the first few times. I love to see the change in their faces when they feel the warm sun or the cold snow or when they feel grass between their fingers for the first time. I love to see the pause that takes place when they are crawling around and then come to a new material—sand! My children have always seemed eager to hold and taste the nature we have just outside our classroom. Sometimes I hold them next to a tree so they can see, touch, and taste the leaves, or offer a snap off of a long piece of grass for them to hold and explore while they are lying in the grass. The outdoors gives us a place to explore our senses like no other space. I'm not sure what I would do without it!

Olivia Wendorf
Infant Teacher
Used with the permission of Olivia Wendorf

CASE STUDIES

Sometimes there can be resistance to increasing children's exposure to outdoor play on the part of colleagues or families. Read Case Study 9.2 to learn about one early learning teacher who was faced with this obstacle, and consider the questions that follow to reflect on what you would do in a similar situation.

CASE STUDY 9.2 Feeling Frustrated About Outdoor Play

Lisa was fortunate to have had the opportunity to take a 36-hour course on outdoor play. For six Saturdays throughout the spring and fall, she met with a group of early learning teachers to learn. They spent most of the time learning outdoors. Even though there were course materials online, that didn't prevent them from learning together in nature. They loaded the materials onto their devices and brought them to the forest. Together the early learning teachers in Lisa's course explored the concepts of curiosity, wonder, risky play, nature pedagogy, and the pedagogy of place. They got to see how the forest changed between their visits, and they became very observant. Lisa was very excited when one of the other teachers showed her a tiny monarch egg on a milkweed plant and weeks later she noticed butterflies in the same spot. Her colleagues at work did not share Lisa's excitement for outdoor play and learning. This dampened her enthusiasm and caused her stress. They did not want the children to play in the rain. Lisa knew from the time she spent outdoors that there was so much to be learned when playing in the rain. Her colleagues often indicated the families as the reason for keeping the children indoors during wet weather. They said that the families did not want their children to catch a cold or to get their clothes wet. Lisa was worried. She knew that winter was coming and that her colleagues would once again complain about children being outside in the cold, snowy weather. She knew that once again, they would suggest that it was the families who wanted the children to remain indoors.

1. Lisa felt isolated in her beliefs about the importance of outdoor play. How might she help her colleagues understand?
2. How might Lisa approach the families to engage them in a discussion about the benefits of outdoor play?
3. What types of invitations would you suggest Lisa might provide when it rains or snows to illustrate the benefits of outdoor play during all seasons?

BOX 9.4 Take It Outside!

Go outside in all types of weather and think about the affordances that each season offers children for playing and learning. Once you have experienced rain, snow, sun, and wind, you will be able to consider ways for children to experience seasonal play.

KEY TERMS

Activity
Experience
Emergent curriculum
Negotiated curriculum
Pedagogy
Programming
Intentionality
Outcomes
Provocations
Invitations
Stance
Service learning
Ecopedagogy
Naturalistic intelligence
Mentoring
Schemas

Diane Kashin

Photo 9.14 Key terms.

Summary

- Children in Canada need access to outdoor play in the four seasons.

- Research suggests that children's opportunities for physically active outdoor play varies depending on the season. Being outdoors is an important predictor of children's physical activity levels, as well as other indicators of healthy development.

- Early learning teachers engage in a weather assessment process when determining whether it is safe for children and teachers to engage in outdoor play.

- Intentionally inviting children to play involves experiential learning. An experience is different than an activity. The term experience implies a deeper level of potential learning. An activity implies a limited provision for children.

- Curriculum is emergent when it evolves from children's interests. Place provides many possibilities for emerging interests. An emergent curriculum is negotiated within a community of learners that includes teachers, children, families, and the community.

- Pedagogy is not the same as curriculum. Curriculum is the content of the potential experiences that children may engage in and what we facilitate. Pedagogy is about how we teach it. Pedagogy is how learning happens.

- Early learning teachers often program according to outcomes based on academic domains (literacy, mathematics, science, and social studies), as well as what have traditionally been considered early learning domains (social and emotional, cognitive, language, physical, and creative development). In addition, consideration is given to the STEAM areas (science, technology, engineering, arts, and math).

- Inquiry-led pedagogy is a way to enhance children's experiences with nature play. The outdoor environment is rich for inquiry learning and service learning. Service learning benefits the world. Environmental stewardship is a form of service learning. This type of curriculum is sometimes referred to as ecopedagogy. The purpose of ecopedagogy is for children to develop an ecological identity that promotes the image of children as citizens of the planet.

- Some researchers have referred to the process of supporting children in realizing their full potential and to benefit their community as *Coyote Mentoring*. Resources such as games, questioning, storytelling, and music making support children's connection to nature. In the previous centuries, this connection happened naturally, as families depended on nature to survive. Elders taught children how to hunt, trap, fish, and gather what they needed at the same time as caring for the natural world. The three elements essential to Coyote mentoring include a cyclical pattern of visits to nature, explorations of nature, and relationship building in nature.

- Children's books can be used as part of the celebration of seasons. Early learning teachers support children to make seasonal discoveries in nature. Each season offers different affordances for play and learning.

- Infants and toddlers learn from their whole bodies and all their senses. Infants and toddlers often repeat behaviours as they explore and discover the world around them, including how their environments may change from one season to the next. These repeated behaviours are patterns or schemas. Schemas can be observed in children's outdoor play experiences.

- Early learning students and teachers use the process of scientific inquiry to support intentionality in outdoor planning and programming, following the steps that include observation, classification, wondering, predicting and hypothesizing, experimenting, testing, exploring, and drawing conclusions and communicating ideas.

- The pond as place offers children significant opportunities to make connections to the environment. When children have the opportunity to visit a pond over the course of the year, their experiences will change; they will develop new knowledge about ponds, water, and vegetation and their connection to place will intensify.

- Early learning teachers have a responsibility to engage families in their outdoor play and learning experiences. By providing digital images of their children's experiences with these materials and documenting the benefits for learning and development, the hope is that families will be encouraged to get outdoors with their children in the evenings, weekends, and holidays throughout the year.

- Outdoor spaces can be designed to support all season play. Researchers have proposed that by adding seasonal plants, natural spaces for children could change in each season. With careful consideration and preparation, outdoor spaces for children can be engaging all year.

- Intentionality with the provision of tools, materials, and supplies will encourage the children to engage in self-directed play.

QUIET REFLECTION

Quietly, as you are outside in your sit spot, try to evoke the sensory experience of each season. In winter, what did you feel when your cheeks were cold and red and snowflakes landed on your eyelashes? In the spring, what did it feel like to have the sun on your cheeks and smell the freshness in the air? What did the raindrops taste like when you caught them with your tongue? In the summer, do you remember what it felt like to be so hot that you needed to take shelter from the sun and find a shady spot? Do you recall what it felt like to jump in a pile of leaves? Was it joyful? What did you smell, taste, and touch when you were in that pile? Think about to how the leaves sounded as you played. You may have found it easy to evoke these feelings. Perhaps it is because they were so strong and powerful. This is what we want children to experience today.

COMMUNITY DIALOGUE

There are ways to seeks like-minded others when early learning teachers feel isolated in their beliefs and values about outdoor play and nature pedagogy. Even if they are not physically in proximity, there are early learning teachers active on Facebook and on Twitter who support and advocate for outdoor play. There are multiple pages and groups to join. Posting on Facebook pages and groups can involve sharing articles and sites that you find inspiring in order to encourage others in dialogue. You can also post and ask for recommendations to support further learning. Early learning teachers also post to seek advice and feedback.

FOR FURTHER THOUGHT AND ACTION

The p.i.n.e. project is a Canadian charitable organization with a mission to build healthy communities, deeply connected to the natural environment. They support, encourage, and teach the mentoring approach to nature connection. Check out their website to see what they can offer you as you become an advocate for outdoor play and learning: https://www.pineproject.org/

RESOURCES

Creating Outdoor Learning Environments is an initiative from the province of Saskatchewan to support children's learning experiences outdoors. The objectives of the document are to: assist with the development of safe and stimulating outdoor learning environments; increase awareness of the benefits of outdoor play for children; and increase understanding of the educator's role in supporting outdoor play. The document can be found here:

http://publications.gov.sk.ca/documents/11/86146-Outdoor%20Learning%20Environments%20Resource%20Booklet.pdf

CHAPTER 10

Supporting Families and Others in Connecting Children's Play to Their Development

A child, more than anyone else, is a spontaneous observer of nature.

(Maria Montessori, 1870–1952)

LEARNING OUTCOMES

After exploring this chapter, you will be able to:

- Describe how outdoor play contributes to children's overall development.

- Discuss the relationship between brain development and outdoor play.

- Describe what community and journeys mean and how these concepts influence children's outdoor play and learning, as well as their connections to observations, engagement, and intergenerational learning.

- Explain the relationship of Maslow's hierarchy of needs to programming and outdoor play.

- Describe how nature nurtures children's well-being.

- Describe the role of early learning teachers and families in promoting children's outdoor play experiences.

CHILDHOOD MEMORIES

When my siblings and I reminisce about our childhood, we talk about going to the brook, running through the culvert, and having the freedom to roam between our play space near our home and those fabulous fields nearby. We think about pulling our toboggans to the hill in the day and on many winter evenings in the dark—and then walking home under the stars in anticipation of having a cup of hot cocoa with marshmallows on top. Now, whenever I have a chance to provide children with experiences that contribute to them feeling free to play in nature, I feel as though I am offering them a glimpse of an old-fashioned childhood.

CHAPTER PREVIEW

Children with opportunities for outdoor play gain a wide range of health, social, and cultural benefits that are associated with their rights as children to play (Park & Riley, 2015). These include the development of connectedness to people and the environment, creativity, aesthetic and kinesthetic awareness, as well as social and cooperation skills (Hirsh-Pasek, Michnick Golinkoff, Berk, & Singer, 2009; Brown, 2015). When children have a chance to play vigorously and explore nature, they release stress. Compared to children who spend less time playing outside, they eat and sleep better. Given these physical and psychological benefits, communities, families, and early learning teachers have a significant role to play in the lives of children (Park & Riley, 2015).

Nurturing children is one of the most important roles of families, early learning teachers, and communities. Children's development is influenced by characteristics of both the family and the child, such as family harmony (Bekkhus, Rutter, Maughan, & Borge, 2011), social and economic factors, the temperaments of the children, families, and early learning teachers, and the educational levels of families and early learning teachers (Ulset, Vitaro, Brendgen, Bekkhus, & Borge, 2017). All children benefit from play that they initiate. This type of play gives them a feeling of freedom. Unstructured, outdoor play environments have more positive developmental and health values for children than any other experiences or activities (McFarland, Zajicek, & Waliczek, 2014). A recurring theme in research literature today suggests "the decline in free play has resulted in the rise of psychopathology in children, particularly increased anxiety, depression, and narcissism" (McFarland, Zajicek, & Waliczek, 2014, p. 527). Play is considered free when it is freely chosen by the children (Dietze & Kashin, 2018).

Somatic problems refer to feeling anxiety about physical symptoms such as pain or fatigue.

Many researchers, including Gill (2007) and Sandseter and Kennair (2011), have identified that children's social, emotional, cognitive, and physical development benefits when play occurs "that is less supervised, less structured, more adventurous and that includes elements of challenge and risk" (Alexander, Frohlich, & Fusco, 2012, p. 157). Similarly, Kemple, Oh, Kenny, and Smith-Bonahue (2016) found that the developmental experiences that children gain from outdoor play cannot be replicated through other means. Ulrich (2002) outlined more than 15 years ago that outdoor play promotes health and prevents mental and **somatic problems**. This perspective has been influenced by great thinkers such as Henry David Thoreau (1854/1955), a philosopher and writer, whose many literary works include those focusing on natural history and the beauty of nature, and John Muir (1911/1987), a naturalist, author, and environmentalist. John Muir wrote about respecting nature and understanding that emotions of humans are influenced by being in nature (Brinkley, 2017). The influence of Muir and Thoreau has led to a school of thought that is fascinated by the way children's dispositions show more positive attributes when they have opportunities to consistently play, engage, and experience an array of environments, including those with wilderness (Brinkley, 2017).

Outdoor play and nature can be viewed in many ways. Early learning teachers benefit from determining what it means to them from a philosophical and practical perspective. For example, does it mean play that occurs in the wilderness or play in open-spaces? Does it mean that outdoor and nature play in the early learning space where plants, trees, and animals are present? Must the space have trees and greenery to be considered outdoor play and nature? How do play spaces with playground equipment fit when defining outdoor and nature play? Often, the view is dependent

Photo 10.1 Learning in variant landscapes.

Photo 10.2 Children benefit from adult support.

on lived experiences, attitudes, and values adopted about how children's play contributes to their health and well-being. Ideally, children will have a variety of experiences in a number of learning landscapes.

As the health, wellness, and academic benefits of outdoor play become increasingly apparent, educators, health professionals, families, and others are concerned about how to address the increased number of children who are not having access to the outdoors or exposure to outdoor environments (Alexander, Frohlich, & Fusco, 2012). Early learning teachers and families have an important role in identifying the types of barriers and challenges that reduce children's access to outdoor play and determining ways in which outdoor play can be advanced (Beyer, Bizub, Szabo, Heller, Kistner, Shawgo, & Zetts, 2016).

Children's environments and experiences in early learning programs are influenced by government policies and procedures, including child/adult ratios, group size, and minimum daily requirements for outdoor play. Despite this, the attitudes of adults have far more influence on children's exposure to and engagement in outdoor play than the actual policies (Norodahl & Johannesson, 2015). "Although specific definitions of 'attitude' vary among social scientists, generally, there is agreement that it refers to a propensity to react in a positive or negative way to external stimuli" (Beyer et al., 2016, p. 254). The attitudes and behaviours that adults exhibit when outdoors have a profound impact on children's desire to play, their depth of play and duration of play, and the types of play that they engage in, which in turn influences their learning (Williams, 2016).

Children require exposure to adults who have an understanding of, and interest in, sharing their positive enthusiasm for outdoor environments. This would suggest that children's sense of curiosity and patterns of connectedness to outdoor environments emerge and increase with exposure to adults who positively respond to play, nature, and exploration of environments (Oke & Middle, 2016). A major role of early learning teachers is to partner with children to identify their interests outdoors and to encourage them to observe the beauty of nature and place. Ideally, as outlined in Figure 10.1, early learning

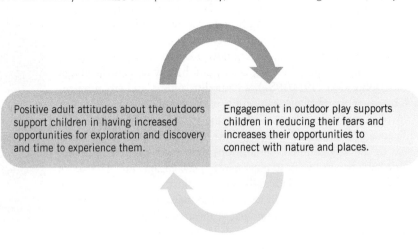

Positive adult attitudes about the outdoors support children in having increased opportunities for exploration and discovery and time to experience them.

Engagement in outdoor play supports children in reducing their fears and increases their opportunities to connect with nature and places.

Results in children's healthy development and attitudes toward outdoor play in nature.

Figure 10.1 Adult attitudes influence children's development.

teachers who enter the profession with positive attitudes toward outdoor play will influence children's connections to the environment enormously (Koc, 2012).

Children benefit from outdoor play environments with adults who role model:

- Planning for experiences and opportunities reflective of children interests;
- Having a philosophy that positions outdoor play as a core value;
- Engaging with children when appropriate during outdoor play;
- Embracing the elements of the outdoor environment in all kinds of weather; and
- Emphasizing that outdoor play is equally valuable to indoor experiences.

To support outdoor play opportunities, early learning teachers facilitate, sustain, and extend the potential types of experiences that children have outdoors. Think about the roles of early learning teachers as they relate to outdoor play experiences. Then, examine the questions in Table 10.1. As you will note, there are many questions and reflections that early learning teachers may consider when thinking about outdoor play and their roles. How early learning teachers approach outdoor play has lasting effects on the lives of children (Ergler, Kearns, & Witten, 2016).

When early learning teachers have a thorough understanding of the relationship of outdoor play to development, they are better prepared to encourage and facilitate play. This includes extending play and scaffolding options that contribute to children leading their own investigations (Brown, 2015) and reaching their highest level of development. Scaffolding is a metaphor that refers to ways of providing support for children as they learn (Zurek, Torquati, & Acar, 2014). Visualize the scaffolding that is erected at a construction site. Early learning teachers use scaffolding as a strategy to support children's learning. Similar to the way that scaffolding is built to just the needed level when constructing a building and then removed when the building is complete, "educators engage in scaffolding by providing the necessary level and type of support that is well-timed to children's needs" (Zurek, Torquati, & Acar, 2014, p. 28). This means that early learning teachers are constantly reflecting upon what they see and hear to determine what would be the most effective strategy to support the next phase of scaffolding.

A certain level of intentionality and preparation is required in order to use scaffolding strategies that support the children in their outdoor play experiences. At times, the opportunities for scaffolding arise spontaneously (Zurek, Torquati, & Acar, 2014). As part of the scaffolding process, Leong and Bodrova (2012) identified that early learning teachers observe children's play and through those observations determine ways in which they can support children with materials, resources, and dialogue that will expand their thinking and experiences during play. Early learning teachers examine how, who, and

Table 10.1 The diverse roles of early learning teachers in outdoor play.

Is sufficient outdoor time provided to children?

What kinds of materials do children have access to in their outdoor learning environments?

What do early learning teachers think about and look for when supporting children's play and learning outdoors?

How are children having opportunities to be creative learners and to develop dispositions that embrace the outdoors?

How do early learning teachers support families in understanding the differences between outdoor play that is child-directed versus adult-directed activities that take place outside?

Photo 10.3 Building forts from sticks and stones.

what children are playing with and then use this knowledge in the scaffolding process. Teachers create options that children may consider and that will ultimately stretch their ideas and motivate them to try new ideas. For example, assume that there is a group of children who are continuously using large sticks and rocks to create forts, as depicted in Photo 10.3. The children have been involved in this play for more than a week. The early learning teachers have been observing and documenting what the children have been captivated by. They use this information to track where the children may be capable of expanding their play. Then, the early learning teachers add new resources that will require children to use new skills, language, and engage in a trial and error process that leads them to discover if and how to use the materials. This expansion may lead children to advance their social, language, problem-solving, planning, and imagining skills.

The African proverb—*it takes a village to raise a child*—has been widely quoted and remains relevant today. The partnerships among families, children, early learning teachers, and communities, or as the proverb states, "villages," are essential in ensuring that children have opportunities to connect and reconnect with nature, the outdoors, and the environment in which they live. The interactions that children have with the people, places, and environments influence how they evolve to appreciate their surroundings (Ergler, Kearns, & Witten, 2016). As outlined in Chapter 5, the Russian developmental psychologist, Uri Bronfenbrenner, had an ecological model that emphasized how the relationship of early learning teachers, families, and others such as government can influence how children develop, think about, and engage in the outdoor environments. The challenge for early learning teachers is twofold; first, early learning teachers require a deep and thorough understanding of the theoretical constructs of outdoor play that they share with families; and second, they personally must embrace and role model in their programming, actions, and curiosity about the outdoor environments.

SETTING THE STAGE FOR OUTDOOR PLAY

Outdoor play aligns with brain development. Children's brains develop and thrive in environments with positive experiences. The basic architecture of the brain is built over time, with a large percentage of the neural connections or synapses being developed during the first six years (Louie & Sherren, 2017). The more children experience positive play outdoors, the more the experiences will remain with them and become part of their healthy brain architecture. As part of the synaptic pruning process, the circuits that are not used are eliminated, while those that are used become more efficient (Louie & Sherren, 2017). Think about children who are intrigued by the wonders of snails and worms. In the right environment, early learning teachers and families support children in looking for them, viewing them, and observing how they move and travel from one location to another. How might this support their brain development and how might it transfer to other experiences? Now think about it in reverse. What happens when early learning teachers or families discourage or stop this level of exploration? How does this affect the structure of brain development?

Bullick (2017) held that the process of building healthy brain architecture is influenced by adults and children engaging in the **serve and return** exchange process. This process influences the formation of relationships and the wiring for language, and it is the foundation for social, emotional, and exploratory functions. The outdoor play environment is rich with opportunities for adults and children to engage in these brain-building exchanges.

Photo 10.4 Snails and worms.

For example, when children express an interest in a frog (a 'serve'), even though an early learning teacher may not be interested in the frog, it is essential that the adult express an interest in their intrigue with the frog (a 'return'). Berry (2017) suggested that this does not mean that adults need to respond to every interest that children express; however, they need enough returns to gain a sense of acceptance and desire to explore. In this chapter, we continue to share how outdoor play aligns with children's development. Outdoor play is an essential component of childhood and is directly related to **higher thinking functions**, including reasoning and planning. As new research becomes available, early learning teachers and families are now positioning outdoor play as an essential need for facilitating the complex connections between the various parts of the brain and development (Jaswal, 2017).

In addition to outdoor play influencing children's brain architecture process, outdoor play is also related to attention restoration theory and behavioural functioning (Bullick, 2017). For many children, the more time they spend indoors, the more they are required to use their energies to manage the noise levels (Stansfield & Clark, 2015). As identified by Stansfield and Clark (2015), this is "because children are exposed to environmental noise and associated pollutants at a time of rapid growth and cognitive development and will perhaps have less developed coping repertoires than adults to deal with environmental noise and less control over noise" (p. 171). Noise levels may influence some children's behaviours in negative ways, especially during the process of their development of self-regulation skills.

Serve and return refers to the exchange that occurs between a child and adult when a child expresses an interest in a person, place, or thing is expressed.

Higher thinking functions refers to the thinking concepts that involve analysis, evaluation, and synthesis of connecting new experiences with previous knowledge. This requires children to learn complex skills, such as critical thinking and problem solving.

THINK ABOUT IT! READ ABOUT IT! WRITE ABOUT IT!

What does serve and respond mean to your practice? Search for examples of serve and return from an outdoor play perspective. How does this influence your philosophy of outdoor play? Review your philosophy and add to it.

Photo 10.5 Piling tree cookies.

Proponents of **attention restoration theory** advocate that children have large periods of time outdoors. Kaplan and Kaplan's (1989) seminal work on attention restoration theory suggested that the natural elements of outdoor play environments bolster children's attention skills and self-regulation strategies. Nature has the capacity to renew attention after exerting mental energy on being in over-stimulating environments, noisy environments, or chaotic environments. Kaplan and Kaplan outlined that there are two attentional systems that influence children's attention. The first is **directed attention** and the second is **soft fascination**. Directed attention requires intensive focus and being able to ignore distractions. This takes prolonged concentration, which takes energy and increases mental fatigue. An example of this with young children would be when they are trying to figure out how they can pile the tree cookies up high without them falling.

Tree cookies are illustrations of items in the environment that are attractive and fascinating to children. **Soft fascination** refers to the sense of wonderment and fascination that is experienced in nature. Outdoor environments that are intriguing, pleasurable, and that have an aesthetic component are classified as soft fascination. Examples of soft fascinations include the sound of wind blowing, the rain hitting the windows, the sunrise, or finding a rainbow.

Early learning teachers look for ways and opportunities to provide children with exposure to natural environments that encourage restoration. Restoration is most effective in environments where children feel the freedom to explore and have a comfort in the environment. In such environments, children reduce the amount of energy required for daily functioning, while supporting their abilities to self-regulate effectively. These environments promote children having their thoughts and ideas wander, wonder, imagine and experience while making connections to what may have been previously disconnected ideas.

During the early years, children require large blocks of time for outdoor play. This contributes to children engaging in longer and more focused play. This results in children being better able to perform more complex skills because they have time to think, ponder, figure out, and pursue their ideas. Focused play opportunities are linked to soft fascination, brain functioning, cognitive development, self-regulation skills, and children's temperaments. This may mean that early learning teachers consider expanding the outdoor play-time beyond the allocated time outlined in regulations.

Similar to attention restoration theory, Gesler, (1992) suggested that because the natural world has long been connected to children's health and well-being, early learning teachers benefit from viewing outdoor play spaces as **therapeutic landscapes**. Beyer et al. (2015) identified that children benefit most from being with adults who value them having consistent access to unstructured, creative play in natural settings.

Unstructured play is a type of play where children choose and engage in play with or without a defined purpose, such as when they begin exploring the use of tree cookies, sticks, and rope. Early learning teachers observe children engaged in the play but do not provide instructions or interfere with the play. This differs from structured play, where there are generally defined goals, such as when children are provided with a block build-ing kit and instructions that they are encouraged to follow when creating a tower.

Unstructured play supports children in having a sense of freedom and control of their environment. They determine the materials, the playmates, the play strategies, and how

Attention restoration theory was developed by Rachel and Stephen Kaplan in the 1980s and is based on the beliefs that children concentrate bet-ter when they spend time in nature.

Directed attention refers to the concentration and focus required when engaged in expe-riences that require problem solving. Direct attention draws upon the inhibitory mecha-nisms of the brain, which helps to block unrelated stimuli.

Soft fascination refers to items in the environment that attract us and keep us stimu-lated in wanting to be in the environment. This experience restores our intellectual energy.

Therapeutic landscapes refers to outdoor places that generate feelings of restora-tion, health, and a sense of happiness.

to manage the successes and opportunities for further development. To support unstructured play, early learning teachers ensure that there are sufficient open-ended, natural materials available such as pine cones, sticks, water, leaves, and rocks for children to choose from without requiring help from adults. As well, materials such as blocks, fabric, and boxes may be added as a way to expand children's options and play opportunities.

Beyer et al. (2015) identified that in order for adults to embrace and be advocates of unstructured play, they must first examine their beliefs about what children acquire from outdoor play. They further suggested that adults develop strategies and processes to address their fears and the barriers that they bring to the environment because children instinctively feel the anxiety of adults in their play space.

The correlation of children's outdoor play to brain development and to learning clearly identifies the importance of adults supporting and promoting children's outdoor play. Bilton (2010) has long advocated that early learning teachers must give outdoor play the same attention, priority, and resources as indoor programming. She identified that adults who view outdoor play as a time for the staff to have a break is putting adults first, not the children. Similar to indoor environments, adults prepare the outdoor environments with invitations that may trigger children's curiosity. They observe and document what children are intrigued with and support them in conversations about their outdoor play. This contributes to children and adults viewing outdoor play as an important part of their daily experience.

As identified by Vygotsky (1981), during the early years, children can be viewed as **apprentices**. As apprentices, children learn social and cognitive skills from the interactions that they have with those who have more knowledge and who role model skills and attitudes that contribute to children acquiring new information. Vygotsky identified that the experiences within children's environments and the cultural contexts influence how the adaptation of experiences and knowledge is internalized.

Apprentices refers to a learning process where a person with particular skills shares their knowledge with another person in order to learn a specific skill.

> **BOX 10.1** **Shedding Light on Outdoor Play—Points of Reflection**

Think about the relationship between the development of the brain and the environment. How can early learning teachers support families and colleagues in taking inventory of their current values, beliefs, and practices and in thinking about how we can elevate the outdoors to have more importance in our daily practices and communities?

Recognizing that adult attitudes have such an impact on children's access to outdoor play and the types that they may engage in, why must we change our practices now? What will this generation of children miss out on—not only in their childhood but throughout their lives—if they do not experience or embrace the great outdoors?

In this chapter, we focus on how children's outdoor play is influenced by early learning teachers and families. Examining outdoor play from the perspective of early learning teachers, families and communities help to connect children to their culture, community, and lived experiences. This contributes to advancing children's curiosity and zest to play outdoors.

OUR VISION FOR OUTDOOR PLAY

Early learning teachers and families play a significant role in the what, if, how, and why children engage in play. Our vision is that for most of their day, children are surrounded by adults who have an interest in and desire to embrace the great outdoors and all of the affordances that the environments offer as a place for play, learning, and discovery.

It is our vision that children are surrounded by adult role models who have an interest in and desire to embrace the great outdoors and all that it has to offer.

Diane Kashin

Photo 10.6 Vision statement.

Social learning theory is based on children learning by observing others.

Family and early learning teachers' attitudes toward outdoor play have a strong influence on the development of children's attitudes (Hutchinson & Baldwin, 2005; McFarland, Zajicek, & Waliczek, 2014). Albert Bandura in the 1960s brought forth the notion of the **social learning theory** (Bandura, 1977). This theory combines both behavioural and cognitive philosophies to form the theory. Bandura (1977) suggested that children and adults learn new behaviours and values through observation, imitation, and modelling from their peers and adults. When adults exhibit positive attitudes about outdoor play and nature and embrace being outdoors, there is a much higher chance that children will adopt a desire to be outdoors than if they do not have such positive role models (Ernst & Tornabene, 2012). For example, think about the early learning teacher who is intrigued with the forest that is located just behind the early learning centre. This teacher often places invitations to the children in the forest. Her love of the forest becomes infectious to the children. Over time, a group of children ask daily if they can visit the forest to see the bugs, smell the trees, or skip along the path. The early learning teacher and children use the forest as a place to talk, discover, and rejuvenate their energy levels.

POSITIONING OUTDOOR PLAY IN THE LIVES OF CHILDREN

Outdoor play environments are places for children to share ideas, observe their peers and adults, and learn how others think about experiences; they are places for problem solving and dealing with ideas that are both successful and unsuccessful. When early learning teachers create play learning environments that model cooperation and collective learning, children develop the skills to accomplish shared goals (Duque, Martins, & Clemente, 2016). As cooperative play requires interaction among children and adults, children gain skills in expressing their thoughts, considering the thoughts of others, and balancing their perspectives with those of their playmates. The more children are exposed to outdoor play environments that emphasize collective play and learning, the more likely they will engage in play that meets both their needs and the interests of their peers (Sachs, Candlin, & Rose, 2003).

A cooperative learning environment aligns with Parten's (1933) classification of children's phases of social play. She suggested that when children begin to share play materials and participate in similar activities, then they are exhibiting associative play behaviours. She suggested that cooperative play is the play that occurs when children determine a common goal and then each child works towards meeting the goal. Cooperative play creates a bond with the group

Diane Kashin

Photo 10.7 A forest invitation.

of children and the adults that are present in their play, which in turn contributes to children gaining a sense of community and belonging.

Early learning teachers plan outdoor play environments so that they are rich with opportunities for children to participate in cooperative play and learning. Think about how children pile leaves in the fall, and then jump in them together. Not only are they learning about science and nature, but they also learn about communication with one another, the boundaries with one another, and the pleasurable feelings attained from being with one another. Cooperative play is often triggered by one child having an idea to build a fort or a snow person and then that idea becoming of interest to others. A joining of ideas and experiences evolves. As outlined in Figure 10.2, other types of experiences may trigger children's desire to participate in collective exploration and learning.

Early learning teachers observe the roles that children exhibit in the outdoor environment. For example, who are the leaders, who are the followers, and who are the children that observe for long periods of time before moving into group play? Duque, Martins and Clemente (2016) identified that early learning teachers analyze children's types of play and the partners in play to better understand how children are contributing to each other's learning. The observations and analysis of documentation serve as means for early learning teachers to understand how the environment, materials in the environment and their role contribute to supporting children in collective and cooperative play.

THEORETICAL FOUNDATION

There are many philosophers, researchers, and educators who over the course of time have contributed to the discussions on the importance of adults and children having access to nature for their development. As mentioned earlier, two of the most prominent proponents are Henry David Thoreau (1817–1862) and John Muir (1838–1914).

Thoreau, known for his book *Life in the Woods* (1854), has long been associated with the beginning of the environmental movement; Thoreau had a particular focus on the role, impact, and influence of the environment on people. He identified the importance of taking lessons learned from the Indigenous peoples to frame perspectives, especially understanding the languages that are embedded in the beauty of the environment (Bieder, 2011).

Muir's early beginnings working on farms and in the forest led him to examine the geological formations of environments. He was one of the first researchers to identify that our environments were endangered in part due to encroaching economic development. His work led him to become an advocate for the environment at all levels of government and community, which gradually evolved into the establishment of the environmental and wilderness protection movement. Muir sought to ensure that all citizens were aware of the beauties and importance of nature. His influence was widespread, including with physicians who began to prescribe outdoor activities as a prescription for children, especially those living in crowded environments (Bieder, 2011).

CURIOUS?

Do you want to learn more about Muir's effort to protect environments and why he began the Sierra Club? Go to http://www.sierraclub.ca/en/about to learn about the work of the Sierra Club in Canada.

Muir and Thoreau influenced the psychologist G. Stanley Hall. In the 1880s he began to observe how children's place of living, especially urban environments, reduced

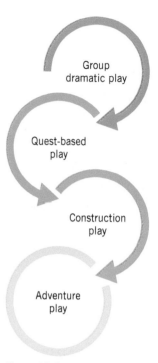

Figure 10.2 Collective play.

- Group dramatic play
- Quest-based play
- Construction play
- Adventure play

Table 10.2 Nature and children's well-being.

Nature Heals	Nature Soothes
Children require exposure to natural settings with plants, trees, and natural products to support their problem-solving and healing processes.	Children require time and access to environments where they experience trees, plants, and other natural elements as a way to support them in gaining a sense of comfort.
Nature Restores	**Nature Connects**
The more time that children have in nature, the more they are able to increase their attention skills and abilities to refresh their ideas and bring meaning to their experiences.	Children who have time in nature have increased opportunities to connect to each other and their environment. Children develop a sense of community.

their connections to nature and felt that it was unnatural. He suggested, "those who grow up without knowing the country are defrauded of that without which childhood can never be complete or normal" (Schmitt, 1990, p. 78). He maintained the importance of children having access to the wilderness or at least country life if they were to become happy and productive citizens.

Influenced by the works of Thoreau, Muir, and Hall, in 1910 the Boy and Girl Scouts movements, under the direction of Ernest Thompson Seton, recognized that young children required programming experiences outdoors that included hiking, nature study, and camping if they were to flourish both from a health perspective and in the development of their **civic virtue**. At the same time, there was increased acknowledgement that children and adults gained physical and psychological benefits from being outdoors. The wilderness became recognized as a restorer of health (Bieder, 2011).

Civic virtue refers to cultivating habits of living that support the individual and success of the community that conforms to a social mode.

According to the University of Minnesota (2017), nature has many ways in which it restores our health. As outlined in Table 10.2, Dietze & Kashin (2017) adapted the University of Minnesota's "How does nature impact our well-being?" to reflect how those principles may transfer to children in early learning programs.

Outdoor play and nature is a place where children heal, restore energy, and make connections. Unstructured play experiences in nature contributes to children increasing their problem-solving skills, cooperation, flexible thinking and self-awareness (Dietze & Kashin, 2018). Figure 10.3 identifies additional health and wellness benefits of outdoor

Figure 10.3 Benefits of outdoor play to children's development.

play environments that are designed for children to participate in self-directed play that they choose to engage in.

From an outdoor play perspective, Ansari & Purtell (2017) suggested that although the majority of play is and should be self-directed, this does not mean that adults are passive observers. Rather, early learning teachers learn to gauge when children would benefit from having interactions with adults, when to become collaborators, and when to interpret and engage with children with the intent of deepening the play or challenging them to think about and experience new play options. Early learning teachers constantly observe, listen, reflect, and use careful judgment of if, when, and how to extend adult prompts that will scaffold children's experiences, thinking, and learning. Building on the work of Dietze and Kashin (2016), Edwards and Cutter-Mackenzie (2011), and Bilton (2010), Table 10.3 outlines the many forms that the supportive roles of early learning teachers take.

As outlined above, early learning teachers have diverse responsibilities in creating environments to support children's play. Early learning teachers require a well-rounded disposition and personal qualities that are supportive of children and families, no matter what their culture, diversity, or beliefs. Solly (2015) suggested that three of the most important traits are flexibility in thinking and practice, the ability to compromise, and pragmatism. Children flourish in environments with adults who have passion and the stamina to be engaged with them and their play (Bilton, 2002; 2014). As depicted in Figure 10.4, it is important that early learning teachers exhibit qualities that align with children's ways of knowing, playing, and learning (Bilton, 2014).

Table 10.3 Supportive roles of early learning teachers.

1.	Child-led play environments draw upon the cultural experiences of children and families. For example, boats, fishing nets, and lobster traps are part of the children's environment in fishing communities.
2.	Child-led play requires access to adults who connect children's play ideas and activities to particular conceptual ideas. For example, when children exhibit an interest in clay and sculpting, they have access to artists who support them in exploring their ideas.
3.	Early learning teachers plan environments that reflect children's current knowledge, experiences, ideas, and peer interests with potential new options for discovery. For example, when children show interests in building forts, teachers provide invitations through the placement of new materials that require children to figure out how to use the materials in their play.
4.	Early learning teachers and families develop dynamic relationships with children, community members, and the environment. For example, when available, families and early learning teachers participate in the outdoor play environment with children.
5.	Early learning teachers support children in developing an appreciation of and care for their natural and constructed environments. For example, children and early learning teachers determine where and what they play with in the forest, how they care for the forest, and what they take from the forest.
6.	Early learning teachers provide children with outdoor play opportunities in varied physical environments. For example, early learning teachers ensure that children have access to a variety of outdoor spaces, such as parks, the early learning space, and community spaces.
7.	Early learning teachers and children make their play and learning visible. For example, children and adults determine what aspects of their outdoor play experiences they write about, document, and share with their families and peers.
8.	Early learning teachers and children create invitations that support active participation and engagement. For example, children and early learning teachers collectively listen to, observe, and contribute materials or ideas to other children's experiences.
9.	Early learning teachers examine the outdoor play environments on their physical properties, the way in which children and adults interact with one another, and the interplay among teachers, children, and the environment. For example, teachers examine the outdoor play space to determine its properties the types of invitations that may be placed in the space to trigger children's curiosity and exploration of various aspects of the space.

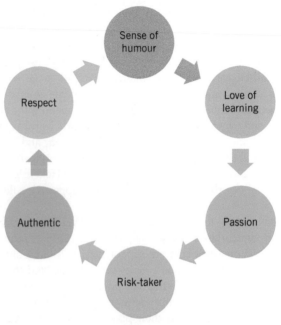

Figure 10.4 Qualities of early learning teachers.

Dietze and Kashin (2017) suggested that early learning teachers exhibit their personal qualities in a number of ways with children, families, and co-workers. For example, when early learning teachers bring a sense of humour to the environment it can be seen in the playfulness that they exhibit with children. Children may find a large pot placed in the outdoor environment with a blank recipe card that says, "Can you add an ingredient to this pot of silly soup?" They may extend this by beginning a rhyming dialogue with children using the word silly as the starting point.

Early learning teachers show their passion and love of learning through their communication with children. Imagine the children finding an intriguing bug in the environment and showing it to the early learning teachers. When the teachers engage in questioning and discussions with the children to examine the bug, they are collectively engaged in learning. They may determine what they know about the bug, what they wish to find out about it, and where they might go to find the answers. Children's depth of inquiry is influenced by the level of interest, curiosity, desire to learn, and by the role modelling of the teachers.

Similar to children, early learning teachers benefit from being comfortable with exhibiting risk-taking behaviours and strategies. For example, when children determine their interest in climbing a tree, an early learning teacher may propose joining up in the tree. Risk-taking may also be exhibited by proposing new ideas and experiences to the children that may be outside the comfort zone of the teacher or colleagues, yet remain very safe and present unlimited inquiry opportunities.

Early learning teachers show respect and authenticity to colleagues and the children as they create ideas, express wonder, and make new discoveries. For example, when children discover the joy that comes from playing in puddles and mud, how an early learning teacher communicates with body language and expresses verbal cues will reflect the values and beliefs about this type of play. Children will get a sense if their desire to explore this natural gift of nature is acceptable to pursue by watching how the teacher responds.

In a study conducted by Bilton (2014) related to outdoor play and staff attitudes, just over 90 percent of the 122 respondents identified their roles as "facilitating, supporting, developing, enhancing, scaffolding, interacting and engaging with children" (p. 946). Just over 30 percent of the respondents indicated that observing children for safety was one of their key roles during outdoor play, while only 7 percent of respondents identified that their explicit role was to teach children specific concepts. Early learning teachers are guided by their program philosophy, beliefs, and values. Throughout this text we have emphasized the importance of self-directed play, rather than teacher-directed activities. Self-directed play is most meaningful to

Photo 10.8 Jumping in the puddle.

children because they determine how to pursue their interest and the depth in which they explore the interest. Think about children becoming interested in apples. How will they learn about the different tastes, colours, ways in which apples can be prepared, and kinds of apples through pictures? Then think about what happens when children decide that after a trip to an apple orchard that they want to open up an apple shop in the dramatic centre to sell apples or set up an apple restaurant where they make applesauce, or offer others to join them to play their taste test game of different types of apples. How do these self-directed experiences influence children's math, science, language, and dramatic skills through meaningful play opportunities? In essence, early learning teachers take the lead from the children and in so doing empower them to decide where, when, what, and how to play.

Although many researchers and early learning teachers support the findings that outdoor play is essential for children's health, wellness, and disposition, there are common barriers and challenges that early learning teachers face (Bilton, 2014; Dietze & Kashin, 2017). Figure 10.5 provides an overview of some of the common concerns that may be influencing children's access to and opportunities for outdoor play.

As you examine the barriers identified in Figure 10.5, which do you envision to be the most challenging barrier to overcome and why? Gehris, Gooze and Whitaker (2014) and Ernst (2012) determined that if early learning teachers do not embrace the outdoor portion of the program, then those attitudes influence the children's experiences or lack thereof. Although lack of storage for loose parts and the environmental conditions (Dietze & Kim, 2014; Oke & Middle, 2016) influence children's outdoor play, good teachers can find ways to support outdoor play and advocate for changes that will address those barriers. Think about preschool children

Photo 10.9 Apples for sale.

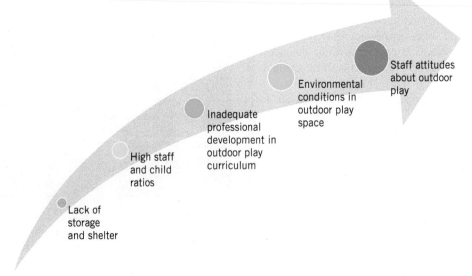

Figure 10.5 Barriers to outdoor play.

who have an interest in hiding behind some of the sheds. Some early learning teachers may view this as an exploratory play experience that includes children in participating in social interactions, planning, and discovering space and place. Others may redirect children because of their fear of them being out of their view or concern that they could participate in play that may not be safe. Early learning teachers who view children as competent and valued rather than as requiring protection will influence how children use their environments and space for their play.

THINK ABOUT IT! READ ABOUT IT! WRITE ABOUT IT!

Bilton (2014) identified that knowing the aims of outdoor play helps early learning teachers to think about their role and responsibilities in outdoor play programming. What do you envision to be the aims of outdoor play? Who decides? What happens if early learning teachers have different aims and values than those of children or families?

Go to http://pubs.sciepub.com/education/2/10/14/index.html to read about Bilton's perspective on the relationship of aims of outdoor play to children's experiences. What are your aims of outdoor play? Write two paragraphs to describe your perspective.

Since outdoor play is so vital to children, early learning teachers consistently and constantly reflect upon their feelings, values, skills, dispositions, and beliefs about the influence of outdoor play in the lives of children. Solly (2015) recommended that early learning teachers individually and collectively answer the following questions:

1. What do we need to change, extend, or develop to add new challenges to the environment that are reflective of children's interests, skills, knowledge, and understanding?

2. How can we offer outdoor play experiences that advance learning opportunities through challenging play?

Photo 10.10 Standard playground.

Photo 10.11 Play space with loose parts.

As shown in Photos 10.10 and 10.11, the outdoor play equipment for the most part offers children physical activity opportunities. Now, look at the types of play that could occur when children have a variety of loose parts. What types of play do you envision evolving in these play spaces?

Children's play opportunities are influenced by environments. More than 100 years ago, Catherine Dodd, influenced by Friedrich Froebel, advocated for young children in group experiences to be given options to have journeys in their communities.

>> **BOX 10.2   Featured Theorist: Catherine Dodd**

Catherine Dodd maintained that children benefit from being in early learning programs with curricula that encourage children to connect with community and *journeys*, a concept that began in Germany in the late 1800s. Journeys refer to being away from the buildings and spaces where programs generally occur and that provide children with a range of environments that they could not otherwise experience (Dodd, 1897). Dodd identified that children benefit from journeys as a way for them to begin to observe, discuss, and discover new geographical and aesthetic attributes of their environments. Today, going beyond the fence has similar characteristics as the historical idea of journeys.

As you think about Dodd's perspective, what might stop early learning programs from taking the children from their early learning settings to engage in journeys in their communities where they may observe, discover, and interact with people, things, and new ideas? If you were going to take the children on a journey, how might you prepare them? What interesting language and concepts might you use to intrigue their imaginations?

PRACTICAL APPLICATIONS

Children's interactions with nature, peers, adults, family, and community are essential components for them to embrace their outdoor environments. This means that children look forward to their outdoor play time, they explore and experiment with a variety of play options such as construction or dramatic and creative play, and they develop meaningful

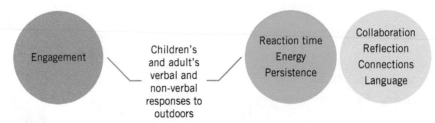

Figure 10.6 Verbal and non-verbal response of children and adults to the outdoors.

relationships with the place, peers, and adults within the environment. Drawing from education psychology, Brown (2015) defined engagement as "the positive affective and cognitive state of self-motivated involvement characterized by initiation, sustained dedication and absorption" (p. 5). As outlined in Figure 10.6, from a constructivist approach early learning teachers and families are encouraged to examine the engagement response to outdoor environments both from the perspectives of children and adults.

According to Williford, Vick Whittaker, Vitiello, and Downer (2013), children's self-regulation skills, depth of play, ability to plan, use of the environment, and positive and negative communication styles are all influenced by their levels of active engagement with peers and teachers. As outlined in Table 10.4, it is beneficial for early learning teachers to observe and reflect upon the teacher and child engagement, peer engagement, task engagement, and negative engagement to determine if and how the outdoor environment may be changed to increase children and teacher engagement opportunities.

As outlined earlier in the text, demographic factors including educational levels of parents and early learning teachers, family income, gender of children, cultural backgrounds, and accessibility to outdoor space all influence children's access to and opportunities for play in the outdoors and in nature (Ernst, 2012).

As you will recall from Chapter 9, infants and toddlers learn from their whole bodies and all of their senses. They are physical thinkers. As children advance into their preschool (ages 2.6 to approximately 4.6 months) and kindergarten (ages 4.6 months to approximately 6 years) phases of development, their worlds expand—from the places and the materials used for their play to the children that they play with. As they begin to develop their independence, having access to outdoor play is a particularly important environment for them because they intuitively want to explore their surroundings. Ideally, because of previous exposure to outdoor play, their sense of curiosity continues. They hone in on their developing skills such as in relationship building and communication through group play, imaginary play, constructive play, and creative play. When children are in outdoor play environments with teachers, materials, and stimulating opportunities such as those derived from invitations, they begin to build upon previous experiences;

Table 10.4 Children's types of engagement.

Teacher and Child Engagement	Peer to Peer Engagement
Refers to the extent to which children and early learning teachers share a positive connection, including their frequent conversations and responses to each other.	Refers to the extent of the connections that children make with one another, including how they share in their play, communicate, and exhibit caring behaviours toward one another.
Child and Task Engagement	**Child Negative Engagement**
Refers to the level of attention, enthusiasms, inquisitiveness, and persistence that a child or children exhibit in their play.	Refers to the frequency and level of aggressive or uncooperative behaviour exhibited towards other children or the early learning teacher.

Source: Based on Williford et al., Understanding how children's engagement and teachers' interactions combine to predict school readiness, *Journal of Applied Developmental Psychology*.

they expand their use of language, including becoming intrigued with reproducing letters of the alphabet and words. They also begin to express their reasoning perspectives about how and why their play may evolve in a particular way. Children require extensive periods of time and opportunities to return to their play materials and structures so that they may think, rethink, and add new dimensions to their original ideas.

PRINCIPLES OF PRACTICE: MATH-BASED PRACTICE

Outdoor play environments are often viewed as laboratories for children to construct and re-construct mathematical knowledge, especially when invitations for exploration are available and require them to think in new ways. This means that early learning teachers and students examine the outdoor play experiences in relation to mathematical properties and concepts.

As important as both mathematics and outdoor play are, Sumpter and Hedefalk (2015) identified that there is a correlation between children's reduction in outdoor play and mathematical skills. For example, children who consistently play outdoors have increased connections with and use of loose parts. They may discuss how tall the pile of snow is or measure how high the tree cookies are piled. They may determine how many cans of sand they need to make the tower the desired height. If children do not have such experiences, there may be gaps in their learning such concepts through play. When you think about the mathematical concepts that can be experienced outdoors, skills such as sorting, identifying shapes, and counting may come to your mind. Those are foundational skills that early learning teachers promote through children's outdoor play. For example, think about the types of questions that could be asked of the children who constructed the design in Photo 10.11. How might you support children in mathematical thinking and reasoning in this situation? Similar to other learning opportunities that are extended to children, the outdoor environment is an important place for them to construct and co-construct play

Photo 10.12 Mathematical concepts in the forest.

that expands mathematical concepts that extend beyond the basic ones outlined above. For example, the early learning teachers may discuss with children concepts such as what is meant by sets and angles. They may extend children's vocabulary by using words such as geometric, patterning, width, depth, and volume, all of which may trigger children's interest in what is meant by these words.

Sumpter and Hedefalk (2015) identified that preschool children benefit from the open discussion of mathematical ideas that they experience and the extension of the concepts, where possible. The achievement of this is dependent on the early learning teacher's ability to ask key questions or provide guidance to children in the right moments. When children are exposed to thinking about mathematical ideas, they develop their reasoning skills, which in turn increases their mathematical sense-making.

To make sense of mathematics, children require many experiences that support them in developing mathematical reasoning skills. Having children describe their **mathematical thinking** (Niss, 2003) ideas helps them internalize the concepts or principles. For example, think of four-year-olds Martie and Samie. They have been constructing a structure out of wooden blocks and sticks for several days. They identified that they wanted to be able to place a large tree cookie on top followed by piling of six rocks. Although they have tried their idea on two occasions without success, in discussions with them, the early learning teacher found out that they believed the more blocks they had, the more stable their structure would be, despite the size of the blocks. **Mathematical reasoning** is related to children's oral language skills as part of the reasoning process used for them to be able to express their ideas and to question other children's arguments about mathematical concepts. **Logical reasoning** is also a key aspect of developing mathematical competence. This concept refers to children being able to identify properties of objects, such as sorting items and working in patterns.

As we think about children's outdoor play experiences and align them with mathematical concepts, one of the core roles of early learning teachers is to encourage children to express their perspectives as a way to co-construct knowledge and skills. Further, Lithner (2008), Sumpter (2013), and Safstrom (2013) all argued that for mathematical skills to flourish during the preschool years, children require early learning teachers who view reasoning processes as a collective process. Sumpter and Hedefalk (2015) suggested "the learning of mathematics depends on the children's participation in processes of collective construction of reality where the reality here is in the context of free play and the chosen subject in focus is mathematics" (p. 3). Early learning teachers use their language, role modelling, and materials to support children in the co-construction of knowledge about mathematical principles. As outlined in Figure 10.7, early learning teachers incorporate core mathematical concepts into children's outdoor play experiences.

Mathematical thinking refers to a process of thinking that is used to solve problems through lived experiences, general reasoning abilities, and skills for communicating responses to solutions.

Mathematical reasoning refers to children being able to observe certain relations between parts such as diagrams and to formulate conclusions in general terms.

Logical reasoning refers to using a systematic series of steps based on mathematical procedures to determine a solution or conclusion.

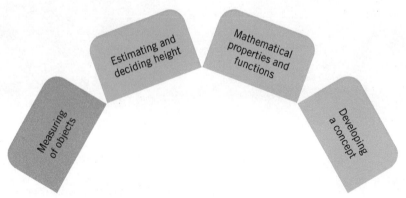

Figure 10.7 Mathematical concepts in outdoor play environments.

Table 10.5 Developing math concepts.

Measuring of objects: A child climbs up on a rock. The early learning teacher begins a conversation about how big the rock is. The child responds that the rock is taller than the child. The child predicts that the rock is taller than three other children as well. The child suggests that a peer get the stick to measure the rock. Then, the children and teacher have discussions about which is taller the rock, the children, the teacher, or the stick. This inspires children to predict the size of other objects and then to measure them using a variety of tools such as sticks, string, other children, and measuring tapes. Children use language such as "I predict", "larger than, smaller than, and bigger than".

Estimating and deciding height: Children are using the blocks for their tower construction. Prior to starting their construction process, each of the children chooses sticks to determine how high they will be able to build the tower before it collapses. Each of the children expresses why they think they can make the tower the height that they are predicting. The teacher synthesizes the children's predictions and asks each of the children to identify their reasons for their predictions.

Mathematical properties and functions: Three children were creating a zoo space for animals with the blocks and sticks. One of the children approached the teacher for the container with the animals in it. As the child took the container back to the construction zone, two of the children started sorting the animals. One child started to place the dogs in cages in the zoo setting, while another child determined that dogs are pets, not zoo animals. Over the course of counting and sorting the animals, discussions occurred about what is a zoo animal, a pet, and a farm animal. The early learning teacher asked children questions such as "is there ever a time that dogs are in zoos?" and "how do you decide what animals are found in zoos versus farms?"

Developing a concept: A group of children were having cookies for a snack. Then, three children decided that anything that was round like the cookies must be cookies. These children made a game of it. They explored their environment for items that were round. They labelled all of the items as cookies. They labelled flowerpots as cookie pots, tree pieces as tree cookies, rounded rocks as rock cookies. As other children observed what the children were doing and saying, they challenged their peers as to how a flowerpot can be called a cookie pot. This process incorporated opportunities for both groups of children to share their perspectives and arguments for the concept.

Table 10.5 provides examples of how mathematical concepts may evolve in outdoor play environments.

Children's foundational math skills begin when mathematic principles are naturally incorporated into their outdoor play environments so that the environment becomes the third teacher—that is, children will begin to view materials for their attributes, construct their understanding of mathematical concepts through their play, engage in conversations among children and early learning teachers, and make connections about math, science, and language concepts.

LEARNING IN PLACE: LEARNING IN THE COMMUNITY

Across Canada, there are many unique **communities**; some with similar characteristics to others, while others have varying and unique characteristics. Some families are more involved in their communities than others. Communities are cultural. Different communities may have geographical differences; they generally offer unique experiences and there are varying family attitudes, local knowledge, and lived experiences. When we combine the concepts of journeys and communities as outlined by Dodd in the late 1800s, there are many benefits for children to participate in journeys in the community. Dietze and Kashin (2017) have taken the concept of journeys and communities and identified them more specifically as **community journeys**. The concept of community journeys differs from that of a field trip. A field trip generally has a defined purpose, such as having the children experience apple picking or going to the fire station. Community journeys refers to children and early learning teachers going on a journey to see what they can experience, without having a defined purpose, but which could include observing, experiencing, seeing, collecting, and meeting people in their neighbourhood. For example, children on a community journey through the main street in Yarmouth, Nova Scotia, recently discovered all of

Communities are places where a group of people live or have a particular characteristic in common.

Community journeys are defined as places, people, and things that contribute to children's learning when exploring their communities.

Photo 10.13 What children see and learn on community journeys.

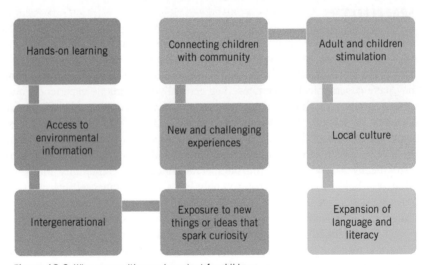

Figure 10.8 Why communities are important for children.

Beverlie Dietze

Photo 10.14 Children learning about weaving and woodworking during their community journey.

Beverlie Dietze

Photo 10.15 Children visit a craftsperson.

the things outlined in Photo 10.13. In addition to their visual discoveries, as outlined in Photos 10.14 and 10.15, they had the opportunity to meet a weaver and a fine wood craftsman.

Community journeys such as the one that the children in Nova Scotia experienced allow them to touch, discuss, and identify their preferences in what they had discovered. The experience supported older adults in having conversations with young children and being able to introduce them to the skills of and their talents in weaving and woodwork. The children expressed their ideas and asked a variety of questions that resulted in further exchanges among the children and adults. Beyond the transfer of knowledge, these types of exchanges contribute to reciprocal learning between different generations. Such **intergenerational learning** promotes respect between generations and contributes to building communities where children and older generations become better connected.

> **Intergenerational learning** refers to learning from individuals from different generations.

After visiting the weaver and craftsperson, four children became intrigued with weaving, while other children spent many days using wood and glue to create wooden frames for their artwork from the wood that the craftsperson had given them. As outlined in Figure 10.8, there are at least nine reasons why early learning teachers build in opportunities for children to have access to community journeys often.

Thinking about the learning that children and families gain from community connections aligns with Indigenous connections to people, environments, and **ways of knowing**. As adults connect children with their outdoor community environments, they role model how to use the outdoor environment as a learning place for play, discovery, observation, and stewardship. For example, in Photo 10.13, what unique learning experiences may evolve from the children's community journey? How might children begin to notice the unique aspects and architecture of buildings? How might this outdoor learning influence their play in the construction area? Then think about the types of discussions you may have with children so that they gain knowledge about why they should protect plants, wildlife, and cultural aspects found in their community. Early learning teachers invest the time to know the assets in a community, so that they can intentionally bring children to their community and the community to the children.

> **Ways of knowing** refers to the way in which we acquire knowledge and incorporate that new knowledge with our previous knowledge and experiences.

Ideally, by roaming and exploring in the community, children will be exposed to the people and the core environmental characteristics of their space, whether it be forests, rolling hills, or unique rock formations. Such awareness connects children to environments (Gehris, Gooze, & Whitaker, 2014). Think about children's communities across Canada. How might community journeys support children in learning about their fishing community? How might community journeys support children in learning about the seniors who live in their community? How might making connections to seniors enrich the lives of children? Early learning teachers support families in understanding ways in which their communities can advance children's curiosity about, interest in, and knowledge related to their environments, while advancing eco-literacy and promoting the adoption of environmentally sustainable communities and lifestyles.

THINK ABOUT IT! READ ABOUT IT! WRITE ABOUT IT!

Communities are incredible places for children to play and learn. What might stop early learning teachers from taking the children to experience their community? Now, there is a movement for children to become involved in community service. Read about how children can make a difference by participating in community service http://startasnowball.com/10-skills-kids-learn-community-service/ and think about what this means for preschool children. Write about how preschool children might support seniors?

PROGRAMMING

Outdoor play is more than opening the doors to the outdoor environment. For children to embrace outdoor play, early learning teachers take care in taking the lead from the children, by choosing materials and creating invitations that build upon previous experiences or skills and that stretch children into new exploration and learning opportunities.

Table 10.6 Maslow's hierarchy of needs and programming.

Self-actualization

Early learning teachers support children in gaining a sense of their abilities by scaffolding materials and invitations that build upon the children's strengths. Children are encouraged to build upon their successes with new challenges and explorations.

Esteem

Early learning teachers provide invitations to children that will spark their curiosity. They encourage the children to try new ideas and experiment with new materials. Children and early learning teachers exhibit respect for peers and families. Pedagogical documentation supports making children's outdoor play visible.

Social Needs

Early learning teachers ensure that children have opportunities to connect, interact, explore, and discover their environments with a variety of playmates. Relationships among children and adults are encouraged.

Safety and Security

Early learning teachers protect children from danger. They support them in taking risks. Rules are kept to a minimum.

Physiological

Early learning teachers support children in consuming healthy food. They role model the importance of children having time and opportunities to participate in outdoor play. Children's rough and tumble play is supported as a way for them to experience human touch and begin the process of learning empathy and self-regulation skills.

Table 10.7 Plan, engage, explore, reflect—moving rocks and boards.

PLAN	Preschoolers show an interest in using large rocks and boards for construction. Early learning teachers place a variety of new rocks, boards, and sticks in the outdoor environment that require more than one child to lift. They arrange the materials and wait for the children to respond to the invitation to move the materials to a large open area more suitable for construction.
ENGAGE	As children show an interest in the new materials, they recognize that the materials cannot be moved individually. They engage in discussions about what resources could be used to move the materials.
EXPLORE	The early learning teachers observe which resources children gravitate to. Do they try to move the materials with a wagon or in a box or a moving dolly? Do they try to carry the rocks or boards in pairs? What is the dialogue amongst the children and how do they engage in the problem-solving process. When children were successful, why and how did this occur? How did this add to their play experiences?
REFLECT	Were there times that children's frustration levels began to surface? Did the children as a team co-construct their strategy for moving the rocks and boards? Was the role that you took as an adult appropriate for the children to gain success? How many failures occurred before success was achieved? What might you do differently next time?

Abraham Maslow proposed a hierarchy of needs in his 1943 paper *A Theory of Human Motivation* that suggested there are specific stages that humans must pass through to become fully functioning (Maslow, 1943). From an early learning teacher perspective, Maslow's hierarchy of needs provides a framework for how early learning programs may support children's development. As outlined in Table 10.6, preschool-aged children still rely on other children and adults to support their needs. Early learning teachers take these needs into consideration as they organize children's outdoor play environments and daily experiences.

Early learning teachers support preschool-aged children in their play by drawing upon their previous experiences and knowledge to incorporate into new experiences. Following the PEER Principle of Plan, Engage, Explore, and Reflect, Table 10.7 illustrates how early learning teachers co-construct opportunities for preschool-aged children to engage in and embrace outdoor play.

As you will note in this example, the early learning teacher took on the role of observer, while the children determined the play and the how the play would unfold. Early learning teachers determine the advantages to the children of extending them the opportunities to problem solve the various aspects of their desired play. They observe and determine when their input and what their input should be to support the children's play.

FAMILY SUPPORT AND ENGAGEMENT

Early learning teachers recognize the importance of children determining their play ideas and the materials that would best support their play idea. This does not mean that adults are passive observers (Williams, 2016). Early learning teachers and families collaborate with children in their play and in facilitating opportunities for them to either deepen or extend their play experiences that leads them to their own investigations (McWilliams, Brailsford-Vaughns, O'Hara, Novotny, & Kyle, 2013). In this chapter, we ask you to think about the core verbal conversations that you can have with children and families about the children's play experiences as a way to expand children's thinking and play ideas. For example, think about what you might share in a conversation with families about the children's community journey and what they experienced. How might your conversation lead a family member to ask questions about the children's day and what they saw? These conversations can serve to bridge the gap between the early learning program and the home environment. Such conversations help families know what has happened at the early learning program and provides them with information that they may draw upon to further expand their conversations with their children. Early learning teachers support family members in viewing community journeys and the people in the community as the way in which children learn about community, culture, and people.

Families are encouraged to take on a supportive role with their children in outdoor play. Waller (2011) suggested that as part of the supportive role, adults must be comfortable in being thinkers and co-constructors of knowledge with children. We ask that early learning teachers work with families to examine how their children's outdoor play can be expanded and appreciated as a family. This is of particular importance today as many children have limited time outdoors (Ulset, Vitaro, Brendgen, Bekkhus, & Borge, 2017). McFarland, Zajicek, and Waliczek (2014) reinforced that when children have families that spend time outdoors, they are more likely to want to spend more time outdoors engaging in exploration, discovery, and in connecting with nature and the beauty of the environments. Generally, families want the best for their children. Programs that partner with families to learn about how their culture, behaviours, attitudes, and interests influence their children's engagement outdoors will ultimately contribute to advancing outdoor play.

Families can be encouraged to share their stories about their outdoor play experiences and adventures with their children, including photos that children may share with their peers. When children and families share their outdoor play stories, the stories may act as a trigger for children to replicate the experiences or the stories at their early learning program. When such experiences are made visible, children, families, and early learning teachers have opportunities to collectively discuss the experiences and build upon them within the early learning program. This expands the partnerships among families and the early learning programs.

ACCESSIBILITY AND DESIGN

All children and families, no matter what their culture or socio-economic standard is, benefit from access to and engagement in outdoor play and their community, although families and individuals may have differing levels of participation (Oke & Middle, 2016). Engagement to the outdoors and community increases physical activity, expands imaginations, problem-solving skills, and connectedness to the environment (Oke & Middle, 2016). The outdoor environment ideally offers children and families a wide range of sensory and physical experiences that include tactile experiences, quiet spaces, motion, and places for discovery of sound, light, and smells. Children and adults benefit from communities that offer space and places for diverse play to occur. These components allow all children and adults to benefit from play and to learn the value of inclusion.

Mobility device refers to equipment or apparatus that aids a person that requires support for their physical movement.

Early learning teachers examine the community for its accessibility for children and families who may use **mobility devices**. They ensure that they choose routes that allow all children to participate in the exploration without being segregated from peers. For example, they examine the crosswalks to determine where the curb cuts are. They examine where the crosswalks are located and the visibility in both directions. Ramps and stairs around the community are examined to ensure that children may manipulate them independently. Surfaces are also examined for stability, including the cracks and unevenness of the surface. Early learning teachers and families engage in dialogue about accessibility requirements so that children and adults collectively can use the outdoor space at early learning programs or in the communities in new, imaginative, and creative ways. Space influences children's social interactions and negotiation skills with peers and adults. Children and families are disadvantaged when the space in the community does not follow accessible principles.

TIPS AND TOOLS FOR OUTDOOR PLAY

Early learning teachers and families support children's outdoor play in subtle and encouraging ways. They embrace children determining their play, while providing them with opportunities for new experiences with materials, peers, and community. Introducing children to the people and things in their immediate environments and communities teaches them about their natural world and the people in their world. Here are some tips for what can be added to the outdoor environment.

- Photos of buildings and pathways that can be found in the community.
- Community-specific materials such as shells, driftwood, fishing nets, rocks, and signs from businesses.
- Visitors as play partners from community members such as artists and woodworkers.
- Maps of possible places that may be visited within the community.
- Cameras for children to use when exploring their communities.

ON THE GROUND—PROFESSIONAL REFLECTIONS: "WHY I LOVE OUTDOOR PLAY"

>> **BOX 10.3** **Why I Love Outdoor Play**

Growing up, I always loved the outdoors. Playing in old cars, the wheat fields, swimming in the ponds and making forts with tree stumps have great memories for me. After entering into the field of Early Childhood Education, I brought my love for outdoors to each childcare centre I worked at. The only pitfall was being required to follow someone else's curriculum and what they thought was the best time for children to be outdoors. It wasn't until I opened my own preschool that I determined the importance of following the lead of the children at all times. The first two years we had dirt and loose parts such as logs, stumps, pallets, boards, buckets, trucks, and lots of water. Most days we spent the entire session outside, just going inside to gather some food and go to the bathroom. Over the years, each group of children and my new learning about the importance of outdoor play spaces would determine the fate of the play yard. As time went on, we would go outside daily; however, if during inside playtime the children were engaged fully, I didn't want to "interrupt" them and would sacrifice our outside time. When we did go outdoors, it wasn't long enough, as parents would soon

be there to pick up the children. The children did not want to leave, as they had just gotten into their play. It wasn't until I engaged in a professional development series on outdoor play that I realized I was sacrificing something very detrimental to the children by not spending more time outdoors. I changed my practice to ensure that we got outdoors daily. I started providing children with invitations during the wintertime that I would typically do in the springtime. The children have spent much more time outside playing, exploring, painting, creating, and sometimes just hanging out. Everywhere I go now, I always feel the urge to express my feelings and thoughts when it comes to outdoor play whether it be to a friend, colleague, or a parent. It is so valuable and it's slowly slipping away from children. I realize that I must be the best advocate for the children and share all my new knowledge learned recently, as well as my personal history to keep outdoor time and play alive! My attitude matters.

Angela Roy
Early Childhood Educator

CASE STUDIES

Sometimes there can be tension between families and early learning teachers, due in part to differing expectations or philosophies related to how children's play correlates to their learning. Read Case Study 10.1 to learn about how an early learning teacher faced with tension with a family related to outdoor play. Consider the questions that follow to reflect on what you would do in a similar situation.

≫ CASE STUDY 10.1 Connecting Children to Community

Melissa had been working in an early learning program for more than eight years. The program emphasized that outdoor play and community connections were essential in children's daily experiences at the centre. Melissa and the children had great relationships with a local artist, store-keepers, and seniors. Weekly, the children and Melissa decided what maps they would use of their community, where they would explore, and who they would visit. For the most part, families appreciated how this approach supported children in learning about their environment and the people in their community. Children often took photos of where they had been and what they had explored. Sometimes they brought back treasures that they had found or learned about along the way. One family began to express concerns that their children were spending more time outdoors and in the community than they were comfortable with. They wanted to know that their children were safe in the early learning fenced yard, rather than roaming around the community. Melissa overheard one

family discussing their concern with another family. Then, two days later, the two families approached Melissa to express their concerns further. Melissa had been thinking about this since she first became alerted to the concern. She knew the benefits of her approach were an expansion in the children's ideas and discoveries, that ultimately are transferred to their play.

1. Melissa felt that the families were questioning her philosophy about how outdoor play and communities influence children's development. How might she support families in understanding how this supports children's learning and development?
2. How might Melissa approach the families to engage them in a discussion about the benefits of children having these experiences?
3. How might Melissa encourage families to become partners in the explorations and transfer the explorations to co-construction in outdoor play?

≫ BOX 10.4 Take It Outside!

Go for a walk in your community—look up, look down, and look across. What do you see that could be used to spark children's curiosity about their community? How might you share your findings with the children? Once you have experienced this, how do you share the benefits with the families?

KEY TERMS

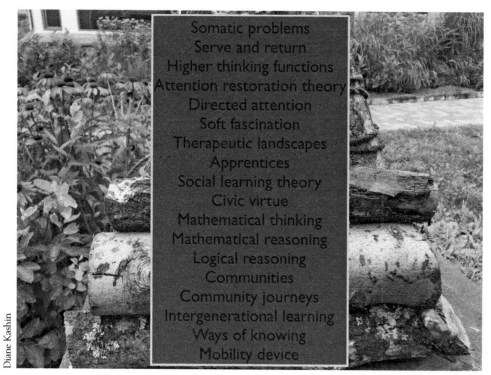

Somatic problems
Serve and return
Higher thinking functions
Attention restoration theory
Directed attention
Soft fascination
Therapeutic landscapes
Apprentices
Social learning theory
Civic virtue
Mathematical thinking
Mathematical reasoning
Logical reasoning
Communities
Community journeys
Intergenerational learning
Ways of knowing
Mobility device

Diane Kashin

Photo 10.16 Key terms.

Summary

- Outdoor play and nature have more positive developmental and health values than indoor experiences or activities. Outdoor play contributes to the reduction of stress and the enhancement of self-regulation skills.

- Children's social, emotional, cognitive, and physical development flourish in less supervised, less structured, and more adventurous and risk-taking environments.

- Early learning teachers and families have an important role in identifying the types of barriers and challenges that reduce children's access to play and to determine ways in which outdoor play can be advanced.

- The attitudes of adults have more impact on children's exposure to and engagement in outdoor play than actual government policies and procedures.

- Children benefit from outdoor play environments with adults who role model a philosophy that positions outdoor play as a core value, with experiences that are scaffolded and reflective of children's interests and materials that embrace the elements of the outdoor environment.

- Early learning teachers require a deep and thorough understanding of the theoretical constructs of outdoor play that they share with families and role model in their programming, actions, and demonstrated curiosity about outdoor play environments.

- Outdoor play aligns with brain development. The more children experience positive play outdoors, the more those experiences will remain with them and become part of their healthy brain architecture.

- Building healthy brain architecture is influenced by adults and children engaging in the serve and return exchange process. This process influences the formation of relationships and the wiring for language, and it is foundation for social, emotional, and exploratory functions.

- Children's brain architecture and attention restoration are influenced by outdoor play. Attention restoration theory is based on the beliefs that children concentrate better when they spend time outdoors.

- Therapeutic landscapes refer to outdoor play places that generate feelings of restoration, health, and a sense of happiness.

- Unstructured play provides children with the opportunities to choose and engage in the play with or without a defined purpose. Unstructured play supports children in having a sense of freedom and control of their environment.

- Children can be viewed as apprentices whereby they gain new knowledge and skills from individuals with particular skills.

- Social learning theory is based on children learning through observing others.

- David Thoreau and John Muir are two prominent proponents of children needing access to nature and the wilderness.

- Research suggests that nature heals, soothes, and restores and also connects children to their environments.

- There is an array of roles that early learning teachers play, including examining the barriers and challenges to children having opportunities for outdoor and nature play.

- Early learning teachers examine the levels of teacher and child engagement, peer-to-peer engagement, child and task engagement and child negative engagement during their outdoor play experiences.

- As part of preschool children's development, their independence increases and their worlds expand from the places and the materials used in their play.

- The outdoor play environment can become rich with mathematical concepts, thinking, reasoning, and logical reasoning with the experiences, materials, and discussions among adults and children.

- Communities are rich with play and learning experiences. Community journeys are defined as the places, people, and things that contribute to children's learning when exploring their communities.

- Intergenerational learning refers to learning from individuals from different generations.

- Communities support children in engaging in new, challenging, and hands-on learning experiences with people in the community and the community culture.

- Abraham Maslow's hierarchy of needs (physiological, safety and security, social needs, esteem, and self-actualization) provides a framework of how outdoor play environments support children in their development.

- Early learning teachers and families collaborate with children in their play and in facilitating opportunities for them to deepen and extend their play experiences that leads them to their own investigations.
- All children and families benefit from having access to and engagement in outdoor play and their community.
- Families and children are encouraged to share photos of buildings, pathways, materials, and maps that can be found in their community.

QUIET REFLECTION

Quietly go to a place in your community that is intriguing to you. What is it about that place that is intriguing to you? Is it the smell, the sounds, the architecture of the buildings, the trees and grasses, and /or the people that make the community place intriguing? If you were to share this community place with children, what might you tell them about the space? Is there a particular season that makes the place more intriguing than in other seasons? How does the place support you in restoring your energy or imagining new ideas or possibilities? How might you document your place to share with others? How might the place support children in engaging in a community journey? How do you think children would feel in your community place?

COMMUNITY DIALOGUE

Wild About Vancouver (WAV) is a unique outdoor play education festival that offers practical ways to support children and families in engaging in outdoor play regularly. WAV aims to connect families, networks for organizations, schools, youth programs, and the broader citizenry of Vancouver who have an interest in promoting outdoor play. Go to http://www.wildaboutvancouver.com/.

FOR FURTHER THOUGHT AND ACTION

Do you believe that children and early learning teachers should spend time connecting with places, things, and people in the community? If so, how is this a different process from taking children on walks in their neighbourhood? Do you think the children get the same benefit from the experience if the people come to the centre and early learning teachers put things from the community in the environment? Why or why not?

RESOURCES

The Early Childhood Education Journal of the Early Childhood Education Council of the Alberta Teacher's Association is intended to assist early learning professionals in increasing their professional knowledge, stimulate new thinking, explore new ideas, and offer various points of view. Check out their website to see what they are focusing on and how their research can inform outdoor play: http://www.ecec-ata.com/.

CHAPTER 11

Documentation and Assessment of Children's Outdoor Play Environments

What we see changes what we know. What we know changes what we see.

(Jean Piaget, 1896–1980)

LEARNING OUTCOMES

After exploring this chapter, you will be able to:

- Explain the relationship between documentation and assessment of outdoor play space.

- Discuss how pedagogical documentation supports early learning teachers in understanding children's interests in outdoor play and their capabilities in their play.

- Describe the differences between documentation and pedagogical documentation.

- Outline strategies that early learning teachers may use when beginning the process of developing pedagogical documentation.

- Discuss how pedagogical documentation supports family engagement.

CHILDHOOD MEMORIES

When I was very little, my family had the opportunity to visit relatives who lived near a wonderful place that they called an adventure playground. For the week that we visited, I spent every day playing with all the materials that were available. My favourites were the tires. Each day I tried to do something different with them—stacking, balancing and rolling them. Each day my father took photos of my experiences. He printed them and put them in a photo album. I still have that album. I am so grateful that my father documented my time in the adventure playground. When I look back, I have nice feelings inside and I can see now the value of outdoor play, loose parts, and documentation. I make sure that all of these are featured prominently in my practice with children today.

CHAPTER PREVIEW

Children's learning in outdoor environments can be enhanced through the practice and process of **pedagogical documentation**, which makes learning visible. Outdoor learning environments that are continuously assessed for their play value, the opportunities that they provide to children, and the ways in which they can be improved ultimately results in children having space that supports their curiosity and development. **Assessment** is a concept that relates to pedagogical documentation—once learning is made visible, the analysis of the learning is a form of assessment. It also relates to a process of evaluating the physical space that children have access to in their daily experiences. Continuous assessment of the outdoor space and analysis of documentation provides an opportunity to make the learning processes of children visible; a practice that Malaguzzi (1998) referred to as leaving traces:

> Teachers must leave behind an isolated, silent mode of working, which leaves no traces. Instead they must discover ways to communicate and document the children's evolving experiences at school. They must prepare a steady flow of quality information targeted to parents but appreciated by children and teachers. (pp. 69–70)

Tarr (2010) suggests that pedagogical documentation requires observations of children not only from the lens of a particular learning or skill, but also through a "lens of curiosity" so that early learning teachers keep the possibilities open for "seeing" interests, learning, and the strengths that children bring to the outdoor play environment. Assessment requires a lens of collaborative reflection so that a continual evaluation of spaces, places, and materials occurs.

According to Wien (2011), the term pedagogical documentation was introduced by Dahlberg, Moss, and Pence (1999) and is associated with the Reggio Emilia Approach. "Pedagogical documentation has its origins in the innovative and, today, world-famous municipal early childhood services in the Northern Italian city of Reggio Emilia" (Dahlberg & Moss, 2004, p. 6). Educators from Reggio Emilia make records of the events that take place and use the documentation as part of action research. This has come to be known as *pedagogical documentation*. Pedagogical documentation has an important role in supporting reflective practice (Dahlberg, Moss, & Pence, 1999).

Early learning teachers capture digital images that are used to create documentation to inform them of children's capabilities. At the same time, the images can help to assess how the outdoor play space contributes to their play. For example, examine the series of photos depicted in the collage (Photo 11.1) that were taken during an afternoon play experience. Beginning with the image in the upper left corner you will see a sequence of events. What story do the photos tell you about the children's interests, learning, and strengths? What do you notice about the environment? How did the environment support children's play? Now, how would you use the information gained from the photos to influence the invitations that you would provide the children the next day?

In this chapter we focus on the process of documentation as it relates to children's outdoor play experiences and how the documentation can be used to inform and influence planning, programming, and the presentation of the outdoor play space (Basford & Bath, 2014; Dietze & Kashin, 2018). When thinking about assessing space and interpreting children's play experiences through documentation, early learning teachers draw upon their knowledge about children's interests, ideas, learning, development, and understanding (Basford, 2015), rather than thinking about examining the documentation to identify and compare children's abilities. Not all documentation is pedagogical. To be pedagogical, the documentation requires interpretation from others and is used to lead

Pedagogical documentation is a process that makes children's learning visible. With analysis and interpretation, the documentation can reveal curriculum directions (Dietze & Kashin, 2016).

Assessment of outdoor space refers to examining and determining the characteristics, value, quallty, and influence that the outdoor space has on children's outdoor play options and opportunities.

Gill Robertson

Photo 11.1 Capturing images of children at play.

the direction of the curriculum (Dietze & Kashin, 2017). When an early learning teacher amasses a collection of observations that are shared via emails, panels, or bulletin boards/ display boards indoors or outdoors, there is ample opportunity for that documentation to become pedagogical.

We advocate for early learning teachers to adopt a pedagogical documentation process that involves collaboration amongst children, families, and other early learning teachers. Adapting a collaborative process helps to foster a democratic practice in early learning programs (Moss, 2007). Pedagogical documentation that is collaborative helps to ensure that children's voices are being heard and that they are being included in the process. As outlined in Table 11.1, there are distinct differences between what pedagogical documentation is and what it is not.

Child observation has an extensive history in early childhood education programs and has been associated with the 19th century child study movement that began with G. Stanley Hall. Until recently, observations were focused mainly on determining whether a child is conforming to a set of predetermined standards. As early learning teachers gain knowledge about and skills in developing and understanding the significance of

Table 11.1 Aspects of pedagogical documentation.

Pedagogical documentation is:	Pedagogical documentation is not:
■ Gathering evidence and artifacts of children's play. ■ Reflecting upon and analyzing the artifacts. ■ Presenting the collection through a documentation process that makes children's learning visible in the early learning environment. ■ Collaborating with multiple people on ideas, reflections, and perspectives.	■ A recording of what the children did on a particular day without analysis. ■ A photo collection of children at play without interpretation. ■ A portfolio created of children's work and placed on shelves and not used to support future curriculum directions. ■ A recording-keeping document that lists the skills that children exhibit.

pedagogical documentation, traditional observations will no longer be the norm. Pedagogical documentation, by contrast, is focused on seeking an understanding of the children's play experiences, their processes of play and their capabilities. It seeks to make visible children's strengths and competence. Pedagogical documentation is child-centric and culturally appropriate rather than prescribed (Dietze & Kashin, 2017) and may draw upon different theories and philosophies (Fleet, Honig, Robertson, Semann, & Shepherd, 2011).

When early learning teachers focus on children's strengths in observations, rather than their weaknesses or gaps in development, pedagogical documentation helps them view children as capable and competent. Malaguzzi (1994) clarifies the image of children from the perspective of the Reggio Emilia approach as follows:

> Our image of children no longer considers them as isolated and egocentric, does not see them only engaged in actions with objects, does not emphasize only the cognitive aspects, does not belittle feelings or what is not logical and does not consider with ambiguity the role of the affective domain. Instead our image of the child is rich in potential, strong, powerful, competent, and most of all connected to adults and other children. (p. 10)

Early learning teachers assess the outdoor environment to determine if and how it aligns with children's play ideas, experiences, capabilities, and competencies. This requires early learning teachers to have an understanding of how the space, place, and materials contribute to children's opportunities to be successful in their outdoor play experiences.

In this chapter, the assessment of the outdoor play space will be discussed from the perspective of examining it to determine if, how, when, and where the outdoor environment supports children's sense of curiosity and wonder. How effective are these spaces? What tools can early learning teachers use to assess outdoor play environments? How can these assessments support and be used in conjunction with pedagogical documentation to ensure the outdoor play spaces provide ample play opportunities? Children's outdoor play is highly influenced by individual, child, and social connections, and by environmental factors. Early learning teachers need to take these factors into consideration (Anbari & Soltanzadeh, 2015).

As outlined in Figure 11.1, Dietze and Kim (2014), Anbari and Soltanzadeh (2015), and others examine children's outdoor play space from a variety of perspectives. Assessing the space and how children use the space is a complex process that is foundational to program planning.

The assessment of children's outdoor play spaces coupled with documentation provides early learning teachers and children with valuable information about the space and the materials within that space. As early learning teachers examine the space through

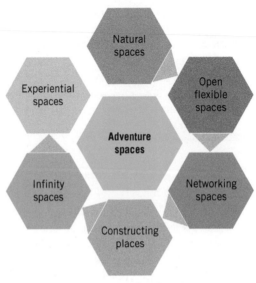

Figure 11.1 Characteristics of outdoor play spaces.

documentation, they also take into consideration how the space is organized, and how the time allocated for outdoor play influences the children's outdoor play engagement (Anbari & Soltanzadeh, 2015). The discussions of the documentation with children and families will provide insight into how children feel about the environment and their play experiences.

Kim (2015) discovered in a study on outdoor play pedagogical documentation that by placing documentation outdoors at the children's level and near where the play occurred, the children's voices become more prominent in the process. The result was that the early learning teachers were more knowledgeable about the children's interests and could use that information in planning and programming. Thus, the documentation became pedagogical. Examine Photos 11.2 and 11.3 and imagine what children might do or say when they view the documentation. What could be the children's reactions to it, perceptions of it, and engagements with it during outdoor play?

Katarina Josipovic

Photos 11.2 and **11.3** Outdoor play documentation.

Kim (2015) interviewed children about their outdoor play documentation and found that they "perceived that outdoor play pedagogical documentation is a reflective tool where they can revisit, interpret, and analyze their previous outdoor play, which yielded new ideas about the outdoor play" (p. 90). Kim suggested that children were more confident in their outdoor play and expressed more profound thoughts, ideas, and emotions about their outdoor play when they had viewed documentation outdoors and then had the materials, space, and opportunities to recreate the play episodes. This finding reinforces the importance of early learning teachers looking and listening closely and carefully when children view the pedagogical documentation.

Documentation highlights how children express themselves in multiple ways when playing in natural environments. For example, some children find the outdoor environment to be invigorating. When they find themselves in an open field, they will run. When they come upon a sloping hill, they will roll. Other children are very excited about what they find when they are exploring all that nature has to offer—the flora, fauna, and mini beasts. Early learning teachers use these observations to make meaning of children's play and to theorize about children's thinking and interests. These observations are foundational to answering questions about children's play. When analyzed, this becomes **action research** that provides insights into programming intentions and the types of materials that will support a potential expansion of play options.

Nevella Schepmyer

Photo 11.4 Examining bugs in a specimen jar.

Recording observations during the documentation process and reflecting upon them in a way that seeks to find meaning and insights into children's play is a core element of early learning teachers' professional practice (Morrison, 2013). Imagine what this child may have said about the bugs in her specimen jar in Photo 11.4. What questions might early learning teachers ask the child to find out more about her thoughts?

Using clipboards and sticky notes to record informal observations helps to capture information that provides insight into and an understanding of children's play. This is a less cumbersome way than a more formal observation method, such as anecdotal observations. The data collected differs as well. For example, early learning teachers would not focus on recording how the child holds the jar, whether she uses a pincer or palmer grasp. These types of observations are not necessary or significant to the process of pedagogical documentation. Rather, early learning teachers are more focused on learning more about the child's thought processes. During the observation phase of pedagogical documentation, early learning teachers encourage children to develop their own observational skills and to incorporate what they see with what they imagine. Early learning teachers encourage children to look closely and to articulate their ideas verbally and/or pictorially. Not only do children gain skills and knowledge about making their learning visible, the information supports early learning teachers in assessing if the environment is supporting their play and learning interests.

Action research in this context refers to a process used to examine and reflect upon a situation or problem among children, early learning teachers, and families as collaborative partners in the community of practice, with the goal of continuous improvement.

SETTING THE STAGE FOR OUTDOOR PLAY

Outdoor play environments are essential places for children to develop foundational skills in play, learning, communicating, networking, critical thinking, and problem solving (Villanueva et al., 2016). Emerging evidence suggests that how the outdoor play environments are designed contributes to children's health and development (Villanueva et al., 2016). As part of connecting children with and to their outdoor environments, early

Diane Kashin

Clipboards
Nature journals
Magnifying
glasses
Binoculars
Measurement
tools
Collection bottles
Field guides

Figure 11.2 Resources for Looking Closely.

learning teachers encourage them to explore and discover the various attributes of the environment, including patterns and connections that are embedded in the outdoor environment. These observations serve as curiosity triggers (Dietze & Kashin, 2018). This can be done in a non-directive way by encouraging children to use their different senses to experience and explore the world (Wilson, 2016). Within the environment, a variety of resources are available that support children in identifying their ideas and inquiries and to record them. As part of the process, early learning teachers role model to the children as to how they can gain new information when they take the time to **look closely**. Consider the following resources for studying nature as adapted from Rubin (2013) and featured in Figure 11.2. The process for looking closely is depicted in Figure 11.3.

As children become familiar with their natural world, they can become keen observers and learn to deepen their observations to go beyond subjective opinions, such as the turtle "is cute," to objective observations that focus on describing the turtle's behaviour, for example, when the head retracts into the shell. Children learn to differentiate between **subjective** and **objective observations**. In describing both the behaviours they observe in the natural world and the features they see, such as the turtle's shell is "hard and shaped like a dome," children learn through role modelling. Children benefit from being encouraged to use all of their senses during the observations and to stop, slow down, look closely, and notice. Early learning teachers exhibit and role model these principles to the children when observing aspects of the outdoor play environments.

There are four phases or basic elements of pedagogical documentation, as seen in Figure 11.4. Observation leads to documentation or recording. Recording may take the form of photos, audio, or videotapes.

Look closely is a strategy to encourage children's observations in nature.

Subjective observations refers to an expression of ideas, thoughts, or opinions without having necessary experience or facts.

Objective observations refer to describing what you see, feel, hear, or smell.

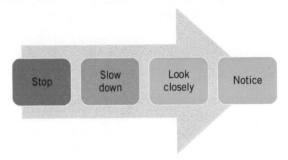

Stop | Slow down | Look closely | Notice

Figure 11.3 Stop, slow down, look closely, and notice.

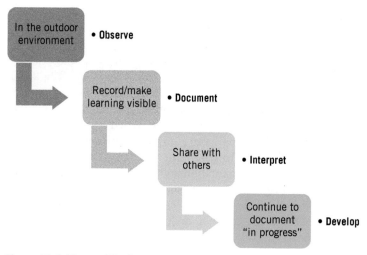

Figure 11.4 Phases of the documentation process.

Collecting data also involves including samples of the children's representations in the documentation. When these representations are shared with others and widely interpreted, documentation continues to develop. For example, children may be interested in drawing or writing what they see, think, or wonder about their outdoor explorations. These representations shared with others encourages visible thinking. *Seeing, Thinking and Wondering* is a visible thinking routine that helps children to focus their experiences as shown in Box 11.1. Think about how the pedagogical

---

CURIOUS?

Learn more about visible thinking routines by clicking this link: http://www.visiblethinkingpz .org/VisibleThinking_html_files/03_ThinkingRoutines/03c_Core_routines/SeeThinkWonder/ SeeThinkWonder_Routine.html

Photo 11.5 Pedagogical documentation contributes to seeing, thinking, and wondering.

Suzanne Gabli

documentation illustrated in Photo 11.5 supports children in the concept of seeing, thinking, and wondering.

Collecting documentation refers to a process that can involve examining observation notes, printing photos, and examining children's representations of their learning. The documentation becomes pedagogical only when it is interpreted and analyzed by early learning teachers and others, including the children and families, to create a curriculum path. Based on the documentation, what will the next step be to continue to support the children's learning and interests? To determine this, early learning teachers need to share the documentation and to be open to possible challenges and criticisms. Early learning teachers accept this as part of the journey in their role as an action researcher. They take the perspectives of others to develop their documentation to the point that it becomes pedagogical.

When early learning teachers view pedagogical documentation as a "process to explore all of our questions about children" (Ontario Ministry of Education, 2014, p. 21), they make the documentation accessible to others (children, families, other educators, community members) and invite interpretations of what is seen, providing multiple perspectives. These perspectives help adults to look at what is happening in a program at any one time and contributes to the creation of a curriculum path that is authentic to those involved.

THINK ABOUT IT! READ ABOUT IT! WRITE ABOUT IT!

Some early learning teachers may be familiar with the term 'pedagogical narration'. Is it the same as pedagogical documentation or is it different? Why are there two different terms? Read the article at http://www.jbccs.org/uploads/1/8/6/0/18606224/pedagogical_narration .pdf. How does this relate to what you have been examining in the chapter?

Pedagogical documentation without an analysis is equivalent to a mere record (Fleet et al., 2012). Seeking to find meaning, early learning teachers read and re-read documentation, trying to see how it aligns with an image of children as competent and capable in their outdoor experiences. By critically reflecting and analyzing interpretations, teachers look for ways that the documentation aligns with their provincial frameworks. Going beyond alignment with provincial frameworks requires deeper analysis. For example, how does the documentation reflect democracy and voice? How does it reflect that all children feel a sense of belonging and well-being and are able to engage and express themselves? Sharing the documentation with others is an invitation to engage in the interpretation. Early learning teachers celebrate the feedback and view it as part of the "in progress" process. Reflections and interpretations of others can have a significant influence on moving outdoor play programming forward in ways that reflect meaningful curriculum.

It is through pedagogical documentation that early learning teachers and children gain insight into how their environments serve the children. For example, early learning teachers

Table 11.2 Pedagogical documentation and learning.

Type of Assessment	Children and Early Learning Teachers	The Early Learning Teacher and the Environment
Assessment for learning	The early learning teacher reflects upon and interprets documentation to determine how to scaffold materials and play options.	The early learning teacher examines the documentation to determine how the children are using the environment and the materials within the environment. The reflections and interpretations will influence the types of invitations and materials that are placed in the outdoor environment that will challenge the children and extend their learning.
Assessment as learning	The early learning teacher listens carefully as children review the documentation and how they embarked upon a particular experience.	The early learning teacher uses the information that children share about how they embarked upon an experience to guide the placement of materials that could lead children to replicate aspects of an experience while adding new aspects to the process.
Assessment of learning	The early learning teacher and children create documentation to illustrate their play, capabilities, and interests.	The early learning teacher examines the documentation to ensure that the outdoor environments and the materials align with the children's capabilities and interests.

Source: Based on Early childhood education (Kindergarten)—Saskatchewan (2010)—Curricula. 2. Competency-based education—Saskatchewan. Saskatchewan. Ministry of Education. Curriculum and E-Learning. Humanities Unit.

may wonder why they rarely see children using a particular part of the play space, while other areas attract children on a daily basis. The Saskatchewan Kindergarten Curriculum identifies the importance of assessment being authentic. As outlined in Table 11.2, we have adapted the three areas of assessment from the Saskatchewan Kindergarten Curriculum to illustrate how pedagogical documentation influences the assessment of outdoor play environments.

The Reggio Emilia approach views children as having capacities to communicate with other children and adults and to express their thoughts through a wide range of languages (Edwards, Gandini, & Forman, 2011). Early learning teachers who create unique, innovative options in the outdoor play environments inherently set the tone for children to utilize the synthesis of a variety of languages. This ultimately enhances their thinking skills (Edwards et al., 2011). Pedagogical documentation becomes an effective process that captures and documents the various means of how children exercise their curiosities, communicate with others, and express their opinions (McKenna, 2005). Pedagogical documentation is an effective strategy to use to document children's voices (Kim, 2015). Examine Photo 11.6 where Nadine, an early learning teacher has created a collage using a digital format to record an outdoor play experience. In the documentation, the child is encouraged to come up with her own theory about a caterpillar she discovered. In this way, Nadine has included the child's voice in the documentation, demonstrating a view of the child as capable and competent.

Early learning teachers, children, and families interact with a variety of visuals that include collections of notes, video recordings, photos, and children's representations such as their drawings that serve to reconstruct learning processes to create

During our morning time outside, Audrey found 2 caterpillars. When she came inside, Mme. Dickson helped Audrey persevere in her search to identify the caterpillar. Audrey confirmed her theory that they were Wooly Bear caterpillars like ones we had found last year. During our afternoon time outside, Audrey and Nico decided to dig for more eggs. Instead of eggs they discovered the longest worm of the day. Jackson shared his knowledge that worms have 2 bums.

Nadine Osborne

Photo 11.6 Digital documentation depicting outdoor play.

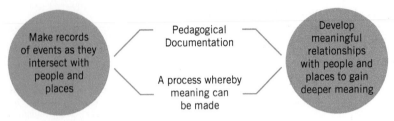

Figure 11.5 Pedagogical documentation to record meaning.

an authentic record for dialogue, reflection, and analysis (Gandini & Kaminsky, 2004). According to Rinaldi (2006):

> Documentation, therefore, is seen as visible listening, as the construction of traces (through notes, slides, videos, and so on) that not only testify to the children's learning path and processes, but also make them possible because they are visible. For us this means making visible, and this possible, the relationships that are the building blocks of knowledge. (p. 68)

When early learning teachers embed documentation into their practice, their pedagogy and curriculum decisions supporting outdoor play experiences are clearly based on the real lived experiences of children. It is complex because as a process, pedagogical documentation involves the interpretation of the documentation to discern meaning. It is telling the story of children's connections to the outdoor environment, peers, and materials within the space.

Digital devices that take photos are important resources for early learning teachers and children to use to capture their experiences. Often photos of special events are taken, such as a trip to a park or the zoo, and then displayed with notes saying "the children had fun in the park" or "the children enjoyed seeing the animals at the zoo". These descriptors lack meaning and show limited interpretation of the actual experience that children were engaged in and how the experience added value to children's learning and development. As outlined by Fleet, Patterson and Robertson (2012), pedagogical documentation "is not a real-time movie or a record of events, but a subjective set of frozen moments that provoke, inform, record, and provide opportunities for further thinking, wonder, able to be offered back to children for comment and reflection" (p. 7). As depicted in Figure 11.5, it is a process whereby early learning teachers seek meaning about children's outdoor play experiences. Documentation is intended to communicate to the children that they are citizens with rights. They need to feel valued and in turn they will be invaluable to the curriculum process as analytical contributors.

In Photo 11.7, early learning teachers collected notes from an ongoing investigation that the children were involved in about growing seeds that were eventually transplanted to an outdoor garden. The documentation was shared with the children and families indoors and later moved and shared outdoors. Because the documentation was visible and aesthetically pleasing, it drew children, families, and other teachers to engage with it. Thought was given to the placement of the documentation so that children

Diane Kashin

Photo 11.7 Documenting a seed investigation.

Table 11.3 Forms of documentation.

Professional Journals	Early learning teachers keep professional journals to record their observations and ideas about children and their outdoor play experiences.
Documentation Panels	These visual, artistic representations—often referred to as "panels"—reveal children's thinking and theory building and, as identified in Reggio Emilia, allow for a hundred languages to be spoken, often without an audible word (Dietze & Kashin, 2016).
Learning Stories or Narratives	Learning stories are a form of observation and documentation that are written in narrative story format. The early learning teacher watches and listens to the children while they explore through play. Photos are taken and notes written. Then a story is created that can be shared with children and their families (Pack, 2015). Learning stories are written for and to the child and the family. Learning stories, similar to other forms of documentation, focus on a child's strengths and dispositions to learn.
Samples of Children's Representations	During the collection of documentation, children's representations of their learning can be archived. For instance, if the children are investigating snails they may draw the snail, create snails from clay, paint snails, or construct snails using another medium such as wire.
Observation Notes	These can be recorded in professional journals, collaborative documentation books, or on sticky notes.
Photographs and Videos	Videos recorded on tablets or smartphones can be stored along with digital photos that may to be added to panels or portfolios.
Portfolios	Portfolios have been popular in early learning for many years. Portfolios are seen as involving a "purposeful, multifaceted process of collecting documentation of children's growth, progress, and effort over time" (Hanson & Gilkerson, 1999, p. 81). Portfolios can be made available for the children to access in their outdoor environment.
Documentation Software Applications	Documentation software is available to download for free or based on a fee per child or per group. These applications often connect to provincial frameworks and have features to share with families.

and families would have access to it and provide their perspectives on it. A number of documentation resources were used to collect the research emanating from the seed investigation.

The documentation tools used in the seed investigation are featured in Table 11.3. Consider each form of documentation as sources of data that may be analyzed by the early learning teachers, the children, and the families.

Documentation takes many forms and can be found in various parts of the early learning environment. According to McNally & Slutsky (2016), documentation is not always permanent or in panel form. Children may view documentation books and portfolios on a daily basis when they are placed in the environment and accessible. These resources, along with panels, should be made available to the children in their outdoor environment because when they view the documentation in their outdoor spaces they see that outdoor play is valued.

CURIOUS?

Do you want to learn more about software applications? Check out this example: https://www.storypark.com/

OUR VISION FOR OUTDOOR PLAY

Pedagogical documentation requires early learning teachers to view one of their roles to be that of researcher. Researchers use many resources to collect data and to seek evidence of the depth and breadth of learning that children are experiencing in the outdoor play space. This information becomes the framework for the type of materials to which children have access and the environmental designs for outdoor play. Researchers determine a strategy, such as using a professional journal, for recording children's words and ideas about their outdoor play experiences. These recordings become the starting point for visual reflection to commence.

Our vision is that early learning teachers view themselves as researchers when they engage in the pedagogical documentation process as illustrated in Photo 11.8. The documentation collected serves as the research data to be analyzed. All subjects of the research—children, families, and teachers—are included in the process. In the analysis of the documentation, early learning teachers think about the interpretations and reflect upon the following:

■ How can you continue to build on children's interests and ideas?

■ How can you scaffold the children's learning and create opportunities for further challenges?

■ How can you provide meaningful and authentic experiences to build on the learning processes of children?

■ How can you change the outdoor environment and materials to support children's explorations and discoveries?

The interpretation process is made richer when there are multiple perspectives. Early learning teachers are open to and solicit the views of others. These perspectives will inform practice and shape future curriculum directions.

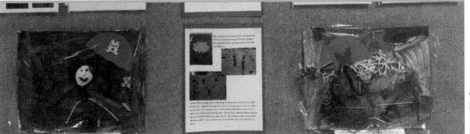

Photo 11.8 Vision statement.

POSITIONING OUTDOOR PLAY IN THE LIVES OF CHILDREN

Pedagogical documentation as a tool for professional practice and professional learning is considered revolutionary. Pence and Pacini-Ketchabaw (2008) noted that "those who have reconceptualized early childhood practices by using pedagogical documentation as a revolutionary tool are not fixed in guidelines that provide one view of the child; rather, they are opened to multiple voices, multiple interpretations—opened to diversity" (p. 248). There are advantages to taking the time to create, amass, and analyze documentation so that it can be used pedagogically. There are benefits to early learning teachers, children, and families such as those depicted in Figures 11.6, 11.7, and 11.8.

Buldu (2010) suggested that pedagogical documentation can galvanize a professional learning community and create opportunities for early learning teachers to work together and collaboratively analyze what children have been learning. Pedagogical documentation has the potential for early learning teachers to reflect on their image of children, their own role, and the role of families and community in children's play and learning. Documenting and interpreting children's learning experiences contribute to a richer and deeper understanding about what and how children think (Jablon, Dombro,

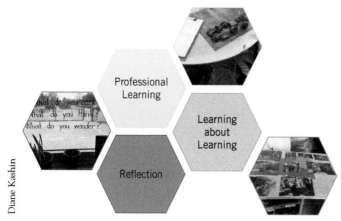

Figure 11.6 Benefits to early learning teachers.

Figure 11.7 Benefits to children.

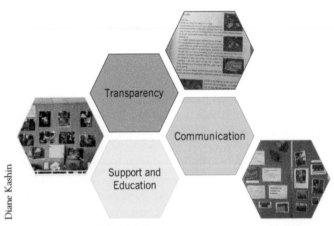

Diane Kashin

Figure 11.8 Benefits to families.

& Dichtelmiller, 2007) and how they exhibit their interests. Continuous documentation that incorporates children's engagement in diverse experiences generates an authentic picture of children's different development levels, skills, curiosity, personalities, and strategies that they use in their play (Forman & Hall, 2005). To view children's play outdoors from the perspective of its importance to their learning and development requires reflection. Reflective practice supports ongoing professional learning.

As outlined in Photos 11.9 and 11.10, there is value to children seeing themselves reflected visually in their environment as the subjects of outdoor play pedagogical documentation. Children benefit when their families are considered partners in their learning experiences, and documentation makes that learning visible and accessible to others. For example, when family members converse with children about their day outside playing in the snow, because they have viewed digital documentation of their experience, children will exhibit pride and a sense of accomplishment. Documentation provides increased opportunities for the learning to be extended at home. In addition, families have visual

Angela Roy

Photo 11.9 A family member views the documentation of her child at play.

Beverlie Dietze

Photo 11.10 A child and a family member view documentation of the child at play.

evidence of their children's daily experiences. This can lead to enhanced communication and increased support between the families and the early learning teachers. Figures 11.6 to 11.8 taken together depict the joy that children and families may experience from outdoor play pedagogical documentation.

Children are more likely to be active participants in their own learning process when documentation is continuously provided and utilized in their environment (Dietze & Kashin, 2017). Pedagogical documentation entices children to take a leading role in their learning journey in part because they develop an increased sense of confidence and curiosity by revisiting their work and thinking about what they have been doing (Malaguzzi, 1998). The use of pedagogical documentation in practice facilitates the scaffolding process of children's ideas and learning and helps them expand their interests, take a more active role in their learning, and promote self-awareness (Buldu, 2010). By revisiting their learning moments through pedagogical documentation, children can revise previous theories that they had established and enhance their thinking with the support of others such as peers and early learning teachers (Kim & Darling, 2009).

Pedagogical documentation provides opportunities to build relationships with the wider community (McKenna, 2005). Inviting community members to view and offer their feedback on documentation broadens children's perspectives.

Families want what is best for their children (Ontario Ministry of Education, 2014). Documentation provides a way in which families can view the quality of the outdoor play experiences that children are engaged in. Thus, they can rest assured that their children are receiving quality care and education. This is of particular importance for families who believe children learn more during the indoor portion of the program than they do outdoors (Sandseter & Sando, 2016). Seeing their children's outdoor play experiences and engaging in dialogue about how these experiences contribute to learning skills necessary for later academic environments help families understand their importance to child development. Buldu (2010) speculated that:

> While it is not easy to adopt and implement pedagogical documentation, it holds potential in highlighting children's learning processes, increasing children's motivation, interest and participation in learning processes, helping them to reflect on and contribute to improve their own learning. (p. 144)

Pedagogical documentation reinforces communication among children, their families, and early learning teachers (Buldu, 2010). By exchanging information, families can learn strategies from early learning teachers (Buldu, 2010). From an outdoor play perspective, documentation may serve as a means to help families enhance the outdoor learning experiences for their children.

THEORETICAL FOUNDATION

Democracy is often associated with **politics**. With regards to documentation, democracy refers to involving people directly in matters that affect them. Democracy from this perspective can be understood as a mode of being in the world, as a form of living together (Dietze & Kashin, 2016). Democracy refers to a way of life that maximizes "opportunities for sharing, exchanging and negotiating perspectives and opinions" (Moss, 2011, p. 2). Democracy "is a way of relating to self and others; an ethical, political and educational relationship that can and should pervade all aspects of everyday life" (Moss, 2011, p. 2). Democratic practice requires intention, supportive conditions, and thinking differently about daily practices. Democratic practice requires democratic professionalism (Oberhuemer, 2005).

Politics refers to the activities associated with the governance of a country or organization that are aimed at improving a situation, status, or position based on a particular set of beliefs or principles.

Table 11.4 The four elements of democratic practice.

Diversity	Democratic practice involves making a commitment to respect diversity. All children should see themselves in the documentation showing them that they are respected and belong. The documentation should feature outdoor learning to show value for diverse learning experiences.
Multiple Perspectives	Democratic practice strives to bring forth multiple perspectives and opens up documentation to be interpreted by others as a way to allow and invite differing perspectives.
Curiosity, Uncertainty, and Subjectivity	Democratic practice involves early learning teachers being in a constant state of uncertainty as they use their curiosity about children's learning to continue to build their documentation collection and to analyze what it reveals. What documentation reveals is not always objective. It can be subjective. Subjectivity is an accepted part of the process.
Critical Thinking	Democratic practice involves using critical thinking, which involves making clear and reasoned judgments that are well thought out. Pedagogical documentation as a process that takes time helps early learning teachers become critical thinkers.

This means that early learning teachers "bring an important perspective and a relevant local knowledge to the democratic forum; they also recognise that they do not have the truth nor privileged access to knowledge" (Moss, 2007, p. 13). Moss (2007) suggested that democratic practice flourishes in learning communities that exhibit the four elements featured in Table 11.4, as adapted by Dietze and Kashin (2017).

THINK ABOUT IT! READ ABOUT IT! WRITE ABOUT IT!

Do you think early learning programs are political places? Read this article http://www.child-encyclopedia.com/child-care-early-childhood-education-and-care/according-experts/democracy-first-practice-early and reflect on your experiences in early learning. Write a reflection about what you have read and what you have experienced about politics.

Documentation supports a democratic process. What this means is that all those involved—families, early learning teachers, children, and the community—have contributions to make to the process. Think about different ways that families can access documentation and get involved in the documentation process. How can the documentation process be presented to families so that they want to view it and contribute to it? By using multiple means to share documentation with families, it will be more likely they will be engaged and lend their perspectives (Dietze & Kashin, 2017). In striving for a democratic practice, early learning teachers involve children in the documentation process. For example, consider that you are exploring the metamorphosis of a caterpillar to butterfly. How might you involve the children? How do you determine the artifacts that will be used to make learning visible? Imagine what happens for the children when they see their own printing in the documentation. How does this contribute to their learning and their involvement in making their learning visible?

Diane Kashin

Photo 11.11 From caterpillar to butterfly.

Including children in the documentation process also involves a need to consider ethical practice. Everyone represented in the documentation must be informed about how the documentation will be used. With young children this means having consent from families to post children's images and their work. When sharing documentation, early learning teachers maintain respect for children's privacy and confidentiality. If a family does not agree to share a child's image on social media or on panels or bulletin boards, then this request must be honoured. Early learning teachers examine the informed consent from families to ensure that no child depicted in the documentation is shown in a negative light or that sharing of the documentation will harm the child in any way (Ontario Ministry of Education, 2015). Tarr (2011) stated that:

> Both educators and researchers must negotiate their way amongst the continually flickering shadows of the ethical dilemmas that arise when we work with visual images intended to bring visibility to the lives of children in ways that include their voices in a collaborative endeavor. (p. 16)

Consider the points below when thinking about ethics in pedagogical documentation. These have been adapted from *Pedagogical Documentation Revisited: Looking at Assessment and Learning in New Ways* (Ontario Ministry of Education, 2015).

1. How have you included children in the documentation in ways that are ethical and respectful?
2. Why did you choose this image or video clip over others to represent learning?
3. What should I do when I have images that may show one child in a less than positive light?

Ethical and democratic practices are considered essential parts of the pedagogical documentation process, as early learning teachers strive to be collaborative and inclusive. Even in the beginning stages of the pedagogical documentation process, where early learning teachers are observing children, their place within the group is considered.

Thinking of ethics and politics in early learning environments may involve rethinking or **reconceptualizing** prior perspectives. Reconceptualization is a current process in early learning that seeks to challenge notions of universal truth. It is about questioning what are known as grand narratives (Bloch, Swadener, & Cannella, 2014), or the notion that there is only one accepted view. In a postmodern world, grand narratives are viewed with skepticism; there is instead a desire to seek localized narratives or stories. In the profession of early learning this means seeking multiple perspectives to inform practice and recognizing diversity and complexity (Bloch et al., 2014). This can be accomplished in the process of pedagogical documentation.

One of the leading scholars of reconceptualization in Canada is Veronica Pacini-Ketchabaw, who has focused her research on the common relations children have with places, materials, and other species (Pacini-Ketchabaw, 2013).

Reconceptualizing refers to rethinking a concept or idea that leads to new visioning of a perspective, concept, or idea.

BOX 11.2 Featured Theorist: Veronica Pacini-Ketchabaw

A leading researcher and university professor, Pacini-Ketchabaw has interests in pedagogical documentation, reconceptualization, and common world relations. Pacini-Ketchabaw studies the real-life worlds that children inherit, inhabit, and share with others—human and otherwise. She is researching how these life-worlds are shaped by environmental damage and global inequalities. For more information on Pacini-Ketchabaw see https://www.edu.uwo.ca/faculty-profiles/veronica-pacini-ketchabaw.html

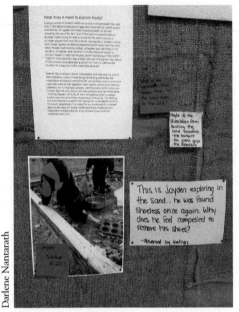
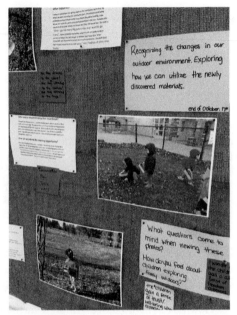

Darlene Nantarath

Photos 11.12 and **11.13** Encouraging the perspectives of others.

Reconceptualization supports a key element of documentation. This requires multiple perspectives to inform the process. The way documentation is shared with others will encourage feedback from families and others. Examine Photos 11.12 and 11.13 and reflect on how the interpretations of others are encouraged.

PRACTICAL APPLICATIONS

One of the greatest challenges of incorporating pedagogical documentation into practice is time. As identified by Fleet, Honig, Robertson, Semann and Shepherd (2011) documentation requires large blocks of thinking and writing time. They suggested that early learning teachers think about "how much time do you spend IN your role and how much time do you spend ON your role?" (p. 18). They suspect that early learning teachers spend less time on their role than in the role, due in part to staffing models and the feeling that there is limited time to step away from the children to think and reflect. Strategies that learning programs may consider include the following:

1. Documentation becomes richer when early learning teachers think, talk, and write in small groups. Bringing groups of early learning teachers together to examine, reflect, debate, and determine ways to document children's play enriches thinking and the pedagogical documentation process.

2. Talking theory is an important practice because early learning teachers come to the environment with a variety of theories and understandings of those theories by which they come to understand their work and which guides their practice. Group meetings, such as staff meetings, provide a venue for early learning teachers to collectively theorize their work.

3. Examining ratios and schedules may help to provide early learning teachers with time away from the children that is used to think about and document learning without violating the required ratios.

Table 11.5 Strategies to support novice documenters.

Thinking	Doing	Reflecting
■ Think about what you will document and why. ■ Think about how you will document what you are trying to capture and why—will it be text, video, photos, or combinations? ■ Think about what the role of the children and families will be and why? ■ Think about how the documentation will influence your assessment of the outdoor play space and the materials within it.	■ Observe children at play and collect the data (visual and textual) that capture what you are trying to explore. ■ Review the artifacts. ■ Identify the lens that will influence how the story is told. ■ Select and organize the artifacts that support your vision for the story. ■ Examine the documentation to determine how it speaks to you. ■ Share the documentation with colleagues, children, and families as the starting point of pedagogical transformation. ■ Determine where the documentation will be displayed outdoors and why. ■ Add to the documentation as new learnings evolve.	■ What story or insights do you gain from the documentation? ■ How does it influence programming, scaffolding, and discussions with children and families? ■ What insight do you gain about children's interests and capabilities? ■ What patterns or trends do you see emerging? How do you use that information going forward? ■ How do children's voices influence your reflections? ■ How does the result of the interaction that occurred with the pedagogical documentation inform how you embrace children and outdoor play in your practice? ■ What might you do differently next time? ■ What assessment of space and place can be made by the documentation presented?

4. Identifying time to document with children is essential to creating quality documentation. When children are engaged in the process, their learning becomes visible. Moreover, collaborating with the children allows for documentation to unfold as part of the regular day.

Although there is no one right way to engage in the process of documentation, increasingly, technology is used as a tool to support the creation of documentation. Even though video recordings are effective in gaining a better understanding of children than other media, Flannery, Quinn, and Schwartz (2011) found that photographs were favoured over video recordings and are better able to support children in being part of the documentation process.

Practising creating documentation using various technologies and in various forms such as digital or hard copy will help educators find the ideal format and tool. As outlined in Table 11.5, novices benefit from engaging in a thinking, doing, and reflecting process. Examine Photo 11.14. Why might an early learning teacher document play in various outdoor play spaces? What would an early learning teacher learn about children when exploring the documentation in different parts of the play space?

PRINCIPLES OF PRACTICE: ENVIRONMENTAL-BASED PRACTICE

Early learning teachers often view outdoor play environments as places for children to participate in active physical play and the socialization that evolves from that play. Incorporating tenets of environmental awareness dates back to Piaget (1962). He suggested that understanding

Photo 11.14 Pedagogical documentation placed in various locations in the outdoor play space.

Suzanne Gabli

Table 11.6 Examining environmentally based concepts and practices.

Concept	Thinking and Reflections	Practice
Connections between people and the natural world	What are my roles and responsibilities in fostering children's care for the environment now and for future generations?	■ Discuss with children why and how to care for our environments. ■ Incorporate loose parts that are appropriate for outdoor play.
Respect for the environment	What is my role in illustrating the importance of preserving, conserving, and enhancing the environment?	■ Model how to reduce consumption of commercial materials. ■ Model caring principles in relation to the environment such as reducing waste, preserving water, reusing materials, and using the environment while maintaining respect for nature.
Recognition that people are dependent on the environment	What do I know about the relationship between a child's quality of outdoor play and learning and the quality of the environment?	■ Observe where and how children use the outdoor environment. ■ Discuss and document with the children their connections to the environment. ■ Examine how children's outdoor play changes in the seasons and how children embrace those seasons.

assimilation and accommodation is best achieved when teachers have experiences in their local environments. He determined that children's play and learning is much richer when it occurs outdoors in stimulating environments.

Exposing children to environmental sustainability concepts during their early years will influence the dispositions, values, and behaviours that they adopt toward sustainable practices (Kellert, 2005). This requires early learning teachers to think about the pedagogy of sustainability in broad terms. Children need to develop the skills and knowledge to identify as community and global citizens and model practices that will sustain and improve both our natural and social environments (Haas & Ashman, 2014). Early learning teachers incorporate opportunities for children to learn about **ecosystems** as part of their outdoor play "lived" experiences. Incorporating opportunities for learning about ecosystems contributes to many aspects of children's development, including, but not limited to, science, language, problem solving, and critical thinking skills. Supporting children in learning about ecosystems is foundational to children becoming environmentally literate citizens.

Beckford & Nahdee (2011) suggested that Indigenous epistemologies offer a framework for early learning teachers to consider when incorporating environmentally based practices into early learning programs. Indigenous environmental philosophies can guide early learning teachers in thinking about and recognizing the interconnectedness among human beings, nature, and other living things. Table 11.6 illustrates how early learning teachers may begin to advance their thinking about how environmentally based perspectives may be woven into children's outdoor play experiences.

Once early learning teachers have determined their perspective on environmentally based practices, they use it as a foundation to guide their discussions with colleagues. As outlined in Table 11.7, the *Early Childhood Environmental Education Programs: Guidelines for Excellence* (NAAEE, 2016), provides early learning teachers with core perspectives for framing environmentally sustainable practices in early learning programs.

Ecosystems refer to systems or networks of interconnecting parts and interactions among the parts with the environment.

CURIOUS?

Do you want to learn more about *The Giving Tree* story by Shel Silverstein? Go to https://www.youtube.com/watch?v=A5y-ZQv1JaY. How does this story relate to environmental sustainability?

Table 11.7 Guidelines for integrating environmental practices into early learning programs.

Systems	Children live in and learn about systems: families, communities of people, animals, and plants. How is systems learning visual in the outdoor play environment? How do children and families learn about outdoor play?
Interdependence	Children and adults are connected to each other and to nature. What we eat, drink, breathe, and wear is drawn from nature and has an impact on nature as well. How do children and families learn through outdoor play ways in which we are connected to nature? How do we support children in learning about the sun, water, wind, and rain?
The importance of where one lives	Children benefit from knowing the sights, sounds, and smells of their own habitat and the local environment. How do early learning teachers support children in looking closely at their environment? How do children learn to describe the smells and sounds that they hear? What role does the early learning teacher have in advancing these connectors with the children?
Integration and infusion	Environmental learning is best integrated with experiences in a variety of outdoor places and spaces through curricular areas (literacy, creative arts, mathematics, science, health, daily routines). How is literacy and math incorporated into outdoor play? How is creative arts different outdoors from indoors for children? How does that change the way in which creative arts is offered?
Roots in the real world	Children require direct experience with authentic materials outdoors; sorting leaves and seeds, digging for worms, and identifying local birds, insects, and plants are all activities that may help children become grounded in the natural world. What happens to children if they are not exposed to some of these important real-world materials? Think about urban early learning programs that have synthetic grass and no trees. How do children connect with nature if they are in synthetic spaces?
Lifelong learning	Curiosity about the world, creative thinking, problem solving, and collaborative learning are essential components for lifelong learning. What happens to children who are not given the options of unique materials and stimulation to advance their desire to learn and to experience? What happens if children have limited time outdoors or are hurried when they are outdoors? How does that restriction on their outdoor play influence their learning?

Source: Adapted from North American Association for Environmental Education (NAAEE) (2016). *Early Childhood Environmental Education Programs: Guidelines for Excellence.* Washington, DC.

For many early learning teachers, thinking about the environment and making it explicit in the program may be a challenge to consistently carry out. Think about what you might introduce the children to in their environments now. Is it through gardening and harvesting vegetables? Is it adopting a particular place in your community and caring for it? Is it illustrating particular reusable practices?

Environmentally based principles are most effective with children when early learning teachers collectively examine their environments, highlight potential options for nurturing healthy environments, and negotiate ways in which their outdoor play experiences are considerate of the environment. For example, think of children who may want to climb a tree to swing up and down on a particular branch. As an early learning teacher, you recognize that such an experience may allow the children to practise physical movements such as balance and how to use their body in the space. However, as an advocate for the environment, you know that it is vital for children to think about how the experience may affect the health of the tree. What types of questions might you pose to the children? What type of environmental scan may you complete with the children to determine the viability of their potential play experience with the tree?

We share with you seven core principles that support early learning teachers in their quest to support children in becoming environmentally connected and concerned citizens. They are:

■ Ensuring children feel a sense of belonging to a particular place and that they can influence and make a difference to the environment.

■ Creating environments in a range of spaces and places with materials and resources where children can engage, explore, and make choices and decisions that influence their experiences in their world.

- Providing children with invitations that extend responsibility to them for following through on actions that support care for the environment.
- Facilitating opportunities for children to learn about life cycles, make connections to the outdoor environment, and observe the beauty of the trees, the plants, skies, and the place.
- Ensuring that the outdoor play opportunities contribute to children gaining new thinking and problem-solving skills, while expanding their decision-making about their play and the world around them.
- Advocating for and implementing schedules that allocate large portions of time for outdoor play in all kinds of weather and seasons.
- Becoming connected with their community—the people, the places, the environment, and the resources within the environment that contribute to their curiosity about nature and engagement with their outdoor play environments.

The experiences that early learning teachers extend to the children influence how they connect to their world. Children require early learning teachers who support them in learning about the importance of the environment. Such support will encourage children to develop positive habits in relation to the environment and become catalysts for environmentalism among their peers, families, and communities.

LEARNING IN PLACE: THE WORLD AS PLACE

Common worlds refer to the notion that we share our existence with other beings, non-living entities, technologies, landforms, discourses and forces.

Big ideas refer to concepts that underpin the work of early learning students and teachers.

French author and anthropologist Bruno Latour (2004) asks us to think about the nature of nature as we approach our lives situated in **common worlds**. This notion requires thinking about a big idea. Dietze and Kashin (2016) describe **big ideas** as theoretical concepts that underpin early learning practice. When we think of concepts deeply and critically we can stimulate ideas that will lead to a better world. The big idea of a common world is one that is inclusive to all beings, human and otherwise. Common world pedagogies (Taylor, 2013) prepares young children to inherit and co-inhabit multispecies worlds. Common worlds do not assume harmony or balance in perfect equality but accept that when children connect and communicate with other inhabitants of the world, such as animals, that new channels for thinking and living are opened up (Pacini-Ketchabaw, di Tomasso, & Nxumalo, 2014).

THINK ABOUT IT! READ ABOUT IT! WRITE ABOUT IT!

Think about how you could bring the big idea of common worlds to a group of school-aged children. Look for and read some examples at: http://commonworlds.net/. Write out some of your own suggestions.

PROGRAMMING

Early learning teachers consider and assess how the outdoor space supports school-aged children in their play. The depth and breadth of the outdoor play that is undertaken by school-aged children is strongly influenced by the friendships that they have and the greenery within the outdoor space (Mårtensson, Jansson, Johansson, Raustorp, Kylin, & Boldemann, 2014). School-aged children require open-ended play spaces and places

Table 11.8 Plan, engage, explore, reflect—offering outdoor space and place to school-aged children.

PLAN	School-aged children require spaces that support active outdoor play for small and large group play. Assess outdoor play space to determine where the children may engage in quiet, small group play and more active play. Plan how your space can accommodate children wanting to use equipment, engage in pretend play, participate in rough and tumble play, embark on chasing games, or organize a specific game. How can you plan for and support the varying interests of the children and how will you support or facilitate the play?
ENGAGE	Present the space and materials in an invitational way that encourages children in determining how and where they will engage in their play options. Engage the children in documenting their play and how they use the space.
EXPLORE	Listen to, observe, and question the children about what they need in the space and how they will use the outdoor environment for their play. Engage the children in making changes to the play space that would support their outdoor play in new ways.
REFLECT	How did the children use the space? What types of play did they participate in and how did the space support or detract from the play? What did you learn about the children from observing them in play or through the documentation? How do school-aged children use the space differently than younger children do?

to play both games and more open-ended play. Pellegrini and Smith (1998) urged early learning teachers to think about outdoor play with school-aged children from the perspective of physical activity play. They defined physical activity play as:

> Physical activity play, specifically, may involve symbolic activity or games with rules; the activity may be social or solitary, but the distinguishing behavioural features are playful context combined with […] moderate to vigorous physical activity. (p. 1)

Mårtensson et al., (2014) determined that physical activity play amongst school-aged children combines aspects of high imaginative, verbal, and physical content. Games with codified rules are dominant in school-aged outdoor play.

Following the PEER Principle of Plan, Engage, Explore, and Reflect, Table 11.8 illustrates considerations when planning for outdoor play environments for school-aged children.

FAMILY SUPPORT AND ENGAGEMENT

Outdoor play pedagogical documentation offers early learning teachers the opportunity to engage in dialogue about children and the importance and benefits of outdoor play with families and the children. Often, when families are given the opportunity to share their perspectives about their children and their play, early learning teachers gain different insights about the interests and capabilities of children from what they observed in the early learning setting. Having strong, reciprocal relationships with families enables early learning teachers to gain an image of the child beyond the early learning program. Families identify core information about children's outdoor play patterns and interests. As early learning teachers listen to and observe the reactions of children and families to the documentation, the diversity of families and cultures becomes evident. Similarly, families have the opportunity to view, observe, make connections, and see their children in a new light (Fleet et al., 2011).

Early learning teachers recognize the importance of ensuring that the dialogue with children and families is respectful and engaging. As families observe how their reflections are informing programming ideas, assessment of past experiences, and opportunities for new experiences, they are more likely to share their thoughts and impressions. In this chapter, we ask you to consider how children and families can contribute to making the outdoor play documentation pedagogical. Then, how do their perspectives influence how the outdoor play space is presented to the children? How might families contribute to supporting some of the outdoor play interests expressed by the children? How might you encourage families to share aspects of children's outdoor play experiences to expand the pedagogical documentation and ultimately the children's play options?

ACCESSIBILITY AND DESIGN

Dietze and Kim (2014) identified that early learning programs have a responsibility to ensure that the outdoor spaces are designed to support all children in having access to the play environments. Pedagogical documentation provides insight into the outdoor play spaces and opportunities to assess their features and potential further development.

Dietze and Kim (2014) identified the following as core design features:

1. Play zones that include flexible, green, affinity, quiet learning, and seasonal zones that are accessible to children and families.

2. Play environment elements that include a variety of surfaces, play shelters, beautiful objects, sunshine and shade, and wildlife habitats.

3. Physical movement and risk-taking experiences that are challenging and include places for children to climb, jump, run, use tools, experience elements of the environment, and engage in rough and tumble play.

4. Loose parts that include natural, recycled, re-purposed, and manufactured parts.

5. Experiential play areas that include places for children to engage in: mud, water, and sand play; construction and dramatic play; and art, music, math, and science play.

6. Involving families in pedagogical documentation and locally appropriate curriculum.

When assessing outdoor play space through pedagogical documentation and the reflections that evolve from the documentation, early learning teachers ensure that the space and materials support the capabilities and interests of children. The space changes as children's interests evolve and their skills develop. Assessing play spaces provides a framework for creating environments that support all areas of children's development (Spencer & Wright, 2014).

TIPS AND TOOLS FOR OUTDOOR PLAY

Wien (2011) identified five steps in pedagogical documentation that we have interpreted as useful strategies and have depicted in Figure 11.9. Let's consider these from an outdoor play perspective. Getting into the habit of documentation in the outdoor environment requires having the tools available for documenting and recognizing that there are many worthy moments to document that can occur at all times of the day, especially during outdoor play. If you are a beginner, you will probably find that your documentation is descriptive in that it recounts the experiences of the children. The more you share and open yourself up to the interpretations of others, the more you will develop your potential and capacity to think and look deeper. This will help you develop your comfort level in sharing your documentation publicly.

If others are going to engage with your documentation, think about the aesthetics of what you have documented. Consider the white space that surrounds your photos and collections of artifacts. Avoiding visual clutter will help you recognize how the components of your documentation interact with each other, creating an aesthetically pleasing visual for the human eye to view. When you view documentation not only as a way to make the learning of children visible, but also to see it as a way to grow and develop as an early learning teacher, you conceptualize documentation as research and professional learning. First attempts at

Figure 11.9 Strategies for engaging in the pedagogical documentation process.

documentation are placeholders in your progression towards pedagogical documentation as you work to study, interpret, plan, and carry forward. Pedagogical documentation is a process. At first, you take time to interpret and theorize about children's learning. You make the learning visible by sharing your theories and opening yourself up to the interpretations of others. In doing this, your documentation reveals a greater depth of meaning.

ON THE GROUND—PROFESSIONAL REFLECTIONS: "WHY I LOVE OUTDOOR PLAY"

>> **BOX 11.3**   **Why Do I Like Outdoor Play Pedagogical Documentation?**

Throughout my practice, the most interesting and unique dialogues I have had with children occurred outside. I believe that the questions, creativity in play, and learning is most insightful and intriguing while outdoors. These are the reasons why I am fond of outdoor play pedagogical documentation. Developing outdoor play pedagogical documentation has supported me in acknowledging those invaluable outdoor play moments by making children's thinking and learning—and my learning—visible. Outdoor play pedagogical documentation has become a core part of my professional practice. It is a magical tool that helps me comprehend children's outdoor play while considering a variety of perspectives from individuals; and, therefore, it effectively helps me support children's outdoor play.

One of the real treasured and meaningful moments for me was when I had conversations with children about their outdoor play pedagogical documentation. Children shared unthreaded stories beyond what I observed and documented. They generated new theories, ideas, and plans for their outdoor adventures. Having a dialogue with children about their outdoor play pedagogical documentation was when I had most of my "aha" moments about their perspectives on their outdoor play experiences, genuine interests, and thinking processes. It became evident to me that children are capable of reflecting upon and meaning making through the use of outdoor play pedagogical documentation. The use of outdoor play pedagogical documentation also helped me discover the true joy of being outdoors

(Continued)

with children. I couldn't wait to go outside to explore how children would react to their outdoor play pedagogical documentation, what they would do based on our conversations about the documentation, and how I could be part of their outdoor play experiences. I was really **present** during children's outdoor play time because I wanted to pay close attention to how they experimented with their new ideas, solved problems, and interacted with each other, materials, and environments. Having pedagogical documentation that focuses on children's outdoor play

motivates me to engage in continuous research that will help me support children in their play and to share that research with other educators and children's families. My values about outdoor play and the importance of children's voices are evident through the use of outdoor play pedagogical documentation.

Bora Kim
Instructor
Early Childhood Education Program, Lethbridge College

CASE STUDIES

Change in practice can be very challenging for early learning teachers and families using the service. Sometimes engaging in new practices is delayed due in part to attitudes expressed by colleagues. This is not necessarily because they are opposed to the new practice but because of their comfort with their current practice. Read the scenario presented in Case 11.1 and reflect upon the questions featured below.

CASE STUDY 11.1   Making Documentation Pedagogical

Situated in eastern Canada, a large early learning program was expanding and therefore required additional early learning teachers. Four of the newly hired teachers had participated in a day-long workshop on strategies for preparing and making documentation pedagogical. When they returned to their early learning program, they were enthusiastic to share their learning with their colleagues. At the workshop they had envisioned some of the areas of outdoor play that they felt would benefit from taking a closer look. At their staff meeting later that week they gave a presentation on their learning and how they felt they could move the concepts forward. Their director was supportive of this new practice and discussed how it may help them in further engaging families, children, and visitors in exploring outdoor play. The keen teachers were surprised when their colleagues expressed concerns about

the time it would take, the purpose, and if it was any different than taking photos and posting them. They questioned who the documentation was for and why. Through discussions over the next few days, it was determined that the time was not right to begin engaging in pedagogical documentation.

1. What are the challenges for the newer early learning teachers if they postpone using their skills and knowledge gained at the workshop?
2. Why do you think that not all team members support this new practice?
3. What are the advantages and disadvantages of the new early learning teachers pursuing their desire to begin conducting observations and completing pedagogical documentation?

BOX 11.4   Take It Outside!

Consider an outdoor play space that is special to you. Record why you think it is special to you. Now, take a camera outdoors and take many photos of the place.

Examine those photos to determine what you see. From the photos do you gain a new appreciation for the space? Did you learn anything new about the space?

KEY TERMS

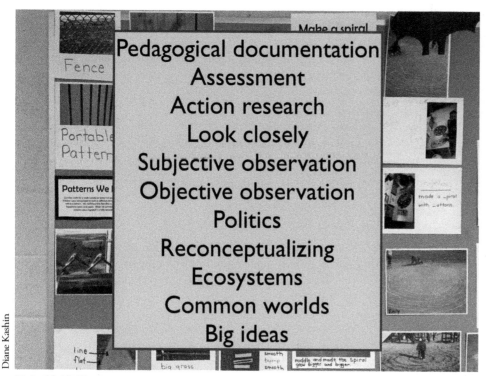

Pedagogical documentation
Assessment
Action research
Look closely
Subjective observation
Objective observation
Politics
Reconceptualizing
Ecosystems
Common worlds
Big ideas

Photo 11.15 Key terms.

Diane Kashin

Summary

- Pedagogical documentation makes learning visible and is a form of assessment. Assessment can also refer to a process of evaluation of the physical space that children play in.

- The term pedagogical documentation was introduced by Dahlberg, Moss, and Pence (1999) and is associated with the Reggio Emilia Approach. Educators from Reggio Emilia make records of the events that take place and use the documentation as part of action research. Pedagogical documentation has an important role in supporting reflective practice.

- Pedagogical documentation is a process that involves collaboration amongst children, families, early learning teachers, and the community, which supports democratic practice in early learning programs.

- Assessment of children's play space involves examining whether the outdoor environment supports children's sense of curiosity and wonder. Assessment of outdoor play environments in conjunction with pedagogical documentation supports their effectiveness.

- Child observation has an extensive history in early childhood education programs. Until recently, observations were focused mainly on determining whether a child conforms to a set of predetermined standards. Pedagogical documentation, by contrast, is focused on seeking an understanding of the children's play experiences, process of play, and capabilities.

■ When early learning teachers focus on children's strengths in observations rather than their weaknesses or gaps, pedagogical documentation helps them view children as capable and competent.

■ A study on outdoor play documentation has identified that by placing documentation outdoors at the children's level and near where the play occurred, the children's voices become prominent, resulting in the process of documentation becoming pedagogical.

■ As part of connecting children with and to their outdoor environments, early learning teachers encourage children to use their different senses to experience and explore the world. Early learning teachers role model to the children how they can gain new information and ideas when they take the time to look closely.

■ There are four basic elements of pedagogical documentation—observation, documentation, interpretation, and development—a phase where the documentation is revised and expanded upon.

■ Documentation can take the form of professional journals, panels, or learning stories. Samples of children's representations, photographs, videos, and observation notes are also forms of documentation. Documentation can be shared with families using software applications. Pedagogical documentation has multiple benefits for children, families, and early learning teachers.

■ Documentation supports democracy in practice. Moss (2007) suggested that democratic practice flourishes in learning communities that exhibit diversity, seek multiple perspectives, and encourage curiosity, uncertainty, subjectivity, and critical thinking.

■ Reconceptualization supports a key element of documentation—the requirement of multiple perspectives to inform the process. The way documentation is shared will encourage feedback from families and others.

■ Practising the creation of documentation using various technologies and in various forms, such as digital or hard copy, will help educators find the format and tools that reflect their perspective. Novice documenters benefit from engaging in a thinking, doing, and reflecting process.

■ Exposing children to environmental sustainability concepts during their early years influences the dispositions, values, and behaviours that they adopt toward sustainable practices.

■ Children who learn about ecosystems through their 'lived' outdoor play experiences contribute to developing environmentally literate skills.

■ The notion of common worlds, in which we share our existence with others, requires thinking about a big idea. Big ideas are theoretical concepts that underpin early learning practice. The big idea of a common world is one that is inclusive to all beings, human and otherwise.

■ When families are given the opportunity to share their perspectives about their children and their play, early learning teachers may gain different insights about the interests and capabilities of children from those they observe in the early learning setting. Having strong, reciprocal relationships with families contributes to early learning teachers gaining an image of the child beyond the early learning program.

■ Core design features of early learning outdoor environments include flexible, green, affinity, quiet learning, and seasonal zones, as well as a variety of surfaces and shelters. Core design features also include opportunities for physical movement and loose parts.

- Five aspects of an educator's progression towards pedagogical documentation include getting into the habit of documentation, becoming comfortable with documentation, utilizing visual literacy skills, making learning visible, and sharing visible theories with others.

QUIET REFLECTION

Quietly, go to a place outdoors that is special to you. What are the environmental characteristics in that space? What do you do to care for that space? How do you preserve that space? If you were to share this place with children, what would you tell them about the space and why? What might you suggest they become familiar with? How would you observe children and assess how they use the space and care for the space? Why is this important, and how does this inform your practice? How could you support children in becoming ambassadors for caring for the place?

COMMUNITY DIALOGUE

Children should be viewed as community members. The concept of community can be both broad and complex. School-aged children are capable of engaging in philosophical dialogue with others in their community about the nature of community. Before taking these philosophical prompts to children, discuss them with other early learning students or teachers. Questions could include "Are animals a part of our community?" and "How should we treat animals?"

Naji & Hashim (2017) confirm that school-aged children are capable of philosophical dialogue and suggest that it involves the following elements:

1. Not only questioning but challenging as well;
2. Making connections with others and seeing relationships;
3. Thinking about what might be possible;
4. Exploring or extending ideas more deeply; and
5. Reflecting critically.

Early learning students and teachers can apply the same elements to their dialogue with others.

FOR FURTHER THOUGHT AND ACTION

There is a worldwide organization devoted to reconceptualization in early childhood education. Learn more about the work that is being done and how you can become a member: http://www.receinternational.org/.

RESOURCES

Think, Feel. Act: Lessons from Research about Young Children is a resource published by the Ontario Ministry of Education (2014) to support early learning teachers in their work with young children. There are multiple resources available online that are focused on important topics, including pedagogical documentation. When you go to http://www.edu.gov.on.ca/childcare/document.html, you will find a series of videos explaining the process and the practice of pedagogical documentation.

CHAPTER 12

Outdoor and Nature Play— Looking to Research and Practice to Inform the Future

We sometimes talk as if "original research" were a peculiar prerogative of scientists or at least of advanced students. But all thinking is research, and all research is native, original, with him who carries it on, even if everybody else in the world already is sure of what he is still looking for. It also follows that all thinking involves a risk. Certainty cannot be guaranteed in advance.

John Dewey (1859–1952).

LEARNING OUTCOMES

- Describe how research influences children's outdoor opportunities and experiences.

- Outline the sequence of a research process.

- Explain how a charter of ethical research informs the research practice of researchers.

- Outline the characteristics of action research, narrative inquiry, and pedagogical documentation as they relate to children's outdoor play.

- Identify the role of critical friends and mentors in the research process.

- Outline how the types of research outlined by our Canadian researchers inform practice.

CHILDHOOD MEMORIES

When I think back to the time when we tried to make an ice fort, I remember that we ran into trouble. We had no experience in making an ice fort. All we had was a picture. We began rolling snowballs and stacking them on top of each other. That worked for a few layers but soon the snowballs started to tumble. We tried making the snowballs smaller, but then we realized we would not be able to make the fort as high as we had imagined. Then, we took shovels and tried to pile the snow on top of the snowballs that we had made. Some of our snowballs collapsed. Fortunately, my dad arrived at the scene. My dad was always willing to help. Sometimes he asked lots of questions. Thinking back, I can imagine that he asked us questions such as "What are you building?" and "What have you tried?" He probably asked us about the other ideas that we had been thinking about and what resources we had used to help us develop our strategy. Now, as I think about that day, I think that he was helping us use previous experience and combine it with our new ideas. He was introducing us to being active researchers in our play.

CHAPTER PREVIEW

Early learning teachers and children continuously learn. Research informs an early learning teacher's practice and supports his or her continuous learning journey. As Rinaldi (2003) pointed out, research is a word with multiple meanings. If you visualize a researcher in your mind, you may envision someone who works in a scientific laboratory. Scientists as researchers generally seek objectivity in their research. However, teachers as researchers may use a lens of subjectivity to search and research their theories about children's learning. Learning and teaching are connected. We learn to teach and we teach to learn. Malaguzzi (1998) described the connection between teaching and learning as a journey. Malaguzzi suggested that

> Learning and teaching should not stand on opposite banks and just watch the river flow by; instead, they should embark together on a journey down the water. Through an active, reciprocal exchange, teaching can strengthen learning and how to learn. (p. 83)

Teachers and children learn together and learn from each other. Learning and teaching involves constant research that must be made visible (Rinaldi & Moss, 2004). In this chapter, we ask you to reflect on the position of research as it relates to the role of the early learning teacher and informs practice.

Henderson (2012) maintained that teachers who view themselves as researchers think of themselves as knowledge creators, rather than simply as receivers of information. Henderson referred to Rinaldi's (2005) perspective of being a "cultured teacher." "A cultured teacher not only has a multidisciplinary background, but possesses the culture of research, of curiosity, of working in a group: the culture of project-based thinking" (p. 73). As you think about being a cultured teacher, what does it look like for you? What is the relationship between the role of being a knowledge creator with children and active learning? We view knowledge creators as those early learning teachers who, along with the children, exhibit a high level of curiosity and inquiry skills, and continuously construct new learning from the active process of sharing and participating with others. Research becomes one aspect of continuous and professional learning.

Research is a framework of a profession (Dietze & Kashin, 2016). For early learning teachers, it is associated with engaging in inquiry to promote professional changes and social actions. The process of research in early learning programs has changed over the past 10 to 15 years (Jarvie, 2015). Traditionally, research in the educational domain, aimed at improving social contexts (Ampartzaki, Kypriotaki, Voreadou, Dardioti, & Stathi, 2013; Levine, 2002) focused on children's development, with a particular emphasis on cognitive development. The researcher determined the research, set the framework in which the questions would evolve, and established how the research would be conducted (Dietze & Kashin, 2016; Kellett, 2011). This view of research is changing.

Early learning programs are the perfect environments to be "incubators of inquiry" (Pelo, 2006, p. 50). For many researchers coming from an early learning perspective, the tide

Photo 12.1 A place for inquiry.

Suzanne Gabli

is changing on who conducts research, how research is conducted, and how research influences practices in early learning programs. These influences include:

- The recognition that research designs about children and their play include involving children in the process and in giving voice to their ideas and experiences (Dietze & Kashin, 2016).

- The "new" sociologies of childhood with a theoretical framework that emphasizes that children actively influence their social settings and have rights to contribute to the experiences and opportunities extended to them in outdoor play settings. No longer is childhood framed in terms of children's vulnerability and dependency.

- An increasing number of studies that show the benefits and strategies of engaging children in research.

- Educators viewing research as a tool to be used to answer questions in conjunction with children and early learning teachers about their play and learning, rather than as a tool to assess skills and gaps in development.

Later in the chapter, we feature prominent Canadian researchers who focus on varying aspects of outdoor play. A distinction can be made between teachers as researchers who engage in continuous professional learning about teaching and learning and research that is conducted by others in early learning programs. As the interest in outdoor and nature play becomes more prevalent, early learning teachers may have opportunities to be involved in a more formal research process. Early learning teachers may be observed in interactions with children in the outdoor environment. Both you and the children are considered subjects of the research. Researchers who come into early learning programs follow a formal research protocol that has been approved by an ethics department at their academic institution. It is the early learning teacher's role to support children's rights and voices, as well as their own in relation to the research being conducted.

Whenever research occurs and whoever conducts the research, it must be done following ethical practices. As cited in Dietze and Kashin (2016), MacNaughton and colleagues (2010) identified the importance of research in early learning programs being ethical, purposeful, contextualized, credible, imaginative, and equitable. Graham, Powell, and Taylor (2015) suggested that early learning teachers answer questions before engaging in research. These questions have been adapted from Graham et al., and appear in Table 12.1.

When early learning teachers examine their ethical perspectives and act in a way in which children are at the core of the five decision-making process, the children and the researchers benefit. One of the main reasons that early learning programs are encouraged to participate in research is to "make a positive difference in the lives of children"

Table 12.1 Ethical Considerations.

- How can I ensure that the children involved in the research will not be harmed?
- What will be my response if children involved in the research become distressed or upset?
- What information can be given to children so that they are able to give authentically informed consent?
- Are parents always required to provide consent for children to participate in research?
- Are both parents required to provide parental consent?
- What will happen if children and parents have different opinions about research participation?
- If required, what professional services and supports are available for the children?
- Are children required to be paid or are paid for their involvement in the research?

(MacNaughton et al., 2010, p. 4). If research does not benefit children's experiences in early learning programs, one must question why the research is being conducted. As outlined in Box 12.1, the International Charter for Ethical Research Involving Children provides researchers with a framework to guide practice.

CURIOUS?

Do you want to learn more about ethical considerations that researchers consider before engaging in research with children? Go to www.childethics.com. How would you apply this to research that early learning teachers do on a day-to-day basis?

≫ BOX 12.1   Charter for Ethical Research Involving Children

As a research community working with children, we are committed to undertaking and supporting high quality ethical research that is respectful of children's human dignity, rights, and wellbeing. The following seven commitments guide our work:

Ethics in research involving children is everyone's responsibility
We, the research community, including all who participate in undertaking, commissioning, funding, and reviewing research, are responsible for ensuring that the highest ethical standards are met in all research involving children, regardless of research approach, focus, or context.

Respecting the dignity of children is core to ethical research
Ethical research is conducted with integrity and is respectful of children, their views, and their cultures. Involving children respectfully requires that researchers recognize children's status and evolving capacities and value their diverse contributions.

Research involving children must be just and equitable
Children involved in research are entitled to justice. This requires that all children are treated equally, the benefits and burdens of participating are distributed fairly, children are not unfairly excluded, and that barriers to involvement based on discrimination are challenged.

Ethical research benefits children
Researchers must ensure that research maximizes benefits to children, individually and/or as a social group.

The researcher has the primary responsibility for considering whether the research should be undertaken and for assessing whether research will benefit children, during, and as a consequence of, the research process.

Children should never be harmed by their participation in research
Researchers must work to prevent any potential risks of harm and assess whether the need to involve the individual child is justified.

Research must always obtain children's informed and ongoing consent
Children's consent must always be sought, alongside parental consent and any other requirements that are necessary for the research to proceed ethically. Consent needs to be based on a balanced and fair understanding of what is involved throughout and after the research process. Indications of children's dissent or withdrawal must always be respected.

Ethical research requires ongoing reflection
Undertaking research involving children is important. Ethical research demands that researchers continually reflect on their practice, well beyond any formal ethical review requirements. This requires ongoing attention to the assumptions, values, beliefs, and practices that influence the research process and its impact on children.

As outlined by Dietze and Kashin (2016) and MacNaughton, Rolfe, and Siraj-Blatchford (2010), research in early learning programs includes the voices of children, families, and early learning teachers. The process is used to examine questions, gather data from children's play and learning experiences, analyze and interpret the data, and determine how the findings influence practice. The findings generally contribute to advancing knowledge, skills, or abilities about particular practices. We encourage early learning teachers to view and to incorporate research into their practice, "because the process of research examines and improves practice" (Dietze & Kashin, 2016, p. 280). Further, when conducted among early learning teachers and children, research gives children a voice in their program.

SETTING THE STAGE FOR OUTDOOR PLAY

Throughout this text, we have emphasized the benefits of early learning teachers viewing children, families, communities, and cultures as core to programming, philosophy, and practice. From a research perspective, this means that children, families, and communities become valuable partners in "generat[ing] a body of children research knowledge" (Kellett, 2011, p. 1). Early learning teachers who engage in or encourage research with, for, and by children recognize that there are aspects of the process that inform and interact with each other. To seek clarity in the data, early learning teachers analyze the data through a number of lenses as a way to make sense of what they are discovering. For example, in analyzing the outdoor play space, a researcher may examine the data from the perspective of environment, children's engagement, options for play, adult/children interactions, why the research is being conducted, or what the children say about the play experience. The researcher may begin with a primary focus, only to learn that the data leads to additional directions that need to be considered.

As outlined in Chapter 3, there are many topics related to outdoor play that early learning teachers and children may be intrigued to research, such as children and risky play, outdoor play designs, how outdoor play supports children's health, outdoor play curriculum, teacher attitudes and influences, and outdoor play and loose parts. Think about children engaging in outdoor play. What might be some of the questions that you have about their play? What would you like to know more about? What might children like to explore further and learn about? Examine Photo 12.2. What might a research topic be? Now, look at Photo 12.3. What intrigues you and what might you like to learn more about? How would you proceed? What is your core research question?

Photo 12.2 Examining space.

Photo 12.3 How space can trigger research in children's play.

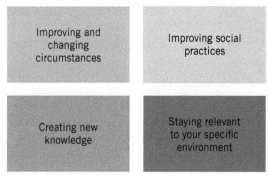

Figure 12.1 Four interrelated aspects of research.

There are many ways for children and early learning teachers to embark on research. As outlined by MacNaughton and Hughes (2009), researchers think about the research process by identifying the question (action), assessing the suitability of the question for the environment and those who may be part of the research (reflection), and deciding whether or not to proceed with the research (action). They suggested that researchers think about the purpose of the research from the basis of four related aspects, as depicted in Figure 12.1.

To focus on increasing the depth and breadth of outdoor play experiences that children have access to, early learning teachers may wish to examine current practices, places of play, and what the children use in their play. What do you see when you examine the space? What do children generally do in the space? How do children engage in the play? What might you like to attempt to change and why? These questions help early learning teachers and children in deciding what their questions are and how new information may inform changes to space, place, or opportunities for play. As illustrated in Photos 12.2 and 12.3, examining space can provide insight into how changes to the environment can influence children's play.

Research is an effective professional learning strategy that supports early learning teachers in improving and changing practice. Early learning teachers benefit from using a new lens to think about outdoor play pedagogies as a way to increase opportunities to make changes to practice. A new lens opens up more possibilities and increases diversity in thinking and problem solving. A new lens requires early learning teachers to be open to exploring new options from current practice and to acknowledge that some of the current practices may not be in the best interest of the children.

MacNaughton and Hughes (2009) identified that early learning teachers consider how **rituals**, customs, and conventions influence their social practice and agenda for change. For example, think about early learning programs that have a schedule or ritual of outdoor play being from 10:00 a.m. to 11:00 a.m. daily. Imagine if through a research process, children and early learning teachers were to determine that they want to change this practice. How would that change be received by colleagues, families, or other children and what would happen if there was not agreement on such a change?

Customs are established by families, communities, and early learning programs. For example, think about celebrating the story of gingerbread in December. Some early learning programs may have established this custom to celebrate the festive season in part as a way to honour the diversity in children's families and beliefs. When the event has been implemented over a period of many years, it becomes a custom. **Conventions** are those actions that are performed on a regular basis to conform to particular rules and regulations.

Rituals refer to a sequence of activities or practices that are performed according to an established set of rules or procedures.

Customs refer to a traditional practice that is followed by a specific group at specific times.

Conventions refer to ways in which actions are consistently carried out within a particular environment, activity, or people.

For example, think about children in an early learning program wanting to climb a tree. However, the teachers and the director have determined that climbing trees is off limits at their program. As a result, children are not allowed to climb the tree. How might a new lens change this thinking?

Changing social practice requires early learning teachers, directors, children, and families to be open to examining the meanings of the rituals, customs, and conventions that have been established in the program. Looking at them more closely may lead to changing practice. Are individuals willing to change behaviours, try new ways of practice, and reflect upon the changes to determine if the change enhances children's access to and opportunities for outdoor play? These are essential questions that when discussed with early learning teams can provide insight into if and how new practices may unfold.

Research is intended to change our thinking patterns, ideas and ideals, knowledge, and practices that will benefit children's play. For example, think about how an early learning teacher and children may view mud play. Imagine that an early learning teacher has the perspective that children can gain skills similar to those they gain from mud with play dough. How might a research experience that focuses on observing children's play with mud change this perspective? How might the early learning teacher gain insight into this question from observing language, social interactions, and creativity that evolves as children play with mud? How would the research lead to "seeing different views, opening new doors; being flexible, trying new ideas" (MacNaughton & Hughes, 2009, p. 12)? How do children benefit from this new knowledge?

Research with children, about children, and for children is based on the children's lived experiences, including the environment and the people that intersect with the children in the environment. Researchers must determine who the partners are in the research, such as the children, colleagues, families, and the employer, as well as what the research question is to support the identified area of research interest.

The Commission of the European Communities (2007) identified basic principles that support roles in being knowledge creators. They include:

- Reflecting on practice in a systematic way;
- Undertaking place-based research;
- Incorporating and evaluating the results of research into practice; and
- Assessing one's own professional development needs as it relates to research.

Mentor refers to a learning and development partnership that has an individual with more experience or knowledge on a particular subject share their knowledge and wisdom with a less experienced or knowledgeable person.

Critical Friend refers to a person that you trust and with whom you have conversations about your practice. This person asks provocative and probing questions that may inspire you to examine your practice with a different lens and bring new perspectives to your work with children and colleagues.

As early learning teachers discover new perspectives from their research, embarking on a change process in practice is most successful when there is a support team present. **Mentors** and **critical friends** can play key roles in examining the data, making conclusions and recommendations, and in changing practice. Healy and Welchert (1990) defined the mentoring process as "a dynamic, reciprocal relationship in a work environment between an advanced career incumbent (mentor) and a beginning (protégé), aimed at promoting the career development of both" (p. 16). Others, such as Lea and Leibowitz (1983) viewed mentoring as an integrative process that includes "teaching, guiding, advising, counselling, sponsoring, role modelling, validating, motivating, protecting, and communicating" (p. 26). Mentoring may occur as a formal or informal process. Effective mentors have coaching, observation, communication, and critical reflection skills. They support the protégé in reflecting on aspects of change, how the change may occur, and how new learning may transfer to practice (Costa & Garmston, 2016).

The term critical friend is derived from critical pedagogy. The concept of critical pedagogy can be traced back to Paulo Freire's best-known 1968 work, *The Pedagogy of the Oppressed*.

The goal of critical pedagogy is for individuals to affect change through social interactions and actions. Costa and Kallick (1993) defined a critical friend as

> a trusted person who asks provocative questions, provides data to be examined through another lens, and offers critiques of a person's work as a friend. A critical friend takes the time to fully understand the context of the work presented and the outcomes that the person or group is working toward. The friend is an advocate for the success of that work. (p. 14)

THINK ABOUT IT! READ ABOUT IT! WRITE ABOUT IT!

Critical friends can be very valuable in supporting early learning teachers in evolving their skills, practices, and beliefs. Why might you want to have a critical friend? Who might be a critical friend with you at this time? Read about Baskerville and Goldblatt's 2009 study on critical friends. Go to these links https://www.pscyholosphere.com/Learning%20to%20be%20a%20Critical%20Friend%20.%20.%20.%20by%20Baskerville%20&%20Goldblatt.pdf

Go to this link https://www.kidsmatter.edu.au/sites/default/files/public/eCritical%20friends.pdf and think about and then write about why you might want a critical friend or be a critical friend.

As outlined in Figure 12.2, Baskerville and Goldblatt (2009) suggested that there may be a five-step process in developing effective critical friend relationships. They concluded

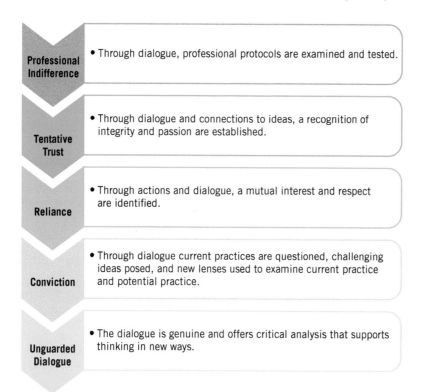

Professional Indifference
- Through dialogue, professional protocols are examined and tested.

Tentative Trust
- Through dialogue and connections to ideas, a recognition of integrity and passion are established.

Reliance
- Through actions and dialogue, a mutual interest and respect are identified.

Conviction
- Through dialogue current practices are questioned, challenging ideas posed, and new lenses used to examine current practice and potential practice.

Unguarded Dialogue
- The dialogue is genuine and offers critical analysis that supports thinking in new ways.

Figure 12.2 Developmental phases of critical friends.

that as the partners engaged in dialogue and exploratory topics, the exchanges and collective learning contributed to the strength of the relationship.

As noted by Dietze and Kashin (2016), critical friends and mentors can provide emerging researchers with feedback that may lead to advancing thinking in new ways or revisiting perspectives as a way to bring clarity to the information. Participating in research is one of the core professional learning methods that stretch early learning teachers to expand their knowledge and competence about how children play and learn. Research flourishes in environments where early learning teachers and children create learning communities. These partnerships build upon their knowledge and extend and examine core questions of practice in a collaborative, creative, and critical way (Dietze & Kashin, 2016). Figure 12.3 provides one research model that helps emerging early learning teachers and children begin their research journeys.

Phase 1: Examining Practice: Looking Closely	
What questions could be explored? Who might be involved in the research and why?	Why is this question of interest to the children or me? How does the research team prepare to engage in the collaborative process?

Phase 2: Preparing to Engage: Looking Closely	
What does the literature say about the question to be explored? What are the ethical questions that need to be examined? What will the research method be and why? How will the research process be mapped?	What requires reflection? How will the children be supported in becoming engaged in the research and why? How is the research method determined? How does mapping the process inform the research process?

Phase 3: Engaging in Research: Looking Closely	
Engage the research team. Gather the data. Analyze the data. Determine what the data highlights. Draw conclusions.	How do the findings deepen knowledge and understandings of practice? How might the findings inform practice? How might a critical friend contribute to new learning? What happens next?

Phase 4: Taking Action and Sharing Findings: Looking Closely	
How are the conclusions used to inform practice? How will the results be shared beyond the research team?	How will the changes to practice be monitored and why? What new questions have evolved from this research?
What new knowledge have you discovered?	

Figure 12.3 Cycle for engaging in research.

OUR VISION FOR OUTDOOR PLAY

It is our vision that early learning teachers will view research as a key professional practice. Research is an important foundational tool for designing programming and facilitating children's outdoor play experiences. Through research, early learning teachers continuously learn about and with the children through discussions, observations, reflections, questioning, documenting, and theorizing (Dietze & Kashin, 2016). As early learning teachers look closely at children's outdoor play, they examine when, if, and, what the benefits are of participating with the children as a co-constructor of learning or as a critical friend.

Niemi and Nevgi (2014) identified that the scope of the changes and the pace in which changes are occurring require early learning teachers to be ready to learn continuously. As part of this continuous learning, understanding how knowledge is created and how early learning teachers contribute to the creation of new knowledge is important for individuals and the field. Niemi and Nevgi suggested that early learning teachers require the following:

It is our vision that early learning teachers engage in research and use evidence to inform decisions. This process is viewed as a crucial element of professional practice.

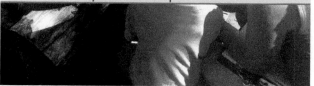

Diane Kashin

Photo 12.4 Vision statement.

- Higher order thinking skills;

- Analytical and research-orientated skills;

- Ability to inquire and assess the validity of knowledge and its different information sources; and

- Competency in identifying problems, arguing, and drawing conclusions.

The concept of early learning teachers being researchers requires thoughtful reflection. Thinking about thinking or **metacognition** is a way to engage in thoughtful reflection. Reflecting on higher order thinking skills is a lens to view research. We encourage early learning students and teachers to reach for the pinnacle of the triangle as depicted in Figure 12.4 in the research process. The figure represents a revised version of Benjamin

Metacognition refers to the process of being aware of and analysing one's thinking and learning process.

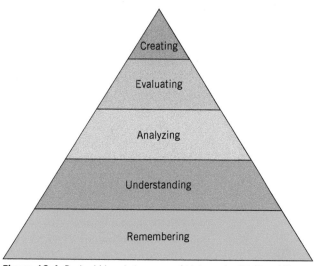

Figure 12.4 Revised bloom's taxonomy of higher order thinking skills.

Photo 12.5 Creating opportunities for risky play.

Bloom's higher order thinking skills (Anderson & Krathwohl, 2001). Using reflection questions and engaging in reflective practice offers early learning teachers a strategy for affecting change in philosophies and practices in early learning environments.

Imagine that you are working in an early learning setting where there is a collective decision to create more opportunities for children to engage in outdoor risky play. You begin at the top of the triangle to program for children to have more challenge in their play. You decide to spend more time in the open field where there are ample opportunities for children to have challenge in their play. Moving downwards you use these reflection questions to apply research to your practice.

- Creating—What experiences have we created to research risky play in practice?

- Evaluating—How have these experiences impacted the children and our practice?

- Analyzing—Do we see patterns, themes, and ideas emerging?

- Understanding—Where else can we use this knowledge that we have created?

- Remembering—How have we recorded the research that we have done?

POSITIONING OUTDOOR PLAY IN THE LIVES OF CHILDREN

Interprofessional practice refers to a collaborate practice among internal and external colleagues that share similar philosophies and goals.

Interprofessional practice involves working alongside other professionals to support children with each bringing an important perspective. Bringing diverse professionals together creates a new and expanded encompassing view of the child (Payler & Georgeson, 2013).

When interprofessional practice aligns with the philosophy, programming, and professional learning of early learning teachers, it can significantly position outdoor play in the lives of children. The purpose of interprofessional practice is to connect with and bring together the expertise of a wide variety of professionals who have a common interest in outdoor play (Payler, Georgeson, & Wong, 2015). As part of that interprofessional practice, early learning teachers benefit from examining research on outdoor play from a variety of disciplines and perspectives. For example, as you will read later in the chapter, we are featuring Canadian researchers who have a common interest in outdoor play, each examining it from a different lens. When early learning teachers examine research from different disciplines, it helps to understand the complexity of the subject and the diversity in thought. Broadhead, Meleady, and Delgado (2008) suggested that early learning teachers who engage with a wide range of professionals, in multiple ways, including reviewing their research, develop a broader view of the relationship of outdoor play to children's development and learning.

The attitudes and the context of the thinking of early learning teachers has a direct correlation

Photo 12.6 Learning outside.

on the environments and experiences that are extended to children's outdoor play (Luís & Roldão, 2017). Luís & Roldão, (2017) observed that how early learning teachers use new learning and knowledge and how they transfer that new learning is influenced by experience (implicitly or explicitly) and through the personal theories that they develop. Buitink (2009) suggested that there are three characteristics that support early learning teachers in amalgamating new learning. The first is the quality of the content and how it is related to current knowledge and experiences; the second is richness of application of theory; and the third is the structure of theory. How these characteristics are exhibited will vary amongst early learning teachers because of the variety of individual "lived experiences" that influence their quest for knowledge and the transfer of knowledge to practice. As an example, imagine that you were given an article by Ellen Sandseter on risky play. You read the article, but your life experience and current beliefs do not include children being able to play near a fire or to climb to the tops of trees. You struggled with how the research would inform your practice in a Canadian context. Now, you have an opportunity to travel to Norway to learn directly from Ellen Sandseter and to observe children participating in climbing trees, walking along steep banks, and playing near a fire. This new "lived experience" now helps you to be able to make the connections of theory to practice and enables you to incorporate aspects of risky play into your environment.

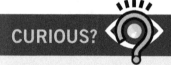

CURIOUS?

To learn more about Ellen Sandseter and her research on risky play go to: https://ellenbeate-hansensandseter.com/

Buitink (2009) suggested that using research to inform practice takes time. Applying theory requires early learning teachers to be comfortable in seeking advice on their ideas and engaging in discourse to formulate how theory transfers to practice. This may mean that through the process there are mistakes or situations that may not have been anticipated or experienced previously. Ideally, synthesizing how a theory transfers to practice requires time and a plan of action that is developed with colleagues and the children. A critical friend or mentor may also provide great wisdom and support when transferring theory to practice.

The experiences that early learning teachers acquire in early learning programs have a direct influence on their beliefs and values surrounding outdoor play. For example, if early learning teachers are in environments with a focus on outdoor play and view children as capable of engaging in intriguing outdoor play experiences, their approach will differ from those colleagues who view indoor environments as more important. They will exhibit skills that include encouraging children to think, communicate, and problem solve. They will have the ability to transfer research about the importance of outdoor play theory to their practice. Their views will be very different from those who focus on a school readiness curriculum.

Transferring research to practice is more than "showing and telling" (Buitink, 2009) or taking strategies that have been observed and directly transferring them to practice without considering the context and pedagogy of place. It is through questioning of research, practice, and reflections that early learning teachers assimilate new strategies that are informed by evidence-based decisions into their practice.

THEORETICAL FOUNDATION

Action research refers to research that is initiated to solve a problem or engage in a progressive reflective process to seek answers to improve a practice.

When early learning teachers decide to engage in their own research they can use an **action research** methodology. Kurt Lewin (1890–1947) is often associated with coining the term action research (Mills, 2011). Action research aligns with social constructivism and Freire's (1992) pedagogy of hope that views teaching as a "co-operative activity involving respect when people work with each other." This value is grounded in the philosophy of "emancipation through the empowerment of dialogue" (p. 2). When individuals come together to collaborate on sharing ideas or knowledge, new knowledge is created that changes practice (Moore & Gilliard, 2008). Children co-create knowledge within their play space. Early learning teachers listen to the children's voices and embrace the challenges that children offer that may trigger a reconsideration of ways in which play opportunities are designed and implemented.

Action research is a process of systematically examining and reflecting upon an individual or group practice and is interactive as teacher-researchers and children construct knowledge (Abdul-Haqq, 1995; Miller & Pine 1990; Williamson, 1992). Piggot-Irvine (2003) suggested, "the word 'action' in action research is key. It is about making or implementing change, rather than investigating an issue" (p. 28). The process encourages a form of professional development that connects researchers with their practices and in engaging in **reflective inquiry** (Kirkey, 2005).

Reflective inquiry refers to a participatory action research process that stimulates intense reflection on a topic by a group interested in looking closely at the data collected.

Ferrance (2000) categorized action research as:

- *Individual teacher research*: early learning teachers who investigate a single question that evolves from a child, a group of children, or a programming or environmental situation;

- *Collaborative action research*: a group of early learning teachers and children who have an interest in examining a common question that evolves from children's play experiences or observations of the environment; and

- *Program-wide research*: a group of early learning teachers who explore a common question that evolves from children, adults, family, or programming processes.

Borgia and Schuler's (1996) seminal work illustrates how early learning teachers may use action research to guide their practice and model continuous improvement. Think about some of the observations made regarding children's engagement in outdoor play and in the space to which children have access. Now, think about adding new types of loose parts to the space. How might early learning teachers use action research to look closely at if and how the types of active play change when an array of loose parts is introduced in the environment? What might early learning teachers learn by examining if, how, what, and when children play when loose parts are added to the outdoor play environment? How might early learning teachers and children take 'action' after examining the data on what happened when new loose parts were added? Why would this information be important to teachers? This reflective process contributes to early learning teachers being proactive knowers, thinkers, and co-constructors of knowledge rather than depending on the knowledge of others.

Collaborative action research refers to a research method that is conducted by teams for the purpose of improving group experiences and in contributing to the professional learning of the researchers.

Peterson (2016) suggested that there are many benefits to **collaborative action research** in early learning programs. Collaborative action research has a focus on constructing knowledge at the local level. Peterson outlined that collaborative research aligns with "community-first, land-centred theoretical framework for research with Indigenous communities; one that is built on principles of relationship, respect, relevance, responsibility and reciprocity" (p. 38). Collaborative action research begins with partnerships that are formed to ensure that the research is grounded in the understanding of the cultural knowledge about the children and communities where the research will occur.

Another research method that early learning teachers may use is **narrative inquiry**. Narrative inquiry emerged as a qualitative research method in the early twentieth century. There are many ways in which narrative inquiry research can take place. It may involve using texts, such as stories, pedagogical documentation, journals, conversations, interviews, and life experiences to bring meaning to experiences through stories (Meier & Stremmel, 2010). But, it is not merely telling stories; it requires individuals and groups to compare experiences and situations in an effort to understand current practice and to bring insight into potential new ways of practice. It also means revising the

Photo 12.7 Engaging in collaborative action research on outdoor play.

Diane Kashin

stories and/or seeing situations from multiple and new perspectives (Meier & Stremmel, 2010). In essence, through narrative inquiry, early learning teachers develop a deeper understanding of the children, the environment, and the attitudes and values that are associated with programming, cultures, and communities. Through the stories, the truths that early learning teachers hold about their philosophies and practice may become evident and explicit. When early learning teachers collaborate with their peers to share their experiences, learning, and practices, the narrative inquiry process is rich with opportunity to gain new insights into particular situations being explored (Dietze & Kashin, 2016).

Narrative inquiry refers to a process of examining living stories for threads and themes that bring new insight into lived experiences.

Bresler (2013) suggested "in the context of research, the idea of interaction between 'outside' and 'inside' and the possibility of dialogic connection are supported by the postmodern attention to researchers' interactions with participants and in settings" (p. 27). From an outdoor play perspective, narrative inquiry is effective in early learning programs with colleagues who are collegial and collectively have an interest in advancing outdoor play to the next level. When colleagues have a genuine interest in continuous learning and improvement, an environment that is safe to banter concepts back and forth evolves. Bantering is necessary for "aha" moments to be experienced. The bantering and "aha" moments become stimulants for new ideas to surface that shapes professional practice and the changes that occur to support children's outdoor play and learning. In Photo 12.8 an early learning teacher is seen working on a documentation piece that led to an "aha" moment about nature and outdoor play surfacing. Read her narrative in Case Study 12.1. Afterwards, she shared the documentation with colleagues leading to an opportunity to banter.

Jacob Bortolotti

Photo 12.8 Documenting Pippa and the red boots.

≫ CASE STUDY 12.1   The Story of Pippa in the Garden

Documenting young children does not always involve beautiful pictures of engaged children. Documentation is about capturing the thinking process in what inspired children to start their investigations. The world to children is a curious place, trying to unfold piece by piece to what can make sense to them. Through their thinking evolves many theories and explorations. What will change during their discoveries? What directions are taken during this process? Pippa, age 2.5 years old, spends time observing and exploring the outdoors during the month of August, as the gardens and playgrounds are overly filled with greenery, plant life, quietness, and sounds. There is an approach that Pippa takes on the grounds that includes careful steps and caution. She shows a gentleness in her awareness of the plants. She listens carefully to the sounds around her. The curiosity to understand nature, to learn alongside nature, takes time, listening, and observing the environment is evident every day that Pippa is in the garden.

This daily encounter with the outdoors provides the time to build understanding and for questions to emerge that support developing theories. What will happen when plants mix with water? Why does the water change colour as the grass is submerged in it? 'Oh! So much muddy dirt, it fell in the water!' Mixing, dunking, lifting, and labelling the grass as 'spaghetti for mommy and daddy' Pippa's imagination and creativity comes alive in the garden.

1. How should the teacher respond to the questions from her colleagues?
2. In what ways can the story of Pippa and the garden be shared with the child's family?
3. Why is the realization about the importance of time significant for Rosalba and how can she use this as a research question to support the work that she does with children?

Source: Used with the permission of Rosalba Bortolotti.

The "aha" moment for this teacher was the importance of time. She had not rushed to share her documentation that had been collected about Pippa. She slowed the process down, just as the child took a slow and careful approach to her time in the garden. Realizing that supporting children's connection to nature requires a long-term commitment, she shared her documentation with her colleagues. The teacher was not prepared for the bantering that resulted. Her colleagues questioned her about the first line of her story about beautiful pictures of engaged children, and there was a back and forth banter about finding the substance in documentation that goes beyond the descriptive or objective to the interpretative or subjective.

Although not specifically identified in the literature as a narrative inquiry methodology, we suggest that pedagogical documentation could be classified in this category. As you will recall from Chapter 11, pedagogical documentation was highlighted as a form of examining what early learning teachers, children, and families see and wonder about—it is telling a story, similar to embarking on research. Wien, Guyevskey, and Berdoussis (2011) identified that pedagogical documentation is considered a form of research because it is a "research story, built upon a question of inquiry 'owned by' teachers, children and others, about the learning of children" (p. 1). Examining pedagogical documentation from a variety of perspectives—including from the voices of children and others, and interpreting what is seen—follows the principles of research.

We encourage early learning students and teachers to view the pedagogical documentation process as research. Focusing the documentation on outdoor play and sharing the documentation outdoors with others is a newer perspective that can lead to new knowledge

Suzanne Gabli

Photo 12.9 Sharing documentation with others.

creation. This, in conjunction with being a consumer of current professional research will support professional learning and keep you relevant. Increasingly, there are Canadian scholars who are focusing their research agendas on outdoor play. In this chapter we feature five researchers who share aspects of their research and perspectives on outdoor play.

Featured Theorists

We asked our featured theorists to consider what the future holds for outdoor play. What might the next frontier for outdoor play be? Do they have recommendations for early learning teachers just starting out and do they have recommendations for early learning teachers already in practice? As you read about their contributions to research, think about how their information informs your practice. What questions remain for you? How might you gain further information on their work?

》 BOX 12.2   Featured Theorists: Banack, Brussoni, Elliot, Harwood, Zimanyi

Featured Theorists

Hartley Banack, Ph.D., University of British Columbia: Hartley shares his perspective on why teachers should learn about outdoor play and learning outdoors. Mariana Brussoni, Ph.D, University of British Columbia: Mariana provides insight into her work on risky play and environments. Enid Elliot, Ph.D. Camosun College: Enid shares

principles of outdoor play that evolved from work with an advisory committee. Debra Harwood, Ph.D., and the Educators of the Rosalind Blauer Centre for Child Care, Brock University: They share their story of how shifting of theories informed their practice. Louise Zimanyi, M.Ed., Humber College: Louise shares her story of children and their encounter with willows.

Hartley Banack, Ph.D. Lecturer and Coordinator, University of British Columbia

I have been talking, thinking, and writing about stories in relation to outdoor learning experiences (Banack & Berger, in press), for some time now. I offer you my story of outdoor learning and how I both experience and affect how time spent outdoors infuses and influences education.

Complexity resonates with me, for one of the many benefits of outdoor learning includes a demand for educators and learners to respond to changing conditions that cannot be controlled (e.g., rain, cold, darkness) when outdoors. Learning is no longer precisely organized the way it might be in the classroom. Outdoor learning is a story of rich complexity, of how *where* we learn is an essential, yet under-explored, educational question. In my story, I use *where* in a rather specific way. *Where* includes physical places (indoors/outdoor), as well as non-material (thought, memory) and digital/analogue textual/visual (cyberspace, books, movies) places. All of these are distinct iterations, and thus understandings, of *where*. This way of thinking also means that you can be in two *wheres* at the same instant!

Where is thus an umbrella concept that includes outdoors. It is important to broadly consider the idea of the *where* in learning. Particularly, this importance is noted when we consider how outdoor learning has been marginalized and ignored by education, in general. Often, education is divided into the larger groupings of curriculum and pedagogy. With just two main considerations, outdoor learning has to *fit* into one or the other (or both) categories. Thus, outdoor learning has been regularly promoted as but another curricular and/or pedagogical consideration. In this struggle of belonging, outdoor learning has ebbed and flowed, often relegated to a position of low priority, in the wake of other more urgent and particular curricular and pedagogical concerns or demands.

Also recall, as mentioned above, at least three ingredients are required for complexity to exist, and curriculum and pedagogy offer but two. This is why *where* is an imperative consideration for education, as it decouples outdoor learning from curriculum and/or pedagogy and it invites a third educational criteria, which results in a modelling better able to consider learning. So, my story is a story of *where*. I invite discussion of education and learning with these three points, in their simultaneous co-emergence: Curriculum (what), Pedagogy (who, who), and Place (where). Please understand, this story is not a linear or logical story, much in the way that outdoors is complex and chaotic in its nature. In this spirit, my tale also wanders.

This story invites you to consider time spent outdoors as a significant *where* of learning. In this story, *where* children play, learn, and experience life is as important as what and how they play/learn/experience and who they experience/learn/play with, and when they learn/play/experience, and so on. There is no doubt that learning outdoors is facilitated by teachers who craft learning experiences that take place outdoors. In my story, teachers are central characters in the effort to increase time spent outdoors for learning and play.

Teachers are the agents who decide *where* learning experiences happen. If a teacher plans for learning to happen outdoors, then outdoor learning happens. It is really that simple, especially when we are talking about local outdoor learning. However, if a teacher complains about rain and cold, then children do not go outdoors for learning on cold and wet days, and if a teacher finds the outdoors dirty and scary, then their children do not go outdoors often. The autonomy of the educator, in relation to *where* learning happens, is significant. As an academic, I know the benefits of being outdoors for personal/social, physical, and mental health, the development of an environmental/sustainable ethic and practice, and for the attainment of high quality learning experiences that stick with us; therefore, I make it an emphasis to be outdoors. I have noticed that through my invitation to shift learning outdoors, pre- and in-service teachers will regularly include outdoor

Jen Winkel

Photo 12.10 Worm measurement.

learning in their microteaching lessons. I believe that more attention needs to be paid to *where* we are when we are engaged in learning experiences (from pre-school, to K-12, to post-secondary levels), and that if we really believe in the benefits of being outdoors, for ourselves and our students, then this begins by taking learning outdoors.

Where does not only exist outdoors or indoors or even online, but includes all notions of *where* (i.e. utopia, nowhere, memory) (Banack, in press). I distinguish *where* from curriculum, described as a *what* question in my story, and pedagogy, *who* and *how* questions (and, of course, all questions have *whys* and *whens*). *Where* learning experiences happen seems to be an under-considered part of education and schooling, from preschool right through post-secondary. Year after year, learning happens in *the classroom*.

My work has aimed to disrupt this pattern by increasing the actual amount of time spent outdoors; thus providing outdoor learning experiences that inspire teachers to shift their own learning experiences outdoors. By inviting outdoor occurrences into learning, children become more comfortable being and learning outdoors. Many educators, it seems, have not really considered *where* their own learning has occurred or that they have personal responses/reactions to outdoor learning that influence their practices and educational dispositions. (This includes outdoor enthusiast teachers who teach outdoor education programs/ courses; teachers who engage in outdoor learning in their own lives; as well as *fancy pants* teachers who do not wish for their professional clothing to be soiled outdoors; and those who find the outdoors scary or dangerous.) As the *where* of learning has been underexplored in general, outdoor learning seems caught in a tangle of personal feelings and not assessed for its educational, ethical (environmental/sustainable) and health benefits.

Aligning with research looking at changing practices of teachers, I have noticed through my work with teachers that they are prone to replicating their personally lived learning practices in their own teaching, often without even recognizing this. Much of teacher education is predicated on explorations of practices and their consideration in relation to learning experiences that teachers create (i.e., the language we use in our lessons, the content to which we expose students, etc.). With the emphasis on reflective practice, it seems curious that many teachers still assume that indoor learning is *de facto* *where* better learning occurs. Generally, the *where* of learning has been a much under-considered question. I actively move learning experiences outdoors, requesting that students experience outdoor learning by engaging in learning outdoors.

I believe that an essential aspect of outdoor learning begins with actually shifting our practices outdoors, as an act of experiential learning, and to appreciate outdoor learning (for example, how to practice outdoor learning; how it feels to be outdoors; the views of peers; how the learning experiences stick with them) through the outdoor learning experiences we share.

Through my professional involvement in and around outdoor learning—in formal, informal, and non-formal contexts—I have noticed fluctuations in feelings around outdoor learning over the years. I attribute these changes to changing imperatives in curriculum and/or pedagogy, rather than as a departure from a uniquely distinct category, that of *where*. I urge teachers and researchers to shift more of their attention to the distinct domain of outdoor learning, and, more generally, to the *where* of learning. Through such a shift, particularly at the level of the individual teacher, I believe that it is possible that educational practices change over time, and that the story of a pre-schooler in 2017 may be vastly different from that of a Grade 12 student with respect to the benefits of time spent outdoors, especially for learning.

Mariana Brussoni, Ph.D. Associate Professor, University of British Columbia

Approximately 60% of Canadian children attend some form of childcare (Sinha, 2014). For many children the outdoor play spaces in childcare centres serve as their main experience of outdoor play. The quality of these spaces and the play that children are allowed to engage in influences their development and wellbeing. Despite their importance, little attention is paid to these outdoor environments. In fact, trends indicate that they have become increasingly restricted and limiting due to a heightened focus on risk reduction and perceived safety concerns (Wyver et al., 2009).

My research program uses an injury prevention and developmental psychology lens to examine children's every day freedoms in outdoor play. Because risk-taking in play currently faces significant cognitive and environmental barriers, I have focused on risky play.

Risky play is defined as thrilling play involving uncertainty and includes six categories: play at speed, at height, with dangerous tools (e.g., hammers, saws), near dangerous elements (e.g., fire, water), rough and tumble play, and play where there is a chance of getting lost (Sandseter, 2007). I have examined the effects of risky play on children's health and development, as well as cognitive barriers (e.g., caregiver fear), and environmental limitations (e.g., impoverished play environments). Our research, summarized below, shows the importance of supporting children's opportunity for freedom and risk-taking in play, and we have developed tools for early learning teachers to help them provide rich play environments.

Our systematic review examining research related to the relationship between risky outdoor play and health and development found positive associations with physical activity and social health, and negative associations with sedentary behaviours (Brussoni et al., 2015). Importantly, our research did not find a link between risky play and negative outcomes, including injury. Other research has also indicated the importance of risky play in promoting risk-management skills, resilience, self-confidence, mental health, and independence (Hüttenmoser, 1995; Lavrysen et al., 2015; LeMoyne & Buchanan, 2011; Sandseter & Kennair, 2011).

This research highlights the limitations of typical approaches to injury prevention that focus on injury rates and patterns, rather than considering the child's developmental and other needs. To illustrate, the injury data indicate that falls from play equipment are a leading cause of hospitalization (BC Injury Research and Prevention Unit, n.d.). A glance at these data would suggest that fall heights need to be lowered, greater attention needs to be paid to the surfacing under the play equipment, and close supervision is necessary to ensure children are following strict safety rules (Fuselli & Yanchar, 2012). This approach fails to recognize that, while it is important to provide children with play environments that limit the likelihood of serious injuries, risk-taking is a fundamental aspect of children's play, necessary for enabling their exploration and understanding of the world (Smith, 1998; Sutton-Smith, 2001). This approach also neglects the myriad of research and data indicating that serious play-related injuries are extremely rare, particularly given the numbers of hours that children spend on play equipment. In recognition of these limitations, many injury prevention professionals have moved towards an approach that seeks to keep children as safe as *necessary*, rather than as safe as *possible* (Brussoni et al., 2015). In basic terms, it is recommended that play providers focus on addressing *hazards* that have the potential to cause serious harm (for example, sources of harm that are not obvious to the child, such as broken equipment), but maintain risks that let children recognize and evaluate the challenge.

We conducted an intervention study to increase access to nature and risky play opportunities in two childcare centres that had impoverished play spaces. In an effort to increase the affordances available for play and access to nature, we spent $8000 to add natural materials and loose parts (e.g., plants, sand, water) as sources of play, using the Seven Cs play space design criteria to guide placement of materials (Herrington, Lesmeister, Nicholls, & Stefiuk, 2007). Play in environments with natural elements tends to be more complex and of longer duration than in equipment-based playgrounds (Luchs & Fikus, 2013; Samborski, 2010). Furthermore, ongoing and repeated exposure to nature benefits physical activity, emotion regulation, social development, and readiness for learning (Gill, 2014; Gray et al., 2015; Thompson, Oliveira, Wheeler, Depledge, & van den Bosch, 2016). A greater dose of nature is associated with more benefits (Shanahan et al., 2016). Childcare centres are ideal venues for inclusion of nature, given children's daily access.

Even with a modest intervention and limited time frame, our findings showed significant effects on children's outcomes (Brussoni, Ishikawa, Brunelle, & Herrington, 2017). Early childhood educators expressed greater satisfaction with the space post-intervention and perceived positive changes in children's behaviours, trends that were supported by our data. Children's depressed affect decreased significantly, which could be associated with an increase in the quality of the play environment, but also with greater exposure to nature, since contact with nature is associated with improved mental health. Antisocial behaviour was rare at both centres but further decreased after the intervention. Prosocial behaviour increased, as did instances of independent play. Early childhood educators reported that they spent less time managing difficult behaviours or manufacturing play after the intervention.

Through my research and consultations with parents, early learning teachers, licensing officers, landscape architects, and many others, I have identified many fears that act as potent barriers to children's risk taking in play:

- *Injury*: Serious injury or death resulting from risky play is extremely rare. Statistics Canada data indicate only one death over a period of 12 years, resulting from a fall from play equipment. To put this in perspective, you are several times more likely to be struck by lightning. Recent research on injury rates in Norwegian Early Childhood Centres indicated a rate of 0.13 minor (simple first aid treatment) injuries per child (Sando, Sandseter, Pareliussen, & Egset, 2017). As such, a typical child would have to spend almost eight years in childcare before they were there long enough to have a minor injury. For readers interested in seeing the latest injury statistics, visit the Canadian Atlas of Child & Youth Injury Prevention (http://injuryevidence.ca).

- *Licensing Officers*: Early childhood educators (ECEs) may preemptively limit or ban risky play activities on the assumption that licensing officers (risk managers, insurance providers) would not allow them. The licensing regulations are not prescriptive and are open to interpretation. It is important to have open dialogue with licensing officers, and the materials and tools outlined below could help facilitate these conversations.

- *Parents*: ECEs might be worried about parents' reactions to even a minor injury or dirty/ripped clothing at pick-up time, and concerned about liability resulting from a more serious injury. Childcare centres that have successfully implemented programs grounded in risky play outline some key steps in their process that have helped them manage these concerns. First, they have had extensive internal consultations to develop their own play philosophy and ensure that all staff feel comfortable supporting it and understand how it applies to their work. Second, they have prepared educational materials and had ongoing conversations with parents to educate them on the importance of risky play. Third, they have implemented mechanisms to support continuous and ongoing dialogue among the ECEs about their experiences and challenges supporting risky play (e.g., as a regular item on a staff meeting agenda); as well as ongoing communication with parents, such as documenting instances of their child engaging in risky play to help illustrate to parents how it has influenced and benefited the child. This ongoing and open communication can help address emerging issues before they become major concerns, as well as help avoid knee-jerk (and often counter-productive) reactions that sometimes follow a serious incident.

There are a number of readily available tools and resources that can support early learning teachers manage the challenges described above.

- *OutsidePlay.ca*: We have developed an online tool to reframe parents' perceptions of risk and make a personalized plan for changing their behaviour. This tool is accessible to anyone at https://outsideplay.ca/ and is being used by many childcare centres and programs to help educate parents on the importance of risky play.

- *Position Statement on Active Outdoor Play*: This evidence-based document provides an overview of the relevant literature and resulted from extensive consultation with experts and agencies across a range of disciplines. It can be accessed at http://www .haloresearch.ca/outdoorplay/ and lists specific recommendations for different target audiences, including encouraging ECEs to embrace the outdoors for play opportunities more often and in all weather (Tremblay et al., 2015). It has already proven influential in shifting policies and has been supported by the Chief Medical Officers of Health from every province and territory in Canada.

- *Tools to help with the design of outdoor play spaces*: We developed the Outdoor PLAY-book (http://outdoorplaybook.ca/) as an online guidebook giving the latest research and best practices for outdoor play space design. While it is focused on schools, the principles are readily applicable to early childhood spaces. To help with planning design modifications, we developed an audit tool for early childhood centres' outdoor play spaces based on the Seven Cs design guidelines. This 27-item checklist helps ECEs to examine the play that is occurring and evaluate the play space based on each of the Cs to determine where their efforts would be best spent in modifying the play space. The tool can be accessed in the SAGE Handbook of Outdoor Play and Learning (Herrington, Brunelle, & Brussoni, 2017) or by contacting me.

- *Risk Benefit Assessment*: The Child and Nature Alliance of Canada (CNAC), which includes Forest School Canada, is developing a Risk Benefit Assessment (RBA) framework modelled on the tool developed by the UK's Play Safety Forum (Ball, Gill, & Spiegal, 2012). A risk benefit assessment process allows for a more balanced and child-centred consideration of the play space or activity and facilitates inclusion of nature and natural materials in children's play spaces.

I am encouraged by the many exciting changes that are currently taking place in Canada and elsewhere and the increasing recognition of the importance of children's outdoor play space environments and opportunities for freedom and risk-taking in play. At the same time, it is clear that continued focus and momentum is needed to address the many barriers to play. We are still some way off from being in a position where children everywhere have the freedom to play how and when they choose in high quality outdoor play environments. Furthermore, in order to support the diverse children living in Canada, we must increase our efforts to understand and support play for children with different socio-economic and cultural backgrounds, including indigenous, immigrant, and refugee children. There is no one-size-fits-all approach to play and the limited research that is available indicates important differences in conceptions of play that need to be taken into account in providing sensitive contextualized support to children and their families. Supporting all children's needs will help foster rich experiences for everyone, support healthy child development, and attenuate the impact of social disadvantage.

Diane Kashin

Photo 12.11 All children should experience the richness of the outdoor environment.

Enid Elliot, Ph.D. Program Leader, Early Learning and Care, Camosun College

Research on outdoor play from a collaborative standpoint has led to the creation of a set of principles that emerged from an advisory group, which met for a year and a half before we started our research. The principles are as follows:

- *Connecting deeply with nature: environmental stewardship*: Teachers and students would nurture their relationship with nature with care, compassion, and a sense of wonder for the physical world in which they live by fostering a 'Sense of Wonder', curiosity, and inquiry. Further, they would do so by encouraging a sense of responsiveness, caring, and commitment to the environment and by supporting an understanding of ecology and sustainability.

- *The environment as another teacher*: The value that all living things and systems are interconnected is a central concept to the program. Spending significant periods of time in the outdoors should support children's growing awareness of their intertwined connections with natural landscapes and phenomenon. By moving freely in outdoor spaces, learning by looking into and with nature rather than at it, developing self-confidence in natural landscapes, engaging with the sensuality of nature, engaging in unstructured and spontaneous play, and enjoying the sensory awareness of being engaged outside can all provide a rich learning situation.

- *Learning collaboratively as a part of a community*: Through a growing sense of place, children will begin to appreciate their connections within their local community that includes family, neighbours, friends, and local nearby nature. The children will learn and teach with a kindergarten teacher, early childhood educator, and community members, such as First Nations Elders, CRD parks educators, and Royal BC Museum curators, grandparents and parents and build a sense of belonging and community by developing a sense of attachment to their "larger community" (Berry, 1988).

- *Physical and Mental health*: With consistent and sustained interaction with the natural environment, children's physical and mental well-being can benefit, as being in a green setting fosters improved mental health and provides multiple opportunities for movement (Kuo, 2010). By exploring their physical abilities, children have opportunities to take risks and become comfortable in their bodies.

- *Aboriginal ways of knowing*: The forest the children would be entering each morning has been a special place of gathering and engagement for several Coast Salish First Nations bands (Turner & Hebda, 2012; Turner et al., 2000).

All of these principles were meant to guide and question our program. The discussion of our principles was an important step in our process. The process of developing our key ideas provided opportunities for discussion with our wider community. We immediately got feedback on our proposal to include Aboriginal Ways of Knowing; several people within the Indigenous community suggested our wording gave the impression that we were assuming a universal Aboriginal understanding of nature. Each aboriginal band and First Nation have narratives and knowledge unique to their land. We were grateful for this feedback and changed the term to *local traditional knowledges*. Through this, we began to understand that we needed to focus on sharing with the children the narratives that belong to the place in which they would be playing and learning. This particular aspect of our vision was complex and had multiple layers; even before the program started, we were learning to think about it carefully.

The other aspect we are investigating more deeply is the living, breathing world as a teacher. This fits with the connection to local Indigenous knowledge. The world beyond humans has much to share with us. Children connect in their own ways without the mediation of educators. There is much to be learned here and acknowledged in our pedagogy.

The children had experiences that were different from ones that they would have found in a classroom, because outside, IN the living breathing world, what Merleau-Ponty calls "the flesh of the world" (Merleau-Ponty, 1962) reaches out to them and invites them to know what Thomas Berry calls "the larger community" or "the comprehensive Earth community" (Berry, 1988) or what Affrica Taylor calls "common worlds" (Taylor, 2013). A sense of community is strong among the children and educators.

When outside, the children formed communities of safety where they trusted the teachers as well as their classmates to care for them, physically and emotionally. Encouraging the children to take responsibility for themselves and each other was part of our risk-management plan. Building this community of safety, the children were all given a kit of band-aids, Kleenex, a 'space blanket,' and emergency food to carry in their backpacks. They learned how to behave if they sighted a predator (there are cougars and bears in the school's habitat), what to do if they stepped on a wasps' nest, and how to negotiate how high they felt safe to climb or what to do if they got lost in the forest. Being in charge of a major component of their own safety allowed children to understand their own limits rather than imposed ones, and that their safety depended on everyone's safety. Within this community of children, self-regulation was more about regulating one's self within the group and the group dynamics helping a child find a place. To a child who insisted on barking all morning, the children explained that she could be a fairy dog and fairy dogs "don't bark." Rather than have to be quiet because her barking was annoying, the children found a way for her to still be a dog, but a quiet one.

Children shared learning with each other as well as the teacher and educator. "I will meet you at the cedar tree." "That is an invasive species" "I am going to make an old age home for my worm, she is old and pregnant." Or they determined what trees might the local First Nations choose for a canoe and why. They absorbed information from each other, as well as their teachers, community experts, and the Aboriginal Support educator who journeyed with them one day a week.

The greater-than-human community offers many opportunities for learning and different ways to express that learning. The children learned about paradox; for example, 'when is my stick also your stick'? One day Enid was walking down the trail with four children, and three children had sticks and were comparing their stick's characteristics. The fourth child complained that she did not have a stick; without missing a beat, the child beside her broke his stick over his knee and gave her half of his stick and said, "now you do." They learned about metaphor and poetry. For example, with a break in the clouds and a bit of blue sky, a child said, "the sky is waving at us." Caring for the other creatures of the forest was an issue when the anthills that the children had been exploring had been covered with sticks and stones from others who had been walking in the forest. Some of those people were children from the older grades in their school who, with the spring weather, had started coming into the forest. Upset by the violation to the ants' homes, the children made signs and posted them by the anthills, then visited some of the other classes to explain that the anthills were the ants' homes and should be respected.

While the outdoors is a place of possibilities and of invitations, it is also a place of uncertainty; outside of the four walls, there were many opportunities for children to engage with life, materials, and the relationships that rocks, trees, and owls offered them. One never knew what would present itself. Children were usually ready to see and seize the opportunities, and the educators learned to do the same, responding to the questions and concerns that arose from the current situation in which the children were engaged.

Focusing on the children's inquiries became the educator's goal, rather than following a set lesson plan. They used narrations, children's questions and theories, and their own observations and discussions with the children to see where to build the teaching/learning. Working together carefully, they thought about what children seemed to be exploring and where their questions lay; they took notes of children's ideas and decided which ideas they might follow.

Working as a team, they were able to question each other when it seemed one might be settling for an easy answer to the children's explorations. Was it really birds the children were focused on or was it woodpeckers or nests as homes? What was the entry point of children's interests? They tried not to hijack the children's discussions and manipulate them, but rather collaborate. The children were clear about their preferences and interests, as they would often drift away from the teachers when something did not interest or intrigue them. Without walls, children are less contained within the space; place, the very fabric of the forest and land that they walked on, sat on, and lay on, enticed children to explore. Without the walls it was easier to drift away from an uninteresting lesson. As Orr (2013) says, "the place itself becomes agent in the curriculum" (p. 184).

Being outside with children meant the teachers had to be ready for anything and willing to not know everything. There is so much to wonder about when in the forest. A dead owl may be in the path; worms may be everywhere as the rain pours down; mushrooms and bright red fungi might have sprouted overnight. There are multiple stories to share—why worms come out in the rain, why cedar is a powerful ally, the history of immigrants and settlers—plants and people.

Debra Harwood, Ph.D., and the Educators of the Rosalind Blauer Centre for Child Care, Brock University

As researchers and educators supporting and transitioning to an outdoor nature-based program, we had several research questions at the outset of our study. What play opportunities does the forest offer? What developmental benefits are realized by the children in a nature-based program? How do interactions and ways of relating unfold in the forest? These initial questions have changed over the years as each new discovery led to more questions. We soon realized that our constructivist theoretical framework and human-centric focus limited gaining a complete understanding of the complexities involved in the nature-based program. Thus, the essence of our research approach has changed dramatically.

Theoretically, we now align our ideas with the notion of human-centrism as a "grossly inadequate conceptual framework for responding to the challenges of growing up in an increasingly complex, mixed-up, boundary blurring, heterogeneous, interdependent and ethically confronting world" (Taylor et al., 2012, p. 81). In our study, the children and educators' lives in the forest were inseparable from the animals, birds, ants, sticks, deer, rocks, and so on. Additionally, throughout the first year of the study we experienced tensions in the forest (e.g., human garbage, a dead raccoon, rights of animals, colonialism) that challenged our original conception of "innocent child and 'pure' nature in early childhood education" (Nxumalo, 2015, p. 21). We found nature was enmeshed, entangled, and indivisible from the children's and educators' experiences. This shift in thinking and understanding provoked us to seek new theoretical and methodological frameworks (see also Harwood & Collier, 2017). Our research project has been a journey, our story of questioning the role, context, and pedagogical implications of adult/child/animal/nature/culture entanglements in one Ontario forest early childhood program.

The context for our study is a nature-based program that supports the immersion of eight preschool-aged children and their two educators into the natural, unstructured forest located on a university campus in Ontario. Typically, the children engage in play in the forest two mornings each week from September to June. The children refer to their program as 'forest school,' and philosophically the model does adhere to the principles of regular and repeated access to the same natural space, and emergent, experiential, and play-based learning (MacEachren, 2013).

Initially, we were curious about the benefits and effects of nature programming on children, educators, and their families, utilizing a mixed-method research design in the first and second year of the study. The initial study comprised a mosaic approach of data collection tools (Clark & Moss, 2001), including accelerometers, photos, videos, researcher notes, educator journals, surveys, conversational interviews, and GoPro cameras worn by the children. Like others (O'Brien & Murray, 2006; Slade, Lowery, & Bland, 2013), our study's early findings have hinted at a myriad of developmental benefits gained from the forest program. For example, children were twice as physically active in the forest in comparison to a 'typical' day in a childcare centre, with more unique opportunities for vigorous types of play afforded in the forest (Harwood, Reichheld, McElhone, & McKinley, in press). Yet, the more time we spent in the forest coupled with the abundance of data collected and analyzed, the more we came to question *who are we in relation to these children, this forest place, this entangled world?* Our encounter with a dead raccoon was a pivotal moment in the research project, and the animal's presence in the children's lives highlighted the affective and fluid relations that exist between children and nature. We transitioned to considering the ways in which one is "with and of nature, not [simply just] in it" (Dickinson, 2013).

We are currently engaged in rethinking our project using a post-humanist lens. A post-humanism conceptual framing invites the possibilities of considering the influence of the learning child's human social cultural milieu, as well as their more-than-human contexts within the spaces and places where children and teachers coexist (Barad, 2007; Haraway, 2008; Somerville, 2011; Taylor & Giugni, 2012). In our project, we have found that children often think relationally with the objects in their forest environments (rocks, sticks, raccoons). Ideas, concepts, and understandings are formed from the intra-actions that occur in the forest. So, the child's entanglement with a stick, for example, forges something new. The stick, much like the child, is agentic, acting upon the child as the child in turns acts upon the stick (Harwood & Collier, 2017). Seemingly, it is not possible to separate the child from nature as they are one in the same. Thus, new research questions are emerging, such as how might educators foster intra-actions in the forest and support a relational pedagogy with the natural world? As these new questions emerge, we have also queried the appropriateness of our research process and our "habitual anthropocentric style of seeing" (Hultman & Lenz Taguchi, 2010, p. 527). We look forward to the possibilities of new ways of seeing and deepening our emerging understanding of the ways in which adults/children/animals/forests are entangled and enmeshed.

Louise Zimanyi, M. Ed., Professor, ECE, Humber College

Two towering and deeply furrowed 150-year old cracked willow trees, as outlined in Photos 12.12 and 12.13, situated along the Humber River watershed and surrounded by Canada's most biologically diverse ecosystem (Humber Arboretum, n.d.) are the heart of a recently launched Forest Nature Program (FNP) for children aged 2.5 to 4 years at Humber College in Toronto (Zimanyi, 2016).

Located in *Adobigok* (Place of the Alders in the Ojibwe Language), the 105-hectare traditional territory of the Ojibwe Anishnabe Aboriginal people, including several First Nations communities (Charles, n.d), the *oziisigobiminzh* or willow tree provides opportunities for climbing, explorations of light and shadow, watching chickadees swoop from branches and land on eager outstretched hands offering sunflower seeds, noticing how wind and rain, snow, and sun change the tree, and exploring the inside of a storied tree cracked wide open following a windstorm.

The FNP is a collaborative initiative of the Early Childhood Education (ECE) department within the School of Health Sciences, the Humber Arboretum and the Humber Child Development Centre, supported by the Aboriginal Resource Centre at Humber.

Louise Zimanyi

Photos 12.12 and **12.13** Willow encounters.

Building on previous nature education initiatives within ECE and a commitment to innovative practice in teaching and learning, the FNP provides children regular and repeated opportunities to play and learn in a natural setting and develop a stronger and more knowledgeable connection with and in the natural world. The program was piloted and launched in 2016 within the context of a growing forest school movement in North America (Forest School Canada, 2014) that values place-based, situated, and embodied learning in nature (Sobel, 2008) as developmentally beneficial (Gill, 2011) because it supports children's attachment to nature, mitigating what is commonly known as "nature deficit disorder" (Louv, 2005, 2014) and fostering a global interest in environmental stewardship (IUCN, 2012).

While the importance of embodied learning in nature is increasingly being acknowledged in the early years, early learning programs are dominated by Euro-Western child-centred pedagogies that see nature as separate from culture (Taylor, 2013) and are unaware of and/or neglect Indigenous ways of knowing. They do not address or take responsibility for supporting children's collective and relational engagements (Hultman & Lenz Taguchi, 2014) in increasingly complex, inherited (Haraway, 2008), colonized, and ecologically challenged life worlds (Pacini-Ketchabaw, Taylor, Blaise, Finney, 2015).

Increasing interdisciplinary work within early childhood studies, critical place pedagogies, post-structural and materialist feminist philosophies, the ecological humanities, post-humanist geographies, and Indigenous onto-epistemologies reflect a growing body of work that is contesting, reconfiguring, refiguring, and re-storying colonized pedagogical practices in early childhood education (Taylor & Pacini-Ketchabaw, 2015a; Tuck, McKenzie, & McCoy, 2014). This includes a shift away from child-centred developmental environmental pedagogies toward pedagogies that bring attention to children's entanglements within multiple human and more-than-human relations.

While seemingly addressing present-day environmental concerns, mainstream twenty-first century early childhood education is still rooted in early twentieth century child-centred child developmental theories (Piaget, 1970). Taylor & Pacini-Ketchabaw (2015a) highlight that while "children in contemporary early childhood settings are inheriting increasingly complex and challenging common worlds, mainstream child-centered pedagogies seldom support children to engage meaningfully with them" (p. 4) neglecting or doing little to acknowledge or address the pedagogical significance of connectedness and relations with place, plants, and animals, and belonging.

Thinking with place (Taylor & Pacini-Ketchabaw, 2015), relating to place as "intrinsically storied" (Nxumalo & Cedillo, 2017, p. 103), seeing place as pedagogical (Greenwood, 2012), understanding that "wisdom sits in places" (Patterson as cited in Feld & Basso, 1996, p. 70) and engaging with the materiality of place and human and non-human assemblage (Duhn, 2012) or children's relations with other living beings and things in their "common world" environments (Common World Childhoods Research Collective, 2016; Taylor, 2013) challenges many nature-based, child-centred early childhood education programs (modelled on forest schools in northern Europe) that seek grand solutions to the ecological problems we are facing in the twenty-first century.

The emerging scholarship in early childhood education highlights the possibilities of place-learning through unsettling child-centred learning, resituating childhood and pedagogies by focusing upon children's relations with other living beings and things in their local "common world" environments (Common World Childhoods Research Collective, 2016). Rooted in Indigenous beliefs of the deep and inseparable connectedness of children and the world (Martin, 2007; Ritchie & Rau, 2010) "common worlds" is used to describe how children, educators, parents, and researchers co-inhabit with other species and as a framework to investigate and situate childhood within children's relations with more-than-the-human-world (Common World Childhoods Research Collective, 2016).

A challenge in qualitative research methodology is to search for an approach that is inclusive and not extractive, one that will "challenge the very core of knowledge production and purpose" (Kovach, 2010, p. 46), yet still can bridge and privilege both Indigenous and Western worldviews. Indigenous research frameworks (Martin & Mirraboopa, 2003; Kovach, 2010; Smith-Tuwahi, 2012) and common worlds and multi-species ethnographies (Pacini-Ketchabaw, Taylor, & Blaise, 2016) are relevant methodologies to specifically anchor and direct the research questions; to explore and understand multiple ways of knowing, being, and doing; to provide ways to "write theory through stories" (Stewart, 2011, p. 445); to explore "ontological, ethical, and ecological knots in multispecies contact zones" (Haraway, 2010); to do what Kovach proposes, "break with polarities and create a new ethical space" (2010, p. 223) for collective wisdom.

My research examines how conceptualizations of place through common world paradigms, methodologies and pedagogies, and Indigenous relational presences may be used to reconceptualize, decolonize, and re-story place-based early childhood studies and support children's emplaced connectedness and ethical relations through lived and collective reciprocity. My research questions ask how might places within Abdigok (the Humber Arboretum) be collectively known and experienced differently through place-specific stories, thinking relationally in common worlds with Indigenous onto-epistomologies that attend to the more-than-human relationalities of place? By thinking with place, how might collective engagement and inquiry—alongside educators, children, and Indigenous peoples working in Adobigok—with the more-than-human world contribute to re-storying young children's place encounters and reshaping place-connected pedagogies?

This research challenges the belief that humans are somehow exceptional and hyper-separated from nature and considers how might we relook at how place (land, water, air) that connects us, "through its materiality, a materiality which is dynamic, constantly changing, shaped by daily cycles of seasons and weather, and the activities of all the living creatures, including humans" (Somerville & Green, 2012, p. 5) helps us "slow down, to be present enough to notice the multiple presence of others" (Instone & Taylor, 2015, p.137).

Though not yet widespread, there are increasing examples of pedagogical and paradigmatic shifts that reflect useful principles of attending to children's relations and emplacement in children's common worlds through collective inquiry (Taylor, 2013). This often "require[es] fieldwork that (repeatedly) immerses the researcher with children and educators in the contexts of the Entities and to watch, listen, wait, learn. In Nunavut, thinking with *nunangat* or land, ice and water (Rowan, 2017); decolonizing and restorying 'natural' forest encounters in early childhood programs, Nxumalo (2015); thinking with and listening to water, exploring watery pedagogies in early childhood classrooms (Pacini-Ketchabaw & Clark, 2016); learning with ants and worms (Taylor & Pacini-Ketchabaw, 2015b); learning about place by 'becoming frog' (Somerville, 2013); seeing trees stumps as storied worlds (van Dooren and Rose, 2012); the bodily effect of rain, wind and sunshine and learning with weather through 'weathering' (Neimanis & Walker, 2014); mutual engagement with the weather world (Ingold, 2007) weather worlding (Rooney, 2016), "where human, non-human and elemental conditions are entangled in a collective world-making (p.2),..that explore "complexities in the mutual and co-implicated happenings between weather and children" (p. 4) through embodied walking in weather (Ingold, 2015), connections made through returning to place.

The central, agentic, and pedagogical significance of being with place, materials, and elements, land, water, and weather encourage children to question both chosen and inherited relations that are different from them (Taylor, 2013), practice a relational ethics (Whatmore, 2002) and learn how to co-exist with the elements and multispecies. This shift from an anthropocentric-human centred to an earth-centred, bio-centric worldview (Kimmerer, 2015) is what philosopher Joanna Macy calls "The Great Turning"—the essential adventure of our time, shifting from the age of industrial growth to the age of life-sustaining civilization" (as cited in Kimmerer, 2015, n.p.).

PRACTICAL APPLICATIONS

Reading the words of the featured researchers is intended to inform practice. As well, engaging in research individually and collaboratively can also influence your work with children in a powerful way. Early learning students and teachers can follow the same PEER Principle of Plan, Engage, Explore, and Reflect to create an opportunity for action research.

Table 12.2 Plan, engage, explore, reflect—creating new knowledge through research.

PLAN	Early learning teachers examine their practice to determine what some of their core questions are related to a variety of aspects of outdoor play, such as how children use space; the types of individual and group play that children engage in; how children embrace the outdoors; and the roles and responsibilities of early learning teachers. Then, plan what, where, when, how, and who will participate in the research.
ENGAGE	Using the plan, engage in examining literature, data gathering, analyzing, and seek to understand what is seen and thought about from the data. Engage others, such as children, critical friends, or mentors to bring meaning to the findings.
EXPLORE	Listen to the voices of children, colleagues, critical friends, or mentors about what they see and think, and what their thoughts are on how findings might transfer to practice. Examine what changes may mean to practice. How might the changes be made and how will the results be recorded? What are the roles of the children, families, colleagues, and researchers?
REFLECT	Did the research process help to clarify the question? How did the process and the findings bring new knowledge to the researcher, children, families, colleagues, and the program? What did you learn from the process? What additional questions surfaced? What surprised you? What do you do next?

TIPS AND TOOLS FOR OUTDOOR PLAY RESEARCH

Research on outdoor play improves the experiences that children have outdoors. Although there are many ways in which research may be conducted, it is most effective when the early learning teachers and teams of teachers embrace the process. The research methodology chosen will be dependent on the question to be explored. We encourage potential research teams to identify a topic or topics that support investing the time to seek answers to. The research process is intended to be satisfying for the researchers, the children, and the overall program. Therefore, it is helpful for teachers who are interested in beginning the process to identify the elements of their practice or aspects of children's outdoor play that they wish to investigate.

The research team benefits from determining what lens they will use to engage in the research. For example, if the team values and beliefs are that children have specific scheduled time outdoors in the morning and in the afternoon, then their approach will be very different to an early learning program that follows the children's lead by supporting children in having the outdoor time that supports their play episodes. Ideally, early learning teachers will think about the story they want to form and tell.

Research requires the researcher to be open to their discoveries and to make a commitment prior to investing in the research that they will use the results to inform practice. Otherwise, one must question why invest the time in the process. The process of research is to contribute to fostering a reflective and continuous growth and development process amongst early learning teachers. Investing time and energy into the research process increases the potential to improve and advance children's outdoor play experiences. Yes, the time is right to engage in research and to seize the power of inquiry. After all, the children are the reason that we make an investment in research!

ON THE GROUND—PROFESSIONAL REFLECTIONS: "WHY I LOVE OUTDOOR PLAY"

>> BOX 12.3   Why I Love Outdoor Play

When I began working with children after becoming an early learning teacher, the focus of my practice was on the indoor environment. I would take children outside, as this was a mandatory licensing requirement, but all I would do was supervise them as they played with the same equipment and materials day after day. I regret not taking children beyond the fence where there was a field and trees. At the time I was learning about the principles of the Reggio Emilia approach and working hard at moving from a theme-based to an emergent curriculum. After I became a college professor and started teaching early childhood education, I advocated for naturalistic indoor environments with loose parts. Outdoor and nature play were still not on my radar. It was not a significant part of the early learning program. However, I was passionate about professional learning and had started to use social media

to find articles, websites, and blogs about anything to do with play and learning. I came upon an opportunity to take a forest school practitioners course. I knew going into the forest that I was stepping way out of my comfort zone! It had been decades since I had "roughed it" and had long been a creature of comfort. I tend to avoid the cold, the wet, and the bugs. My knife skills outside my kitchen have never been used and while I consider myself a great cook, I have cut myself often. I also bump into things on a regular basis and am considered a klutz. I think it is because I am always in my head, thinking deeply about teaching, learning, and relationships. I am always coming up with visions and ideas. In the forest, I got out of my head. I became mindful of my surroundings and took on challenges carefully. I listened with deep consideration to what I was being taught by those more knowledgeable than myself. I used a

>> BOX 12.3   Why I Love Outdoor Play (*Continued*)

bow saw, whittled with a knife, and tied knots. I came out of the forest more confident of my capacity to learn new things and more aware of my surroundings, especially the natural ones. Building on that transformative experience, I took every opportunity I could to spend time outdoors as a workshop participant and a workshop facilitator. As the chair of the York Region Nature Collaborative, I have had the honour of spending time in nature with children, families, and early learning teachers. I became convinced of the importance of outdoor play. When Beverlie invited me to be part of a research project designed to build the capacity of early learning teachers to support children's outdoor play experiences, I did not hesitate. Conducting this research and designing curriculum led to new knowledge creation. Being able to facilitate the curriculum both on-line and face-to-face in an outdoor environment that I felt an emotional connection with was transformative. There is nothing I would rather do now than to be in a forest with others. This is why I love outdoor and nature play.

Diane Kashin
Author

>> BOX 12.4   Why I Love Outdoor Play

I grew up outdoors. I walked the forest and cherished the aroma of the trees, tall grasses in the fields, and the overall environment. I laid in the grass; I made mud cakes with daisies on top for my mother; I screamed loudly when I stepped on ants nests, and I splashed in the puddles. That was my reality. I thought that was every child's reality. When I was a faculty member in 1995 at a college in Ontario, I assumed that students came to the environment with similar childhoods. I realized that although they had experiences outdoors, the students appeared to identify with more organized sports activities than pure play. This resulted in me often taking the students on outdoor discovery events. Some students embraced the opportunity, while others were truly bothered by the experiences and being outdoors—they were cold, bored, and clearly didn't think it was as important as the indoor portion of the program. Due to these experiences, at a faculty curriculum meeting, I suggested that we make outdoor play explicit in our program. Unfortunately, my colleagues had different perspectives. As a way to make outdoor play more explicit in my classes, I went on the hunt for a textbook that would have at least a chapter on outdoor play included. I had no luck in finding such a text. I became frustrated because of my beliefs and values that children and adults are healthier and happier when they spend time outdoors, and that adults were joyful when the time outdoors included children. In 1999, I determined that my professional research agenda would focus on outdoor play, including writing my first text ever and the first Canadian textbook that had a chapter specifically on outdoor play. Despite me leaving teaching and moving into college administration, I have maintained my research agenda in outdoor play. Now, as I write about outdoor play and work with early learning teachers, families, and children in a variety of capabilities, I get such a pleasure from observing, listening, guiding, and discovering new knowledge about outdoor play. I also gain so much from supervising students completing their undergraduate or graduate degrees with an interest in children's outdoor play. When our emerging early learning teachers and educators become "hooked" on outdoor play, I feel a sense of hope for our future generations. As part of a current research project, I am working with a municipality to create a playground with only nature and loose parts. As I have observe families coming with their young children to the park, and hear the laughter and screams of joy, and observe the intensity in the play, I know there is nothing better to support communities and our future generation. Similar to Diane, there is no better place for me than being outdoors; whether it is being in the forest, taking a walk in the neighbourhood, or digging in the garden—my body and soul belong outdoors. Finally, I encourage you to open the door and let the children play outdoors.

Beverlie Dietze
Author

CASE STUDIES

Early learning teachers may find it challenging and risky to move from a place of comfort to a commitment to engage in research for the purpose of creating new knowledge that benefits children and their outdoor play experiences. When engaging in research, early learning teachers must be prepared to understand that by participating with children and in research, they may be exposed to times of discomfort and uncertainty as they make meaning of their findings. Read the scenario presented in Case Study 12.2 and reflect upon the questions featured below.

⟫ CASE STUDY 12.2 | Engaging in Research

At a meeting with a think tank group on outdoor play, early learning teachers and directors were asked to volunteer three centres to become pilot sites to engage in an action research project. The purpose of the project would be to examine the types of play that three-year-olds engage in when their outdoor play environment has specific loose parts placed in it. The director and two of the early learning teachers were really excited to volunteer because they thought they would learn so much by looking closely at how children play with loose parts. At the same time, they very clearly knew that they would be on a new learning journey because they did not have experience in action research. They determined they would volunteer to be one of the pilot sites. When they returned to the centre, they suggested that it might be beneficial to present their concept to their colleagues.

They bantered back and forth about how and what they would present. They knew the importance of sharing the benefits to the centre, children, and early learning teachers. Their challenge was they knew so little information about action research that they didn't know how to describe the scope of the project.

1. What are the challenges of taking on this project without having the background in action research?
2. What do you think the challenges might be for the team in presenting the information to their colleagues? What would you recommend they do or learn before they engage in discussions with their colleagues?
3. What are the advantages of the group engaging in this project? Do you think the advantages outweigh the disadvantages?

⟫ BOX 12.5 | Take It Outside!

Plan an outdoor workshop for other early learning teachers or students. After reading this textbook, what experiences can others engage in so that they become comfortable with outdoor play and find their own nature connections?

KEY TERMS

Rituals
Customs
Conventions
Mentor
Critical friend
Metacognition
Interprofessional practice
Action research
Reflective inquiry
Collaborative action research
Narrative inquiry

Diane Kashin

Photo 12.14 Key terms.

Summary

- Research informs an early learning teacher's practice and supports continuous learning.
- Research is a framework of a profession.
- Early learning programs are the perfect environments to be "incubators of inquiry."
- Whenever research occurs, and whoever conducts the research, it must be done following ethical practices.
- Research in early learning programs include the voices of children, families, and early learning teachers.
- Researchers think about the research process by identifying the question (action), assessing the suitability of the question for the environment and those who may be part of the research (reflection), and deciding whether or not to proceed with the research (action).
- Research is intended to change our thinking patterns, ideas and ideals, knowledge, and practices that will benefit children's play.
- Mentors and critical friends can play key roles in examining the data, making conclusions and recommendations, and in changing practice.
- The term critical friend is derived from critical pedagogy. The goal of critical pedagogy is for individuals to affect change through social interactions and actions.
- Researchers have defined the mentoring process as "a dynamic, reciprocal relationship in a work environment between an advanced career incumbent (mentor) and a beginning (protégé), aimed at promoting the career development of both" (p. 16).

- Benjamin Bloom's higher order thinking skills supports early learning teachers in engaging in a reflection process that contributes to affecting change in philosophies and practices in early learning environments.

- Inter-professional practice involves working alongside other professionals to support children, with each bringing an important perspective.

- The attitudes and the context of early learning teachers thinking has a direct correlation on the environments and experiences that are extended to children's outdoor play.

- Research has suggested that there are three characteristics that support early learning teachers in amalgamating new learning. The first is the quality of the content and how it is related to current knowledge and experiences; the second is richness or amplitude of application of theory; and the third is the structure of theory.

- Applying theory requires early learning teachers to be comfortable in seeking advice on their ideas and engaging in discourse to formulate how theory transfers to practice.

- Action research refers to research that is initiated to solve a problem or engage in a progressive reflective process to seek answers to improve a practice.

- Action research is a process of systematically examining and reflecting upon an individual or group practice and is interactive as teacher-researchers and children construct knowledge.

- Studies have categorized action research as individual teacher research, collaborative action research, and program-wide research.

- Collaborative action research refers to a research method that is conducted by teams for the purpose of improving group experiences and contributing to the professional learning of the researchers.

- Narrative inquiry refers to a process of examining living stories for threads and themes that bring new insight into lived experiences.

- From an outdoor play perspective, narrative inquiry is effective in early learning programs with colleagues who are collegial and collectively have an interest in advancing outdoor play to the next level.

- Pedagogical documentation is considered a form of research because it is a research story that is built upon a question of inquiry about the learning of children.

- Increasingly, Canadian researchers are examining various aspects of outdoor play in their research.

- The research methodology chosen to examine aspects of outdoor play will be dependent on the question to be explored.

- The members of the research team benefit from determining what lens they will use to engage in the research.

- Research requires the researchers to be open to their discoveries and to make a commitment prior to investing in the research that they will use the results to inform practice. Otherwise, one must question why one would invest the time in the process.

QUIET REFLECTION

Quietly, go to a place outdoors that is special to you where you can see or imagine children playing and exploring. Think about what questions you have about the environment or how the children play in the environment? Think about why those questions might be intriguing to you? Why might you want to pursue exploring it further, and how? How might research inform your practice? How do you envision moving your questions to a research project? Who might become partners in your research? What makes you excited about the potential of engaging in research? What do you think might be the challenges? What will you do next?

COMMUNITY DIALOGUE

Children, families, colleagues, and researchers are partners in research. The concept of community dialogue and research are interconnected. We encourage researchers to think of community dialogue and research from a constructivist thinking perspective as an array of voices can have many benefits. The differing perspectives facilitate early learning teachers, community members, and participants in the research to engage in thinking, looking, imagining, and determining how new knowledge can be socially constructed. Community dialogue increases ownership in the research and in using the knowledge in ways that contribute to changing practice. Think about an early learning program that is adjacent to a park. How might community dialogue open up new opportunities for the children to engage and embrace that space? How might all children in the community benefit from the space with research and community dialogue? Early learning teachers ideally have a goal of creating a culture of inquiry, problem solving, and community connections, all of which are essential in effective research and knowledge dissemination.

FOR FURTHER THOUGHT AND ACTION

Outdoor Play Canada is a network of leaders and organizations working together to galvanize an outdoor play movement across Canada. This network sprang from the diverse, cross-sector group that collaborated to create the 2015 Position Statement on Active Outdoor Play. Learn more about Outdoor Play Canada and join the movement: https://www.outdoorplaycanada.ca/.

RESOURCES

The Canadian Association of Family Resource Programs (FRP Canada) funded by the Lawson Foundation has published a new magazine called *Play*, and in the inaugural issues you will read articles written from experts on the forefront of Canada's outdoor play movement. This magazine will help you discover what is happening with play in Canada and includes many helpful tips that early learning students, teachers, and families can use in their work with children. You can find the magazine here: http://ow.ly/IVcE30fOgPf

Guidelines for children's physical activity for the early years were released in late 2017. These are the first 24-hour movement guidelines for this age group. They address sleep, sedentary behaviour, and physical activity. Read the guidelines here and consider the important role outdoor activity plays to ensure children get enough movement in their lives. They are available at

https://www.participaction.com/en-ca/thought-leadership/benefits-and-guidelines/0-4.

References

Abdul-Haqq, I. (1995). *ERIC as a resource for the teacher researcher.* ERIC Digest. EED 381530. Retrieved on March 25, 2006, from http://www.ericdigests.org/1996-1/teacher.htm

Acar, H. (2013). Landscape design for children and their environments in urban context. In *Advances in Landscape Architecture.* InTech.

Alexander, P. A., & Grossnickle, E. M. (2016). Positioning interest and curiosity within a model of academic development. *Handbook of Motivation at School*, 188–208.

Alexander, S. A., Frohlich, K. L., & Fusco, C. (2012). Playing for health? Revisiting health promotion to examine the emerging public health position on children's play. *Health Promotion International*, 29(1), 155–164.

Allsup, K. (2016, June 8). Please don't say you allow your child to take risks. [Blog Post]. Retrieved from https://childrengrowing.com/2016/06/08/please-dont-say-you-allow-your-child-to-take-risks/.

Almon, J. (2017). *Playing it up—with loose parts, playpads, and adventure playgrounds.* Annapolis, MD: Alliance for Childhood.

Ampartzaki, M., Kypriotaki, M., Voreadou, C., Dardioti, A., & Stathi, I. (2013). Communities of practice and participatory action research: the formation of a synergy for the development of museum programmes for early childhood. *Educational Action Research*, 21(1), 4–27.

Anbari, M., & Soltanzadeh, H. (2015). Child-oriented architecture from the perspective of environmental psychology. *European Online Journal of Natural and Social Sciences*, 4(3)(s), 137.

Anderson, K., & Ball, J. (2011). Foundations: First nation and Métis families. In D. Long and O. P. Dickason (Eds.), *Visions of the heart: Canadian Aboriginal issues* (3rd ed., pp. 55–89). Toronto: Oxford.

Anderson, L. W., & Krathwohl, D. R., et al. (Eds.) (2001). *A Taxonomy for learning, teaching, and assessing: A revision of Bloom's taxonomy of educational objectives.* Boston, MA: Allyn & Bacon (Pearson Education Group).

Andrachuk, H., Edgar, T., Eperjesi, P., Filler, C., Groves, J., Kaknevicius, J., Lahtinen, R., Mason, J., Molyneux, L., Morcom, L., Petrini, G., Piersol, L., Power, M., & Young, J. (2014). In R. Carruthers Den Hoed (Ed.), *Forest and nature school in Canada: A head, heart, hands approach to outdoor learning.* Toronto: Forest School Canada. Retrieved from: Forest School Canada. Retrieved from http://childnature.ca/wp-content/uploads/2017/10/FSC-Guide-1.pdf

Andreou, N. 2017. Schools turning communities green. *International Schools*, 19(3). Available: https://cloud.3dissue.com/2389/3124/7031/is19-3/offline/download.pdf

Ansari, A., & Purtell, K. (2017). Activity settings in full-day kindergarten classrooms and children's early learning. *Early Childhood Research Quarterly*, 38(2017), 23–32.

Ärlemalm-Hagsér, E., & Sandberg, A. (2011). Sustainable development in early childhood education: in-service students' comprehension of the concept. *Environmental Education Research*, 17(2), 187–200.

Association of Canadian Deans of Education (ACDE). (2013). *Accord on early learning and early childhood education.* Vancouver, BC: Author.

Atherton, F., & Nutbrown, C. (2016). Schematic pedagogy: supporting one child's learning at home and in a group. *International Journal of Early Years Education*, 24(1), 63–79.

Athey, C. (1990). *Extending thought in young children.* London: Paul Chapman.

Athey, C. (2007). *Extending thought in young children.* (2nd ed.). London: Paul Chapman.

Auld, S. (2002). Five key principals of heuristic play. *The First Years: New Zealand Journal of Infant and Toddler Education: Nga Tau Tuatahi*, 4(2), 36–38.

Australian Government (2009). Belonging, being & becoming. The Early Years Learning Framework for Australia. Australian Government Department of Education, Employment and Workplace Relations for the Council of Australian Governments. Available at https://foundationyears.org.uk/files/2012/03/Development-Matters-FINAL-PRINT-AMENDED.pdf

Bachrach, J. S., Playground movement. *Encyclopedia of Chicago.* http://www.encyclopedia.chicagohistory.org/pages/976.html. Retrieved April 6, 2012.

Bakker, A., Smit, J., & Wegerif, R. (2015). Scaffolding and dialogic teaching in mathematics education: Introduction and review. ZDM 47(7), 1047–1065.

Ball, D. J., Gill, T., & Spiegal, B. (2012). *Managing risk in play provision: Implementation guide.* London: Play England. Retrieved from http://www.playengland.org.uk/resources/managing-risk-in-play-provision-implementation-guide.aspx

Banack, H. (in press). Where STEM binds, and ST(eee)EM flows: A case for where in STEM discourse and practice. *Critical Education.*

Banack, H. & Berger, I. (in press). The emergence of early childhood outdoor education programs in British Columbia: A meandering story. *Advanced in Early Childhood Education and Daycares*, Volume 21.

Bandura, A. (1977). *Social learning theory.* New York, NY: Prentice Hall.

Bandura, A. (1997). Self-efficacy: toward a unifying theory of behavioral change. *Psychological Review*, 84(2), 191.

Banning, W., & Sullivan, G. (2011). *Lens on outdoor learning.* St. Paul, Minnesota: Redleaf Press, p. 201.

Barad, K. (2007). *Meeting the universe halfway: Quantum physics and the entanglement of matter and meaning.* Durham, N.C.: Duke University Press.

Barkley, E. F., Cross, K. P., & Major, C. H. (2014). *Collaborative learning techniques: A handbook for college faculty.* San Francisco: John Wiley & Sons.

Barman, J. (2011). Child Labour. In *The Canadian Encyclopedia.* Retrieved from http://www.thecanadianencyclopedia.ca/en/article/child-labour/

Barrow, R. (2014). "Plato". New York, NY: Bloomsbury Publishing.

Basford, J. (2015). Documenting and assessing learning. In K. Brodie, & K. Savage, (Eds.). *Inclusion and early years practice.* London: Routledge, 18–33.

Basford, J., & Bath, C. (2014). Playing the assessment game: an English early childhood education perspective. *Early Years,* 34(2), 119–132.

Baskerville, D., & Goldblatt, H. (2009). Learning to be a critical friend: From professional indifference through challenge to unguarded conversations. *Cambridge Journal of Education,* 39(2), 205–221.

Battiste, M., & Henderson, J. (2009). Naturalizing Indigenous knowledge in eurocentric education. *Canadian Journal of Native Education,* 32(1), 5–18.

BC Injury Research and Prevention Unit. (n.d.). Injury Data Tool. Retrieved February 5, 2013, from http://www.injuryresearch.bc.ca/?idot=injury-hospitalizations

Beckford, C. L., & Nahdee, R. (2011). Teaching for ecological sustainability: Incorporating Indigenous philosophies and practices. *What works? Research into practice research monograph, 36.* Toronto: Ontario Ministry of Education: Student Achievement division.

Bekkhus, M., Rutter, M., Maughan, B., & Borge, A. I. (2011). The effects of group daycare in the context of paid maternal leave and high-quality provision. *European Journal of Developmental Psychology,* 8(6), 681–696.

Belknap, E., & Hazler, R. (2014). Empty playgrounds and anxious children. *Journal of Creativity in Mental Health,* 9(2), 210–231.

Beloglovsky, M., & Daly, L. (2016). *Loose parts 2: Inspiring play with infants and toddlers.* St. Paul, Minnesota: Redleaf Press.

Berry, M. (2017). Filming Interactions to Nurture Development (FIND). Harvard University. Available at https://developingchild.harvard.edu/innovation-application/innovation-in-action/find/

Berry, T. (1988). *The dream of the earth.* San Francisco: Sierra Club Books.

Beyer, K., Bizub, J., Szabo, A., Heller, B., Kistner, A., Shawgo, E., Zetts, C. (2015). Development and validation of the attitudes toward outdoor play scales for children. *Social Science & Medicine,* 133, 253–260.

Bieder, R. (2011). From Thoreau to Muir: Changes in nineteenth century American competition of the environment. *Americana E-Journal of American Studies in Hungry,* VII(2). Available at: http://americanaejournal.hu/vol7no2/bieder

Bilton, H. (2002). *Outdoor play in the early years.* London: David Fulton Publishers.

Bilton, H. (2010). *Outdoor learning in the early years: Management and innovation.* New York, NY: Routledge.

Bilton, H. (2014). *Playing outside: Activities, ideas and inspiration for the early years.* New York, NY: Routledge.

Bloch, M. N., Swadener, B. B., & Cannella, G. S. (2014). *Reconceptualizing early childhood care and education: A Reader.* New York: Peter Lang.

Borgia, E. T., & Schuler, D. (1996). Action research in early childhood education. ERIC Digest, No ED401047. Retrieved from http://ericae.net/edo/ED401047.htm

Bowler, D. E., Buyung-Ali, L. M., Knight, T. M., & Pullin, A. S. (2010). A systematic review of evidence for the added benefits to health of exposure to natural environments. *BMC Public Health,* 10(10), 456, www.biomedcentral.com

Boyle, L. (2008). Environmental experiences in child care. *Putting Children First,* 19, 14–17. Retrieved from http://ncac.acecqa.gov.au/educator-resources/pcf-articles/Environmental_Experiences_in_Child_Care_Sept06.pdf

Bresler, L. (2013). *Knowing bodies, moving minds: Towards embodied teaching and learning.* Boston, MA: Kluwer Academic Publishers.

Brillante, P., & Mankiw, S. (2015). A sense of place: Human geography in the early childhood classroom. *YC Young Children,* 70(3), 16.

Brindova, D., Pavelka, J., Ševčikova, A., Žežula, I., van Dijk, J. P., Reijneveld, S. A., & Geckova, A. M. (2014). How parents can affect excessive spending of time on screen-based activities. *BMC Public Health,* 14(1), 1261.

Bringolf, J. (2008). Universal Design: Is it Accessible. *Multi* 1(2) (Spring/Summer, 2008).

Brinkley, D. (2017). Thoreau's wilderness legacy, beyond the shores of Walden Pond. Available at https://www.nytimes.com/2017/07/07/books/review/douglas-brinkley-thoreaus-wilderness-legacy-walden-pond.html

Broadhead, P., Meleady, C., & Delgado, M. A. (2008). *Children, families and communities. Creating and sustaining integrated services.* Maidenhead: Open University Press.

Bronfenbrenner, U. (1979). *The ecology of human development: Experiments by nature and design.* Cambridge, MA: Harvard University Press.

Brown, J. M., & Kaye, C. (2017). Where do the children play?: An investigation of the intersection of nature, early childhood education and play. *Early Child Development and Care,* 187(5–6), 1028–1041.

Brown, R. (2015). Engaging families through artful play. *International Journal of Education & the Arts,* 16(8).

Brundtland, G. (1988). *World commission on environment and development (WCED). 1987. Our common future: The Brundtland report.* London: Oxford University Press.

Brunelle, S., Herrington, S., Coghlan, R., & Brussoni, M. (2016). Play worth remembering: Are playgrounds too safe? *Children, Youth and Environments,* 26(1), 17–36.

Bruner, J. S. (1966). *Toward a theory of instruction* (Vol. 59). Cambridge, MA: Harvard University Press.

Brussoni, M., Brunelle, S., Pike, I., Sandseter, E. B. H., Herrington, S., Turner, H., ... & Ball, D. J. (2014).

Can child injury prevention include healthy risk promotion. *Injury Prevention, 21*, 344–347. http://doi.org/10.1136/injuryprev-2014-041241

Brussoni, M., Gibbons, R., Gray, C., Ishikawa, T., Sandseter, E. B. H., Bienenstock, A., ... & Pickett, W. (2015). What is the relationship between risky outdoor play and health in children? A systematic review. *International Journal of Environmental Research and Public Health, 12*(6), 6423–6454.

Brussoni, M., Ishikawa, T., Brunelle, S., & Herrington, S. (2017). Landscapes for play: Effects of an intervention to promote nature-based risky play in early childhood centres. *Journal of Environmental Psychology, 54*, 139–150.

Brussoni, M., Olsen, L. L., Pike, I., & Sleet, D. A. (2012). Risky play and children's safety: Balancing priorities for optimal child development. *International Journal of Environmental Research and Public Health, 9*, 3134–3148.

Buitink, J. (2009). What and how do student teachers learn during school-based teacher education. *Teaching and Teacher Education, 25*(1), 118–127.

Buldu, M. (2010). Making learning visible in kindergarten classrooms: Pedagogical documentation as a formative assessment technique. *Teaching and Teacher Education, 26*(7), 1439–1449.

Bullick, T. (2017). Your brain is plastic. *Applemag*. Alberta Health Services. Calgary, AB. Special Reprint 2017–2018.

Burdette, H. L., & Whitaker, R. C. (2005). Resurrecting free play in young children: looking beyond fitness and fatness to attention, affiliation, and affect. *Archives of Pediatrics & Adolescent Medicine, 159*(1), 46–50.

Campbell-Barr, V., Georgeson, J., & Varga, A. N. (2015). Developing professional early childhood educators in England and Hungary: where has all the love gone? *European Education, 47*(4), 311–330.

Canadian Standards Association. (2007). *Children's playspaces and equipment.* Canadian Standards Association.

Cannon, E. N., & Woodward, A. L. (2012). Infants generate goal-based action predictions. *Developmental Science, 15*(2), 292–298.

Carbone, E. T., DiFulvio, G. T., Susi, T., Nelson-Peterman, J., Lowbridge-Sisley, J., & Collins, J. (2016). Evaluation of an Urban Farm-to-Preschool and Families Program. *International Quarterly of Community Health Education, 36*(3), 177–187.

Carlton, M. P., & Winsler, A. (1998). Fostering intrinsic motivation in early childhood classrooms. *Early Childhood Education Journal, 25*(3), 159–166.

Carr, A. (2015). *The handbook of child and adolescent clinical psychology: A contextual approach.* New York, NY: Routledge.

Carr, V., & Luken, E. (2014). Playscapes: a pedagogical paradigm for play and learning. *International Journal of Play, 3*(1), 69–83.

Carson, R. (1956). Help your child to wonder. Released by Cherry Hill, MA: Council of Liberal Churches (Universalist-Unitarian) Incorporated, Division of Education.

Carson, V., Spence, J. C., Cutumisu, N., Boule, N., & Edwards, J. (2010). Seasonal variation in physical activity among preschool children in a northern Canadian city. *Research Quarterly for Exercise and Sport, 81*(4), 392–9.

Carter, M., Cividanes, W., Curtis, D., & Lebo, D. (2010). Becoming a reflective teacher. *Teaching Young Children, 3*(4), 1–4.

Casey, T. (2011) Outdoor play for everyone. In J. White (Ed.), *Outdoor provision in the early years* London: Sage Publications.

Casey, T., & Robertson, J. (2016). Loose parts play: A tool kit. Available: https://www.inspiringscotland.org.uk/wp-content/uploads/2017/03/Loose-Parts-Play-web.pdf

Casey, T. (2007). *Environments for outdoor play: A practical guide to making space for children.* London: Paul Chapman.

Cavallini, I., & Tedeschi, M. (2008). *The languages of food: Recipes, experiences, thoughts.* (L. Morrow, Trans.). Reggio Emilia, Italy: Reggio Children.

Cevher-Kalburan, N., & Ivrendi, A. (2016). Risky play and parenting styles. *Journal of Child and Family Studies, 25*(2), 355–366.

Charles, S. (n.d.). Honouring our Indigenous Roots and Future Commitment. Humber Institute of Technology and Advanced Learning. Retrieved from http://humber.ca/aboriginal/sites/default/files/upload/documents/Online Elder'sCornerHONOURINGOURINDIGENOUSROOT SANDFUTURECOMMITMENTS.pdf

Chawla, L. (1991). Childhood place attachments. In: I. Altman, I. & S. Low (Eds.), *Place Attachment*, 63–86. New York: Plenum.

Chawla, L. (2012). Children's engagement with the natural world as a ground for healing. In K. G. Tidball, & M. Krasny (Eds.), *Greening in the red zone: Disaster, resilience and community greening.* Dordrecht: Springer.

Chawla, L. (2015). Benefits of nature contact for children. *CPL Bibliography, 30*(4), 433–452.

Chawla, L., & Rivkin, M. (2014). Early childhood education for sustainability in the United States of America. In J. Davis & S. Elliot (Eds.), *Research in early childhood education for sustainability: International perspectives and provocations*, 248–265. London: Routledge.

Chawla, L., Keena, K., Pevec, I., & Stanley, E. (2014). Green schoolyards as havens from stress and resources for resilience in childhood and adolescence. *Health & Place, 28*, 1–13.

Cheng, J. C. H., & Monroe, M. C. (2012). Connection to nature: Children's affective attitude toward nature. *Environment and Behavior, 44*(1), 31–49.

Chiao, J. Y., Li, S. C., Seligman, R., & Turner, R. (Eds.). (2016). *The Oxford handbook of cultural neuroscience.* London: Oxford University Press.

Clark, A., & Moss, P. (2001). *Listening to young children: the Mosaic approach.* London: National Children's Bureau for the Joseph Rowntree Foundation.

Coe, D. P., Flynn, J. I., Wolff, D. L., Scott, S. N., & Durham, S. (2014). Children's physical activity levels and utilization of a traditional versus natural playground. *Children, Youth and Environments, 24*(3), 1–15.

Coe, H. (2016). From excuses to encouragements: Confronting and overcoming the barriers to early childhood outdoor learning in Canadian schools. *Journal of Childhood Studies, 41*(1), 5–15.

Cohen, D. (1993). *The Development of Play.* (2nd edition), London, Croom Helm.

Cohen, P. M., & Solnit, A. J. (1993). Play and therapeutic action. *Psychoanalytic Study of the Child, 48,* 49–63.

Colwell, J., & Pollard, A. (Eds). (2015). *Readings for reflective teaching in early education.* London, UK: Bloomsbury Publishing.

Colyer, J, Reimer, J., Watters, D. & Watts, J. (2017). *THINQ Kindergarten: Inquiry-based learning in the kindergarten classroom.* Toronto: Wave Learning Solutions.

Commission of the European Communities. (2007). *Improving the quality of teacher education.* Communication from the commission to the Council and the European Parliament 3.8.2007. Brussels.

Common World Childhoods Research Collective (2016). *Common world childhoods and pedagogies.* Retrieved from: http://www.commonworlds.net/

Constable, K. (2017). *The outdoor classroom ages 3–7: Using ideas from forest schools to enrich learning.* New York, NY: Taylor & Francis.

Cooper, A. (2016). Nature and the outdoor learning environment: The forgotten resource in early childhood education. *International Journal of Early Childhood Environmental Education, 3*(1), 81–95.

Copeland, K. A., Sherman, S. N., Kendeigh, C. A., Kalkwarf, H. J., & Saelens, B. E. (2012). Societal values and policies may curtail preschool children's physical activity in child care centers. *Pediatrics,* peds-2011.

Costa, A. L., & Kallick, B. (1993). Through the lens of a critical friend. *Educational Leadership, 51,* 49–51.

Costa, A., & Garmston R. (2016). *Cognitive coaching: A foundation for renaissance schools.* Lanham, MD: Rowman & Littlefield.

Coster, D., & Gleeve, J. (2008). Give us a go! *Methodology, 4*(3), 1–33.

Couchenour, D., and Kent Chrisman, J. (Eds.). (2016). *The Sage encyclopedia of contemporary early childhood education.* Thousand Oaks, CA: Sage Publications.

Council of Ministers of Education, Canada (2017). CMEC Statement on play-based learning. Available at http://www.cmec.ca/Publications/Lists/Publications/Attachments/282/play-based-learning_statement_EN.pdf

Cree, J., & McCree, M. (2012). A brief history of the roots of forest school in the UK. *Horizons, 60,* 33.

Cremin, T., Glauert, E., Craft, A., Compton, A., & Stylianidou, F. (2015). Creative little scientists: Exploring pedagogical synergies between inquiry-based and creative approaches in Early Years science. *Education 3–13, 43*(4), 404–419.

Cumming, F., & Nash, M. (2015). An Australian perspective of a forest school: shaping a sense of place to support learning. *Journal of Adventure Education and Outdoor Learning, 15*(4), 296–309.

Cutter-Mackenzie, A., & Edwards, S. (2013). Toward a model for early childhood environmental education: Foregrounding, developing, and connecting knowledge through play-based learning. *The Journal of Environmental Education, 44*(3), 195–213.

Dahlberg, G., & Moss, P. (2004). *Ethics and politics in early childhood education.* Florence, KT: Routledge.

Dahlberg, G., Moss, P., & Pence, A. (1999). *Beyond quality in early childhood education and care: Postmodern perspectives.* Levittown, PA: Taylor and Francis.

Daly, L., & Beloglovsky, M. (2014). *Loose parts: Inspiring play in young children.* St. Paul, Minnesota: Redleaf Press.

Davis, J. (2009). Revealing the research 'hole' of early childhood education for sustainability: A preliminary survey of literature. *Environmental Education Research, 15*(2), 227–241.

Davis, J., & Elliott, S. (Eds.). (2014). *Research in early childhood education for sustainability: International perspectives and provocations.* London, UK: Routledge.

Davis, J. M. (2010). Early childhood education for sustainability: Why it matters, what it is, and how whole centre action research and systems thinking can help. *Journal of Action Research Today in Early Childhood,* (Educat), 35–44.

Delpit, L. (1995). *Other peoples children: Cultural conflict in the classroom.* New York: The New Press.

Denham, S. A., Bassett, H. H., Mincic, M. M., Kalb, S. C., Way, E., Wyatt, T., & Segal, Y. (2012). Social emotional learning profiles of preschoolers' early school success: A person-centered approach. *Learning and Individual Differences, 22,* 178–189.

Dennis Jr., S. F., Wells, A., & Bishop, C. (2014). A post-occupancy study of nature-based outdoor classrooms in early childhood education. *Children, Youth and Environments, 24*(2), 35–52.

Department of the Education, Employment and Workplace Relations (DEEWR) (2009). Belonging, Being and Becoming: The Early Years Learning Framework for Australia. Canberra, ACT: Commonwealth of Australia.

Derby, M. W., Piersol, L., & Blenkinsop, S. (2015). Refusing to settle for pigeons and parks: Urban environmental education in the age of neoliberalism. *Environmental Education Research, 21*(3), 378–389.

Dewey, J. (1916). *Democracy and Education: An Introduction to the philosophy of education.* North Chelmsford, MA: Macmillan.

Dewey, J. (1962). *The relation of theory to practice in education.* Association for Student Teaching, [State College of Iowa].

Dewey, J. (1980). *The School and society* (Vol. 151). Carbondale, IL: SIU Press.

Di Santo, A., & Kenneally, N. (2014). A call for a shift in thinking: Viewing children as rights-holders in early childhood curriculum frameworks. *Childhood Education, 90*(6), 395–406.

Diamond, A. 2006. The Early development of executive functions. In E. Bialystok & F. I. M. Craik (Eds.), *Lifespan cognition: Mechanisms of change,* 70–95. New York: Oxford University Press.

Dickinson, E. (2013). The Misdiagnosis: Rethinking "Nature-Deficit Disorder." *Environmental Communication, 7*(3), 313–335. http://dx.doi.org/10.1080/17524032.2013.802704

Dietze, B. (2013). How accessible and usable are our neighbourhood playgrounds for children who have mobility restrictions or use mobility devices? *Canadian Children, 38*(2), 14–20.

Dietze, B. (2016). The risky joys of outdoor play. Available at: http://www.cccf-fcsge.ca/2017/07/25/a-blog-the-importance-of-increasing-childrens-outdoor-play-opportunities/

Dietze, B., & Kashin, D. (2013). Shifting views: Exploring the potential for technology integration in early childhood education programs/Changement d'opinion: Exploration du potentiel d'intégration de la technologie dans les programmes d'éducation de la petite enfance. *Canadian Journal of Learning and Technology/La revue canadienne de l'apprentissage et de la technologie, 39*(4), 1–12.

Dietze, B., & Kashin, D. (2016). *Empowering pedagogy for early childhood education.* Toronto, ON: Pearson.

Dietze, B., & Kashin, D. (2017). *Building capacity – creating specialized outdoor play training to empower children's experiences.* Kelowna, B.C.: Okanagan College. Available at http://outdoorplaytraining.com.

Dietze, B., & Kashin, D. (2018). *Playing and learning in early childhood education* (2nd ed.). Toronto, ON: Pearson.

Dietze, B., & Kim, B. (2014). *An assessment tool in support of creating children's outdoor play environments with a sense of wonder.* Province of Nova Scotia: Department of Health and Wellness.

Dietze, B., Penner, A., Ashley, S., Gillis, K., Moses, H., & Goodine, B. (2014). Listening to faculty: Developing a research strategy in early childhood education. *Transformative Dialogues: Teaching & Learning Journal, 7*(1), 1–15.

Dietze, B., Pye, K., & Yochoff, A. (2013). Risk-taking at the crossroads: Bringing it back into the lives of children and youth. *Relational Child & Youth Care Practice, 26*(4).

Doan, L, (2013). Mentoring needs of novice early childhood educators. *Canadian Children, 38*(2), 21–24.

Dodd, C.I. (1897). "'The school journey in Germany.'" In *Special Reports on Educational Subjects, 1896–7.* Board of Education (Ed.). Vol.1, 512–534. London: HMSO.

Dowdell, K., Gray, T., & Malone, K. (2011). Nature and its influence on children's outdoor play. *Journal of Outdoor and Environmental Education, 15*(2), 24.

Drown, K. K. C., & Christensen, K. M. (2014). Dramatic play affordances of natural and manufactured outdoor settings for preschool-aged children. *Children, Youth and Environments, 24*(2), 53–77.

Duhn, I. (2012). Places for pedagogies, pedagogies for places. *Contemporary Issues in Early Childhood, 13*(2), 99–107.

Duque, I., Martins, F. M. L., & Clemente, F. M. (2016). Outdoor play and interaction skills in early childhood education: approaching for measuring using social network analysis. *Journal of Physical Education and Sport, 16*(4), 1266–1272.

Dyment, J., Davis, J., Nailon, D., Emery, S., Getentet, S., McCrea, N., & Hill, A. (2014). The impact of professional development on early childhood educators' confidence, understanding and knowledge of education for sustainability. *Environmental Education Research, 20*(5), 660–679.

Eager, D., & Little, H. (2011, August). Risk deficit disorder. In Proceeding of IPWEA International Public Works Conference.

Eberle, S. G. (2014). The elements of play: Toward a philosophy and a definition of play. *American Journal of Play, 6*(2), 214.

Edwards, C., Gandini, L., & Forman, G. (2012). *The hundred languages of children: The Reggio Emilia approach in transformation.* (2nd ed.). Westport, CT: Ablex Publishing Corporation.

Edwards, C. P., & Gandini, L. (2015). Teacher research in Reggio Emilia, Italy: Essence of a dynamic, evolving role." *Voices of Practitioners, 10*(1), 89–103.

Edwards, S., & Cutter-Mackenzie, A. (2011). Environmentalising early childhood education curriculum through pedagogies of play. *Australasian Journal of Early Childhood, 36*(1), 51.

Ehlert, L. (2005). *Leaf man.* Boston, MA: Houghton Mifflin Harcourt.

Elder, L. (2007). Our concept and definition of critical thinking. *The Critical Thinking Community.* Available at http://www.criticalthinking.org/pages/our-concept-of-critical-thinking/411

Elkind, D. (2012). *The Many Modes of Experience and Learning: The Grandmasters of ECE. Exchange.*

Elkind, D. (2013). *The hurried child,* (25th anniversary edition). Cambridge, MA: Da Capo Press.

Elkind, D. (2015). *Giants in the nursery: A biographical history of developmentally appropriate practice.* St. Paul, Minnesota: Redleaf Press.

Elliott, S. (2014). *Sustainability and the Early Years Learning Framework.* Mt Victoria, NSW: Pademelon Press.

Engdahl, I. (2015). Early childhood education for sustainability: The OMEP World Project. *International Journal of Early Childhood, 47*(3), 347–366.

Epstein, A. S. (2014). *The intentional teacher: Choosing the Best Strategies for Young Children's Learning* (Revised ed.).Washington DC: National Association for the Education of Young Children.

Ergler, C., Kearns, R., & Witten, K. (2016). Exploring children's seasonal play to promote active lifestyles in Auckland, New Zealand. *Health & Place,* (41), 67–77.

Ergler, C. R., Kearns, R., Witten, K., & Porter, G. (2016). Digital methodologies and practices in children's geographies. *Children Geographies, 14*(2), 129–140.

Ernst, J. (2014). Early childhood educators' use of natural outdoor settings as learning environments: an exploratory study of beliefs, practices, and barriers. *Environmental Education Research, 20*(6), 735–752.

Ernst, J., & Tornabene, L. (2012). Preservice early childhood educators' perceptions of outdoor settings as learning environments. *Environmental Education Research, 18*(5), 643–664.

Ernst, J. A. (2012). Early childhood nature play: A needs assessment of Minnesota licensed childcare providers. *Journal of Interpretation Research, 17*(1), 7–24.

Feld, S., & Basso, K. H. (Eds.) (1996). Wisdom sits in places: Notes on a western Apache landscape. In *Senses of place*. Santa Fe, NM: School of American Research Press, 13–51.

Ferrance, E. (2000). Action research. LAB: A Program of the Education Alliance. Northeast and Island Regional Education Laboratory at Brown University. Providence, RI.

Ferreira, J., & Davis, J. (2015). Using research and a systems approach to mainstream change in early childhood education for sustainability. In J. Davis (Ed.), *Young children and the environment: Early education for sustainability* (2nd ed., 301–316). Cambridge: Cambridge University Press.

Fishbaugh, A. S. (2011). *Celebrate Nature!: Activities for Every Season*. St. Paul, Minnesota: Redleaf Press.

Fjørtoft, I. (2004). Landscape as playscape: The effects of natural environments on children's play and motor development. *Children, Youth and Environments, 14*(2), 21–44.

Flannery Quinn, S. M., & Schwartz, K. (2011). Preservice teachers' perceptions of pedagogic documentation techniques in early childhood teacher preparation. *Journal of Early Childhood Teacher Education, 32*(1), 39–54.

Fleet, A., Honig, T., Robertson, J., Semann, A., & Shepherd, W. (2011). *What's pedagogy anyway? Using pedagogical documentation to engage with the early years learning framework*. New South Wales, Children's services central.

Fleet, A., Patterson, C., & Robertson, J. (2012). *Conversations: Behind early childhood pedagogical documentation*. NSW: Pademelon Press.

Florez, I. R. (2011). Developing young children's self-regulation through everyday experiences. *YC Young Children, 66*(4), 46.

Foltz, M. A. (1998). *Designing navigable information spaces*, MSc Thesis, MIT, Cambridge, MA.

Forest School Canada. (2014). *Forest and nature school in Canada: A head, heart and hands approach to outdoor learning*. R. Carruthers Den Hoed (Ed.). Toronto: Author. Retrieved from http://childnature.ca/wp-content/uploads/2017/10/FSC-Guide-1.pdf

Forman, G., & Hall, E. (2005). Wondering with children: The importance of observation in early education. *Early Childhood Research and Practice, (7)*2.

Forman, G. E., & Fyfe, B. (2012). Negotiated learning through design, documentation, and discourse. In C. P. Edwards, L. Gandini, & G. E. Forman (Eds.), *The hundred languages of children: The Reggio Emilia experience in transformation* (2nd ed., 247–71). Westport, CT: Ablex Publishing Corporation.

Franklin, M. B. (2008). Words in play: Children's use of language in pretend. In E. Goodenough (Ed.), *A place for play*. A companion volume to the Michigan television film "Where do the children play?"

Freire, P., (1992). *Pedagogy of hope: reliving pedagogy of the oppressed* (R. R. Barr, Trans. 2004 ed.). New York: Continuum Publishing Company.

Freire, P. (1968). *Pedagogy of the oppressed*. (M. Bergman Ramos, Trans.). New York: Herder & Herder. Original work published.

Fritz, R. W., Smyrni, K., & Roberts, K. (2014). The challenges of bringing the waldkindergarten concept to North America. *Children, Youth and Environments, 24*(2), 215–227.

Fröbel, F. (1889). *Autobiography of Friedrich Froebel*. Syracuse, NY: CW Bardeen.

Froebel, F. (1974). The education of man (Rev. ed.). Clifton, NJ: *Augustus M. Kelley (Original work published 1887)*.

Fromberg, D. P., & Bergen, D. (1998). *Play from birth to twelve and beyond: Contexts, perspectives, and meanings*. New York: Garland Publishing Inc.

Frost, D. J. L. (2009). Back to nature and the emerging child saving movement: Restoring children's outdoor play. *C&NN Leadership Writing Series, 1*(3), 1–13.

Frost, J. (2012). Evolution of American playgrounds. *Scholarpedia, 7*(12), 30423.

Frost, J. (2015). Designing and creating playgrounds. *The handbook of the study of play*, 425–434.

Frost, J. L. (2010). *A history of children's play and play environments: Toward a contemporary child-saving movement*. New York, NY: Routledge.

Frost, J. L., & Sutterby, J. A. (2017). Outdoor play is essential to whole child development. *YC Young Children, 72*(3), 82.

Frost, J. L., Brown, P., Sutterby, J. A., & Thornton, C. D. (2004). *The developmental benefits of playgrounds: Research results from leading experts on playgrounds and child development*. Onley, MD: Association for Childhood.

Frost, J., Wortham, S. C., & Reifel, S. (2012). *Play and child development*. (4th ed.). Upper Saddle River, NJ: Pearson.

Fullan, M. (2013). Great to excellent: Launching the next stage of Ontario's education agenda. Toronto: Ontario Ministry of Education. Retrieved from: www.edu.gov.on.ca/eng/document/reports/FullanReport_EN_07.pdf

Fuselli, P., & Yanchar, N. L. (2012). Preventing playground injuries. *Paediatrics & Child Health, 17*(6), 328–30.

Galinsky, E. (2010). *Mind in the making. The essential life skills every child needs*. New York, NY: Harper Collins.

Galvan, J. L., & Galvan, M. C. (2017). *Writing literature reviews: A guide for students of the social and behavioral sciences*. London: Routledge.

Gandini, L., & Kaminsky, J. A. (2004). Reflections on the relationship between documentation and assessment in the American context: An interview with Brenda Fyfe. Innovations in early education: *The International Reggio Exchange, 11*(1), 5–17.

Gandy, S. K. (2007). Developmentally appropriate geography. *Social Studies and the Young Learner, 20*(2), 30.

Gardner, D. M. (2011). *Parents' influence on child social self-efficacy and social cognition*. Milwaukee, WA: Marquette University.

Gardner, H. E. (2008). *Multiple intelligences: New horizons in theory and practice*. New York, NY: Basic Books.

Gehris, J. S., Gooze, R. A., & Whitaker, R. C. (2014). Teachers' perceptions about children's movement and learning in early childhood education programmes. *Child: Care, Health and Development, 41*(1), 122–131.

Georgeson, J., & Campbell-Barr, V. (2015). Attitudes and the early years workforce, *Early Years, 35*, 321–332.

Gesler, W. M. (1992). Therapeutic landscapes: medical issues in light of the new cultural geography. *Social Science & Medicine*, 34(7), 735–746.

Gibson, E. J. (1982). The concept of affordances in development: The renascence of functionalism. In W. A. Collins (Ed.), *Minnesota symposia on child psychology, the concept of development*, 15, 55–81. Lawrence Erlbaum Hillsdale, NJ.

Gibson, J. J. (2014). *The ecological approach to visual perception: classic edition*. New York, NY: Psychology Press.

Gill, T. (2007). *No fear: Growing up in a risk averse society*. Lisbon: Calouste Gulbenkian Foundation.

Gill, T. (2011). *Children and nature: A quasi-systematic literature review of the empirical evidence*. London: Greater London Authority. Retrieved from https://timrgill.files.wordpress.com/2011/11/children-and-nature-literature-review.pdf

Gill, T. (2014). The benefits of children's engagement with nature: A systematic literature review. *Children, Youth and Environments*, 24(2), 10–34. http://doi.org/10.7721/chilyoutenvi.24.2.0010

Gill, T. (2016, June 15). The R word: risk, uncertainty and the possibility of adverse outcomes in play. [Blog Post]. Retrieved from https://rethinkingchildhood.com/2016/06/15/risk-uncertainty-adverse-outcomes-play/

Gleave, J., & Cole-Hamilton, I. (2012). *A world without play: A literature review*. Barnet, England: Play England and BTHA.

Goldschmied, E., & Jackson, S. (1994). *People under three: Young children in day care*. London: Routledge.

Goldstein, J. H. (2013). Technology and play. *Scholarpedia*, 8(2), 30434.

Gopnik, A. (1996). The scientist as child. *Philosophy of Science*, 63(4), 485–514.

Gopnik, A., Glymour, C., Sobel, D. M., Schulz, L. E., Kushnir, T., & Danks, D. (2004). A theory of causal learning in children: causal maps and Bayes nets. *Psychological Review*, 111(1), 3.

Gopnik, A., Meltzoff, A. N., & Kuhl, P. K. (2000). *The scientist in the crib: What early learning tells us about the mind*. William Morrow Paperbacks.

Gore, A. (2006). *An inconvenient truth: The planetary emergency of global warming and what we can do about it*. London, UK: Rodale.

Graham, A., Powell, M., Taylor, N., Anderson, D. & Fitzgerald, R. (2013). Ethical research involving children. Florence: UNICEF Office of Research - Innocenti.

Graham, A., Powell, M. A., & Taylor, N. (2015). Ethical research involving children: encouraging reflexive engagement in research with children and young people. *Children & Society*, 29(5), 331–343.

Gray, C., & MacBlain, S. (2015). *Learning theories in childhood*. Thousand Oaks, CA: Sage Publications.

Gray, C., Gibbons, R., Larouche, R., Sandseter, E. B. H., Bienenstock, A., Brussoni, M., . . . Tremblay, M. S. (2015). What is the relationship between outdoor time and physical activity, sedentary behaviour, and physical fitness in children? A systematic review. *International Journal of Environmental Research and Public Health*, 12(6), 6455–6474. http://doi.org/10.3390/ijerph120606455

Gray, P. (2008). The value of play I: The definition of play provides clues to its purposes. *Psychology Today*, 1–5.

Gray, P. (2013). *Free to learn: Why unleashing the instinct to play will make our children happier, more self-reliant, and better students for life*. New York: Basic Books.

Gray, P. (2014, April 7). Risky play: Why children love it and need it. [Blog Post]. *Psychology Today*. Retrieved from https://www.psychologytoday.com/blog/freedom-learn/201404/risky-play-why-children-love-it-and-need-it

Greenman, J. (2005). *Caring spaces, learning places: Children's environments that work*. Redman, WA: Exchange Press, Inc.

Greenwood, D. (2012). A critical theory of place-conscious education. In R. B. Stevenson, M. Brody, J. Dillon, and A. E. J. Wals (Eds.), *International handbook of research on environmental education* (93–100). New York: Routledge.

Grimmer, T. (2017). *Observing and developing schematic behaviour in young children: A professional's guide for supporting children's learning, play and development*. London, UK: Jessica Kingsley Publishers.

Gronlund, G., & Rendon, T. (2017). *Saving Play: Addressing standards through play-based learning in preschool and kindergarten*. St. Paul, Minnesota: Redleaf Press.

Gruenewald, D. A. (2003). The best of both worlds: A critical pedagogy of place. *Educational Researcher*, 32(4), 3–12.

Gruenewald, D. A., & Smith, G. A. (Eds.). (2014). *Place-based education in the global age: Local diversity*. London: Routledge.

Gundersen, V., Skår, M., O'Brien, L., Wold, L. C., & Follo, G. (2016). Children and nearby nature: A nationwide parental survey from Norway. *Urban Forestry & Urban Greening*, 17, 116–125.

Haas, C., & Ashman, G. (2014). Kindergarten children's introduction to sustainability through transformative, experiential nature play. *Australasian Journal of Early Childhood*, 39(2), 21.

Hanson, M. F., & Gilkerson, D. (1999). Portfolio assessment: More than ABCs and 123s. *Early Childhood Education Journal*, 27(2), 81–86.

Haraway, D. (2010). Staying with the Trouble: Becoming Worldly with Companion Species: Cultural Studies Lecture. Retrieved from https://people.ucsc.edu/~haraway/CultStud_Nov2011.html

Haraway, D. J. (2008). Otherworldly conversations, Terran Topics, Local Terms. In S. Alaimo and S. Hekman, (Eds.), *Material feminisms* (157–187). Indianapolis, IN: Indiana University Press.

Hartas, D. (Ed.). (2015). *Educational research and inquiry: Qualitative and quantitative approaches*. London: Bloomsbury Publishing.

Harwood, D., & Collier, D. R. (2017). The matter of the stick: Storying/(re) storying children's literacies in the forest. *Journal of Early Childhood Literacy*, 17(3), 336–352.

Harwood, D., Reichheld, S., McElhone, S., & McKinley, B. (in press). I can climb the tree!: Exploring young children's play & physical activity levels in the forest. *The International Journal of Holistic Early Learning and Development*.

Hashemnezhad, H., Heidari, A. A., & Mohammad Hoseini, P. (2013). Sense of place and place attachment. *International Journal of Architecture and Urban Development*, 3(1), 5–12.

Healy, C. C., & Welchert, A. J. (1990). Mentoring relations: A definition to advance research and practice. *Educational Researcher*, 19(9), 17–21.

Healy, K. (2016). There's no bad weather, only bad clothes! Retrieved from https://www.natureplaywa.org.au/there-s-no-bad-weather-only-bad-clothes

Hedefalk, M., Almqvist, J., & Östman, L. (2015). Education for sustainable development in early childhood education: a review of the research literature. *Environmental Education Research*, 21(7), 975–990.

Heft, H. (1988). Affordances of children's environments: A functional approach to environmental description. *Children's Environments Quarterly*, 29–37.

Hemmeter, M. L., Santos, R. M., & Ostrosky, M. M. (2008). Preparing early childhood educators to address young children's social-emotional development and challenging behavior: A survey of higher education programs in nine states. *Journal of Early Intervention*, 30(4), 321–340.

Henderson, B. (2012). Teacher research effects on professional development and professional identity. *Voices of Practitioners*, 7(1), 1–6.

Henderson, K. E., Grode, G. M., O'Connell, M. L., & Schwartz, M. B. (2015). Environmental factors associated with physical activity in childcare centers. *International Journal of Behavioral Nutrition and Physical Activity*, 12(1), 43.

Herrington, S. (2007). *Seven Cs: An informational guide to young children's outdoor playspaces*. Vancouver, BC: University of British Columbia.

Herrington, S., & Lesmeister, C. (2006). The design of landscapes at child-care centres: Seven Cs. *Landscape Research*, 31(1), 63–82.

Herrington, S., Brunelle, S., & Brussoni, M. (2017). Outdoor play spaces in Canada: As if children mattered. In T. Waller, E. Ärlemalm-Hagsér, E. B. H. Sandseter, L. Lee-Hammond, K. Lekies, & S. Wyver (Eds.), *The SAGE handbook of outdoor play and learning* (143–165). London: Sage Publications.

Herrington, S., Lesmeister, C., Nicholls, J., & Stefiuk, K. (2007). *Seven C's: An informational guide to young children's outdoor play spaces*. Vancouver: Consortium for Health, Intervention, Learning and Development (CHILD). Retrieved from http://www.wstcoast.org/playspaces/outsidecriteria/7Cs.pdf

Hill, L. T., Stremmel, A. J., & Fu, V. R. (2005). Teaching as inquiry: Rethinking curriculum in early childhood education. *Education Review/Reseñas Educativas*.

Hirsh-Pasek, K., Golinkoff, R. M., & Berk, L. E., Singer, D.G. (2009). *A mandate for playful learning in preschool: Presenting the evidence*. New York, NY: Oxford University Press.

Hollister Sandberg, E., & McCullough, M. B. (2010). The development of reasoning skills. In E. H. Sandberg & B. L. Spritz (Eds.). *A clinician's guide to normal cognitive development in childhood* (179–98). New York: Routledge.

Holmes, R. M., Romeo, L., Ciraola, S., & Grushko, M. (2015). The relationship between creativity, social play, and children's language abilities. *Early Child Development and Care*, 185(7), 1180–1197.

Houghton, S., Hunter, S. C., Rosenberg, M., Wood, L., Zadow, C., Martin, K., & Shilton, T. (2015). Virtually impossible: limiting Australian children and adolescents daily screen based media use. *BMC Public Health*, 15(1), 5.

Houser, N. E., Roach, L., Stone, M. R., Turner, J., & Kirk, S. F. (2016). Let the children play: Scoping review on the implementation and use of loose parts for promoting physical activity participation. AIMS PUBLIC HEALTH, 3(4), 781–799.

Howell, A. J., Passmore, H. A., & Buro, K. (2013). Meaning in nature: Meaning in life as a mediator of the relationship between nature connectedness and well-being. *Journal of Happiness Studies*, 14(6), 1681–1696.

Hughes, A. M. (2015). *Developing play for the under 3s: The treasure basket and heuristic play*. London, UK: Routledge.

Hultman, K., & Lenz Taguchi, H. (2010). Challenging anthropocentric analysis of visual data: A relational materialist methodological approach to educational research. *International Journal of Qualitative Studies in Education*, 23(5), 525–542. Retrieved from https://www.researchgate.net/publication/233130100_Challenging_anthropocentric_analysis_of_visual_data_A_relational_materialist_methodological_approach_to_educational_research

Humber Arboretum (n.d). *Ecosystems*. Retrieved from http://humber.ca/arboretum/explore/ecosystems.html

Hung, R. (2014). In search of ecopedagogy: Emplacing nature in the light of Proust and Thoreau. *Educational Philosophy and Theory*, 46(13), 1387–1401.

Hunnicutt, B. K. (1990). Leisure and play in Plato's teaching and philosophy of learning. *Leisure Sciences*, 12(2), 211–227.

Hutchinson, S. L., & Baldwin, C. K. (2005). The power of parents: Positive parenting to maximize youth's potential. *Recreation and youth development*. Venture, State College, PA, 243–263.

Hüttenmoser, M. (1995). Children and their living surroundings: Empirical investigation into the significance of living surroundings for the everyday life and development of children. *Children's Environments*, 12(4), 403–413.

Ingold, T. (2007). Earth, Sky, Wind, and Weather. *Journal of the Royal Anthropological Institute*, 13(s1), S19–S38.

Ingold, T. (2015). *The life of lines*. New York, NY: Routledge.

Innis, G. (2012). Problem-solving skills begin in preschool. Available at http://msue.anr.msu.edu/news/problem_solving_skills_begin_in_preschool

Institute for Agriculture and Trade Policy, 2011 *Farm to Preschool Program Models*. Retrieved from: http://www.farmtopreschool.org/programmodels.html

Instone, L., & Taylor, A. (2015). Thinking about Inheritance through the Figure of the Anthropocene, from the Antipodes and in the Presence of Others. *Environmental Humanities*, 7, 133–150.

International Union for the Conservation of Nature (IUCN) (2012). *Children's right to connect to nature*. WCC-2012-Res-101-EN, International Union for the Conservation of Nature, World Conservation Congress, 2012. Retrieved from https://portals.iucn.org/library/sites/library/files/resrecfiles/WCC_2012_RES_101_EN.pdf

Jablon, J. R., Dombro, A. L., & Dichtelmiller, M. (2007). *The power of observation for birth through eight*. (2nd ed.). Washington, DC: NAEYC.

Jardine, D. (2010). *Ecopedagogy: Sage encyclopedia of curriculum studies*. New York: Sage Publications.

Jarvie, W. K. (2015). Qualitative research in early childhood education and care implementation. *International Journal of Child Care and Education Policy*, 6 (2), 35–43.

Jarvis, P., Swiniarski, L., & Holland, W. (2016). Early Years Pioneers in Context: Understanding theories about early childhood education and care. Abingdon, VA: Routledge.

Jaswal, Y. (2017). A matter of nature and nurture. *Applemag*. Alberta Health Services. Calgary, AB. Special Reprint 2017-2018.

Jayanandhan, S. R. (2009). John Dewey and a Pedagogy of Place, *Philosophical Studies in Education*, 40, 104–112.

Jennings, R. (2014). *The discovery of wild things: Assessing children's play in naturalized playgrounds*. Unpublished PhD Thesis, Prescott College, Prescott, AZ.

Jones, E. (2012). The emergence of emergent curriculum. *YC Young Children*, 67(2), 66.

Jones, E., & Nimmo, J. (1994). *Emergent curriculum*. Washington, DC: NAEYC.

Jones, M., & Shelton, M. (2011). *Developing your portfolio: Enhancing your learning and showing your stuff*. New York, NY: Routledge.

Kahriman-Ozturk, D., Olgan, R., & Guler, T. (2012). Preschool Children's Ideas on Sustainable Development: How Preschool Children Perceive Three Pillars of Sustainability with the Regard to 7R. *Educational Sciences: Theory and Practice*, 12(4), 2987–2995.

Kamii, C. (2014). Physical-knowledge activities: Play before the differentiation of knowledge into subjects. In *Learning Across the Early Childhood Curriculum* (57–72). Bingley, UK: Emerald Group Publishing Limited.

Kaplan, R., & Kaplan, S. (1989). *The experience of nature: A psychological perspective*. CUP Archive.

Kashin, D. (2009). *Reaching the top of the mountain: The impact of emergent curriculum on the practice and self-image of early childhood educators*. Koln, Germany: Lambert Academic.

Kashin, D. (2017). Invitations, provocations and reflective practice. Retrieved: https://tecribresearch.wordpress.com/2017/05/14/invitations-provocations-and-reflective-practice/

Katz, L. G. (1993). *Dispositions as educational goals*. ERIC Digest: ED363454.

Keeler, R. (2008). *Natural playscapes: Creating outdoor play environments for the soul*. Redmond, WA: Exchange Press.

Keeler, R. (2016). *Seasons of play: Natural environments of wonder*. Lewisville, NC: Gryphon House.

Keeler, R. (2017). Play: Rising Up! In Almon, J. (Ed.), *Playing it up-With loose parts, playpods, and adventure playgrounds*, Annapolis, MD: Alliance for Childhood.

Kellert, S. (2005). *Building for life: Designing and understanding the human-nature connection*. Washington, DC.: Island Press.

Kellett, M. (2011). Empowering children and young people as researchers: Overcoming barriers and building capacity. *Child Indicators Research*, 4(2), 205–219.

Kemple, K. M., Oh, J., Kenney, E., & Smith-Bonahue, T. (2016). The Power of outdoor play and play in natural environments. *Childhood Education*, 92(6), 446–454.

Kernan, M. (2006). *The place of the outdoors in constructions of a 'good' childhood: an interdisciplinary study of outdoor provision in early childhood education in urban settings*. Unpublished PhD Thesis, University College Dublin, Dublin, IE.

Kernan, M. (2007). *Play as a Context for Early Learning and Development. A Research Paper*. Dublin: NCCA.

Kernan, M., & Devine, D. (2010). Being confined within? Constructions of the good childhood and outdoor play in early childhood education and care settings in Ireland. *Children & Society*, 24(5), 371–385.

Kilvington, J., & Wood, A. (2010). *Reflective playwork: For all who work with children*. London: Continuum International Publishing Group Ltd.

Kim, B. (2015). *"Sometimes I like to see what I'm doing": Children's voices in outdoor play pedagogical documentation*. Unpublished PhD Thesis, Mount Saint Vincent University, Halifax, NS.

Kim, B. S., & Darling, L. F. (2009). Monet, Malaguzzi and the constructive conversations of preschoolers in a Reggio-inspired classroom. *Early Childhood Education Journal*, 37, 137–145.

Kimmerer, R. W. (2015). *Interactive Dialogue of the General Assembly on Harmony with Nature*. Retrieved from http://harmonywithnatureun.org/content/documents/302Correcta.kimmererpresentationHwN.pdf

Kirkey, T. L. (2005). Differentiated instruction and enrichment opportunities: An action research report. *The Ontario Action Researcher*. Retrieved from: http://oar.nipissingu.ca/pdfs/v833e.pdf

Kleppe, R., Melhuish, E., & Sandseter, E. B. H. (2017). Identifying and characterizing risky play in the age one-to-three years. *European Early Childhood Education Research Journal*, 25(3), 370–385.

Kloos, H., Baker, H., Luken, E., Brown, R., Pfeiffer, D., & Carr, V. (2012). Preschoolers Learning Science: Myth or Reality? In *Current Topics in Children's Learning and Cognition*. InTech. Open Access Publisher, 3, 45–55.

Knight, S. (2011). *Risk & adventure in early years outdoor play: Learning from forest schools*. London: Sage Publications.

Knight, S. (2013). *Forest school and outdoor learning in the early years*. London, UK: Sage Publications.

Koc, K., (2012). Using a dilemma case in early childhood teacher education: Does it promote theory and practice connection? *Educational Sciences: Theory & Practice*, 3153–3163.

Kovach, M. (2010). *Indigenous methodologies: Characteristics, conservations and contexts*. Toronto: University of Toronto Press.

Krechevsky, M., Mardell, B., Filippini, T., & Tedeschi, M. (2016). Children are citizens: the everyday and the razzle-dazzle. *Innovations in Early Education*, December 2016, 4–16.

Ku, F. (2010). Parks and other green environments: Essential components of a healthy human habitat. National Recreation and Park Association.

Kuh, L. P., Ponte, I., & Chau, C. (2013). The Impact of a natural playscape installation on young children's play behaviors. *Children, Youth and Environments, 23*(2), 49–77.

Lai, E. R. (2011). "Critical Thinking: A Literature Review." Research report. San Antonio, TX: Pearson. http://images.pearsonassessments.com/images/tmrs/criticalthinkingreviewfinal.pdf

Larimore, R., & Sobel, D. (2016). A case study of expanding a nature-based early childhood program from preschool into the K-5 curriculum in public schools in Midland, Michigan. Unpublished Document. Antioch University, Keene, NH.

Lascarides, V. C., & Hinitz, B. F. (2013). *History of early childhood education* (Vol. 982). New York, NY: Routledge.

Latour, B. (2004). *Politics of nature*. Cambridge, MA: Harvard University Press.

Lao, K. L. (2017, March). Teacher knowledge for early mathematics education in a technology-rich environment-in the eyes of practitioners. In Society for Information Technology & Teacher Education International Conference (pp. 68–71). Association for the Advancement of Computing in Education (AACE).

Lavrysen, A., Bertrands, E., Leyssen, L., Smets, L., Vanderspikken, A., & De Graef, P. (2015). Risky-play at school. Facilitating risk perception and competence in young children. *European Early Childhood Education Research Journal, 25*, 89–105. http://doi.org/10.1080/1350293X.2015.1102412

Lawrence, E. (1952). *Frederick Froebel and English Education*. London: University of London Press.

Lea, D., & Leibowitz, Z. B. (1983). Mentor: Would you know one if you saw one? *Supervisory Management, 28*(4), 32–35.

Lee, A. C. K., Jordan, H., & Horsley, J. (2015). Value of urban green spaces in promoting healthy living and wellbeing: prospects for planning. *Risk Management and Healthcare Policy, 8*, 131–137.

Lefleur, G. (2014). *Ojibwe elders' experiences of peace: To teach our well-being with the earth*. Unpublished PhD Thesis. Faculty of Education, Brock University, St. Catharines, ON.

Leggett, N., & Newman, L. (2017). Play: Challenging educators' beliefs about play in the indoor and outdoor environment. *Australian Journal of Early Childhood, 423*(1), 845–853.

Leichter-Saxby, M., & Law, S. (2017). Pop up adventure play. In J. Almon, (Ed.), *Playing it up-with loose parts, playpods, and adventure playgrounds*. Annapolis, MD: Alliance for Childhood.

LeMoyne, T., & Buchanan, T. (2011). Does "hovering" matter? Helicopter parenting and its effect on well-being. *Sociological Spectrum, 31*(4), 399–418. http://doi.org/10.1080/02732173.2011.574038

Leong, D. J., & Bodrova, E. (2012). Assessing and scaffolding: Make-believe play. *YC Young Children, 67*(1), 28.

Lester, S., & Russell, W. (2008). *Play for a change*. London: National Children's Bureau.

Lester, S., & Russell, W. (2010). *Children's right to play: An examination of the importance of play in the lives of children worldwide*. Working Papers in Early Childhood Development, No. 57. Bernard van Leer Foundation. PO Box 82334, 2508 EH, The Hague, The Netherlands.

Levin, D. E. (2015). Technology Play Concerns. *Play from Birth to Twelve: Contexts, Perspectives, and Meanings*, 225–232 In D. Fromberg & D. Bergen (Eds). *Play from birth to twelve: Contexts, perspectives, and meanings*. New York, NY: Routledge.

Levine, E. (2002). One kid at a time. *Educational Leadership, 59*(7), 29.

Lewis, P. J. (2017). The erosion of play. *International Journal of Play, 6*(1), 10–23.

Li, J., Hestenes, L. L., & Wang, Y. C. (2016). Links between preschool children's social skills and observed pretend play in outdoor childcare environments. *Early Childhood Education Journal, 44*(1), 61–68.

Liebschner, J. (1991). *Foundations of progressive education: The history of the national Froebel society*. London, UK: Lutterworth Press.

Lindon, J., & Rouse, L. (2013). *Child-initiated learning*. Albert Park, Australia: Teaching Solutions.

Lithner, J. (2008). A research framework for creative and imitative reasoning. *Educational Studies in Mathematics, 67*(3), 255–276.

Lloyd, A., & Gray, T. (2014). Place-based outdoor learning and environmental sustainability within Australian primary school. *The Journal of Sustainability Education, 10*, 1–15.

Louie, J., & Sherren, N. (2017). Our brain thrives on connections. *Applemag*. Alberta Health Services. Calgary, AB. Special Reprint 14–17.

Loukaitou-Sideris, A., & Sideris, A. (2009). What brings children to the park? Analysis and measurement of the variables affecting children's use of parks. *Journal of the American Planning Association, 76*(1), 89–107.

Louv, R. (2005). *Last child in the wood: Saving our children from nature-deficit disorder*. Chapel Hill, NC: Algonquin Books.

Louv, R. (2014). *The nature principle*. Chapel Hill, NC: Algonquin Books.

Luchs, A., & Fikus, M. (2013). A comparative study of active play on differently designed playgrounds. *Journal of Adventure Education & Outdoor Learning, 13*(3), 206–222. http://doi.org/10.1080/14729679.2013.778784

Luís, H., & do Céu Roldão, M. (2017). Early childhood teachers' learning and professional development. *European Scientific Journal, 13*(15).

MacEachren, Z. (2013). The Canadian forest school movement. *Learning Landscapes, 7*(1), 219–233.

MacMillan, M. (1919). Nursery schools, *The Times Educational Supplement, 13.2*.

MacNaughton, G., & Hughes, P. (2009). *Doing Action Research in Early Childhood Studies: A step by step guide*. Berkshire, England: Open University Press.

MacNaughton, G. M., Rolfe, S. A., & Siraq-Blatchford, I. (2010). *Doing early childhood research: International perspectives on theory & practice*. New York, NY: McGraw-Hill.

Malaguzzi, L. (1994) Your Image of the Child: where teaching begins. *Exchange*, 3, 52–61.

Malaguzzi, L. (1998). History, ideas, and basic philosophy. An interview with Lella Gandini. In C. Edwards, L. Gandini, & G. Forman (Eds.), *The hundred languages of children: The Reggio Emilia approach to early childhood education* (2nd ed., 49–97). Westport, CT: Ablex Publishing Corporation.

Maller, C. (2009), Promoting children's mental, emotional and social health through contact with nature: A model. *Health Education*, 109(6) 1–21.

Marano, H. E. (2011). Why parents should stop overprotecting kids and let them play: An interview with Hara Estroff Marano and Lenore Skenazy. *American Journal of Play*, 3(4), 423–442.

Mårtensson, F., Boldemann, C., Söderström, M., Blennow, M., England, J. E., & Grahn, P. (2009). Outdoor environmental assessment of attention promoting settings for preschool children. *Health & Place*, 15(4), 1149–1157.

Mårtensson, F., Jansson, M., Johansson, M., Raustorp, A., Kylin, M., & Boldemann, C. (2014). The role of greenery for physical activity play at school grounds. *Urban forestry & Urban Greening*, 13(1), 103–113.

Martin, K. (2007). Ma(r)king tracks and reconceptualising Aboriginal early childhood education: An Aboriginal Australian perspective. *Childrenz Issues*, 11(1), 15–20. Retrieved from http://search.informit.com.au/document Summary;dn=367385701511095;res=IELFSC

Martin, K., & Mirraboopa, B (2003): Ways of knowing, being and doing: A theoretical framework and methods for Indigenous and Indigenist research. *Journal of Australian Studies*, 27(76), 203–214. Retrieved from http://www.integrativescience.ca/Principles/TwoEyedSeeing/

Martin, L. (2015). The promise of the Maker movement for education. *Journal of Pre-College Engineering Education Research (J-PEER)*, 5(1), 4.

Maslow, A. H. (1943). A theory of human motivation. *Psychological Review*, 50(4), 370–396.

Maxwell, J. A. (2012). *Qualitative research design: An interactive approach*. (Vol. 41). Thousand Oaks, CA: Sage Publications.

Maxwell, L. E., Mitchell, M. R., & Evans, G. W. (2008). Effects of play equipment and loose parts on preschool children's outdoor play behavior: An observational study and design intervention. *Children Youth and Environments*, 18(2), 36–63.

Mayer, F. S., Frantz, C. M., Bruehlman-Senecal, E., & Dolliver, K. (2009). Why is nature beneficial? The role of connectedness to nature. *Environment and Behavior*, 41(5), 607–643.

Maynard, T., & Waters, J. (2007). Learning in the outdoor environment: a missed opportunity? *Early Years*, 27(3), 255–265.

Maynard, T., & Waters, J. (2014). *Exploring outdoor play in the early years*. Open University Press, McGraw Hill Education. www.openup.co.uk.

McClelland, D. C. (1987). *Human motivation*. Cambridge, MA: Cambridge University Press.

McClintic, S. (2014). Comparing loose parts outdoors and indoors. *Texas Child Care Quarterly*, 38(3), 16–19.

McClintic, S., & Petty, K. (2015). Exploring early childhood teachers' beliefs and practices about preschool outdoor play: A qualitative study. *Journal of Early Childhood Teacher Education*, 36(1), 24–43.

McClure, N. (2010). *Mama, is it summer yet?* New York, NY: Harry N. Abrams.

McFarland, A. L., Zajicek, J. M., & Waliczek, T. M. (2014). The relationship between parental attitudes toward nature and the amount of time children spend in outdoor recreation. *Journal of Leisure Research*, 46(5), 525.

McFarland, L., & Laird, S. G. (2017). Parents' and early childhood educators' attitudes and practices in relation to children's outdoor risky play. *Early Childhood Education Journal*, 46(2), 1–10.

McKenna, D. (2005). Documenting development and pedagogy in the Swedish Preschool: The use of portfolio as a vehicle for reflection, learning and democracy. *Frontiers: The Interdisciplinary Journal of Study Abroad, Special Issue: Undergraduate Research Abroad*, 12, 155–178.

McLeod, S. (2012). The zone of proximal development. Retrieved from http://www.simplypsychology.org/Zone-of-Proximal-Development.html

McMillan, M. (1930). *The nursery school*, London: Dent.

McNally, S.A., & Slutsky, R. (2017). Key elements of the Reggio Emilia approach and how they are interconnected to create the highly regarded system of early childhood education. *Early Child Development and Care*, 187(12), 1925–1937.

McNichol, H., Davis, J. M., & O'Brien, K. R. (2011). An ecological footprint for an early learning centre: identifying opportunities for early childhood sustainability education through interdisciplinary research. *Environmental Education Research*, 17(5), 689–704.

McWilliams, S., Brailsford, A., Vaughns, A., O'Hara, L., Novotny, S., & Kyle, T. J. (2014). Art play: Stories of engaging families, inspiring learning, and exploring emotions. *Young Children*, 69(2), 32.

Meier, D. R., & Stremmel, A. J. (2010). Reflection through narrative: The power of narrative inquiry in early childhood teacher education. *Journal of Early Childhood Teacher Education*, 31(3), 249–257.

Meltzoff, A. N., Kuhl, P. K., Movellan, J., & Sejnowski, T. J. (2009). Foundations for a new science of learning. *Science*, 325(5938), 284–288.

Merleau-Ponty, M. (1962). *Phenomenology of Perception [Phénoménologie de la Perception]*. New York, NY: Routledge & Kegan Paul.

Merrill, J. (1916). The kindergarten of today. In *Paradise of childhood: A practical guide to kindergardners* by Eward Wiebe. Springfield, MA: Milton Bradley Company.

Mezirow, J. (1997). Transformative learning: Theory to practice. *New directions for adult and continuing education*, 1997(74), 5–12.

Michalko, R. (2009). The excessive appearance of disability. *International Journal of Qualitative Studies in Education*, 22(1), 65–74.

Miller, D. M., & Pine, G. J. (1990). Advancing professional inquiry for educational improvement through action research. *Journal of Staff Development, 11*(3), 56–61.

Miller, D., Tichota, K., & White, J. (2009). *Young children learn through authentic play in a Nature Explore Classroom.* Lincoln, NE: Dimensions Foundation.

Miller, E., & Almon, J. (2009). Crisis in the kindergarten: Why children need to play in school. *Alliance for Childhood (NJ3a)* 1–72.

Mills, G. (2011). *Action research: A guide for the teacher researcher.* Toronto, ON: Pearson.

Mills, K. (2017). Adventure playgrounds and the maker movement. In J. Almon (Ed.), *Playing it up: with loose parts, playpods and adventure playgrounds.* Annapolis, MD: Alliance for Childhood.

Misiaszek, G. W. (2015). Ecopedagogy and citizenship in the age of globalisation: Connections between environmental and global citizenship education to save the planet. *European Journal of Education, 50*(3), 280–292.

Mitchell, T (2013). Loose parts benefit all children. *HighScope Extensions, 27*(2), 14–15.

Moore, R. (1996). The need for nature: A childhood right. *Social Justice, 24*(3), 203–220.

Moore, R. A., & Gilliard, J. L. (2008). Preservice teachers conducting action research in early education centers. *Journal of Early Childhood Teacher Education, 29*(1), 45–58.

Moore, R. C., & Marcus, C. C. (2008). Healthy planet, healthy children: Designing nature into the daily spaces for childhood. In S.R. Kellert, J. Heerwagen, & M. Mador (Eds.), *Biophilic design: The theory, science, and practice of bringing buildings to life* (153–203). Hoboken, NJ: Wiley.

Morrison, G. S. (2013). *Fundamentals of early childhood education.* Upper Saddle River, NJ: Pearson.

Moss, P. (2007). Bringing politics into the nursery: early childhood education as a democratic practice. *European Early Childhood Education Research Journal, 15*(1).

Moss, P. (2011). Democracy as first practice in early childhood education and care. *Encyclopedia on Early Childhood Development: Child Care – Early Childhood Education and Care.* Retrieved from http://www.child-encyclopedia.com/sites/default/files/textes-experts/en/857/democracy-as-first-practice-in-early-childhood-education-and-care.pdf

Moss, P. (2016). Loris Malaguzzi and the schools of Reggio Emilia: Provocation and hope for a renewed public education. *Improving Schools, 19*(2), 167–176.

Moustakas, C. (1990). *Heuristic research: Design, methodology, and applications.* Thousand Oaks, CA: Sage Publications.

Moyles, J. (2014). *The excellence of play.* Open University Press, McGraw-Hill Education, London, UK.

Muelle, C. (2013). *The history of kindergarten: From Germany to the United States.* Florida International University, USA.

Retrieved from http://digitalcommons.fiu.edu/cgi/viewcontent.cgi?article=1110$&$context=sferc

Muir, J. (1987). *My First Summer in the Sierra. 1911.* The Eight Wilderness Discovery Books, 185–288.

Mukherji, P., & Albon, D. (2014). *Research methods in early childhood: An introductory guide.* Thousand Oaks, CA: Sage Publications.

Mulryan-Kyne, C. (2014). The school playground experience: opportunities and challenges for children and school staff. *Educational Studies, 40*(4), 377–395.

Munroe, E., & MacLellan-Mansell, A. (2013). Enhancing outdoor play experiences for young First Nations children in Nova Scotia: Examining the barriers and considering some solutions. *Canadian Children, 38*, 25–33.

Murray, M. (2011). Taking an active part: Everyday participation and effective consultation. In J. White (Ed.), *Outdoor provision in the early years* (105–113). London: Sage Publications.

Murray, R., Ramstetter, C., Devore, C., Allison, M., Ancona, R., Barnett, S., ... & Okamoto, J. (2013). The crucial role of recess in school. *Pediatrics, 131*(1), 183–188.

Na, I. S. (2011). *Snow rabbit, spring rabbit: A book of changing seasons.* New York, NY: Knopf Books for Young Readers.

Naji, S., & Hashim, R. (2017). *History, theory and practice of philosophy for children.* New York, NY: Routledge.

National Council for the Social Studies. (2010). *National curriculum standards for social studies: A Framework for teaching, learning, and assessment.* New York, NY: National Academic Press.

Nedovic, S., & Morrissey, A. M. (2013). Calm active and focused: Children's responses to an organic outdoor learning environment. *Learning Environments Research, 16*(2), 281–295.

Neill, P. (2013). Open-Ended Materials Belong Outside Too! *HighScope Extensions, 27*(2), 1–8. Available from: http://www.highscope.org/file/NewsandInformation/Extensions/ExtVol27No2_lowrez.pdf

Neimanis, A. (2015). Weather writing: A feminist materialist practice for (getting outside) the Classroom. In P. Hinton and P. Treusch (Eds.), *Teaching with feminist materialisms: Teaching with gender: European women's studies in international and interdisciplinary classrooms* (141–157). Utrecht: Atgender.

Neimanis, A., & R. L. Walker (2014). Weathering: climate change and the "thick time" of transcorporeality. *Hypatia 29*(3), 558–575.

Nell, M. L., Drew, W. F., & Bush, D. E. (2013). *From play to practice: Connecting teachers' play to children's learning.* Washington, DC: National Association for the Education of Young Children.

Nicholson, J., Baurer, A., & Woolley, R. (2016). Inserting child-initiated play into an American urban school district after a decade of scripted curricula. *American Journal of Play, 8*(2), 228–271.

Nicholson, S. (1971). How not to cheat children, the theory of loose parts. *Landscape Architecture, 62*(1), 30–34.

Niehues, A. N., Bundy, A., Broom, A., & Tranter, P. (2015). Parents' perceptions of risk and the influence on children's everyday activities. *Journal of Child and Family Studies,* 24(3), 809–820.

Niehues, A. N., Bundy, A., Broom, A., Tranter, P., Ragen, J., & Engelen, L. (2013). Everyday uncertainties: reframing perceptions of risk in outdoor free play. *Journal of Adventure Education & Outdoor Learning,* 13(3), 223–237.

Niemi, H., & Nevgi, A. (2014). Research studies and active learning promoting professional competences in Finnish teacher education. *Teaching and teacher education,* 43, 131–142.

Nimmo, J., & Hallett, B. (2008). Childhood in the garden. *YC Young Children,* 63(1), 32.

Niss, M. (2003). Mathematical competencies and the learning of mathematics: The Danish KOM project. *Third Mediterranean conference on mathematics education* (pp. 115–124).

Nolan, A., & Raban, B. (2015). *Theories into practice: understanding and rethinking our work with young children and the EYLF.* Blairgowrie, Victoria, AU: Teaching Solutions.

Norodahl, K., & Johannesson, I. (2015). Children's outdoor environment in Icelandic educational policy. *Scandinavian Journal of Educational Research,* 59(1), 1–23.

North American Association for Environmental Education. (2010a). *Excellence in environmental education: Guidelines for learning (K-12).* Washington, DC. http://resources.spaces3.com/89c197bf-e630-42b0-ad9a-91f0bc55c72d.pdf

North American Association for Environmental Education (NAAEE) (2010b). *From research to practice: Connecting children to nature.* Available at: https://naaee.org/news/newsroom/connecting-children-nature-executive

North American Association for Environmental Education (NAAEE). (2016). *Early childhood environmental education programs: Guidelines for excellence.* Available at https://cdn.naaee.org/sites/default/files/final_ecee_guidelines_from_chromographics_lo_res.pdf

Nutbrown, C. (2011). *Threads of thinking: Schemas and young children's learning* (4th ed.). London: Sage Publications.

Nxumalo, F., (2015). Forest stories: Restorying encounters with "natural" places in early childhood education. In V. Pacini-Ketchabaw & A. Taylor (Eds.), *Unsettling the colonialist places and spaces of early childhood education.* New York: Routledge.

Nxumalo, F., & Cedillo, S. (2017). Decolonizing place in early childhood studies: Thinking with Indigenous onto-epistemologies and Black feminist geographies. *Global Studies of Childhood,* 7(2), 99–112.

Oberhuemer, P. (2005). Conceptualising the early childhood pedagogue: Policy approaches and issues of professionalism. *European Early Childhood Education Research Journal,* 13(1), 5–2.

O'Brien, L., & Murray, R. (2006). A marvellous opportunity for children to learn. *A participatory evaluation of forest school in England and Wales.* Farnham, UK: Forest Research.

Ogden, J. A. (2000). Skeletal injury in the child. New York, NY: Springer. *Springer Science & Business Media.*

Oke, A., & Middle, G. J. (2016). Planning playgrounds to facilitate children's pretend play: A case study of new suburbs in Perth Western Australia. *Planning Practice & Research,* 31(1), 99–117.

Olsen, H., & Smith, B. (2017). Sandboxes, loose parts, and playground equipment: a descriptive exploration of outdoor play environments. *Early Child Development and Care,* 187(5–6), 1055–1068.

Olsen, H. M. (2015). Planning playgrounds: A framework to create safe and inclusive playgrounds. *Journal of Facility Planning, Design, and Management,* 3(1).

Omatseye, B. O. J., & Momodu, B. E. (2014). An appraisal of the Froebelian 'Children's garden': the living connection in nature, play and learning. *Sophia: An African Journal of Philosophy,* 15(1), 11–18.

Ontario Ministry of Education. (2014). *How does learning happen? Ontario's pedagogy for the early years.* Ontario: Queen's Printer. Author.

Ontario Ministry of Education. (2015). *Pedagogical documentation revisited: Looking at assessment and learning in new ways.* Capacity Building Series. Ontario: Queen's Printer. Author.

Ontario Ministry of Education (2016). *21st century competencies: Foundation document for discussion.* Ontario: Queen's Printer. Author.

Opp, Karl-Dieter (2009). *Theories of political protest and social movements: A multidisciplinary introduction, critique, and synthesis.* London, UK: Routledge.

Orr, D. (2013). Place and Pedagogy. *NAMTA Journal,* 38(1), 183–88.

Ostroff, W. L. (2016). *Cultivating curiosity in K–12 classrooms: How to promote and sustain deep learning.* Alexandria, VA: ASCD.

Ouvry, M. (2003). *Exercising muscles and minds: Outdoor play and the early years curriculum.* London, UK: Jessica Kingsley Publishers.

Pacini-Ketchabaw, V. (2013). Frictions in forest pedagogies: Common worlds in settler colonial spaces. *Global Studies of Childhood,* 3(4), 355–365.

Pacini-Ketchabaw, V., & Clark, V. (2016). Following watery relations in early childhood pedagogies. *Journal of Early Childhood Research,* 14(1), 98–111. doi: 10.1177/1476718X14529281

Pacini-Ketchabaw, V., & Nxumalo, F. (2015). Unruly raccoons and troubled educators: Nature/culture divides in a childcare centre. *Environmental Humanities,* 7(1), 151–68.

Pacini-Ketchabaw, V., di Tomasso, L., & Nxumalo, F. (2014). Bear-child stories in late liberal colonialist spaces of childhood. *Journal of Childhood Studies,* 39(1), 25–53.

Pacini-Ketchabaw, V., Taylor, A., & Blaise, M. (2016). Decentring the human in multispecies ethnographies. In C. Taylor & C. Hughes (Eds.), *Posthuman research practices in education* (149–67). London: Palgrave Macmillan.

Pacini-Ketchabaw, V., Taylor, A., Blaise, M., de Finney, S. (2015). Learning how to inherit in colonized and ecologically challenged life worlds in early childhood education: An introduction. *Journal of Childhood Studies,* 40(2), 1–3.

Pack, J. (2015). Learning stories. *Teaching young children* December/January 2016, Vol. 9(2).

Palmer, S. (2015). *Toxic childhood: How the modern world is damaging our children and what we can do about it.* London: Orion.

Park, M., & Riley, J. (2015). Play in natural outdoor environments: A healthy choice. *Dimensions of Childhood, 43*(2), 22–28. Available at http://www.southernearlychildhood.org/upload/pdf/Dimensions_Vol43_2_ParkRiley.pdf

Parks Canada. (2014). *Connecting Canadians with nature—An investment in the well-being of our citizens.* Ottawa, ON: Author.

Parks Canada (2016). *The Nature Playbook – Take action to connect a new generation of Canadians with nature.* Ottawa, ON: Author. Retrieved: http://www.parks-parcs.ca/english/nature-playbook.php

Parsons, A. (2011). *Young children and nature: Outdoor play and development, experiences fostering environmental consciousness, and the implications on playground design.* Unpublished PhD Thesis, Virginia Polytechnic Institute and State University, Blacksburg, VA.

Parten, M. (1933). Social play among preschool children. *Journal of Abnormal and Social Psychology, 28*, 136–147.

ParticipACTION. (2015). The biggest risk is keepings kids indoors. The 2015 ParticipACTION Report Card on Physical Activity for Children and Youth. Toronto: ParticipACTION; 2015.

Pathway to Stewardship: A Framework for Children and Youth (2016). Available at https://sustainablepeterborough.ca/wp-content/uploads/2016/02/PATHWAY-TO-STEWARDSHIP-APRIL-2016.pdf

Payler, J. K., & Georgeson, J. (2013). Personal action potency: early years practitioners participating in interprofessional practice in early years settings. *International Journal of Early Years Education, 21*(1), 39–55.

Payler, J., Georgeson, J., & Wong, S. (2016). Young children shaping interprofessional practice in early years settings: Towards a conceptual framework for understanding experiences and participation. *Learning, Culture and Social Interaction, 8*, 12–24.

Pearson, D. G., & Craig, T. (2014). The great outdoors? Exploring the mental health benefits of natural environments. *Frontiers in Psychology, 5*, 1–4.

Pearson, J., & Kordich Hall, D. (2017). Adversity, failure & resilience. *Reaching IN … Reaching OUT*, 36. Available at: http://launchbox-emailservices.ca/mail/v.aspx?SI=190352&E=caroline.cote@ocdsb.ca&S=59&N=13383&ID=9989&NL=135

Pellegrini, A. D., & Smith, P. K. (1998). Physical activity play: The nature and function of a neglected aspect of play. *Child Development, 69*(3), 577–598.

Pelo, A. (2006). Growing a culture of inquiry: observation as professional development. *Exchange, Nov/Dec*, 50–53.

Pelo, A. (2009). A pedagogy for ecology. *Rethinking Schools, 23*(4), 30–35.

Pelo, A. (2013). The goodness of rain: Developing an ecological identity in young children. *Children, Youth and Environments, 23*, 3.

Pence, A., & Pacini-Ketchabaw, V. (2008). Discourses on quality care: the "investigating quality" project and the Canadian experience. *Contemporary Issues in Early Childhood, 9*(3), 241–255.

Peterson, S. S. (2016). Developing a play-based communication assessment through collaborative action research with teachers in northern Canadian Indigenous communities. *Literacy, 51*(1), 36–51.

Phillips, N. (2016). *Returning to our natural roots: Learning to love nature with children (A Workshop Series for Early Childhood Educators).* Unpublished PhD Thesis, Mount Saint Vincent University, Halifax, NS.

Piaget, J. (1930). *The Child's Conception of Physical Causality.* (Trans. by M. Gabain.) London: Kegan Paul; New York: Harcourt.

Piaget, J. (1962). *Play, dreams and imitation in children.* London: NY: Routledge.

Piaget, J. (1970). *Piaget's theory.* New York: Wiley.

Piaget, J. (1970). *Science of education and the psychology of the child.* Trans. D. Coltman, New York: Oxford University Press.

Piaget, J., & Cook, M. (1952). *The origins of intelligence in children 8*(5),. New York: International Universities Press.

Piggot-Irvine, E. (2003). Key features of appraisal effectiveness. *International Journal of Educational Management, 17*(4), 170–178.

Plowman, L., McPake, J., & Stephen, C. (2012). Extending opportunities for learning: the role of digital media in early education. In S. Suggate & E. Reese (Eds.), *Contemporary debates in child development and education.* (95–104). Abingdon: Routledge.

Porto, A. F. (2017). *Constructing Nature with children: A phenomenological study of preschoolers' experiences with (in) a natural environment.* Unpublished PhD Thesis, Kent State University, Kent, OH.

Prellwitz, M., & Skär, L. (2007). Usability of playgrounds for children with different abilities. *Occupational Therapy International, 14*(3), 144–155.

Pressoir, E. (2008). Preconditions for young children's learning and practice for sustainable development. In *The contributions of early childhood education to a sustainable society.* Paris: UNESCO. http://unesdoc.unesco.org/images/0015/001593/159355E.pdf

Priest, C. (2010). The benefits of developing a professional portfolio. *YC Young Children, 65*(1), 92.

Prince, H., Allin, L., Sandseter, E. B. H., & Ärkemalm-Hagsér, E. (2013). Outdoor play and learning in early childhood from different cultural perspectives. *Journal of Adventure Education & Outdoor Learning, 13*, 183–188. doi:10.1080/14729679.2013.813745

Prochner L. (2015) The history of kindergarten as new education: Examples from the United States and Canada, 1890–1920. In: Willekens H., Scheiwe K., Nawrotzki K. (eds) The Development of Early Childhood Education in Europe and North America. Palgrave Macmillan, London.

Pushor, D. (2012). Tracing my research on parent engagement: Working to interrupt the story of school as protectorate. *Action in Teacher Education*, 34(5–6), 464–479.

Pyle, A., & Danniels, E. (2016). Using a picture book to gain assent in research with young children. *Early Child Development and Care*, 186(9), 1438–1452.

Pyle, A., & Danniels, E. (2017). A continuum of play-based learning: The role of the teacher in play-based pedagogy and the fear of hijacking play. *Early Education and Development*, 28(3), 274–289.

Raczka, B. (2014) *Summer Wonders*. New York: Open Road Media.

Rafferty, S. (2013). *Ecological encounters in outdoor early childhood education programs: Pedagogies for childhood, nature and place*. Toronto: York University.

Ramani, G. (2012). Influence of a playful, child-directed context on preschools children's peer cooperation, *Merrill Palmer Quarterly*, 58, 159–190.

Redman, E. (2013). Advancing educational pedagogy for sustainability; developing and implementing programs to transform behaviours. *International Journal of Environmental Science Education*, 4(1), 1–34.

Relph, E. (1976) *Place and Placelessness*. London: Pion.

Riley, K. E., & Park, C. L. (2015). How does yoga reduce stress? A systematic review of mechanisms of change and guide to future inquiry. *Health Psychology Review*, 9(3), 379–396.

Rinaldi, C. (2003). The teacher as researcher. *Innovations in early education: The international Reggio exchange*, 10(2), 1–4.

Rinaldi, C. (2005). *In dialogue with Reggio Emilia: Contextualising, interpreting and evaluating early childhood education*. London: Routledge.

Rinaldi, C. (2006). Documentation and research. In *dialogue with Reggio Emilia, listening, researching and learning*. (97–101). NY: Routledge.

Rinaldi, C. (2012). The pedagogy of listening. In Edwards, C., Gandini, L., & Forman, G. (2012). *The hundred languages of children: The Reggio Emilia approach in transformation*. (2nd ed.). Westport, CT: Ablex Publishing Corporation.

Rinaldi, C., & Moss, P. (2004). What is Reggio. *Children in Europe*, 6, 2–3.

Ritchhart, R., & Perkins, D. (2008). Making thinking visible. *Educational Leadership*, 65(5).

Ritchie, J., & Rau, C. (2007). Ma wai nga hua? 'Participation' in early childhood in Aotearoa/New Zealand. *International Journal of Educational Policy, Research and Practice: Reconceptualizing Childhood Studies*, 8(1), 101–116. Retrieved from http://journals.sfu.ca/iccps/index.php/childhoods/article/viewFile/12/16

Ritchie, J., & Rau, C. (2010). Poipoia te tamaiti kia tū tangata: Identity, belonging and transition. *First years: Ngā Tau Tuatahi*, 12(1), 16–22.

Rivkin, M. (1998). "Happy Play in Grassy Places": The Importance of the Outdoor Environment in Dewey's Educational Ideal. *Early Childhood Education Journal*, 25(3), 199–202.

Rogers, S., Waite, S., & Evans, J. (2017). Outdoor pedagogies in support of transition from Foundation Stage to Year 1. In S. Waite (Ed.) *Children learning outside the classroom: From birth to eleven* (2nd ed.), 94–104. London, UK: Sage Publications.

Rooney, T. (2016). *Weather worlding: Learning with the elements in early childhood. Environmental Education Research*. DOI: 10.1080/13504622.2016.1217398

Rose, S., Spinks, N., & Canhoto, A. I. (2015). Case study research design. *Management Research: Applying the principles*, 1–11. New York, NY: Routledge.

Rousseau, J. J. (1889). *Emile or concerning education*. (E. Worthington, Trans.) Boston: D. Heath & Co. (Original work published in 1762).

Rousseau, J. J. (1911). *Emile or Education, trans*. B. Foxley, London and Toronto: J.M. Dent and Sons.

Rowan, M.C. (2017). *Thinking with Nunangat in proposing pedagogies for/with Inuit early childhood education*. Unpublished PhD Thesis, University of New Brunswick, Fredericton, New Brunswick.

Rubin, L. (2013). *To look closely: Science and literacy in the natural world*. Portland, Maine: Stenhouse Publishers.

Rupiper, M. (2016). Mud, marvellous mud. Community Playthings. Available: https://www.communityplaythings.com/resources/articles/2016/the-benefits-of-mud-play

Sachs, G., Candlin, C., & Rose, K. (2003). Developing cooperative learning in the EFL/ESL Secondary classroom. *RELC Journal*, 34(3), 338–369.

Säfström, A. I. (2013). *Exercising mathematical competence: Practising representation theory and representing mathematical practice*. Unpublished PhD Thesis, Göteborgs Universitet. Göteborg, Sweden.

Sahoo, K., Sahoo, B., Choudhury, A. K., Sofi, N. Y., Kumar, R., & Bhadoria, A. S. (2015). Childhood obesity: causes and consequences. *Journal of Family Medicine and Primary Care*, 4(2), 187.

Samborski, S. (2010). Biodiverse or barren school grounds: Their effects on children. *Children, Youth and Environments*, 20(2), 67–115.

Samuelsson, I. P., & Kaga, Y. (Eds.). (2008). *The contribution of early childhood education to a sustainable society* (1–136). Paris: UNESCO.

Sando, O. J., Sandseter, E. B. H., Pareliussen, I., & Egset, C. K. (2017). Injuries in Norwegian early childhood and care (ECEC) institutions. *Nordic Early Childhood Education Research Journal*, 14, 1–15. http://doi.org/10.7577/nbf.1698

Sandseter, E. (2016, June 14). Risky play? Adventurous play? Challenging play? [Blog Post] Retrieved from https://ellenbeatehansensandseter.com/

Sandseter, E. B. (2010). Scaryfunny: a qualitative study of risky play among preschool children. 2010: 69. *Norges teknisk-naturvitenskapelige universitet, Trondheim*.

Sandseter, E. B. H. (2007). Categorising risky play—how can we identify risk-taking in children's play? *European Early Childhood Education Research Journal*, 15(2), 237–252.

Sandseter, E. B. H. (2009). Affordances for risky play in preschool: The importance of features in the play environment. *Early Childhood Education Journal*, 36(5), 439–446.

Sandseter, E. B. H. (2010). *Scaryfunny: A qualitative study of risky play among preschool children*. Unpublished PhD Thesis, Norwegian University of Science and Technology.

Sandseter, E. B. H. (2011). Children's risky play in early childhood education and care. *Child Links, 3*, 2–6.

Sandseter, E. B. H., & Kennair, L. E. O. (2011). Children's risky play from an evolutionary perspective: The anti-phobic effects of thrilling experiences. *Evolutionary Psychology, 9*(2), 257–284.

Sandseter, E. B. H., & Sando, O. J. (2016). "We don't allow children to climb trees": How a focus on safety affects Norwegian children's play in early-childhood education and care settings. *American Journal of Play, 8*(2), 178.

Sandseter, E. B. H., Ärlemalm-Hagsér, E., Allin, L., & Prince, H. (2012). Call for papers for themed edition of the *Journal of Adventure Education and Outdoor Learning: Outdoor play and learning in early childhood from different cultural perspectives*.

Santer, J., Griffiths, C., & Goodall, D. (2007). *Free play in early childhood: A literature review*. London, England: National Children's Bureau.

Santoro, N., Reid, J. A., Crawford, L., & Simpson, L. (2011). Teaching Indigenous children: Listening to and learning from Indigenous teachers. *Australian Journal of Teacher Education (Online), 36*(10), 65.

Saracho, O. N. (2013). *An integrated play-based curriculum for young children*. New York, NY: Routledge.

Sarama, J., & Clements, D. H. (2009). *Early childhood mathematics education research: Learning trajectories for young children*. New York, NY: Routledge.

Saskatchewan Curriculum (2010). Kindergarten. Saskatchewan. Ministry of Education. Curriculum and E-Learning. Humanities Unit. Available at http:www.edonline.sk.ca/bbcswebdav/library/curricula/English/Master_K_Curr_2010_Final.pdf

Saxby-Leichter, M. & Law, S. (2015). *The new adventure playground movement*. London: Notebook Publishing.

Schleien, S. J., & Miller, K. D. (2006). *A community for all children: A guide to inclusion for out-of-school time*. Department of Recreation, Parks & Tourism. University of North Carolina, Greensboro, NC.

Schmitt, P. (1990). *Back to nature: The Arcadian myth in urban America*. Baltimore: The Johns Hopkins University Press.

Schoonover-Shoffner, K. (2013). Holistic or wholistic? *Journal of Christian Nursing, 30*(3), 133.

Schweizer, S. (2009). *Under the sky: Playing, working and enjoying adventures in the open air*. Vancouver, BC: Rudolf Steiner Press.

Scriven, M., & Paul, R. (1987, August). Critical thinking as defined by the National Council for Excellence in Critical Thinking. In 8th Annual International Conference on Critical Thinking and Education Reform, Rohnert Park, CA (25–30).

Seidel, T., & Stürmer, K. (2014). Modeling and measuring the structure of professional vision in preservice teachers. *American Educational Research Journal, 51*(4), 739–771.

Seltenrich N. (2015). Just what the doctor ordered: Using parks to improve children's health. *Environmental Health Perspectives, 123*(10), 255–259.

Shanahan, D. F., Bush, R., Gaston, K. J., Lin, B. B., Dean, J., Barber, E., & Fuller, R. A. (2016). Health benefits from nature experiences depend on dose. *Scientific Reports, 6*(1), 28551. http://doi.org/10.1038/srep28551

Shanker, S. (2016). *Self-reg: How to help your child (and you) break the stress cycle and successfully engage with life*. Toronto: Penguin Random House Canada.

Sinha, M. (2014). *Child care in Canada*. Ottawa: Statistics Canada.

Siraj-Blatchford, I. (2007). Creativity, communication and collaboration: The identification of pedagogic progression in sustained shared thinking. *Asia-Pacific Journal of Research in Early Childhood Education, 1*, 3–23.

Siraj-Blatchford, I., Sylva, K., Laugharne, J., Milton, E., & Charles, F. (2006). Monitoring and evaluation of the Effective Implementation of the Foundation Phase (MEEIFP) Project Across Wales, Cardiff: WAG.

Slade, M., Lowery, C., & Bland, K. (2013). Evaluating the impact of forest schools: A collaboration between a university and a primary school. *Support for Learning, 28*(2), 66–72.

Smirnova, E. O., & Riabkova, I. A. (2016). Psychological Features of the Narrative-Based Play of Preschoolers Today. *Journal of Russian & East European Psychology, 53*(2), 40–55.

Smith, G. A., & Sobel, D. (2014). *Place-and community-based education in schools*. New York, NY: Routledge.

Smith, P. K., Cowie, H., & Blades, M. (2015). *Understanding children's development*. John Wiley & Sons.

Smith, S. J. (1998). *Risk and our pedagogical relation to children: On the playground and beyond*. Albany, NY: State University of New York Press.

Smith-Tuhiwai, L. (2012). *Decolonizing methodologies: Research and Indigenous peoples* (2nd ed.). London: Zed Books.

Sobel, D. (1996). *Beyond ecophobia: Reclaiming the heart in nature education* (No. 1). Great Barrington, MA: Orion Society.

Sobel, D. (2004). Place-based education: Connecting classroom and community. *Nature and Listening, 4*, 1–7.

Sobel, D. (2005). *Place-based education: Connecting classrooms & communities* (2nd ed.). Great Barrington, MA: The Orion Society.

Sobel, D. (2008). *Children and nature: Design principles for educators*. Portland, ME: Stenhouse Publishers.

Sobel, D. (2016). *Nature preschools and forest kindergartens: The handbook for outdoor learning*. St. Paul, Minnesota: Redleaf Press.

Solly, K. S. (2015). *Risk, challenge and adventure in the early years: A practical guide to exploring and extending learning outdoors*. London, UK: Routledge.

Somerville, M. (2011). Becoming-frog: Learning place in primary school. In M. Somerville, B. Davies, K. Power, S. Gannon, & P. de Carteret (Eds.), *Place, pedagogy, change* (65–80). Rotterdam: Sense Publishing.

Somerville, M. (2013). *Water in a dry land: Place-learning through art and story*. London and New York: Routledge.

Somerville, M., & Green, M. (December 2012). Place and sustainability literacy in schools and teacher education. Presentation at the Australian Association for Research in Education conference. Retrieved from https://www.researchgate.net/publication/275534777_PLACE_AND_SUSTAINABILITY_LITERACY_IN_SCHOOLS_AND_TEACHER_EDUCATION

Spencer, K. H., & Wright, P. (2014). Quality outdoor play spaces for young children. *Young Child, 69*(5), 28–34.

Spodek, B., & Sarracho, O. (2003). On the shoulders of giants: Exploring the traditions of early childhood education. *Early Childhood Journal, 31*(1), 3–19.

Stansfeld, S., & Clark, C. (2015). *Curriculum Environment Health Report* 2:171. doi: 10.1007/s40572-015-0044-1

Stepaniak, J. R. (2015). *Increasing parent involvement through parent education in an early childhood program: An action research study.* Unpublished PhD Thesis, Capella University, Minneapolis, MN.

Stewart, K. (2011). Atmospheric attunements. *Environment and Planning D: Society & Space, 29*(3), 445–53.

Stewart, N., & Moylett, H. (2012). *Development matters in the early years foundation stage (EYFS).* London: Early Education: The British Foundation for Early Childhood Education.

Stuhmcke, S. M. (2012). *Children as change agents for sustainability: An action research case study in a Kindergarten.* Unpublished PhD Thesis, Queensland University of Technology, Brisbane, Australia.

Sumpter, L. (2013). Themes and interplay of beliefs in mathematical reasoning. *International Journal of Science & Mathematics Education, 11*(5).

Sumpter, L. & Hedefalk, M. (2015). Preschool children's collective mathematical reasoning during free outdoor play. *The Journal of Mathematical Behaviour, 39*(2015), 1–10.

Sutherland, D., & Swayze, N. (2012). Including Indigenous knowledges and pedagogies in science-based environmental education programs. *Canadian Journal of Environmental Education (CJEE), 17*, 80–96.

Sutton, M. J. (2011). In the hand and mind: The intersection of loose parts and imagination in evocative settings for young children. *Children, Youth and Environments, 21*(2), 408–424.

Sutton-Smith, B. (2001). *The ambiguity of play.* Cambridge, MA: Harvard University Press.

Suzuki, D. (2014). *The David Suzuki reader: A lifetime of ideas from a leading activist and thinker.* Vancouver, BC: Greystone Books Ltd.

Swank, J. M., Cheung, C., Prikhidko, A., & Su, Y. W. (2017). Nature-based child-centered group play therapy and behavioral concerns: A single-case design. *International Journal of Play Therapy, 26*(1), 47.

Szczytko, R., & Stevenson, K. (2017). How kids learn in nature. *Parks & Recreation, 52*(5), 37–37.

Tamm, M. P. M. (1999). Attitudes of key persons to accessibility problems in playgrounds for children with restricted mobility: a study in a medium-sized municipality in northern Sweden. *Scandinavian Journal of Occupational Therapy, 6*(4), 166–173.

Tandon, P. S., Saelens, B. E., Zhou, C., Kerr, J., & Christakis, D. A. (2013). Indoor versus outdoor time in preschoolers at child care. *American Journal of Preventive Medicine, 44*(1), 85–88.

Tarr, P. (2010). Curiosity, curriculum and collaboration entwined: Reflections on pedagogical documentation. *Canadian Children, 35*(2), 10–14.

Tarr, P. (2011). Reflections and shadows: Ethical issues in pedagogical documentation. CAYC. *Canadian Children, 36*(2), 11–16.

Taylor A. (2013). *Reconfiguring the natures of childhood.* New York: Routledge.

Taylor, A., & Guigni, M. (2012). Common worlds: Reconceptualising inclusion in early childhood communities. *Contemporary Issues in Early Childhood Education, 13*(2), 108–20.

Taylor, A. & Pacini-Ketchabaw. V. (2015a). Introduction: Unsettling the colonial places and spaces of early childhood education in settler colonial societies. In V. Pacini-Ketchabaw and A. Taylor (Eds.), *Unsettling the colonial places and spaces of early childhood education* (11–25). New York: Routledge.

Taylor, A & Pacini-Ketchabaw, V. (2015b). Learning with children, ants, and worms in the Anthropocene: Towards a common world pedagogy of multispecies vulnerability. *Pedagogy, Culture & Society, 23*(4), 507–529. Retrieved from http://www.tandfonline.com/doi/abs/10.1080/1468136 66.2015.1039050

Taylor, A. F., Kuo, F. E., & Sullivan, W. C. (2001). Coping with ADD: The surprising connection to green play settings. *Environment and Behavior, 33*(1), 54–77.

Teague, K. D. (2015). *Restraints on design: Adventure playgrounds and landscape architecture.* Arlington, TX: The University of Texas at Arlington.

The British Columbia Injury Research and Prevention Unit (2015). http://www.injuryresearch.bc.ca/injury-insight-childs-play-why-its-time-to-pop-the-bubble-wrap/

Thompson, C. W., Oliveira, E. S., Wheeler, B. W., Depledge, M. H., & van den Bosch, M. A. (2016). *Urban green spaces and health: A review of the evidence.* Copenhagen, DK. Retrieved from http://www.euro.who.int/__data/assets/pdf_file/0005/321971/Urban-green-spaces-and-health-review-evidence.pdf?ua=1

Thoreau, H. D. (1995). *Walden, or life in the woods.* 1854. Minneola, NY: Dover.

Titchkosky, T. (2008). To pee or not to pee. *Canadian Journal of Sociology, 33*(1), 37–60.

Tolme, P. (2017). A surprising number and variety of North American wildlife species are quietly disappearing. The National Wildlife Federation. https://www.nwf.org/Magazines/National-Wildlife/2017/Feb-March/Conservation/Biodiversity

Tovey, H. (2014) 'Outdoor Play and the Early Years Tradition' in Maynard, T., Waters, J. (2014) *Exploring Outdoor play in the Early Years,* Maidenhead: Open University Press.

Tovey, H. (2016). *Bringing the Froebel approach to your early years practice.* London, UK: Taylor & Francis.

Tovey, H. (2017). Adventure, risk and challenge in play outdoors. *The Routledge international handbook of early childhood play*, 168–180.

Tremblay, M. S., Gray, C., Babcock, S., Barnes, J., Bradstreet, C. C., Carr, D., & Brussoni, M. (2015). Position statement on active outdoor play. *International Journal of Environmental Research and Public Health*, 12(6), 6475–6505. http://doi.org/10.3390/ijerph120606475

Tuck, E., McKenzie, M., & McCoy, K. (2014). Land education: Indigenous, post- colonial, and decolonizing perspectives on place and environmental education research. *Environmental Education Research*, 20(1), 1–23. Retrieved from http://dx.doi.org/10.1080/13504622.2013.877708

Turner, N., & Berkes, F. (2006). Knowledge, learning and the evolution of conservation practice for social-ecological system resilience. *Human Ecology*, 34:479. https://doi.org/10.1007/s10745-006-9008-2

Turner, N., & Hebda, R. (2012). *Saanich ethnobotany: Culturally important plants of the WSÁNEC people*. Victoria, BC: Royal BC Museum.

Turner, N., Ignace, M. B., & Ignace, R. (2000). Traditional ecological knowledge and wisdom of aboriginal peoples in British Columbia. *Ecological Applications*, 10(5), 1275–1287.

Turner, N. J., Ignace, M. B., & Ignace, R. (2000). Traditional ecological knowledge and wisdom of aboriginal peoples in British Columbia. *Ecological Applications*, 10(5), 1275–1287.

Tzuriel, D., & Flor-Madual, H. (2010). Prediction of early literacy by analogical thinking modifiability among kindergarten children. *Journal of Cognitive Education and Psychology*, 9(3), 207–26.

Ulrich, R. S., Simons, R. F., Losito, B. D., Fiorito, E., Miles, M. A., & Zelson, M. (1991). Stress Recovery During Exposure to Natural and Urban Environments. *Journal of Environmental Psychology* 11(3): 201–230.

Ulset, V., Vitaro, F., Brendgen, M., Bekkhus, M., & Borge, A. I. (2017). Time spent outdoors during preschool: Links with children's cognitive and behavioral development. *Journal of Environmental Psychology*, 52, 69–80.

Umbreit, M., Coates, R., & Vos, B. (2003). Community justice through peacemaking circles. *Contemporary Justice Review*, 9, 7–21.

Underwood, K., & Killoran, I. (2012). Parent and family perception of engagement: Lessons from early years programs and supports. *Canadian Journal of Education*, 35(4), 376.

Undiyaundeye, F. A. (2013). How children learn through play. *Journal of Emerging Trends in Educational Research and Policy Studies*, 4(3), 514.

UNESCO (2005). United Nations' decade of education for sustainable development. Retrieved from http://unesdoc.unesco.org/images/0014/001486/148654e.pdf

United Nations High Commission for Human Rights (1989). Convention on the Rights of the Child. Geneva: UNCHR. https://downloads.unicef.org.uk/wp-content/uploads/2010/05/UNCRC_united_nations_convention_on_the_rights_of_the_child.pdf. Retrieved June 18, 2017.

United Nations Treaty Collection (2014). *Statement of treaties and international agreements*. United Nations: New York, NY.

University of Minnesota (2017). How does nature impact our wellbeing? Available at https://www.takingcharge.csh.umn.edu/enhance-your-wellbeing/environment/nature-and-us/how-does-nature-impact-our-wellbeing

Valentine, G. (1997). A safe place to grow up? Parenting, perceptions of children's safety and the rural idyll. *Journal of Rural Studies*, 13(2), 137–148.

Vandermaas-Peeler, M., & McClain, C. (2015). The green bean has to be longer than your thumb: An observational study of preschoolers' math and science experiences in a garden. *International Journal of Early Childhood Environmental Education*, 3(1), 8–27.

Vandermaas-Peeler, M., McClain, C., & Fair, C. (2017). "If I'm in the grass and these boots overflow, I could water the plants": Exploring the natural world as service learning with young children. In *Service Learning as Pedagogy in Early Childhood Education* (193–211). New York, NY: Springer International Publishing.

van Dooren, T., & Rose, D. B. (2012). Storied-places in a multispecies city. *Humanimalia: A Journal of Human/Animal Interface Studies*, 3(2), 1–27. Retrieved from: http://www.depauw.edu/humanimalia/issue%206/rose-van%20dooren.html

Vecchi, V. (2010). *Art and creativity in Reggio Emilia: Exploring the role and potential of ateliers in early childhood education*. London: Routledge.

Vergeront, J. (2013). Museum notes: Place matters. Retrieved from http://museumnotes.blogspot.com/2013/07/place-matters.htm

Villanueva, K., Badland, H., Kvalsvig, A., O'Connor, M., Christian, H., Woolcock, G., ... & Goldfeld, S. (2016). Can the neighbourhood built environment make a difference in children's development? Building the research agenda to create evidence for place-based children's policy. *Academic Pediatrics*, 16(1), 10–19.

Voce, A. (2016, June 8). The trouble with 'risky play'. [Blog Post]. Retrieved from https://policyforplay.com/2016/06/08/the-trouble-with-risky-play/?fb_action_ids=10154040579166609&fb_action_types=news.publishes.

Vygotsky, L. S. (1978). *Mind in society: The development of higher psychological processes*. Cambridge, MA: Harvard University Press.

Vygotsky, L. S. (1981). The genesis of higher mental functions. In J. V. Wertsch (Ed.), *The concept of activity in Soviet psychology*, 144–188. New York, NY: Sharpe.

Waite, S., Huggins, V., & Wickett, K. (2014). Risky outdoor play: embracing uncertainty in pursuit of learning. *Exploring outdoor play in the early years*. Maidenhead: Open University Press/McGraw-Hill, 71–85.

Waller, T. (2011) Adults are essential: The roles of adults outdoors. In J. White (Ed.), *Outdoor provision in the early years*. London: Sage Publications, 35–44.

Waller, T., Ärlemalm-Hagsér, E., Sandseter, E. B. H., Lee-Hammond, L., Lekies, K., & Wyver, S. (Eds.). (2017). *The SAGE handbook of outdoor play and learning*. London: Sage.

Waller, T., Sandseter, E. B. H., Wyver, S., Ärlemalm-Hagsér, E., & Maynard, T. (2010). The dynamics of early childhood spaces: opportunities for outdoor play? *European Early Childhood Education Research Journal*, 18(4), 437–443.

Walton, R. M. (2013). *Early childhood educators' experiences of the Ontario full-day early learning: Promises to keep*. Unpublished PhD Thesis, University of Western Ontario, London, ON.

Wass, R., & Golding, C. (2014). Sharpening a tool for teaching: The zone of proximal development. *Teaching in Higher Education*, 19(6), 671–684.

Waterman, A. S. (2014). *Service-learning: Applications from the research*. Mahwah, NJ: Lawrence Erlbaum Publishers.

Waters, J., & Maynard, T. (2010). What's so interesting outside? A study of child-initiated interaction with teachers in the natural outdoor environment. *European Early Childhood Education Research Journal*, 18(4):473–483.

Watts, A. (2013). *Outdoor learning through the seasons: An essential guide for the early years*. London: Routledge.

Weintraub, B. (2010). *It's only natural*. Arlington, VA: National Recreation and Park Association.

White, R. (2004). Young children's relationship with nature: Its importance to children's development & the earth's future. *White Hutchinson Leisure & Learning Group*, 1–9. Available at https://www.whitehutchinson.com/children/articles/childrennature.shtml

Whitebread, D., & Coltman, P. (Eds.). (2015). *Teaching and learning in the early years* (4th ed.). London, UK: Routledge.

Whitebread, D., Basilio, M., Kuvalja, M., & Verma, M. (2012). The importance of play. *Brussels, Belgium: Toy Industries of Europe (TIE)*. Retrieved from http://www.importanceofplay.eu/IMG/pdf/dr_david_whitebread_-_the_importance_of_play.pdf on 16 October 2015.

Whittaker, J. V. (2014). Good thinking! Fostering children's reasoning and problem solving. *Young Children*, 2(3), 80–89.

Wien, C. A. (2011). Learning to document in Reggio-inspired education. *Early Childhood Research & Practice*, 13(2), n2.

Wien, C. A. (2015). *Emergent curriculum in the primary classroom: Interpreting the Reggio Emilia approach in schools*. New York, NY: Teachers College Press.

Wien, C., Guyevskey, V., & Berdoussis, N. (2011). Learning to document in Reggio-inspired education. *Early Childhood Research and Practice*, 13(2).

Williams, D. (2016). Playworker: The adult role in outdoor play and learning. Available at http://www.firstdiscoverers.co.uk/playworker-outdoor-learning/

Williford, A. P., Vick Whittaker, J. E., Vitiello, V. E., & Downer, J. T. (2013). Children's engagement within the preschool classroom and their development of self-regulation. *Early Education & Development*, 24(2), 162–187.

Willis, J., Weiser, B., & Kirkwood, D. (2014). Bridging the Gap: Meeting the needs of early childhood students by integrating technology and environmental education. *International Journal of Early Childhood Environmental Education*, 2(1), 140–155.

Wilson, E. O. (1984). *Biophilia: The human bond with other species*. Cambridge: Harvard University Press.

Wilson, R. (2008). *Why children play under the bushes*. Retrieved from http://www.earlychildhoodnews.com/earlychildhood/article_view.aspx?ArticleID=412

Wilson, P. (2010). *The playwork primer. Alliance for childhood*. PO Box 444, College Park, MD 20741.

Wilson, R. (2012). *Nature and young children: Encouraging creative play and learning in natural environments*. London, UK: Routledge.

Wilson, R. (2016). *Learning is in bloom: Cultivating outdoor explorations*. Lewisville, NC: Gryphon House, Inc.

Wilson, R. A. (1994). *Environmental education at the early childhood level*. Troy, OH: North American Association for Environmental Education.

Witt, S. (2017). Storying the outdoors. In S. Pickering (Ed.), *Teaching outdoors creatively*. New York, NY: Taylor & Francis, 59–70.

Woods, A. (2016). *Elemental play and outdoor learning: Young children's playful connections with people, places and things*. New York, NY: Taylor & Francis.

Woodward, A. L. (2009). "Infants' Grasp of Others' Intentions." *Current Directions in Psychological Science* 18(1): 53–7. http://web.mit.edu/course/other/i2course/www/devel/wco.pdf

Woolley, H. (2013). Now being social: The barrier of designing outdoor play spaces for disabled children. *Children & Society*, 27(6), 448–458.

Wyse, S. (2011). What is the Difference between Qualitative Research and Quantitative Research? http://www.snapsurveys.com/blog/what-is-the-difference-between-qualitative-research-and-quantitative-research/

Waller, T., Ärlemalm-Hagsér, E., Sandseter, E. B. H., Lee-Hammond, L., Lekies, K., & Wyver, S. (Eds.). (2017). *The SAGE handbook of outdoor play and learning*. Thousand Oaks, CA: Sage.

Young, J., Haas, E., & McGown, E. (2010). *Coyote's guide to connecting with nature*. Santa Cruz, CA: OWLLink Media.

Zamani, Z. (2016). 'The woods is a more free space for children to be creative; their imagination kind of sparks out there': exploring young children's cognitive play opportunities in natural, manufactured and mixed outdoor preschool zones. *Journal of Adventure Education and Outdoor Learning*, 16(2), 172–189.

Zimanyi, L. (2016). *Forest nature program: Outreach engagement strategy*. Humber College Institute of Technology and Advanced Learning. Toronto.

Zurek, A., Torquati, J., & Acar, I. (2014). Scaffolding as a tool for environmental education in early childhood. *International Journal of Early Childhood Environmental Education*, 2(1), 27–57.

Index

Note: Page numbers followed by '*f*,' '*t*,' and '*b*' represent figures, tables and boxes respectively.

Research (*continued*)
  in practice *vs.* academic research, 56
  principles, 64, 64*f*, 329
  professional reflections, 75–76,
    336–337
  professional vision, 61, 61*f*
  programming, 73, 73*t*
  qualitative, 59
  quantitative, 59
  self-activated play, 71
  setting the stage, 57–60, 312–316
  theoretical foundation, 63–70,
    320–335
  tips and tools for, 75, 336
  types of, 59, 60*f*
  vision, 60–61, 317–318
Researcher, teacher as, 56–57
Resiliency, 16
Resiliency skills, 210
Resources, for looking closely, 284, 284*f*
"Rewilding children," 72
Rights-based practice, 16
Rights-integrative approach, 10, 16
Rights perspective, 8
Risk assessment, 139, 143, 147
Risk management, 137
Risk(s), 89
  learning about, 142–143
  perceptions, 133
  toddlers learning about (case study),
    142
  vs. hazards, 135
Risk-taking, 16, 33, 260. *See also* Risky
  play
  advantages of, 133, 138
  barriers to, 327–328
  disadvantages of, 138
  self-regulation and, 139
  vision statement, 141
Risk-taking, responsibility, and confidence standard, 147, 148*t*
Risk-taking skills, 112
Risky play, 74
  accessibility and design, 150, 151*f*
  adventure in, 134
  arguments to support, 133–137, 136*f*
  benefits of, 132–133, 135*t*
  case studies, 142, 153
  categories, 144–145
  categories and sub-categories, 66*t*
  challenges, 134
  continuum of, 133–134, 134*f*
  defined, 132, 326
  described, 134–135, 134*f*
  early learning teacher role in, 143–144,
    143*f*

example, 139–140
family support and engagement, 150,
  150*f*
health-based practice, 148
hilltop as place, 148–149
importance of, 140
intrinsically motivated, 140
overview, 132–134
positioning, in children's lives,
  141–144
practical applications, 145–147, 148*t*
professional reflections, 152
programming, 149, 149*t*
self-efficacy, 135
self-regulation and, 139
setting the stage, 137–140
steps to prepare for, 147
theoretical foundation, 144–145
tips and tools for, 151–152
vision, 141
vision statement, 141
Rituals, 313
Rocks, as historical objects for play, 29
Rocky playground (case study), 153
Roosevelt, Theodore, 190
Rousseau, Jean-Jacques, 30–31, 40–41,
  107, 131, 132–133, 158
Routliffe, Barbara, 24
Roy, Angela, 273*b*

S

Sandpit
  as learning place, 99
  loose parts in, 99*t*
  in natural playgrounds, 169
Sandseter, Ellen, 144, 145*b*, 319
Saskatchewan Kindergarten
  Curriculum, 287
Saving Play, 32
Scaffolding, 43, 251
Scaffolding learning, 115
Scaryfunny feelings, 139. *See also* Risky
  play
Schema play, 94–95, 95*t*
Schemas, 94, 94*f*, 238
  by season, 239*t*
  tree cookies by, 5*t*, 95*t*
Schema theory, 94
Schepmyer, Nevella, 76*b*
Science-based practice, 238–240
Seasonal discoveries, 236*t*
Seasonal play, 220–244
  accessibility and design, 242–243
  case studies, 230, 244
  family support and engagement, 242
  overview, 220–222

pond as learning place, 240–241
positioning, in children's lives,
  231–232
practical applications, 234–238
professional reflections, 243
programming, 241–242
science-based practice, 238–240
setting the stage, 223–229
theoretical foundation, 233–234
tips and tools, 243
vision, 229–230
Self-activated play, 71
Self-directed play, 261
Self-discovery, 96–97
Self-efficacy, 135
Self-reflection, 114. *See also* Critical
  thinking
Self-regulation, 33
  defined, 139
  risk-taking and, 139
Sense of belonging, 177
Sense of place, 165
Sensory awareness, outdoor play and,
  109*t*
Serve and return exchange process, 253
Service learning, 231
Seton, Ernest Thompson, 258
Set shifting, 209
Setting the stage, 3–6
  children's development, families and
    others support in, 252–255
  children's development and, 108–110,
    109*t*
  historical and philosophical
    foundation, 30–33
  loose parts, 84–89
  nature-based early learning places and
    spaces, 163–176
  pedagogical documentation and
    assessment, 283–289, 284*f*
  research, 57–60, 312–316
  risky play, 137–140
  sustainability/sustainable practices,
    199–204
"Seven Cs," 67, 110
7 Rs of sustainability, 195–196, 195*f*
Skills. *See also* Competencies; *specific
  entries*
  development, loose parts and, 86
Sky, watching, 36
Sobel, David, 35, 89, 179*b*
Social awareness and progress, 193
Social concept construct, 207
Social-constructivism, 33
Social constructivist learning, 33, 34
Social context, learning in, 33